# Integral Finance – Akhuwat

There are many misconceptions and concerns regarding Islamic societies and how Muslim countries have failed to come up with their own localised solutions to socio-economic problems in dealing with poverty alleviation and societal development. This book explores why there is so much disconnect between spirituality and enterprise development in the world today, and how a part of the Islamic world, in fact located in Pakistan, can be part of the solution rather than being central to the problem.

This book builds upon Ronnie Lessem and Alexander Schieffer's theory of 'integral dynamics' which works through a fourfold rhythm of the GENE. Set against a mono-cultural perspective, the authors highlight the ever-increasing and deepening divide between Western and Islamic cultures. Through the course of the book, the authors use the transformational GENE (Grounding, Emergence, Navigation, Effect) rhythm developed by Lessem and Schieffer to take readers through the 4C (Call, Context, Co-creation and Contribution) process, articulated to CAREing-4-Society. They ground their call in Akhuwat's community of Akhuwateers (donors, beneficiaries, borrowers, volunteers and replicators) to explore alternative models of spiritually based finance through an emerging SOUL-idarity paradigm. Furthermore, through these models and Akhuwat's CARE (Community, Awareness, Research, Embodiment) process, they put forward that encouraging community activism, raising awareness of Islamic practices of Qard-e-Hasan, institutionalising their innovative research, and finally transforming and educating the community will provide an alternative to microfinance for poverty alleviation.

Showcasing an unconventional spiritual-financial solution, deeply immersed in spirituality and infused with local moral values and traditions, this book demonstrates how poverty can be alleviated in countries around the world, specifically in developing Muslim countries.

**Muhammad Amjad Saqib** is the founder and chairperson of Akhuwat, the world's largest Qard-e-Hasan Trust. He has also worked as a consultant for various international development agencies, such as the Asian Development Bank (ADB), International Labor Organization (ILO), UNICEF, the World Bank, Canadian International Development Agency (CIDA), USAID and DFID.

**Aneeqa Malik** is a transformation management consultant and Akhuwat UK's senior research and development strategist. She is an action learning (ILM) and research facilitator and a research fellow at TRANS4M's Centre for Integral Development, Hotonnes, France. She is currently on a PHD (Personal Holistic Development) program for TRANS4M's 'CARE-4-Society' module.

## Transformation and Innovation

*Series editors: Ronnie Lessem, Alexander Schieffer*

This series on enterprise transformation and social innovation comprises a range of books informing practitioners, consultants, organization developers, development agents and academics how businesses and other organizations, as well as the discipline of economics itself, can and will have to be transformed. The series prepares the ground for viable twenty-first-century enterprises and a sustainable macroeconomic system. A new kind of R & D, involving social, as well as technological innovation, needs to be supported by integrated and participative action research in the social sciences. Focusing on new, emerging kinds of public, social and sustainable entrepreneurship originating from all corners of the world and from different cultures, books in this series will help those operating at the interface between enterprise and society to mediate between the two and will help schools teaching management and economics to re-engage with their founding principles.

**Integral Innovation**
New Worldviews
*Odeh Al-Jayyousi*

**Evolving Work**
Employing Self and Community
*Ronnie Lessem and Tony Bradley*

**Integral Finance – Akhuwat**
A Case Study of the Solidarity Economy
*Muhammad Amjad Saqib and Aneeqa Malik*

For more information about this series, please visit www.routledge.com/business/series/TANDI

# Integral Finance – Akhuwat

## A Case Study of the Solidarity Economy

**Muhammad Amjad Saqib and Aneeqa Malik**

Routledge
Taylor & Francis Group
LONDON AND NEW YORK

First published 2019
by Routledge
2 Park Square, Milton Park, Abingdon, Oxon OX14 4RN

and by Routledge
711 Third Avenue, New York, NY 10017

*Routledge is an imprint of the Taylor & Francis Group, an informa business*



*British Library Cataloguing-in-Publication Data*
A catalogue record for this book is available from the British Library

*Library of Congress Cataloging-in-Publication Data*
Names: Saqib, Muhammad Amjad, author. | Malik, Aneeqa, 1965- author.
Title: Integral finance - Akhuwat : a case study of the solidarity economy / Muhammad Amjad Saqib and Aneeqa Malik.
Description: New York : Routledge, 2019. |
Series: Transformation and innovation series | Includes bibliographical references and index.
Identifiers: LCCN 2018024443 (print) | LCCN 2018028614 (ebook) | ISBN 9781315183282 (Ebook) | ISBN 9781138740709 (hardback : alkaline paper)
Subjects: LCSH: Akhuwat (Organization : Pakistan) | Finance–Religious aspects–Islam. | Microfinance–Pakistan. | Solidarity–Religious aspects–Islam.
Classification: LCC HG187.P18 (ebook) | LCC HG187.P18 S265 2019 (print) | DDC 332.095491–dc23
LC record available at https://lccn.loc.gov/2018024443

ISBN: 978-1-138-74070-9 (hbk)
ISBN: 978-1-315-18328-2 (ebk)

Typeset in Times New Roman
by Integra Software Services Pvt. Ltd.

**Dedicated to the loving memory of my late father Abdul Latif Malik for always believing in me.**

# Contents

# Figures

# Tables

# Foreword

There emerged from the Arabian Peninsula the foundations of what is known today as the Islamic socio-economic system. In reality, the system started to evolve gradually from the Old Testament in the Bible and then into the New Testament. Amazingly, Aristotle in his masterworks defined money in a manner that somewhat aligns with some of the core principles of the Islamic moral economic system. And of what essence is this model of financial intermediation, or rather partnership mode of finance, without social impact? And how has such socio-communal impact touched the lives of the custodians of the peaceful religion? And again, how has physical finance influenced the spiritual – the philosophy of Mawakhat, or spiritually-based finance?

Why, then, is that spirituality not quickly influencing the Maqasid al Shariah? Whereas the Maqasid speaks of the primary purpose of the Shariah or the intent of the peaceful religion of Islam, such peace-building is targeted at enhancing communal goodwill and human wellbeing. And certainly this is related to the enhancement, the safeguarding and the enthronement of the human self, and of faith, and of intellect, and of prosperity and of wealth. This expansion of wealth within such an integral and communal setting is the foundation of Akhuwat, indeed, a *solidarity bond*, as postulated by the author of this book. Moreover, Philosophy, Principles, Practices and integral Paradigm (4 P's) culminate into TRANS4M's CARE-4-Society: Community activation, raising Awareness, Research-to-innovation and Embodied action.

CARE denotes Community activation through Qard-e-Hasan (benevolent loan); Awakening integral consciousness through knowledge of the sacred; institutionally based innovative Research on *SOUL-idarity Economics*; provision of loans for enterprise building; educating communities; and providing alternatives to microfinance targeted at poverty alleviation – thereby altogether Embodying integral development.

Thus emerge the following research questions: Why was such a fantastic model of Mawakhat, or solidarity economics, effective more than 1,400 years ago and even 500 years ago, but suddenly became less potent in today's world? Why have the poorest nations with such huge Muslim populations not translated the traditional model to one of perpetual posterity except, perhaps, the oil-rich GCC nations and Malaysia? Why has production not exceeded the needs of communities such that export becomes imperative? Why has poverty grown so much that nations look to the interest-based West for economic support, for aid and for Western-based economic prescriptions? Is this due to lack of integral knowledge? Or inability to convert such propositional knowledge to economic prosperity? Perhaps the spiritual or sanctuary, so to speak, or sacred knowledge-base, has indeed been misplaced. The values of the core religious knowledge have been lost. Or maybe the human self, the human self-motivation or the motivational self-creation is what is weakened.

It is amazing that this book seeks a new trajectory of economic knowledge and an extension of existent soul awakening – an allegiance to the path of Tasawwuf, and of Sufism, and a base of soul iteration of the *solidarity impulse*, as per the author's postulation. This, thus, calls for an integral Hikma (wisdom) of SOUL-idarity Economics as per the author's perception of indigenous wisdom (Hikma) locked in the soil of Pakistan and the South Asian region. This Hikma (soul-wisdom) originates from an Eastern noesis of is**h**q (love), ilm (knowledge), akhuwat (solidarity) and a**ma**l (action), as described in this book.

How does one start to translate this into communal socio-economic development? And of what essence is this deep spiritual touch if a good life on Earth cannot be achieved and sustained? Why would divine knowledge just be wasted like the rain water falling heavily into the canal while water is not flowing in the house? This knowledge of the cosmos, influenced by spirituality, must yield communal good life and human wellbeing. As Southern economies become overburdened by the weight of interest-based economic models or neo-liberal economic prescriptions, and they completely lose the direction to economic prosperity, and then find themselves in the big hole of debt slavery, is a model of '*SOUL-idarity Economics'* perhaps the answer?

The new emerging light involves the metempsychosis or rebirth of a new form which this fascinating book displays. The book places '*Infaq*', or spending in the way of Allah, as a life-enriching philosophy, yet a heart-cleansing one. Such a unique approach is founded on '*Iman*', or faith and absolute belief in the oneness of the Creator, the Owner of creation, the Sustainer of creation, and the Controller of creation. Besides enjoying the pleasure of the Supreme Being, the lives of people can be touched positively. Thereby people, after becoming financially stable over time, also extend their hands of fellowship to others. The circle continues in rounds, in communities and over time. Then again, poverty reduces, entrepreneurship increases, production explodes, and inclusive economic development takes place. It is such expansion of societal wealth that translates into the relational epistemology of **Akhuwat's 4 I's**: Iman, Ikhlas, Ihsan and Ikhuwah. Infaq could be considered a 5$^{th}$ I.

This book draws on a new socio-economic path for the poorest communities. This path allows ethical free trade, it allows the welfare model to exist, it supports even extreme cases of state-led development, and it certainly allows interest-free loans for the people. So, those with entrepreneurial zeal are able to demonstrate the strength of their production capacity and innovation on the one hand. And those with limited entrepreneurial opportunities are able to enjoy such support through interest-free loans, which is expected to jump start the motivational self-creation that then leads to further innovation. In this vein, Akhuwat according to Malik and Saqib is a self-sufficient regenerative model of 'reciprocal endowments' (Mawakhat) coming from its borrower's pool of reciprocity.

A renewed world is expected to be created. An intriguing storyline of societal transformation through the Akhuwat structure then will shine its light from Pakistan to Nigeria and from Palestine to Uganda. This measurable ideology can indeed be calculated into development indicators and governance indicators while displaying such a huge impact on investment that society truly extinguishes poverty and income inequality. Plus, it encourages entrepreneurship rather than forcing people to await employment. Further action research in academic centres can then be aligned with specific societal circumstances and implemented in a way that relevant social ontology is drawn upon always. This book is indeed a fascinating one, exposing spirituality in economics and finance – coining a new paradigm of '*integral finance*'.

Dr. Basheer Oshodi (PhD)
Group head – Non-Interest Banking, Sterling Bank, Nigeria; Research fellow – Centre for Integral Social and Economic Research (CISER); Research fellow – TRANS4M, Geneva; Research fellow – Centre for Housing Studies, University of Lagos, Nigeria; Member – American Economic Association (AEA); Member – International Atlantic Economic Society (IAES); Member – Non-Interest Finance Working Group, Nigeria.

# How to read this book

This book presents a distinctive model of Islamic re-distributive model of finance & economics, commonly known and perceived as the largest (interest-free) microfinance organisation, inside and outside of Pakistan. Whereas, I intend to present Akhuwat as a futuristic alchemist for co-creating a SOUL-idarity Hikma (wisdom) through a transcendental contemplation of its 4 I's (Iman, Ikhlas, Ihsan and Ikhuwah), thereby self-sufficiently generating a model of integral finance. This will serve, moreover, as our ongoing collective integral pursuit – to catalyse a model of integral finance and solidarity economics through our Integral Soulidarity Research Academy (iSRA), to be launched in the last quarter of 2018, collaborating with TRANS4M Communiversity, substantially based in the UK at the same time collaborating with Akhuwat in Paksitan.

What this book does not propose is to outline Akhuwat as a microfinance organisation in comparison to other such organisations in Pakistan or in its neighboring countries. While Akhuwat aims to rid Pakistan of poverty just as Muhammed Yunus wished to do with Grameen Bank, Akhuwat parts ways with the the Grameen model in its absolute immersion in the Islamic model of Qard-e-Hasan (benevolent loan), that is, of ridding the society of an imposed scarcity of resources amongst abundance of wealth possessed by the privileged class of the society.

For Akhuwat (brotherhood or Bhai-chara in Urdu) sets in motion its collective impulse of societal reciprocity by emphasising its four stages of self and societal development through its 4I orientation, parallelling with the Integral Dyamics Four Worlds theory, developed by Profs Ronnie Lessem & Alexander Schieffer, co-founders of TRANS4M, centre for Integral Development, France/UK, which makes it, at times, a complex read. Thus, the reader should turn to pages 21-23 of the Orientation section for guidance on how to read this book.

Additionally, considering some of our readers may only be interested in learning about Akhuwat's Qard-e-Hasan (interest-free loans) model and it's many socio-economic operations, in which case, the reader could turn to Chapters 6-8, which elaborates this fully.

## Language and symbolism

Throughout the course of this book you will encounter a significant amount of Urdu and Arabic terms. The usage of such became inevitable, as some terms could simply not be translated into English without exterminating the real essence of the word. Additionally, you will often find the language symbolically laden with Sufi symbolism and terminology.

For example, Akhuwat in Urdu is written with an A, whereas in Arabic it is written as Ikhuwah – with an I, both meaning brotherhood. Now the Arabic Ikhuwah is written with A and I as well. I and A are both pronounced as 'Alif', the first letter of both the Arabic and Urdu alphabets.

Additionally, Mawakhat is defined here as solidarity – a prophetic tradition, originating from the time of hijrah (migration) of Prophet Muhammad from Mecca to Medina, the Islamic holy cities in Saudi Arabia.

Furthermore, to avoid confusion, we are using various typefaces for our readers to mark the distinction between three primary contributors and terminologies.

For example:

- *I, Aneeqa, as the narrator will be using italics whilst expressing my own views.*
- Amjad's quotes and narrations will be boxed.
- Integral inserts are in shaded boxes to mark their distinction.

# Acknowledgements

First and foremost, my heart-felt gratitude, goes out to my TRANS4M-ation mentor Prof Ronnie Lessem, co-founder of TRANS4M, Centre for Integral Development, France, for not only being the Editor of this book but also unlocking the Transformative potential in me by constantly encouraging and equally challenging my imagination to transcend the boundaries of my self-imposed societal conditioning. Along with Prof Alexander Schieffer, co-founder TRANS4M, for their co-joint integral dynamics process that unravelled a soul-dynamic integral paradigm.

For Dr. Amjad Saqib, founder and executive director of Akhuwat Foundation in Pakistan, to act as my Catalyst – releasing the Akhuwat (solidarity) impulse in me and for his constant support sublimating through the infinite source of his (soul) wisdom and for his unyielding faith in me; realising my potential to be a 'revivalist' narrator of a long-forgotten Prophetic tradition of Mawakhat/solidarity amongst communities.

To our beloved Bawa Pir Zia Inayat-Khan, grandson of Hazrat Inayat Khan and present President of The Inayati Order, for his blessings and guidance. For Shaykha Amat-un-Nur, Representative of The Inayati Sufi Order in the South Asian region, as my Spiritual Guide on the path of soul-realisation hence the Soul-idarity Hikma. For through her guidance my soul has transcended the knowledge of metaphysical reality of Tasawwuf transmitting the Gayan of Hazrat Inayat Khan, founder of the Sufi Order in the West in 1914 (London) and teacher of Universal Sufism.

Also extending my gratitude to Akhuwat management team who were a constant source of inspiration – supporting me with my cross-border queries. Particularly to Shahzad Akram, Chief Credit Officer, Akhuwat Foundation. And especially, to Omar Afzal Chaudhry, Trustee Akhuwat UK, for being my solidarity co-conspirator in moments of my highs and lows. Without his constant support this book would have not been completed.

To my family for believing in me and a very special thank you to my dear friend, Tushar Parekh for being my guardian angel and caretaker, throughout the course of writing this book. To my dear friend Mrs Afshan Habib Malik who helped me with Pakistani literature and cultural history by constantly bearing up to my over-intellectualised chatter.

And last but not the least, to my very precious daughter Rida Fatima Jamshed, for being my constant moral support and emotional strength at times of my social dissociation and aloneness.

# Prologue

## Why write this book?

For one of us (Aneeqa Malik) the question arose after emigrating to a new land and facing the challenges that came with it. Although I spent most of my life outside my country of birth and origin, my soul remained attached to my source-identity – the source being my clay moulded out of a soil rich with ancient wisdom and heavily impregnated with mystical lyricism. The lyrics continue to reverberate in the inner silence of my soul – the echoes of the silent wisdom of my Eastern truth. For I grew up absorbing the soul-wisdom of my soil, which to this date reverberates with the wisdom of the mystical giants who formed the Islamic view of my region, Pakistan, through poetry and Sufi preaching which came from a deep inner place. From an Islamic viewpoint and in the South Asian context, the Sufi saints of the region were the people who contemplated the ontological Islamic philosophy, thereafter consciously embedding and embodying cultural values and the wisdom locked in that particular soil. Hence, I term it the soul-wisdom of the soil, which I believe I am carrying within me. Otherwise why else, even after migrating from that land to another, can I feel its resonance? Incidentally, this stands true for the Pakistani diaspora community living in the UK, as I was to find out after working closely with them. Notwithstanding, still cherishing their regional traditions and values, there is a disconnect between their regional and authentic Self (identity) and their (now) adopted reality, i.e., being Pakistani yet British. And the twain have remained abstracted and not fully embraced.

Moreover, I believe I directly received this soul-wisdom of my soil from my mother, who was quite connected to the Eastern Sufi mystics of the Indo-Pak subcontinent. I remember her chanting Heer Waris Shah, Baba Fareed, Bhagat Kabir, Baba Bulley Shah and Sultan Bahu – all are well-revered to this day in Pakistan, more so in the rural areas, where the illiteracy rate is the highest compared to the urban areas. People take guidance and often practise these wisdom traditions in their day-to-day dealings, i.e., the local mystical soul-wisdom of the region along with the cultural traditions of their particular localities – something which I also noticed in people of Pakistani diaspora communities living in the UK. Yet a hesitation to revive these spiritual and wisdom traditions in the 21st century and in a Western culture is what formed the basis of my exploration of the British-Pakistani communities. Moreover, these traditions and their useful practices are dying even in Pakistan and, most significantly, within the urban spaces as the younger generation, mostly educated in English-medium schools, are more adaptive to 'foreign'/Western culture and ways of life than their own local indigenous spiritual traditions.

Additionally, this tradition resonated with the idealistic philosophy of the most revered and acknowledged thinker and national poet of Pakistan, Sir Muhammed Allama Iqbal. He happens to be Amjad Saqib's inspiration too, as he religiously follows and propagates Iqbal's idealism in his public speeches. After being away from my roots (of being), it became pertinent for me to retrace my way back home (Pakistan) by deeply listening and re-living this soul-resonance, i.e., the mystical culture and philosophy of my land. I found it very much present in Akhuwat's model and practices, a phenomenon from Pakistani soils.

### *Why was it important for me to find my way back home?*

In his book *The Soul of Place*, Michael Jones (2014), a transformational speaker and conversation catalyst, and a thought leader with the MIT Dialogue Project and the Executive Leadership Programs at the University of Texas, San Antonio, defines how our relationship with place in nature, art and community deepens our connection with the core energetic patterns that form the undercurrents of life and living systems. He has also been engaged in a variety of place-based initiatives focused on helping communities and organizations find the soul and story of their place, just as it occurred to me after migrating from Pakistan to make UK my then-permanent residence for the past 17 years.

According to Jones, on our human journey, as we leave our familiar (home) ground behind, we carry an anticipated feeling of dread and an ancient fear of the unknown. We are entering a new space, not knowing what to expect, yet the memories of our previous home have a certain attachment which keeps us enticed for the new story to emerge from the old one.

In his words:

> Questions of home remind us we simply cope better with the complexities of the world when we feel rooted in a shared sense of place. Knowing where we come from and where we belong helps us feel more grounded and secure. A sense of place naturally calls for us to care for it in some way. In extending this care, we catch a glimpse of a place in the future we seek to create together
> (Jones, 2014).

For me (Aneeqa) then, it became a personal calling to not only reconnect with my own story integrally, but also narrate a Pakistani story to the world, as quite often, stories of excellence emerging from Pakistan remain globally untold – quite often the diaspora communities are oblivious to these stories too. Personally, I believe that bridging this knowledge gap between the country of origin and diaspora communities could reinforce people's faith in their country of origin, thereby collectively co-creating knowledge that could be bilaterally beneficial. This is particularly useful for members of the Pakistani diaspora who remain concerned due to all the negative publicity Pakistan attracts owing to the negative perception being labelled a terrorist Muslim state as the aftermath of Soviet-Afghan war in 1989.

My inner calling and pusuit to find my own cultural grounding in the UK as an immigrantbecame a consistent yearning after migrating to the UK from Pakistan and constantly grappling with Pakistan's,somewhat mute global presence. In my quest of finding my own voice and place between two countries, namely UK and Pakistan, my soul and soil connection was re-established, especially after taking allegiance to Hazrat Inayat Khan's Sufi order, thereafter coming of a new trans4mational age and pursuing my PHD (Process of Holistic Development) with TRANS4M, Centre for Integral Development, Hotonnes.

### *What is Integral Development about?*

Integral development aspires to make development fully relevant to human life. To live up to this goal, it is concerned with all aspects of human life and hence looks at development, in holistic fashion, from multiple perspectives. It purposefully builds on the most innovative development theory and practice from the four corners of the globe, as well as the world's centre. It is framed to enable and co-engage with others in bringing about integral human systems - each one of them contributing to an integral society and an integral world.

As such embedded within the Integral Worlds approach, as developed by Ronnie Lessem and Alexander Schieffer, are powerful processes of transformation that activate and guide the integral development of individuals, organisations, communities and societies. Two of these processes stand out, and underpin all their transformative engagements around the world: the GENE-process, geared to release the GENE-ius of a human system, and the CARE-process, assisting to fully embody and sustain the integral innovation that stem from their work around the world. (Schieffer & Lessem, 2014)

Thus, my outer calling, working closely with Professor Ronnie Lessem, co-founder of TRANS4M and Integral Development Theory, became a search for alternative models of 'integral finance'. This is a model which integrates all the four worlds integrally as postulated by (Schieffer & Lessem, 2014), coming out of a CARE (Community activation, raising Awareness, Research-to-innovation and Embodied action) model, following a transformational GENE (Grounding, Emergence, Navigation and Effect) rhythm of a particular society. This is, thus, an effort to explore and thereafter release the Pakistani GENE-IUS, locked and (almost) lost in the muddled and often-confused British-Pakistani realities or, in Pakistan's case, lost in their Indian-Pakistani heritage.

Incidentally, my personal call, after taking on a spiritual discipline, also became to explore why financial models and practices were so averse to adopting a spiritual philosophy and if there were any such models that could be studied and (re)presented in such a light.

Through the course of this book, we thus explore this overarching question: Could a particular community or communities, by releasing their community's GENE-IUS – that is, by Grounding in their communal reality, being mindful of what is Emerging (as a new identity or reality), thereon Navigating through with this knowledge to finally Effect a new transformed reality of I and US as a community – unlock their full communal potential?

Furthermore, in an age of global mass migration after the Iraq and Afghan Wars and unrest in Syria, we are living in a world of submerged realities and identities. Now in 2017, after two major events, namely, Brexit and Trump's election – Muslims, especially living in the Western countries, are forced to rethink their religious heritage and allegiances as per the popular belief: that Islamic values do not work within Western cultures. All around Europe governments are passing laws against religious covering, i.e., the burqa ban in some of the EU countries. If ever, in the history of mankind, religion was under scrutiny, it is now – when being of a Muslim identity or heritage in a non-Muslim country is becoming an existential challenge. How, then, do a large majority of Pakistani (Muslim) diaspora living in the UK cope with this? To make matters worse, the younger/fourth generation is finding it hard to make their mark in the mainstream socio-economic arena. My main concern remains how we are passing on our heritage and legacy to the next generation, who are finding it hard to establish a healthy balance between spiritual and entrepreneurial pursuits.

Despite these facts, I am quite hopeful that all is not lost for Muslims, as I personally believe there is a universal call in the times to come for an Islamic renaissance emerging from the West, and the Muslims living in the Western countries are playing a vital role in this process.

As predicted in the Quran and Hadith of the Prophet of Islam.

Abu Huraira reported that the Holy Prophet (peace be upon him) said, '*Hasten to do good deeds before six (things happen): Rising of the sun from the West…*' (Sahih Muslim #7039)

Through my work with ethnic minority communities in and around the UK, I am familiar with many organisations now working on de-radicalising Muslim religiosityAccording to Philip Wood, a UK researcher who teaches and researches the history of the Middle East; are British values really Islamic values? (Wood, 2016)

The question at the core of this debate over British values is whether difference means incompatibility and whether difference can be compromised.

A new term, British Islam, is coined. As per the popular belief that the beliefs and values migrant communities, especially of Muslim and Pakistani origin, have carried with them are incompatibale with British values. Conversley, The Muslim Council of Britain has responded that Muslims and Islam are compatible with UK life. Yet, all I see is the third generation Muslim youths, primarily of Pakistani origin, are living in a submerged and rather subdued reality of identity suppression.

It was thus important for me to retrace my own roots and cultural heritage to fathom how this civilizational confrontation can be resolved and if there is a middle ground for two contrasting philosophies to co-exist. Could a new language that speaks to the heart be developed? A universal language, one that is understood by all without the divide of religion, faith and colour.

Islam is growing more rapidly than any other religion in the world, according to a new report by the Pew Research Center which says the religion will nearly equal Christianity by 2050 before outstripping it around 2070 if current trends continue.

As of 2010, there were an estimated 1.6 billion Muslims around the world, making Islam the world's second-largest religious tradition after Christianity. And although many people, especially in the United States, may associate Islam with countries in the Middle East or North Africa, nearly two-thirds (62%) of Muslims live in the Asia-Pacific region, according to the Pew Research Center analysis. In fact, more Muslims live in India and Pakistan (344 million combined) than in the entire Middle East-North Africa region (317 million).

The question, then, arises for us: How are Muslims shouldering this responsibility of tackling developmental challenges, as most Muslim-majority countries in Asia are considered 'underdeveloped', keeping in mind much of the developmental aid and solutions come from the 'West'? How are Muslim countries who are considered to be poor and underdeveloped contributing to the socio-economic development and its transitional new-age challenges (if at all)?

Therefore, this book is being written at a time when there are many misconceptions and concerns regarding Islamic societies and how Muslim countries have failed to come up with their own localised solutions to socio-economic problems in dealing with poverty alleviation and societal development.

Our main call is to explore why there is so much reticence and disconnect between spirituality and enterprise development in the world today, and how a part of the Islamic world, in fact located in Pakistan, in that respect can be part of the solution rather than being central to the problem. We will as such present a case study which demonstrates how spirituality and religiosity could have an impact on the economic performance of micro-entrepreneurs, especially in a country like Pakistan, which was conceived on a basis of faith. Conversely, could a model like Akhuwat (brotherhood), if introduced and thereafter replicated amongst the underprivileged diaspora communities, help alleviate their socio-economic privation which often comes as a result of their reticence against the prevailing economic culture?

As identified by Professors Lessem and Schieffer (Schieffer & Lessem, 2014):

'Much of development – over the past, and indeed until today – is trapped by a cultural distortion. We can see a "Western" economic and enterprise perspective and a "Northern" political, scientific and technological perspective, dominating the global development scene.' It is what they term a 'mono-cultural dominance' in development. As such, the 'Western' and 'Northern' perspectives on development dominate the global scene, while 'Southern' and 'Eastern' perspectives are either neglected or not authentically expressed.

Drawing from their 'mono-cultural global dominance' perspective, we are also mindful of the fact that there is this ever-increasing and deepening divide between Western and Islamic cultures. At the turn of the 21st century, what with technological advancement and innovation, the West sees Muslim societies, especially from the South Asian regions, as too backwards to offer new and relevant models, Grameen in Bangladesh being the exception to that rule. Here then, we will showcase an unconventional spiritual-financial solution, deeply immersed in spirituality and infused with local moral values and traditions, working successfully in an Islamic (Eastern) country, which is presented as a role model in providing solutions for poverty alleviation in other countries around the world, specifically underdeveloped and/or developing Muslim countries.

It was through this quest for those integrative, successful and innovative models in Pakistan that could be presented to my UK colleagues and stakeholders, that I came across an unconventional (Islamic) spiritual-financial model, Akhuwat Foundation. After a few sittings with its founder and CEO, Dr. Amjad Saqib, I realised that the model he created is not only steeped in spirituality but also is quite unique.

In TRANS4M's four world terms, an economy, in order to flourish over the long term, needs to be aligned with the innermost belief systems of a society or community. Taking this approach forward, we aim to build a case, taking Akhuwat Foundation, an unconventional Islamic socio-economic model, as a case study to show that the closer Muslims are to the ideal, the greater the stability in Islamic societies.

Akhuwat (brotherhood) presents a perfect case study for such, as the model has an unconventionally spiritual approach to financing enterprise, which was borne out of Dr. Amjad Saqib's spiritual inclination and his deep fascination with Islamic philosophy, following the Sunnah (tradition of the Prophet), and local traditions of Bhai-chara (brotherhood).

For Amjad

## The regime of selfish wealth must now be razed

*Dr. Muhammad Amjad Saqib, founder of the world's largest 'economic brotherhood', Akhuwat, joined the elite Civil Service of Pakistan in 1985. Having stood out as a public servant, right when his career was to move towards higher echelons, he resigned in 2003 with the intent to dedicate himself to becoming a social entrepreneur and facilitating societal change through Akhuwat – which had already been founded by him in 2001 and had meanwhile started taking strides towards the force it was to become. The salient feature of his public service career – one that perhaps changed the course of his life – was his last assignment as general manager of Punjab Rural Support Programme (PRSP). It was here that he had the opportunity to closely examine the various initiatives of poverty alleviation, education management, participatory development and conventional microfinance. This made him realise that 'something different had to be done'. This desire to do 'something different', something more effective as a panacea for the poor, spurred him on to conceive and introduce an interest-free microfinance model based on the idea of Mawakhat or brotherhood.*

The year 2000. In those days, I worked for the Punjab Rural Support Programme (PRSP) in Lahore. As a vision of rural development, the Rural Support Programme had gained practical shape after several decades of struggle. Among the many who can be credited with this achievement, two prominent names come to mind: Akhtar Hameed Khan and Shoaib Sultan. Their efforts and that of those before them in the struggle for participatory rural development became consummated in the form of this realisation. An important function of PRSP was to provide small loans to enable people to set up their own ventures and lift themselves out of poverty.

The shackles of poverty could not be shattered, however, because of an inherent curse in the system. Service charges, often exceeding 20%, were being added to these loans. In similar programmes elsewhere, the charges were as high as 50%. Taking out a small loan could be a significant step towards success; therefore, many people protested against these exorbitant service charges. We are well aware of the extent to which every moral system or religion in the world disapproves of the burden of interest. In all fairness, the poor should have the right to acquire loans to set up small enterprises and escape the clutches of poverty, and the loan is Qard-e-Hasan – a loan without interest. When it comes to poverty, instead of monetary benefit, compassion and sacrifice must prevail.

It was at PRSP that I noticed the oppressive economic system at work. A wealthy person borrowed at an interest rate of about 10–12% and a poor person at 30–40%. This was ironic because access to credit made a wealthy man wealthier, but a poor person only acquired two extra morsels or a roof over his head or enabled his child to go to school or his elderly parents to receive medicine. Can there not be an economic system where the fruit of a poor man's toil falls into his own lap?

Akhuwat was the struggle to create such a society, where there is no deprivation and exploitation of the poor and where, in place of rapacity and temptation, the ethos of benevolence and sacrifice rules.

During this period, an opportunity to talk with the pioneer of Grameen Bank, Dr. Muhammad Yunus, arose. He is counted among those people who have altered the course of history. Through his efforts, microfinance received global recognition as a viable tool for alleviating poverty. After acknowledging his services, I drew his attention to the injustice that laced the service charges imposed on small loans for the poor. He expressed his commitment to keeping the service charges as low as possible but suggested that those questioning the very existence of service charges failed to comprehend the system. 'Why don't they design something themselves that is free of interest' he inquired. Aware of the requisites of etiquette, I smiled politely and chose not to argue with him. Following this discussion, however, my impetus to devise a system that would be free of the cancer of interest intensified. Enquiry and endeavour can open closed doors: new paths began to emerge, and a far destination started coming into view. The question was whether I was prepared to embark on that journey.

### *A new dawn; a new resolve*

Akhuwat was eventually launched in March 2001. Modestly and discreetly, we started conferring small loans without interest to the poor while working from within a mosque. We had decided not to run it as a business: self-promotion would be eschewed, nothing would be taken from global agencies or institutions – each rule different, each procedure unprecedented.

> Unusual in state, distinct from the whole world they are
> O Lord! Inhabitants of which habitation these Lovers are?[1]

Akhuwat has a virtue-based approach to poverty alleviation and has designed its various social and economic development activities as an expression of solidarity with the marginalised and disadvantaged groups of people. Akhuwat's vision of development is known as Mawakhat, meaning 'solidarity' – a paradigm of justice and compassion.

Mawakhat refers to the creation of brotherhood between emigrants (Muhajireen) and the helpers (Ansar). The Holy Prophet (peace be upon him established brotherhood between the Muhajireen and Ansar. He paired off each Muhajir with one Ansar and declared them brothers. The generous Ansar gave over one half of their wealth to their new brothers so that they could live comfortably in Medina.

Incidentally, the last few decades have seen the emergence of a number of institutions that used microfinance as a tool for poverty alleviation. These programmes, however, failed to benefit the poorest of the poor because of the huge service charges they imposed on the beneficiaries of these loans. People were also avoiding accessing these loans due to their faith beliefs. Active research during his association with the Rural Support Programmes helped him to fuse the notions of interest-free banking with the principles of microfinance, and he started articulating these innovative ideas. Dr. Saqib was able to mobilise a large number of volunteers to perform various administrative and professional tasks for Akhuwat. This helped him keep the operational costs low, a sine qua non of providing free-of-cost micro-credit. Akhuwat, a novel initiative which banks on civil society, ultimately created new vistas and is now inspiring many other NGOs to follow its suit and contribute to poverty reduction efforts the world over. The model has by now been replicated by many organizations, but at close to $600 million in disbursed amount Akhuwat remains the largest such institution in the world.

Malcolm Harper, the renowned microfinance expert, on his visit to Pakistan made a point of coming to see what we were doing in the name of microfinance. When he arrived at the mosque and witnessed our modus operandi, he observed *'I am not surprised Akhuwat has broken the existing rules of microfinance. What I am surprised about is that in spite of this, they are heading towards success'*.

For Amjad, altruism and sacrifice, passion and perseverance, and the beautiful tropes of tradition form Akhuwat's philosophy of brotherhood (Bhai-chara), but none of this happened by itself.

A lifetime is needed to pluck the string of love
Where today is the bliss in the wounded heart[2]

Akhuwat places a lot of emphasis on and draws its inspiration from 'brotherhood' or solidarity by invoking the doctrine of Mawakhat-e-Medina, which immediately expects communal solidarity amongst believers to the extent that each individual be willing to literally adopt another as a family member.

Pakistan, officially the Islamic Republic of Pakistan, is the sixth-most populous country, with a population exceeding 2.1 million people. It is a state founded on an ideological basis and not on territorial grounds. Incidentally, Pakistan is unique among Muslim countries, as it is the only country to have been created in the name of Islam. Islamic ideology is the philosophy underlying the two-nation theory. Pakistan is purely an ideological state whose foundations were laid on Islamic ideology based on the Quranic teachings and Sunnah. Those who repudiate the two-nation theory and oppose Islamization are not considered friends and well-wishers of the country.

Based on Lessem and Schieffer's analysis, the world is undergoing a profound civilizational crisis in an attempt to outgrow the existing, modernist worldview and forming a new, more sustainable paradigm, what they term as 'alternative to modernity'. As such, this book then aims to explore if 'liberation' from the dominant Western worldview is really an answer to developmental problems for a faith-based country like Pakistan, withholding the fact that the spiritual-financial solution Akhuwat came up with has proved to be successful locally in its local albeit spiritual context. Basing our conclusion on Akhuwat's success due to its founder's vision and leadership qualities emulating from the Prophet's tradition (Sunnah) and taking Iqbal's wisdom, as the philosopher and Muslim visionary of the East.

Furthermore, building on TRANS4M's 'integral approach' as per Ronnie Lessem & Alexander Schieffer

> where personal origination, for one character or another, in one place/society or another, is followed by managerial and organizational foundation. Thereafter, individual leadership has its subsequently, emancipatory place, only when set within a developing self, and organization as well as a particular society. Thus, for Lessem & Schieffer (ibid), integral transformation follows when all of such is not only differentiated but also integrated: self, organization and society, set within a particular world, in relation to other worlds, psychologically and culturally.
>
> (Schieffer & Lessem, 2014)

We thus aim to close-match their new notion of the 'integrator' in the twenty-first century with an Islamic 'spiritual-social innovator' arising from self-individuation through spiritual emulation, emerging from local wisdom traditions and acculturation. Through this new approach to 'spiritual-social innovation', we strive to provide an alternative outlook on societal transformation sought out through spiritual and wisdom integration in a faith-based society. Hoping this somewhat closes the gap and philosophical divide between Islamic spirituality and Western cultural understanding of these traditions.

This book can be approached in two different ways. If the reader is primarily interested in having a deeper look into what role spirituality, mystical traditions in this instance, however subliminally, plays in shaping a society's psyche and/or leadership of a faith-based society, i.e., Pakistan in this case, this book will provide some insight.

However, if the reader wishes to explore an alternative solution to the 'ethical' banking/lending model, or what is termed as 'integral finance' by TRANS4M's 'integral development' model, through an Islamic perspective of separation of profitability from productivity, i.e., interest-free lending and banning of excessive gharar – a term in Islamic jurisprudence which stands for speculative uncertainty deliberately structured within financial contracts in pursuit of profit – it is presented here, in Akhuwat's case.

This is our attempt to initiate a new so(u)lidarity movement by presenting a case study of a unique *integral finance* model. Though it comes from the *holy* East (Pakistan), it could equally be inspirational for the capitalistic debt economies to adopt. Furthermore, it is an attempt to release the Pakistani GENE-IUS (Grounding, Emergence, Navigation and Effect) through the integral 4C (Call, Context, Co-creation and Contribution) model developed by Lessem and Schieffer (ibid), thereby integrally CARE-ing (Community activation, raising Awareness, Research-to-innovation and Embodied action) for Pakistan through Akhuwat's 4I (Iman, Ikhlas, Ihsan and Ikhuwah) GENE-alogy.

## Notes

1 Allama Iqbal (Bang-e-Dra-055)
2 A verse of Altaf Hussain Hali, another poet of sub-continent, who believed in Muslim renaissance along with Iqbal and Sir Sayyed Ahmad Khan

## References

Jones, M., 2014. *The Soul of Place*. Victoria, Bc: Friesen Press.
Lessem, R., & Bradley, T., 2018. *Evolving Work*. Abingdon: Routledge.
Schieffer, A., & Lessem, R., 2014. *Integral Development*. Farnham: Gower Publishing Ltd.
Wood, P., 2016. *Are British values really Islamic values?* Open Democracy UK. Available at: https://www.opendemocracy.net/uk/philip-wood/are-british-values-really-islamic-values

# Part I

# Orientation – spiritual bases of regional cultures

## 1 Initiation: the 4 P's of the SOUL-idarity process in an age of integrality

### *1.1 Preamble*

> 'As a philosophy, Akhuwat cannot fail; if the movement does not succeed, it will not be a failure of the principles and ideals that guide the organisation. Failure could only stem from the waning strength of men and the weakness of their resolve but never from the lack of strength in the idea of Akhuwat itself.'

*In the prologue we have covered our distinctive Akhuwat paths, intertwined spiritually (Islamic) and culturally (Pakistani), whereas my overall orientation was to cross paths with a new discipline, developed by Lessem and Schieffer, which is integral and dynamic, yet holistic in its nature, which truly aligns it with my spiritual purpose.*

As such, Amjad's call was to fight the biggest challenges facing Pakistan – poverty elimination and reviving the spirit of Mawakhat/solidarity endowment. In doing so, he has successfully devised a localised financial solution which veritably came out of the pages of Islamic history and the Prophetic tradition of Mawakhat. This model of finance has been helping Pakistan in two ways: On the one hand, it is providing access to finance for the poorest of the poor of the society, and on the other hand, the resources provided to the poor have been conducive in helping the growth of local micro-enterprises at a grassroots level, thereby generating a self-sufficient economy for Akhuwat's community.

*Whereas I was introduced to Lessem and Schieffer's 'integral dynamics' and their TRANS4M work whilst acting as a research facilitator for one of their PhD students, their holistic fourfold approach, especially the framework they've developed for 'CARE-ing-4- Society' (Community activation, raising Awareness, Research-to-innovation and Embodied action) and 'releasing of GENE-IUS' resonated completely with the work I was involved in, which revolves around community cohesion and social integration in a CARE-ing way. Particularly, their GENE (Grounding, Emergence, Navigation and Effect) model naturally appealed to my inquisitive Sufi/philosophical nature, or as I call it, the soul-wisdom of things.*

*As we, Amjad and I, explored our respective fields, my spiritual path was to meet with the integral. A new trans4mation took place after I became a lifelong ally of TRANS4M, to be taken in as a research fellow of TRANS4M's research community at a later stage.*

*Then, came the proposition of writing a book with Dr. Amjad Saqib, Akhuwat's founder and chairperson, on Akhuwat. This provides us with an opportunity to present Akhuwat as a case study of an integral finance model, having successfully generated a solidarity economy for its community of micro-borrowers through a reciprocal endowment model of Qard-e-Hasan.*

*On a personal level, this is immensely relevant to the work I do, i.e., bridging the Pakistan–global knowledge divide. And as part of my community organisation, The WISE Initiative (WISE stands for Women in Societal Enterprise), wherein we help migrant women to develop their potential to be socially and economically active.*

*My fascination with their unique and distinctive model was equivalently shared by my colleagues at TRANS4M. This in turn plays an important role of providing us with an opportunity to study and explore an Islamic spiritual-finance model serving to promote our collective co-creation of a Centre for Integral Finance & Economics (CIFE), established in London, UK by my TRANS4M colleague, Robert Dellner.*

*Throughout the course of this book, I act as a narrator, along with – in a researcher's capacity – phenomenologically establishing a link between Pakistan and Akhuwat's implicit spiritual philosophy, conjointly in Dr. Saqib's words, and finally, communicating through TRANS4M's integral dynamics process.*

## 2 The process

*I understand it could prove challenging to read or perhaps at times understand the way this book is written, that is, by adopting various methods of inquiry and research processes all stitched together to narrate Akhuwat's story – and that too in light of our own personal and shared knowledge, insights and experiences. If anything, the whole process is more subjectively intuitive and at times transcendental, as it occurred from a deeper state of knowing, which often gets lost in the process of translation.*

*Why subjective? The whole Akhuwat phenomenon, as I perceived it, and as it spoke to me, besides being unique in its economic and financial nature, is also philosophical and spiritual in its approach, as conceived by its founder Dr. Amjad Saqib. Yet, to my dissatisfaction, everywhere I looked, Akhuwat was portrayed as yet another model of Islamic microfinance and not as an integrated model of, for example, Associative Economics as per Rudolph Steiner's postulation, or indeed 'spiritual economics' as my Christian colleague Tony Bradley, based at Liverpool Hope University, also a fellow of TRANS4M, maintains.*

*What is intuitive knowledge?* According to Persian polymath Ibn Sina, also known as Avicenna, every act of cognition involves the illumination of the mind by the active intellect, which bestows upon the mind the form whose knowledge is the knowledge of the subject in question.

The power of creative imagination, which is only perfected in the Universal Man (al-insan al-kamil), is able to create forms in the imaginal world and know these forms ontologically. As maintained by Iranian Islamic philosopher Mulla Sadra, the very existence of these forms is the knowledge of them in the same way that according to Persian philosopher and founder of the Iranian school of Illuminationism, Shabab al-Din Suhrawardi, God's knowledge of the world is the very reality of the world.

In any case, the harmony and balance between intellect and intuition is perfected by Mulla Sadra through his recourse to this intermediate domain and the intermediate faculty of knowing this domain, the faculty which is none other than the power of 'imagination' (takhayyul) residing in the soul and integrally related to the rational, intellectual and intuitive faculties of the soul.

*Why metaphysical?* Tasawwuf (spiritual science) is a branch of Islamic knowledge which focuses on the spiritual development of the Muslim, thereby disciplining the *Self* to act in accordance with authenticated intentions by becoming an empty vessel receiving direct divine guidance.

The subject of Tasawwuf and its goals can be summarised as follows:

- Salvation from ignorance and attainment of gnosis (ma`arifah) – ***intuitive knowledge domain***
- Refinement and purification of the Self (tazkiyah al-nafs) – ***existential knowledge domain***
- Cleansing of the spiritual heart (tasfiyah al-qalb) and the enlightenment of the soul (tajliyah al-ruh) – ***active knowledge domain***
- Sincerity and devotion to the Creator (ikhlas) and detachment from material and worldly concerns (zuhd), and commitment to the service of all the creatures of God – ***social knowledge domain***

*As I immersed myself more deeply into Akhuwat's philosophy of Mawakhat (solidarity) and as it is professed by Dr. Saqib – a Sufi by nature, I sensed that Akhuwat has the potential for defining a new model of finance which is so unique that there might not be a single definition for it, yet it encompasses a universality of many disciplines and cultures in its approach. It is distinct, as no one has dared to experiment with various intersections as Akhuwat has.*

*For example, Akhuwat, as an institution, is fully integrated and conscientious of various societal challenges faced by the Pakistani society, providing solutions (and a societal framework) to assuage the social consequences of abject poverty by providing micro-loans. Yet it does not function or operate merely as a microfinance organisation – giving out micro-loans – but also educates the masses by raising their awareness of 'reciprocal endowment' (Akhuwat's principles of volunteerism and borrowers becoming donors), thereby instilling a communal spirit of Mawakhat (Akhuwat's principle of Qard-e-Hasan, or interest-free loans).*

*This is why I, acting as a narrator, have thus instinctively adopted the transcendental phenomenology method, combined with participatory cooperative inquiry through my Sufi knowledge, and all this is supported by the Transformational theory, developed by Lessem and Schieffer as co-founders of the TRANS4M movement.*

*For I strongly believe that this could only be effectuated through an integral language which is trans-disciplinary and trans-cultural to a consequential transformational effect. Additionally, as I believe, Islam as a religion (faith) and Muslims as a community are evolving as the Muslim population is growing globally. Its many disciplines are becoming more adaptive of universality, especially for its Muslim population living in non-Muslim countries. Therefore, for Akhuwat to have a global visibility and acknowledgment within Islamic finance sectors as a (creative) model of integral finance, TRANS4M's multi-disciplinary integral language is used to present Akhuwat's unique phenomenon.*

Transcendental phenomenology: Clark Moustakas, American psychologist and one of the leading experts on humanistic and clinical psychology, in his book *Phenomenological Research Methods*, states, 'Transcendental phenomenology (TPh), largely developed by Husserl, is a philosophical approach to qualitative research methodology seeking to understand human experience' (Moustakas, 1994).

Cooperative inquiry: This method, also known as collaborative inquiry, was first proposed by John Heron in 1971 and later expanded with Peter Reason. The major idea of cooperative inquiry is to 'research "with" rather than "on" people'.

In the process of writing this book, I have therefore adopted this method rather than using a quantitative research methodology. This cooperative inquiry method of action research was adopted to assimilate qualitative knowledge to inquire into Akhuwat's distinctive model of finance. This included endless discussions with my fellow research colleagues at TRANS4M globally as well as Dr. Amjad Saqib, the founder and visionary behind the Akhuwat phenomenon as well as Akhuwat's management team members.

*As the emergent solidarity impulse initially emanated through Amjad, it was thus important for me to understand the Self, the person: Amjad Saqib, the visionary, or Social Integrator – a term coined by Ronnie Lessem of TRANS4M movement, behind the phenomenon, from this perspective.*

The Transformational GENE: Furthermore, the Transformational GENE rhythm as developed by the integral dynamics process (Lessem & Schieffer, 2013) provided me with an integrative theory which supports any such abstract yet interpretive method of research and narration.

Hence, the inspiration for my SOUL-idarity Hikma GENE emerged from this GENE process, thereby birthing a new integral-spiritual Hikma (wisdom) paradigm.

The fourfold model of integral realities (worldviews), and realms (knowledge domains), provides what they call their static or stabilising elements. The dynamic is provided most especially, and thirdly, by what they term their integral rhythm – grounding to effect, combined with, fourthly, their integral rounds – self-to-organisational-to-societal (their rounds) development.

Such a 'rhythm', then, underlies the recognition and release of a particular individual (self) and collective (community, organisation and society) GENE-IUS (Grounding, Emerging, Navigating and Effecting) (Lessem & Bradley, 2018a).

In an age of integrality, as per our collective call, along with TRANS4M's research community, Akhuwat's dynamic solidarity impulse needed one such medium to research what lies at the heart (core) of such an impulse.

Furthermore, it equips us to translate how the *recursive* (involving an effective, inauthentic 'fall' before a potentially authentic 'rise') *GENE* process, as postulated by my TRANS4M colleague Reverend Tony Bradley (Lessem & Bradley, 2018b).

This same GENE process, as perceived by me, is doing rounds in the 21st century through Amjad's Islamic Pakistani archetypal approach, renewing the Prophetic philosophy of Mawakhat through a bond of solidarity, all of this created through Akhuwat's virtuous circles which I, now, term the multiplier effect of 'barakah (God's bounty) rounds'.

### *2.1 The 4 R's of integral development*

For Schieffer and Lessem (Lessem & Schieffer, 2013), the four main elements of the integral development approach, drawing from their overall 'integral worlds' approach, are what they call the 4 R's: *Realities, Realms, Rounds and Rhythms.* These four constituents are dynamically and interactively interwoven.

These rhythms stimulate and enable dynamic and interactive processes towards authentically addressing the development calling and challenge at hand. They are designed to release the GENE-IUS of a particular self, organisation, community and society.

As such the 4 R's are simplified as:

| | |
|---|---|
| ***Integral Realities:*** | ***South and East, North and West*** |
| ***Integral Realms:*** | ***Nature, Culture, Technology/Systems and Economy*** |
| ***Integral Rhythm:*** | ***Origination, Foundation, Emancipation and Transfomation*** |
| ***Integral Rounds:*** | ***Self, Organisation, Society and ultimately University*** |

The interactive and dynamic engagement of all 4 R's with a specific, underlying inner and outer calling as core, lodged within a particular local context

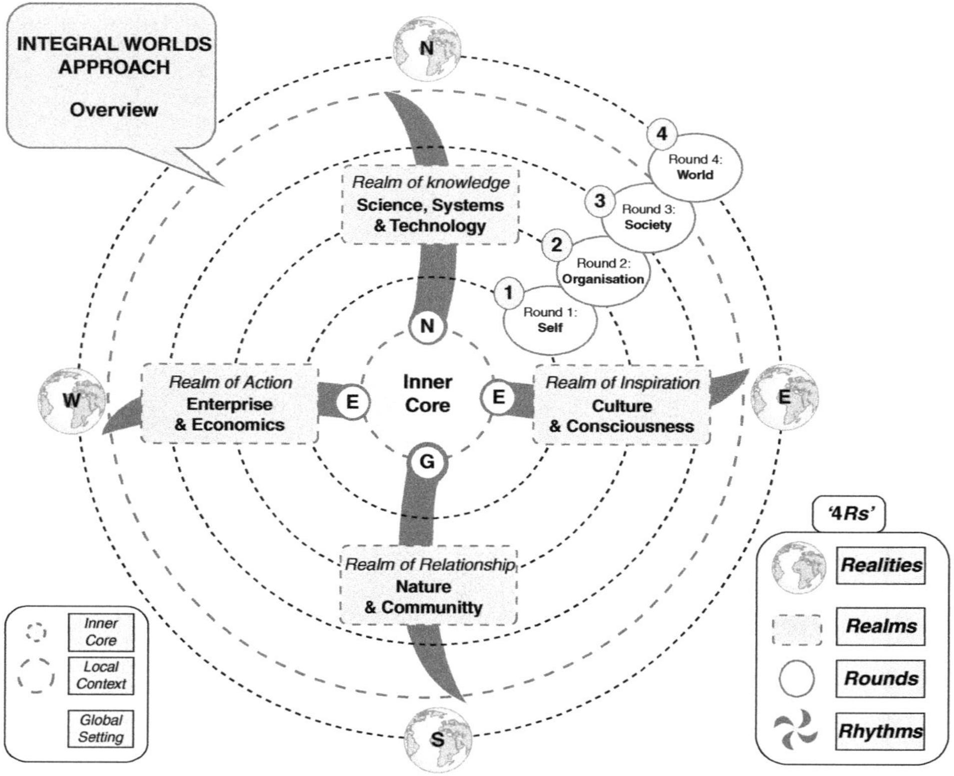


Model developed by Ronnie Lessem & Alexander Schieffer Integral Development (2013)

*Figure I.1* Integral Worlds

and global setting, is reflected in the circular, integral framework of integral development shown below.

As such the four *Transpersonal Rounds* following through the four *Trans-disciplinary Realms* of a particular personal, organisational or societal development calling and challenge are:

- *1st Round of Self Development*
- *2nd Round of Organisational Development*
- *3rd Round of Societal Development*
- *4th Round of University Development*

From an Islamic symbiotic viewpoint, the circle is the most important coded form for imagination of unitary and integrity issue in constitution of the existing universe. The radii of the circle are radiation codes, the circumference of the circle is the reflection code and the surface of the whole circle is the code of existence itself or a specific level of existence. The circular rotation of the planetary system codifies the journey of unity towards the centre. This brings us to the journeying of our *solidarity-gene* rhythm around the four worlds.

### *2.2 Why the four-worlds journey of the solidarity GENE?*

Everything in this universe is marked by a sense of restlessness – the stars, the stones, the trees and man; all are in motion.

Love is the beginning of this journey and beauty its quest. Those who live by this rule are the ones who succeed; those who are indifferent remain at a loss.

In Amjad's words:

*For us, the resonance of journeying through stages of self and communal metamorphosis is all too familiar with the journeying of the soul or pilgrimage (Hajj). The circumambulation resonates with the physical circumambulation around the Kabah, the ultimate spiritual journey for any Muslim.*

Circumambulating the Kabah represents the idea of oneness. In regards to social life, it means not to leave unity and to try to maintain this unity. Its meaning regarding individual life contains deep truths. The sky has seven layers; man has seven souls. Each revolution around the Kabah represents a phase, a stage; man covers a phase and is elevated up to the seventh sky, above the material realm. Besides, it means to rise from the lowest realm of the soul, which has seven realms, to the highest one. That is, from Nafs al-Ammarah (soul commanding to evil) to Nafs al-Mutmainnah (tranquil self), from the animal life to the spiritual life. It is a kind of worship taken from the order of the universe. The planets rotate around the sun, the electrons around the nucleus, the moth around the candle; rotating around such a centre means allegiance to love.

This cyclical procession is called tawaf (circumambulation), the ritual of taking seven rounds around the holy Kabah.

The Arabic verb tafa, from which the term for the circumambulation (tawaf) is derived, has the meaning to '*attain to the summit of a thing by spiralling around it*'. Hence, it is thought that through the tawaf the pilgrim participates with the angels in their circumambulation of the Divine Throne. This is so because cosmologically the Kabah is regarded as the reflection of the archetypal Divine House in the seventh (or fourth) Heaven, above and beyond which stands the Throne of Allah, around which the angels are constantly rotating (Uzdavinys, 2011).

The two complementary ideas of circularity and centrality are involved in the establishment of a haram, a sanctuary, where the physical (man) meets the spiritual (Divine).

For us, this represents the solidarity impulse which pulsates in the centre (Kabah/sanctuary) and the cyclical procession around it spirals down as the Divine bounty (barakah) transcends in circularity. For us, any journey (Hijrah/ migration) one takes to achieve God-proximity and recompense through one's acts of kindness towards fellow beings sets this impulse in motion.

Thus, we draw a parallel with Lessem and Schieffer's (Lessem & Schieffer, 2010) four cultural types or 'worlds' (drawing on Jung's personality types) as a metaphor to both explain trans-cultural and trans-disciplinary differentiation in individual, organisational and societal approaches and to point the way towards their trans-personal and trans-formational integration.

The resultant 'four worlds' integral orientation would also serve to dynamically promote *individuation, continuity and change, research and innovation, learning and development*, and overall *cultural transformation* through a new 'genealogical combination' of *community, sanctuary, university and laboratory.*

The four worlds identified in Lessem and Schieffer's integral theory are figurative labels of Western, Northern, Eastern and Southern to represent four cultural types that can be found simultaneously both 'out there', that is, in society, economically and politically, and 'in here', for us, psychologically and socially, with the newly genealogical combination of 'Southern' community, 'Eastern' sanctuary, 'Northern' university and 'Western' laboratory mediating between the two.

The release of genius, thus, turns the integral-static (four worlds) into an integral-dynamic GENE (*Grounding, Emergence, Navigation and Effect*), releasing GENE-IUS, including I, yoU, and the Synergy between us.

Thus, our solidarity GENE rhythm draws inspiration from the integral four worlds theory of GENE rhythm.

## 3 The structure – 4 P's of SOUL-idarity Hikma – the wisdom of solidarity

Ajaz Ahmed Khan is a senior microfinance advisor with CARE International – Akhuwat's lending partner in the UK. According to him, Akhuwat of Pakistan is probably the purest Islamic microfinance institution and one of the largest anywhere, but is at the same time one of the simplest. Akhuwat, however, is something of a hybrid. In fact, Akhuwat turns the concept of economic man (or woman) on its head (Harper & Khan, 2017).

Such is the phenomenal nature of Akhuwat's paradigm: outwardly simple yet inwardly a whole philosophy of reciprocity, benevolence and compassion.

*It was thus important for me to draw on Akhuwat's implicit inner wisdom of hybridity. This book is therefore interwoven into four layers of our 4P process which draws on Akhuwat's philosophy and processes in a unique way, thereby drawing a parallel with the four rounds of integral dynamics conceived in Lessem and Schieffer's integral GENE orientation*:

- *The Philosophy – Round I: the philosophy of Akhuwat/solidarity (SOUL-idarity)*
- *The Principles – Round II: Akhuwat's four principles*
- *The Practices – Round III: Akhuwat's principles in practice*
- *Integral Hikma Paradigm – Round IV: Akhuwat's integral SOUL-idarity paradigm*

*The Figure I.2 maps out our 4P's in a more illustrative way*:

***Part One (Chapters 1,2 and 3)*** *of the book explores the Mawakhat (solidarity) phenomenon from an Islamic spiritu-philosophical lens. It is that which forms the deeper, implicit layer of Akhuwat's philosophy through the Hikma (wisdom) of solidarity, as identified by me by employing Sufi knowledge (Tasawwuf) consolidated through the knowledge from Islamic philosophers and mystics, blended with the local wisdom traditions of the South Asian region – in our case, Pakistan. This part explores the nature and philosophy of our solidarity GENE impulse, thereby setting the scene for Akhuwat's four principles which constitute Akhuwat's philosophy of Mawakhat. For it was important to unravel this process to further adduce our new SOUL-idarity paradigm as a progression of Akhuwat's philosophy of reciprocity as a transcendental effect of its 4I (Iman, Ikhlas, Ihsan and Ikhuwah) GENE-alogy.*

***Part Two*** *analyses Akhuwat's four principles in the light of our proposed SOUL-idarity paradigm. It accentuates the solidarity impulse, furthermore emphasising the full effect of its four-stage iteration through the integral CARE-4-Society process, whereby CARE stands for Community activation, raising Awareness, Research-to-innovation and finally Embodied action. Drawing a*

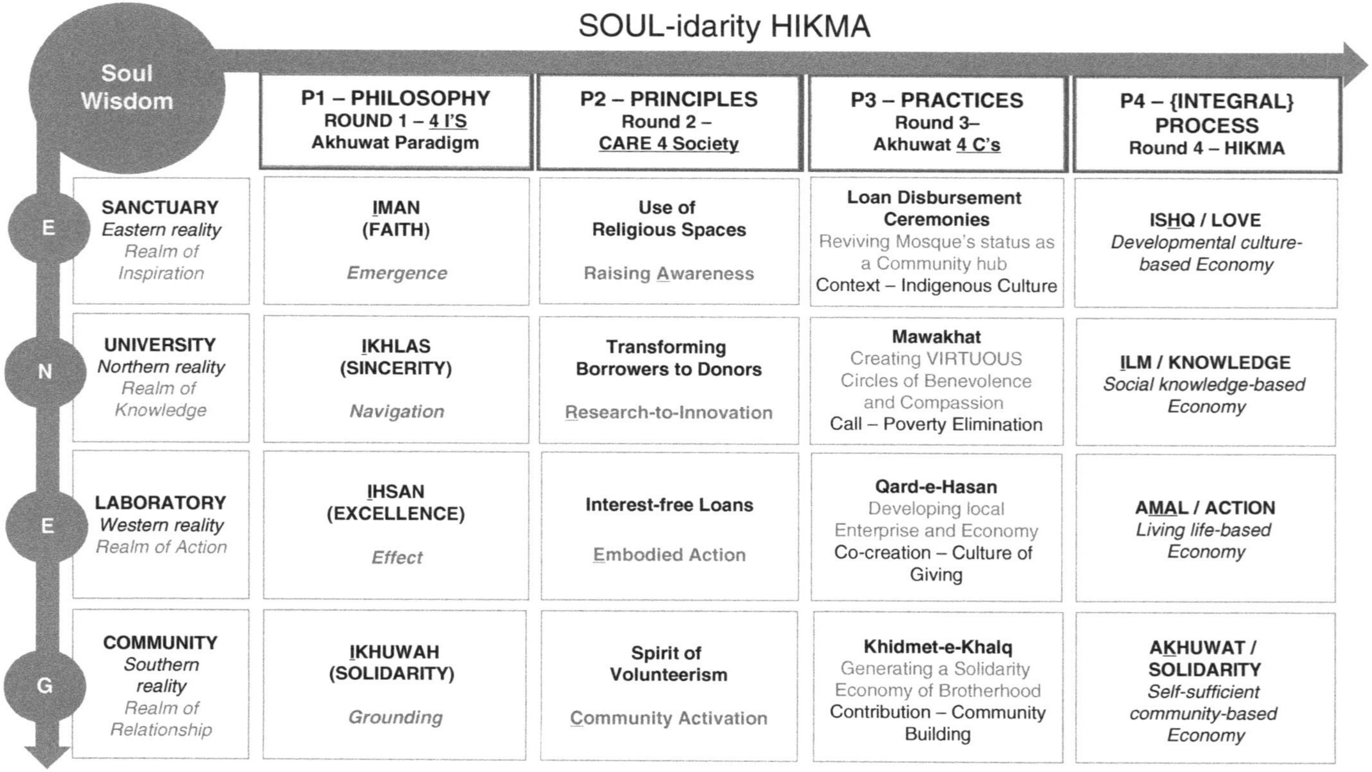


*Figure I.2* 4P SOUL-idarity Hikma

*parallel between Akhuwat's four principles and integral 4C (Call, Context, Co-create, Contribution) process.*

***Part Three*** *of the book is a combination of Part One (Philosophy) and Part Two (The Principles), interpreting Akhuwat's various practices and operations in the light of the aforementioned two disciplines.*

***Part Four*** *is all of this through an integral dynamics transformational GENE noesis, thus conceptualising a new SOUL-idarity wisdom (Hikma) process, emerging from Akhuwat's philosophy and principles, altogether forming a new integral Hikma (born out of ishq, ilm, amal and akhuwat) language for integral finance. The research methods and action research adopted are transcendental phenomenology and cooperative inquiry as per my PHD (Process of Holistic Development) prerequisites.*

### *3.1 How to read this book*

For Khalil Jibran (1883–1931), a Lebanese writer, poet and mystic, thought is a state of *being* rather than a state of mind.

According to Jibran, "The appearance of things changes according to the emotions and thus, we see magic and beauty in them, while the magic and beauty are really in ourselves". *And thus, we expect our readers to read this book, actioning (amal) through our solidarity (ikhuwah) impulse, and by employing their heart (ishq) dimension along with their aql/intellect (ilm), the rational faculty of the soul or mind. And whilst doing that, imagine a new discipline of SOUL-idarity through reciprocity, compassion and benevolence.*

For me particularly, owing to my philosophical nature, transcending the nature and philosophy of a phenomenon is of utmost importance as its ontological progression indicator. For in Amjad's words, Akhuwat is a social movement, notwithstanding the fact it has borrowed the initial 'micro-lending' concept from the all-pervading microfinance movement which gained global awareness through Bangladeshi social-business guru Muhammad Yunus and his Grameen Bank initiative. Where Akhuwat parts ways with the much-lauded microfinance movement is by transcending the boundaries set by the (formal) microfinance industry, by turning the whole movement around in favour of people who not only needed a loan but engage in social ownership, and with reciprocal endowment too, by unequivocally advocating the spirit of Mawakhat/solidarity and association with the lesser-able fellow community members, i.e., the poorest of the poor. In this respect, Akhuwat vends itself as a family of Akhuwateers all working towards bettering the society, displaying a sense of solidarity with each other.

*For that purpose alone, as altruistic as it might sound to many of our readers, my intention is to make visible the 'invisible' impulse: that which – if presumed with the same intention, of reciprocity and ihsan (benevolence) – could help in finding a solution to our cursory man-made social divides between 'the haves' (those who have and can give) and 'have-nots' (those who could do with some taking).*

For behind the constitutional 'poverty elimination' anterior, Akhuwat's overarching call is to build a 'just' and equitable society, just as ordained by Islamic principles and code of conduct. How much it has succeeded in achieving this idealistic purpose is interpreted through the course of this book, albeit through the lens of my Sufistic and inventive 'inner eye'.

*This is how I have perceived it, but how Akhuwat progresses, particularly with its recent endeavours of institutionalising this 'spirit of solidarity' by building an Akhuwat-versity, remains to be seen.*

### *3.1.1 How not to read this book*

As reiterated above, Akhuwat is commonly known and perceived as the largest (interest-free) microfinance organisation, inside and outside of Pakistan. Whereby, I am presenting Akhuwat as a futuristic alchemist for co-creating a SOUL-idarity Hikma (wisdom) through a transcendental contemplation of its 4 I's (Iman, Ikhlas, Ihsan and Ikhuwah), thereby self-sufficiently generating a model of integral finance. This will serve, moreover, as our ongoing collective integral pursuit – to catalyse a model of integral finance and economics through our Centre for Integral Finance and Economics (CIFE), substantially based in the UK, at the same time collaborating with CISER (Centre for Integral Social & Economic Research) in Nigeria, along with our colleagues from Integral Africa, not to mention the whole TRANS4M community.

What this book does not propose is to outline Akhuwat as a microfinance organisation in comparison to other such organisations in Pakistan or in its neighboring countries. While Akhuwat aims to rid Pakistan of poverty just as Muhammed Yunus wished to do with Grameen Bank, Akhuwat parts ways with the the Grameen model in its absolute immersion in the Islamic model of Qard-e-Hasan (benevolent loan), that is, of ridding the society of an imposed scarcity of resources amongst abundance of wealth possessed by the privileged class of the society.

For Akhuwat (brotherhood or Bhai-chara in Urdu) sets in motion its collective impulse of societal reciprocity by emphasising its four stages of self and societal development through its 4I orientation. This is further explained in Chapters 3 and 8.

## *3.2 Language and symbolism*

*Throughout the course of the book you will encounter a significant amount of Urdu and Arabic terms. The usage of such became inevitable, as some terms could simply not be translated into English without exterminating the real essence of the word. Additionally, you will often find the language symbolically laden with Sufi symbolism and terminology.*

*For example, Akhuwat in Urdu is written with an A, whereas in Arabic it is written as Ikhuwah – with an I, both meaning brotherhood. Now the Arabic Ikhuwah is written with A and I as well. I and A are both pronounced as 'Alif', the first letter of both the Arabic and Urdu alphabets.*

*Additionally, Mawakhat is defined here as solidarity – a prophetic tradition, originating from the time of hijrah (migration) of Prophet Muhammad from Mecca to Medina, the Islamic holy cities in Saudi Arabia.*

*Furthermore, to avoid confusion, we are using various typefaces for our readers to mark the distinction between three primary contributors and terminologies.*

*For example*:

- *I, Aneeqa, as the narrator will be using italics whilst expressing my own views.*

| |
|---|
| • Amjad's quotes and narrations will be boxed. |

| |
|---|
| • Integral inserts are in shaded boxes to mark their distinction. |

## 4 Part I: the philosophy of solidarity coming from Islamic knowledge – grounding

*Why is it foremost and important for us to delve into the philosophy of solidarity (Akhuwat)?*

In the Islamic religion, philosophy, or falsafa, used to be the integral prerequisite for deciphering the Quran and the Tradition of Prophet Muhammad (may Allah's peace be upon him).

*The Quran itself is referred to as a falsafa-e-hayat (philosophy of life) in our part of the world, and that's how I became familiar with the word falsafa (philosophy). Or it could be my nature to speculate on the deeper or hidden meanings in everything around me. Retracing back to my earliest memories, all I could recall was how to apply this philosophy to our way of life, which I would only now understand had more to do with the local Hikma (wisdom) of the place (Lahore) rather than coming from a theological source. For example, I remember my mother teaching me the philosophy of life by reciting Heer Waris Shah or Mian Muhammad Baksh. Both are revered Punjabi mystic poets.*

As Satish Kumar, an Indian activist and editor now living in England, alludes to in his book, "we will be ill-equipped to care for the soil, nourish the soul and nurture society without the power of imagination manifested in the enchantment of poetry, the spell of songs. For him, the trinity of soil, soul and society is an inspiration that came out of Tagore's poetry". (Kumar, 2013)

*Thus it could be true for me then, as one learns one's mother tongue from their mother, so should be true that one knows one's soul connection with the soil through Hikma (wisdom) locked in that soil. Nobody taught me that philosophy – but perhaps my mother did, through her Eastern way of BEING;*

*hence, it's a coming of age for me. This could also be the reason for me to decipher Akhuwat's implicit philosophy in that light to give it a wider acknowledgment.*

The same rings true for Amjad, as he recalls the same wisdom of the soil coming to him through his teacher asking him to repetitively write one particular verse from Iqbal's poetry on his slate to instil it into his consciousness. The words were etched onto his soul and this is how he grew up with a deep knowledge and reverence for the Prophet of Islam as the only guide leading him on the path to (inner) knowledge/ilm.

For we believe and, hence, propose this further through our first chapter, that the soul-wisdom is an intrinsic knowledge that comes directly through the heart channel, i.e., by loving (ishq): loving one's mother, the teacher, the community, the soil, and so on and so forth.

The sense perceptions, thus, get activated by the 'feelings' we have for a place, person and even the God-entity. For how does one see God, to then love HIM/HER? It can only come from feeling HIS presence around us. And this I refer to as the eminence of solidarity, which will be further elaborated on in Chapter 3.

From lessons of love/ishq, we now proceed to the lessons of the Book (Ilm) – in our case, the ultimate Book: falsafa-e-hayat, the Quran – as our book holds a lot of Quranic references and ordinations. It is therefore important to particularise it further before moving on to Chapter 1.

### *4.1 The philosophy of the word/book (scripture and Sunnah)*

رَبِّ زِدْنِي عِلْماً *(Rabbi zidni ilma)*

*O my Lord! Advance me in knowledge. [Surah Ta-Ha (20):114]*

The Quran advises its readers to seek knowledge for the sake of seeking Allah, for seeking knowledge is a form of worship. And knowing makes one God-fearing and, more importantly, God-aware. In Surah Al-Fatir, Allah Almighty says: 'Only those fear Allah, from among His servants, who have knowledge. Indeed, Allah is Exalted in Might and Forgiving. (Surah Al-Fatir [35]:28).

For a Muslim, the ultimate knowledge source is the Quran, also referred to as Shariah (word of God). In Sufi, or mystic, traditions, there are four stages or paths that lead to the development of the soul – also known as Tazkiya (spiritual development) in Sufi terminology – to gain its existential knowledge and truth of Being.

These are: Shariah (exoteric path), Tariqah (esoteric path), Haqiqah (mystical truth) and Marifa (final mystical knowledge, unio mystica).

After gathering knowledge from the Quran (Shariah), one has to turn inward to decipher the deeper truths of the scripture and texts. The spiritual path leads to a complete surrender to God's word and ordination, as well as training one to take the path of *Ihsan* – spreading excellence and beauty on Earth and amongst one's community.

Henry Corbin (Corbin, 1993), a French philosopher and professor of Islamic Studies at the École Pratique des Hautes Études in Paris, in his seminal work on Eastern and Islamic philosophy explored 'The Sources of Philosophical Meditation in Islam' by drawing a comparison with the Western esoteric understanding of the tradition. In his book *History of Islamic Philosophy*, translated into English by Philip Sherrar, exploring the spiritual exegesis of the Quran, he probes how Muslims themselves have failed to take on the mystical and the philosophical nature of the Quran.

Corbin alludes to Islamic philosophy as the work of thinkers belonging to a religious community characterised by the Quranic expression ahl al-kitab: a people in possession of a sacred book, a people whose religion is founded on a book that 'came down from Heaven', is revealed to a prophet and is taught to the people by that prophet. Properly speaking, the 'people of the book' are the Jews, the Christians and the Muslims.

All these communities are faced with the problem of the basic religious phenomenon which is common to them all: the phenomenon of the Sacred Book, the law of life within this world and guide beyond it. The first and last task is to understand the true meaning of this Book. But the mode of understanding is conditioned by the mode of being of he or she who understands; correspondingly, the believer's whole inner ethos derives from his/her mode of understanding. The lived situation is essentially hermeneutical: a situation, that is to say, in which the true meaning dawns on the believer and confers reality upon his/her existence. This true meaning, correlative to true being – truth which is real and reality which is true – is what is expressed in one of the key terms in the vocabulary of philosophy: the word Haqiqah.

> The term designates, among many other things, the *true meaning* of the divine Revelations: a meaning which, because it is the *truth* of these Revelations, is also their *essence*, and therefore their *spiritual meaning*. One could thus say that the phenomenon of the 'revealed sacred Book' entails a particular anthropology, even a certain definite spiritual culture, and that it postulates, at the same time as it stimulates and orientates, a certain type of philosophy.
>
> (Corbin, 1993)

Early Islamic philosophy began in the 2nd century AH of the Islamic calendar (early 9th century CE) and lasted until the 6th century AH (late 12th century CE). This time period is known as the Islamic Golden Age, and its achievements influenced the development of modern philosophy and science. For Renaissance Europe, the influence representedne of the largest technology transfers in world history.

It was during this period of Islamic history that some of the most renowned Islamic philosophers, like Al-Farabi, Al-Ghazzali, Ibn Rushd and Ibn Arabi reigned and shaped Islamic thought. Hence, our book references and relies on the work of these mystic philosophers. Our intention is to revive this philosophical thinking of Islamic tradition. Also, our barakah rounds contemplation took guidance from the extensive work of these great philosophers of the 9th–12th centuries.

The work of these old philosophers is still followed, as since the end of the Golden Age Islamic intellectual culture has suffered from a philosophical deficit. While there are a few philosophical thinkers in the Islamic world, even they are mostly confined within Western institutional and empirical limits.

But we believe all is not lost, for there are practitioners such as Amjad Saqib who have taken this into their stride to practise this wisdom tradition (Mawakhat) in a practical setting (Akhuwat).

How this practice is conceptualised and pursued by the masses remains to be seen in the future.

*Conversely, I believe the most crucial work in the field of Islamic philosophy is being done within esoteric societies, to keep the mystical – which is the philosophical tradition of Islam – alive. For example, Pir Zia Inayat-Khan, the grandson of Hazrat Inayat Khan, is the Pir (spiritual leader) and president of the Sufi Order International and founder of Suluk Academy and the Seven Pillars House of Wisdom.*

'The Suluk Academy provides participants with the opportunity to take their spiritual education and inner life to new depths. The process fosters authentic personal transformation by shepherding participants through recognizable stages of self-discovery that lead to deep realization and greater awakening. This type and manner of study draws diverse 'seekers' from various spiritual backgrounds, traditions, cultures, lifestyles and occupations' (Suluk Academy.org).

*What I am doing through my own work, in association with Akhuwat and TRANS4M, is to transform such paths of individual transcendence into an organisational (Akhuwat) and societal (Pakistan) form, as well as ultimately world-wide Tran4mative outreach.*

In Islamic tradition, searching for knowledge is jihad, teaching it to those who do not know is charity, and reviewing and perfecting it is like tasbeeh (a form of dhikr that involves the repetitive utterances of short sentences in the praise and glorification of Allah).

For how we value knowledge nowadays differs from the way knowledge was perceived as sacred within the historical traditions of communities. Notwithstanding the fact, in our world today people value knowledge but are unable to distinguish between preaching and thinking and consequently putting that knowledge into practice, which is something Islam and the Quran emphasise. And this is what I find unique in Akhuwat's case, as not only are they putting the knowledge coming directly from the Quran and the Prophetic Sunnah into practice, but they are also reinventing and creating new awareness and knowledge through their practices and operations, on both a micro (finance) and macro (economic) SOUL-idarity basis.

For example, their loan disbursement ceremonies are held inside sanctuaries (mosques, churches and temples), raising awareness with a renewed purpose, as the whole purpose of creating religious spaces in most Abrahamic religions was to congregate communally in them for various reasons, from prayer gatherings to discussing matters of communal concern and benefit.

In doing so, Akhuwat has demonstrated the belief that without action (amal), knowledge (ilm) is of a sectional use only.

Indeed, within Muslim societies, there's a dire need for critical thinkers who force Muslims to think and not only yield feel-good narratives that create comfort bubbles and inhibit thought, but also lead by example and action. It is only through reading and engaging in philosophical discourses that the intellectual level of the Muslim community will rise, thereby claiming their rightful stature globally.

Equally important is this knowledge creation and raising awareness of this fact in reference to Pakistan, as this book presents Akhuwat's financial model, which is set within a Pakistani society. Through its distinctive model of Mawakhat (solidarity), Amjad has successfully generated a solidarity bond by raising awareness of his community through the practical example of a historic Prophetic tradition – of Hijrat-un-Nabwi (the Prophet's symbolic emigration from Mecca to Medina).

### *4.1.1 The spirit of the essence – the universal law of being*

In addition to preaching and spreading religion, almost every prophet sent to Earth was tasked to purify people's souls. Tasawwaf and Suluk (Sufism and the Sufi path) is the reality and the spirit of Islam. All the orders of Sufism pursued the same spirit of Islam, which involves cleansing of the soul and correction of the inner self.

The word Sufi comes from the term Tasawwuf, which is a branch of sciences of the sacred law that originated within the Muslim community, called an ummah, meaning, significantly for our purposes, *community*. From the first, the way of such people was also considered the path of truth and guidance by the early Muslim community and its notables: the companions of the Prophet (Allah bless him and give him peace), those who were taught by them, and those who came after them.

Another most-cherished aspect of Tasawwuf, for me, is the need to take to the middle path, or the 'centre ground', when it comes to applying Quranic knowledge or ordinance to matters of faith, arguably also in the middle, in between self, organisation and society.

Islam has a unique view on spirituality, as it encompasses all aspects of the Muslim's life. In present times, Muslims living in secular societies especially take the spiritual path, which emancipates them from relying on the more scholarly version of Islam, which as of late has lost its credence in the secular Western societies. On the other hand, having a spiritual or philosophical understanding of religion warrants the kind of knowledge (ilm) that transcends directly from the heart. God-consciousness is an essential element in Islamic spiritual practice; without it, the Muslim's behaviour and attitude are corrupted.

It is with this heart erudition that we embark on a journey – of a new discovery of knowledge; of our SOUL-idarity GENE rhythm – which is spiritual, thus, universal and, hence, all-encompassing and integrally dynamic.

*For a few years now, my work through my consultancy, The Loop Global Management, has revolved around bridging the knowledge gap that exists between individuals, communities, organisations and countries. My idealised quest for bridging the divide between social and spiritual, and between sacred and commercial, has often made me wonder why the gap between the spiritual and the material arises in practice, as I constantly notice this total disconnect between practice and principles within work and other spheres of daily life. Therefore, throughout the course of this book, I tend to explore this divide and why people are often so averse to the idea of bringing the spiritual into their commercial realm or, even if they did, they'd probably be merely paying lip-service, conventionally via so-called philanthropy, to what should really transcend and transform the dynamics of how we seek individual and organisational growth and upliftment, financial or otherwise. What I often find interesting to note is how people equate material and/or monetary success with growth, notwithstanding how Islam emphasises carrying on our acts in accordance with Allah's will.*

Is financial growth morally or spiritually uplifting for all? If so, how do we make the implicative nature of the spirit of things more definitive by transcending the essence with such awareness?

As previously communicated, Pakistan is a land of many mystic heavyweights. Some of them were direct descendants of the Prophet Muhammad (peace be upon him) and the four caliphs of Islam after the death of the Prophet. These Sufi saints are hugely revered in Pakistan, with disciples carrying on their soul-wisdom traditions.

## *4.2 Navigating through Pakistan – the 4C process (Chapter 2)*

Akhuwat and Pakistan are integrally netted together as being a faith-based organisation and country, whereby the Mawakhat philosophy of solidarity between brothers was well-received by most, especially those having knowledge of its historic and religious significance. As a matter of fact, Pakistan ranks near the top of the world in illiteracy. In that respect, for most people religious knowledge comes directly from religious places, e.g., mosques, churches and religious scholars; Akhuwat, thus, acknowledges this fact.

Additionally, both Amjad and I have a cardinal connection with Pakistan. Therefore, in Chapter 2 we will be exploring our collective soil connection with Pakistan through an integral 4C (Call, Context, Co-creation and Contribution) mediation developed by Lessem and Schieffer (2013).

Navigating through Pakistan's Call, along with our collective Call to Contribution, we will examine how Akhuwat and Amjad are institutionally CARE-ing for Pakistan through Akhuwat's various operations and our collective endeavours.

Parallel to the 4Cs process, in Chapter 5 we will explore Akhuwat's four principles by engaging with institutionalising *CARE* (Community activation, raising Awareness, Research-to-innovation and Embodied action) rhythm. This constitutes the second part of a dual rhythm towards full-fledged integral development. Together, the four CARE functions enable us to fully 'CARE-4-Society'. CARE, as a whole, is one of the key transformative trajectories of TRANS4M, enabling the gradual actualisation of a social innovation in a real-life context.

## 5 Part II: the solidarity impulse – emergence

Part two, after drawing from the philosophy of the solidarity impulse, explores the emergence of the impulse in Akhuwat's four principles (engaging religious spaces, Qard-e-Hasan, reciprocal endowment and reviving the spirit of volunteerism). The intention is to delve deeper into the spirit of the solidarity impulse and see what instigates that impulse – and the consequential effect this brings, using Akhuwat's living example of one such model of Mawakhat.

By employing the phenomenological 'I' and 'me' model of William James, an American philosopher and psychologist, scholars of human development study the phenomenological relation of the Self to other processes. In a phenomenological model, the 'I' and the 'me' interact to give an individual's self-consciousness its particular form.

*What makes an experience conscious is a certain awareness one has of the experience while living through or performing it. This became evident in Amjad's case whilst working with abjectly poor groups of people in rural areas. His direct contact with these people and their sufferings became the stimulus, lying at the core of Akhuwat's philosophy. And he rightly says that philosophies do not fail if they are borne out of phenomenon.*

*Therefore, the I in our SOUL-idarity intimation is the Self, which awakens the soul of solidarity between groups and communities.*

*From this end, I was intrigued to seek a deeper understanding of the Akhuwat paradigm, as every time I had a meeting with Amjad, he would keep emphasising Akhuwat's philosophy more than its practicality in, say, the financial world or its community of borrowers.*

*Amjad's philosophical call resonated deeply with mine, for being on a spiritual path trains one to look for deeper meaning in the 'spirit' of things. Spirituality means different things to different people, whereby, from an Islamic viewpoint; true spirituality is 'nearness' to Allah by performing every action with this intention to gain pleasure of Allah.*

*And this was what I found evident in Amjad's philosophy and principles of Akhuwat. For example, whenever someone asks him about Akhuwat's business model of interest-free loans and his organisation's sustainability, his answer would come from this deeper realm of tawakul (reliance on Allah), which is almost too altruistic to believe or put into practice in a pragmatic worldview.*

*It thus became inevitable for me to look deeper into the Sufistic philosophy of his Akhuwat paradigm, given his Sufi nature and the mystical influences of how Islam is practised in the South Asian region, Pakistan in our case. Incidentally, it all echoed with my own submission to the spiritual path I had been on for the past nine years. For having spent the formative years of my life in Saudi Arabia, a religiously Islamic country, and being born into a Muslim family, faith had never been as challenging as it turned out to be after my migration to a liberal and pluralistic society. What I was about to find out as I embarked on the spiritual path was never experienced whilst being in my familiar Muslim surroundings. The more I familiarise myself with the philosophical side of my faith, the more it starts resembling my true and transcendental nature. For this was also around the time when the events around the world started projecting Muslims in a rather negative light, albeit rightly so, owing to the fanatic tendencies seeping into the 'spirit' of Islam after the Afghan-Soviet War resulted in a new creed of fanatic Muslim sect emerging, now known to the world as Talibanisation. Muslims around the world are now seen as practising a medieval religious doctrine that is failing to keep pace with the post-modern free-thinking societies. Consequently, Muslims in secular societies have a sense of insecurity within their own communities. Religious fanaticism and 'my version of Islam is better than your version of Islam' rhetoric has divided them from within. The current-day narrative, as I would overhear many a British Muslim saying, is 'I am a secular Muslim and believe in reforms but would love to maintain my orthodoxy'. One can't help but wonder how maintaining one's orthodoxy works in a secular society. For orthodoxy is almost considered a taboo in a postmodern era, and is also considered primitive and outdated. Also, to my understanding, Islam as such does not demand orthodoxy; on the contrary, it is an ever-evolving phenomenon. But who are those people who believe and practise it as such? Our quest continues.*

Thus, in our view, in an era of post-normal truth, if anything could bind communities together it is only through having a deeper understanding of human nature (psychology) and the role humans play in the divine universal order (philosophy) as the custodians of this planet (ecology). For the disconnect between faith as practised (rituals) and as understood through a philosophical standpoint (the principles of creation) has been the main cause of all the havoc that extremism is playing in our world today.

This, therefore, forms the basis of our SOUL-idarity, the encompassing theme of our book.

### *5.1 The barakah rounds*

The Arabic word barakah is the establishment of divine goodness in something; from whence it exudes cannot be sensed by people, nor can it be outwardly quantified, nor is it limited by anything, but rather something with barakah in it is called mubarak and has an unexplainable increase and benefit in it from Allah. An example is when one gives charity, barakah enters one's remaining wealth such that it increases in benefit without increasing in the actual amount.

*In Part II of our book, we will explore the barakah dimension in more depth through Akhuwat's example of reciprocity and the solidarity economic model. For now, let us continue to our integral four-worlds journeying as our main and overall mandate.*

### *5.1.1 Akhuwat's 4I genealogy*

*In the light of the above, that is, the Islamic philosophy and intuitive knowledge, Akhuwat's 4I genealogy is a categorical postulation of Akhuwat's fourfold principles.*

*The 4 I's are Iman, Ikhlas, Ihsan and Ikhuwah.*

*This postulation comes as a result of an absolute contemplation of three main Islamic principles: Islam, Iman and Ihsan, as illustrated in Figure I.3.*

Chapter 4 draws purposefully on Akhuwat's 4I genealogy, building on these fundamental principles, thereby coupling it with Akhuwat's four principles in parallel to the integral CARE model developed by Lessem and Schieffer.

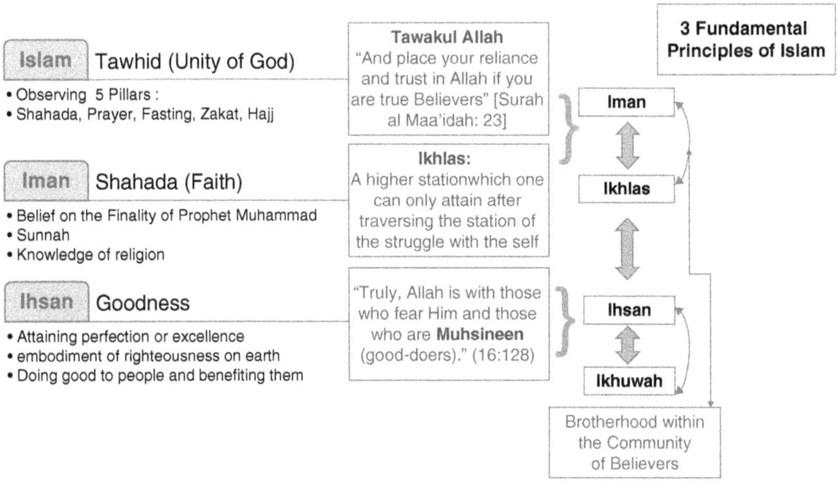


*Figure I.3* Fundamental Islamic Principles

*5.1.2 Solidarity amongst communities*

*Our research is also inspired by past and present-day thought leaders, from present-day 'critical thinkers' like Ziauddin Sardar, Jim Khalili and Hourani to 9th century mystic philosophers, the likes of Al-Farabi and Ibn Khaldun from the Arab world as well as the 19th century visionary mystic philosopher and poet Muhammed Iqbal and the founder of the Inayati Sufi Tariqah, Hazrat Inayat Khan from the Indian subcontinent. This includes many great thinkers from the North and West.*

*The one common thread we will be picking up from all these great thinkers – the mind and spirit activists – is their common love and concern for human communities at large and Muslim communities in particular. Al-Farabi envisions a 'virtuous city' (al-madinat al-fadilah) and how it could be perfected for its citizens to live in accordance with the laws of nature/universal Islamic law. Ibn Khaldun, on the other hand, expounds on asabiyyah, the group feeling, a term used by the Prophet of Islam (may peace be upon him).*

*Community building has been at the core of Islamic and every other tradition and societal development throughout the course of the history of our world. Societies were and are shaped when the communal spirit of the society was fully transcended and harnessed through the Ihsan/benevolence of its virtuous citizens through the Ubuntu*[1] *spirit of 'I am because WE are'.*

*While the ever-pressing call in the 21st century is to rekindle the spirit of community-building through social businesses, the word community is becoming definitive for 'groups': groups and communities of spiritual solidarity, political groups and so on and so forth. Our main call and most earnest wish is to look for systems and groups and communities that are working to develop integrative processes to lead universal solidarity movements that could bind communities together. Hence the need to study and showcase those phenomena, such as Akhuwat in our case.*

## 6 Part III – what is Akhuwat's philosophy

*What then is Akhuwat's philosophy?*

*Akhuwat's model is quite unique in the way the world knows microfinance and poverty. This model is inspired by the hijrah (migration) of the Prophet of Islam from Mecca to Medina, two of the holiest cities for Muslims, in Saudi Arabia. And the story starts more than 1400 years ago, in the time of the Prophet (peace be upon him) of Islam. The story starts with self-sacrifice, migrating (taking a leave) from one's own self and CARE-ing for others and sharing what you have with your brothers. This is a story of Mawakhat (brotherhood) and solidarity amongst the Medina (virtuous city) community.*

*This pertinent story of hijrah (migration) in the history of humankind gave birth to the concept of spiritual brotherhood, Mawakhat. The Mawakhat model adopted by the Ansar (helpers) of Medina under the guidance of Prophet Mohammad (peace be upon him) sets the precedent for how a model integral community and city should look. Although the physical migration in this case happened more than 1400 years ago in Mecca, what I identified in Akhuwat's case was the reiterative renewal of the Mawakhat GENE rhythm at play: the inner moral core of an Islamic community activating the GENE of sharing one's abundance with their needy brothers and sisters.*

*By adopting this philosophy and Sunnah emulation of Prophetic Mawakhat in practice, they successfully generated a solidarity economy based on the four Islamic principles of Iman, Ihsan, Ikhlas and Ikhuwah (4 I's). In doing so, not only did they set a precedent for others to follow in the Muslim world, but they also laid the foundation for an alternative model of microfinance through community activation and participation.*

*According to* Javaid Saeed, *former tutor at Columbia College and the University of South Carolina, the failure of Muslims in understanding and applying the Quranic doctrines in their totality is actually the cause of Muslim societies being generally static and not economically developed in the way they should have. According to Saeed, the Muslim condition compared to the more developed countries of the world is very weak and humiliating: they exist at the mercy of the countries of Europe and America, they receive most of the essential things of life from the more developed countries of the world, and many Muslim countries receive economic aid from foreign countries.* (Saeed, 1994)

*From this viewpoint, Akhuwat has exemplified an immaculate financial model of communal and self-reliance, for in their entire history they've always banked on the benevolence of the affluent members of the society. At the same time, prototypically, they channel the obligatory zakat and sadqah money to the rightful deserving people of the society, i.e., the micro-entrepreneurs, hence they have successfully created a cyclical model of gift economy.*

### *6.1 Akhuwat's reciprocal ecosystem*

*In Part III of the book, we will further establish a link with the barakah dimension in more depth through Akhuwat's example of reciprocity and the solidarity economic model. Akhuwat, through their members donation program (MDP), has successfully generated a reciprocal monetary ecosystem which, notwithstanding the fact it was generated through the benevolence of its civil society, has successfully helped 2.3 million needy families by providing them with a recourse to make their own livelihood rather than depending on charity or dole money. Chapter 6, therefore, demonstrates this using Akhuwat's practical example of drawing more rounds of barakah (bounty), spiralling out of its main pool of solidarity economy.*

#### *6.1.1 The multiplier of the law of benevolence – success initiatives*

Chapter 7 draws on Akhuwat's successive initiatives as a result of a benevolent ecosystem owing to its philosophy of compassion and Ihsan.

Akhuwat, starting off as a loan facilitator for Pakistani micro-entrepreneurs to earn a dignified livelihood for themselves, over a period of 17 years outgrew its loan-facilitator portfolio to now act as a waqf (trust) overlooking its multiple initiatives, which include building a fee-free university for poor students who cannot continue their higher education due to lack of resources.

## 7 Part IV – integral finance to integral SOUL-idarity paradigm

Thus, in Chapter 9 we conclude with our integral finance theorisation of an economy generated with the impulse of solidarity pulsating through the Transformational GENE rhythm, transcribing through a SOUL-idarity Hikma (the soul-wisdom of solidarity).

### *7.1 The Hikma of SOUL-idarity*

In Chapter 1, we summarise a new postulation of SOUL-idarity wisdom (Hikma), transpiring from Akhuwat's 4I genealogy which in turn originate, ontologically, from the Islamic principles of Islam, Iman and Ihsan.

The concluding part then draws upon the Hikma noesis further to transcend the intentionality of solidarity as per German Philosopher Husserl's theory of 'intentionality of consciousness', cognition especially when occurring through direct knowledge or intuition.

Taking Akhuwat's example as a reference of solidarity noesis, our Hikma constituting ishq/love, ilm/knowledge, akhuwat and amal/action is the soul (intention) of SOUL-idarity.

### *7.2 iSRA – institutionalising the spirit of solidarity*

From an integral developmental and transformational standpoint, for Akhuwat to CARE-4-Society, or Pakistan, (Community activation, raising Awareness, Research-to-innovation and Embodied action) in an integral way, what we see lacking is the need to institutionalise all the research it has accumulated in the field of 'turning microfinance on its head', in the words of microfinance expert Malcolm Harper, in a research academy of Integral Islamic Finance.

Now with the advent of Akhuwat University – being built under Akhuwat Education Services' initiative – the challenge for Akhuwat is to establish it as a Centre for Integral Research, thereby taking a lead in the Muslim world and reviving the tradition of philosophic knowledge creation, keeping up with their belief system and faith tradition. This formidable task might seem unimaginable at the moment, but with Amjad's indomitable spirit and stubbornness to persuade and inspire his community of Akhuwateers, this institution should set a precedent in the contextualisation of SOUL-idarity Hikma.

## 8 Guiding thoughts and questions

The distinction between the spiritual and the religious became more obvious in the popular mind during the late 20th century with the rise of secularism and the advancement of the New Age movement. And with the failure of globalisation, therein arose a need for a universal discipline which could bridge the divide between various cultures and faith disciplines for people to co-exist in harmony. Yet, with two major phenomena in 2016, that of Brexit and Trumpism, the global world stands more divided than ever before. Whereas there is less tolerance for religion, religious philosophies are also drawing more inwardly. Therefore, most religious practices are falling short of their essence.

This book is a call-to-action for making the implicit nature of spirituality a more practical apparatus to bridge this Self-societal divide.

This book is, thus, written with the intention to explore and pose the following guiding questions:

- Communities could generate successive models of finance that befit their beliefs, as apparent via Akhuwat's model of solidarity economy. Could there be an awareness of the process that gives birth to such models?
- Or is it in the nature of SOUL-idarity to manifest itself through the process witnessed in Akhuwat's reciprocity paradigm?
- Could this reciprocity, originated through the multiplier effect of *barakah (abundance) rounds* or virtuous circles as expounded by Amjad, sustain micro-communities?
- Or conversely, could micro-communities (in need) generate their own micro-economies through self-sufficiency?
- Spirituality means doing things differently for different people. Could there be a universal value of doing things spiritually and with the intentionality of such?
- By presenting Akhuwat's model of solidarity economy, which is generated through a spiritual discipline, could this universal value, then, be embraced, adopted or even replicated universally?

## References

Corbin, H., 1993. *History of Islamic Philosophy.* London: Kegan Paul International in Association with Islamic Publications Ltd.

Harper, M., & Khan, A. A., 2017. *Islamic Microfinance: Shari'ah Compliant and Sustainable?* Rugby: Practical Action Publishing Ltd.

Lessem, R., & Bradley, T., 2018a. *Evolving Work.* Abingdon: Routledge.

Lessem, R., & Bradley, T., 2018b. *Introducing Evolving Work: Employment of Self and Community.* Abingdon: Routledge.

Lessem, R., & Schieffer, A., 2010. *Integral Economics: Releasing the Economic Genius of Your Society (Transformation and Innovation).* Abingdon: Routledge.

Lessem, R., & Schieffer, A., 2013. *Integral Dynamics.* Abingdon: Routledge.

Moustakas, C., 1994. *Phenomenological Research Methods.* Thousand Oaks: SAGE.

Saeed, J., 1994. *Islam and Modernization: A Comparative Analysis of Pakistan, Egypt, and Turkey.* London: Praeger.

# 1 Akhuwat

## A community built on the paradigm of Mawakhat/solidarity

### 1 Preamble

Previously, we briefly charted the roadmap of our book which, from the very onset, talks about Akhuwat, an organisation in Pakistan which has been facilitating poor people by providing them with interest-free loans, mobilising them to be self-sufficient by starting or growing their own micro-businesses rather than relying on charitable means.

Pakistan ranks as the sixth-largest country in the world when it comes to population. After gaining independence from the British in 1947, it thereafter separated from its neighbouring, now rival, country India. It is still facing massive challenges internally and on the global stage as the first Muslim nuclear country. Along with socio-economic and geo-political challenges, what is simmering underneath and within its national psyche is the trauma of migration and partition. With an overpopulation of varied races and diverse tribal and urban cultures and with a growing dearth of resources and infrastructure, what is important for Pakistanis at this point in time is to invoke a spirit of communal solidarity amongst themselves. There is a common belief in Pakistan that it owes its survival amongst all odds to its compassionate civil society and kind-hearted benevolence of its people, as they have always (and are still) played a huge role in its sustainability by contributing from their abundance of wealth and generosity, mostly considered as their religious duty – a Prophetic tradition of Mawakhat, whereby every one member of the society is responsible for another less-fortunate member by sharing from their wealth. Akhuwat banks its sustainability on this generosity of Pakistani civil society, along with reviving this spirit of Mawakhat with one's brothers – Akhuwat, literally means brotherhood.

Akhuwat, therefore, stands out as a unique example of a community originated with this spirit of Mawakhat and reciprocity. In this opening chapter of the book, we thus ground ourselves in this spirit of solidarity, taking Akhuwat's living example to explore what emerges from deep within the core of a faith-based, primarily Muslim community. What is the spirit and chemistry of one such community? And more importantly, what evokes this spirit and why is it even important to cultivate this spirit of compassion and solidarity amongst communities?

In our context, as I believe, the Pakistani nation is still holding on to the trauma of separation and, as a relatively young nation, it needs to develop a sense of camaraderie and community activation skills to generate a societal and developmental self-sufficiency, given the fact its global image has been tarnished by fanaticism and terrorism. This is the overarching reason for presenting Akhuwat as a model community from Pakistan, being a successful model of raising awareness through their on-the-ground practical work by mobilising and thereby successfully building a community of Akhwateers, that is, its donors, borrowers, volunteers, replicators and government institutions, thereby generating a reciprocal economy of solidarity.

According to Schieffer & Lessem (2014b):

> With every human system being in continuous evolution, so does integral worlds incorporate an inbuilt transformational rhythm, which makes the entire approach dynamic. It is a rhythm that we could equally trace back to natural and cultural systems and their respective evolution. We call this rhythm the GENE (an acronym for Grounding, Emerging, Navigating, Effecting), representing a fourfold spiralling force, activating the entire integral worlds model.
>
> The GENE rhythm is embedded in the diverse reality views and knowledge realms of the integral worlds, bringing them all together in transformative interaction. While we see the GENE as a spiralling, iterative, ever-unfolding force, we nevertheless start most of our transformational processes in the South, thereby beginning with a conscious grounding in a given context and issue, before we then engage in its transformation.

This chapter, thereafter, postulates an innovative articulation of SOUL-idarity (a term coined by me) GENE rhythm, inspired by the Integral Dynamics Theory, thereby activating a society's particular GENE-IUS developed by Lessem and Schieffer of TRANS4M, Centre for Integral Development, Geneva.

Whereby the integral GENE rhythm starts its journey from the integral worlds Southern realm of community building, our Eastern solidarity GENE starts spiraling from the integral worlds Eastern realm of Culture and Spirituality, in the context of Pakistan being a spiritually-inspired, faith-based country wherein development starts from the *Self*, firstly through solidarity (proximity) gained through Iman (faith) and God-realization – the solidarity impulse thus pulsating within as a divinely transcendental effect of Ishq/love, consequently translating into solidarity with the community, society and universe. For Islamic tradition and ethics hold the central position in Pakistani society's inner moral core, as per Lessem and Schieffer's postulation of integral development of self, organisation, community and eventually the society.

Our solidarity GENE rhythm postulation in the context of Akhuwat's Mawakhat backdrop spirals through the integral four rounds philosophy, categorised as per our own circumstances and challenges going through our own individual distinctive paths. As explained in the introduction of this part, the four integral rounds are of the self, organisation, society and ultimately universe, as per Lessem and Schieffer's postulation of integral dynamics.

This chapter, thus, provides an overview of our 4P process in four rounds as categorised below:

**Round 1: The Philosophy (P1):** This refers to the oriental philosophical dimensions of aql (intellect) and Islamic mystical philosophy of Being as opposed to the occidental pragmatic ways of Doing. From a more personal 'relational' expression, the narration is drawn from my (Aneeqa's) migration and spiritual development and challenges, interwoven with Amjad's conception of Mawakhat philosophy, all taking place in the East, i.e., Pakistan within an Eastern (holistic) orientation.

**Round 2: The Principles (P2):** This covers Akhuwat's organisational development as perceived by Aneeqa's spiritual and integral/trans4mational positioning along with Amjad's deep comprehension of spiritual-societal challenges faced by Pakistan.

**Round 3: The Practices (P3):** This further explores Akhuwat's fourfold paradigm in the light of Islamic spirituality, albeit in local (Pakistani) phenomenal wisdom (Hikma) settings.

**Round 4: The Integral Hikma Process (P4):** This rounds it off by proposing an integrated process of SOUL-idarity through employing the inner wisdom (the philosophy) with the outer wisdom (universal development), transpiring from all three previous disciplines, i.e., the philosophy (self-development), the principles (organisational development) and the practices (societal development).

## 2 Initiation: philosophy of SOUL-idarity – the nature and spirit of communitas

We start with Amjad's dream of solidarity between the passionate souls:

> Akhuwat is a dream of the times to come that is envisioned by the truly ardent ones. Great dreams, after all, always gleam in the eyes of passionate souls. It is not the dominion of the highly intellectual. Wherever there's a mention of a great dream, I remember Allama Iqbal, I remember Mohammed Ali Jinnah, and I remember Sir Syed Ahmed Khan.
>
> I also dreamt of Akhuwat, a social movement that could end man-made caustic divide between the haves and the have-nots of the society. A society where everyone can live by their own realities.
>
> This dream has become the first phase of the destination of love, the beginning of the arduous paths of passion, the desire to return to people the respect taken away from them, and the struggle to revive their self-honour. *Akhuwat, veritably, is a common man's legacy.*

*As the main theme of our book and the title of the first part implies, we aim to explore spiritually inspired bases of a solidarity-inspired Islamic economic model of Qard-e-Hasan (benevolent loan) and Mawakhat (brotherhood). Thereby, we further delve deeper into the nature of benevolence (Ihsan) and its multiplier effect/s spreading throughout communities built with purity of intention (Ikhlas) and divine purpose (Iman).*

*Thereby, in this chapter, from time to time we will also be tracing our steps back to the origin of hijrah (migration), the first ever migration that took place in the history of Islam and the importance it holds to this date in the lives of all Muslims. Although this story is more confined to history books now, in Akhuwat's case, this was what drew my attention, that is, identifying its explicit reference within Akhuwat's philosophy which places the Sunnah (Tradition of the Prophet) in all its practical entirety, i.e., the philosophy as well as the practicality of this tradition to tackle the societal affliction of abject poverty in Pakistani society. It was heartening to note, when there is a universal call to bridge the divide between religious philosophies and their practicality in our daily life, an organisation exists that is not only placing focus on following one such philosophy, rather it has had the courage to practise as such within an open public domain, i.e., amongst the microfinances of our world. Thereby, they are reviving the practice in an innovative way. One might find it hard to believe this model exists in current times and is going from strength to strength by transforming the lives of people, thereby following their collective (inner) call to create just and equitable economies and financial models which are people-friendly (reciprocal) or what Dr. Muhammad Yunus* (Yunus, 2003) *terms 'people-worthy'. For this instigated the writing of this book, thereby further immersing myself into the philosophy of Mawakhat by setting the solidarity impulse into motion and its spiralling emergence of a new SOUL-idarity Hikma (wisdom) after-effect.*

This brings us to the initiation phase of our SOUL-idarity GENE in this section of Chapter 1, exploring the chemistry and psyche of the communitas, taking Akhuwat as an example of a solidarity community, having generated an economy of solidarity by practically following the Sunnah of the Prophet of Islam. It was after the Prophet's (may peace be upon him) migration to Medina that he set a precedent for a perfect model of an integrally gratified community.

*The guiding question that we aim to explore and, thus, find an answer to in this section is what truly activates such communities' inner core and what holds them together thereafter?*

This question is probed firstly through a philosophical take on SOUL-idarity, as a result of an integral Hikma (ishq, ilm, amal and akhuwat) noesis, as perceived by me (Aneeqa), working implicitly through Akhuwat's four principles. As such, Akhuwat's philosophy consists of

- **Engaging Sanctuaries (religious places)**
- **Granting Qard-e-Hasan (benevolent/interest-free loans)**

- **Reciprocal Endowment (borrowers becoming donors)**
- **Reviving the Spirit of Volunteerism (solidarity within community)**

The emergent effect is a ***solidarity bond*** generated through individual (Self) and collective (communal) actualisation, by being conscious of the ever-present barakah (divine bounty) that keeps rebounding through the upward-downward spiralling of vertical axis (the arc of ascent) and horizontal axis (the arc of descent). Consequentially, giving birth to a new discipline that we, in our integral language, term the **integral finance paradigm of SOUL-idarity** as an after-effect of journeying through the 4 R's of integral dynamics as developed by Schieffer and Lessem (2014b).

This is further elaborated throughout the book and more so in Chapter 3 and the concluding chapter.

## *2.1 The integrality of solidarity – community spirit*

As proposed by Lessem & Schieffer, through their seminal work on Community Activation (Lessem & Schieffer, Community Activation: Embeddedness, 2014):

> *that "the natural collective starting point for working with society is the immediate community. Starting there, rather than with society as a whole, helps us to bring things back to human scale, back into a sphere where interaction is possible and tangible".*
>
> *In their book they also cite UK-based Geoff Mulgan, founder of the British think tank Demos, who has a similar reason why he prefers community as a starting point.*
>
> 'Community' *is deliberately a different word from society. It may refer to neighbourhoods or workplaces, but to be meaningful it must imply membership in a human-scale collective: a scale at which it is possible to encounter people face to face and to nurture human-scale structures within which people can feel at home. Social science is ill at ease with such ideas.*
>
> *Mulgan reminds us that we often not only overlook social realities that many communities are facing, but that we also detach ourselves from what makes communities 'tick'. He invites us to take a fresh look at the notion of community.*
>
> *The first is the simple recognition of people's social nature, and one might add, of the sociability, sense of fairness, sympathy and duty that evolutionary psychologists now see as hardwired into our genetic make-up. Two hundred years of history have done much to nurture institutions for freedom and equality, but very little for the fraternity and solidarity that hold societies together. Yet, this softer value – a social capital that enables people to work together, to trust each other, to commit to common causes – has proved absolutely critical to societal success, whether in narrow economic terms of in terms of well-being.*

As per our main call and as the central theme of our book suggests, with Akhuwat – the *SOUL-idarity* of brotherhood present in one such community as quoted above – every member of the society looks after their needy brothers' and sisters' communal needs. We assume, and as is dictated phenomenologically, it is the spirit of Bhai-chara that binds people to their communities or a particular Biradari, an Urdu word for fraternity or clan, that they are born into. From a Sufistic perspective, it is a fraternity of individual-to-collective souls which transcends the spirit of SOUL-idarity.

According to Hazrat Inayat Khan (1977), the destined climactic transcendental experience of unveiling of one's soul comes for every being – it must come – it will come, yet its coming is unpredictable.

Through this chapter we will explore this question to make a connection with the soul (and spirit) of solidarity as observed in Akhuwat's community of Akhuwateers: Is it, in effect, an allegiance of compassion (Ihsan) which is further strengthened by coming together in times of need as alluded to by Hazrat Inayat Khan?

Moreover, it is believed in the Sufi spiritual traditions that this awakening comes after going through a trauma or life-changing experience, or in Mevlana Rumi's words, 'The wound is the place where the Light enters you' (Rumi, 1995).

We believe this is true for communities after going through a collective trauma, e.g., famine, migration, poverty and so on: in this particular case, the Pakistani society that has collectively suffered the trauma of partition some 70 years ago, albeit is still nurturing the wounds and aftereffects of that trauma.

This sets the scene for our main theme of the book, i.e., Akhuwat/solidarity with brotherhood within a community, in this case, an ecology of poor and destitute in Pakistani society, divided by class and status, yet attached through the *inner moral core* of their faith and *culture of giving*. (Chapter 2)

As proposed by Schieffer and Lessem (2014a),

> A development process begins with a 'calling' and a 'challenge' originating within an individual, at times also within an organisation, a community, or even a society.
>
> A 'challenge' is linked to a perceived imbalance (inwardly or outwardly) and matched by the 'calling' to respond and a sense of being 'response-able' (having the capacity to) address the imbalance.

*In this section we explore how the spirit of a community's soulful awakening, which Hazrat Inayat Khan alluded to, mutates within a particular community, thus activating the SOUL-idarity GENE of the communitas. What are the attributes that collectively activate a community's SOUL-idarity in a particular spiritual culture and setting?*

From times immemorial, human beings have stuck with own kind and have formed their own clans, tribes and communities, what we also call a Biradari or Bhai-chara in Urdu. All the major religions and especially the Abrahamic religions are full of fables of communities taking centre stage in such activation by often migrating to another land or even finding a new religious tradition that transpired into societal transformation.

*This calls for mentioning another theme that emerged for one of us (Aneeqa): hijrah (migration), which merges with the overarching theme of my PHD (Process of Holistic Development) calling, Soulidarity with Universality. And the prime example, which is also the philosophy of Akhuwat's practical work, is solidarity with one's fellow brothers in times of need. As per my call-to-contribution unfolding, I will be exploring how this model of solidarity (Akhuwat) could be utilised for the diaspora communities in the UK, so they can self-sufficiently co-create their own micro-economies which are in line with their faith system, values and philosophies.*

We now turn to the philosophy of the solidarity manifestation – establishing a link between soul-wisdom of So(u)lidarity, exemplifying it through our own spiritual (soul's) and professional (physical) journeys.

## 3 Section 1: the coming of soul-wisdom – the philosophy

We start with Amjad's message of love (Ishq):

### 3.1 My message is love, wherever it arrives

During my association with Punjab Rural Support Programme (PRSP) in the year 2000, microfinance was becoming the rage. I remember how one day, a few friends accompanied me to look at some work done by PRSP in a village named Jia Bagga in Punjab District. My friend, Dr. Kamran Shams, once asked a woman what difference a loan of Rs. 10,000 (100 USD) had made to her life. The woman answered that previously, her children used to eat one roti (piece of flatbread) at night, but now they can afford to eat two rotis. In this statement is concealed the entire narrative of poverty. That day, as we arrived back to Lahore from Jia Bagga, among many topics, poverty was passionately discussed.

I had long wished to create a micro-lending institution, but one devoid of interest. Often, I would get hold of my friends and take them to remote villages. The work of PRSP was appreciated, but almost all of them had an issue with the condition of interest. I asked my friends whether an initiative where small loans could be granted interest-free would be feasible and if they'd support such an initiative. All hands were raised. After some time, I again invited these friends and a few other people to a presentation of the features of a new institution – interest-free loans based on solidarity and compassion. I coined the name Akhuwat – brotherhood in English – for this endeavour. All of the individuals present were civil servants and microfinance was not their discipline, so the responsibility for shaping this idea into an institution was bequeathed to me. This was the most important duty I had ever assumed in my life.

During the first two years, we worked discreetly. We had faith but were not too certain of the chosen path. We did many things at Akhuwat that had not been done previously in the field of microfinance. We wanted a system that would be simple, straightforward and transparent. Instead of profit, altruism and volunteerism would prevail. None of us favoured interest, but there is hardly anyone out there who opposes it systematically but also presents an alternate solution or system. We wanted to go beyond sermons and advice, into the thicket of the thorns of practice. If vehemence picks not the plough, then it is a mere claim. If passion breaks not the mould, it is raw.

The first loan was granted in March 2001, but Akhuwat was not registered until two years later, in 2003. However, within those two years of intense struggle and hardship, the dream began to attain the hue of reality. We had absolutely no capital or human resources, but we had plenty of criticism, ridicule, and taunts about our 'shallow pockets'. When underprivileged borrowers went to the bank, they were forced to stand and wait for hours. When respect becomes conditional to wealth, it is not surprising that the poor receive none at a bank. We vowed to treat each person with dignity and respect. We had instances where our branches were robbed, workers were assaulted and some who were not awarded loans threatened us. Once a police officer felt offended and detained four Akhuwat staff members for hours without any legal process. One fanatic even threatened the murder and kidnapping of our staff members. Still, the fire of passion was never extinguished. All of these trials and tribulations notwithstanding, whenever an elderly person or a widow prayed with their hands raised for us, all of these were effaced.

*In Section 1 of this chapter, we start by continuing with our personal journeys, engaging through our soul(ful) purposes and the experiences that came as a result of being on our distinctive paths which were life transforming for both of us, that which I term transcendence of the soul-wisdom. This soul-wisdom, as I personally experienced, transcends as one gets disciplined and trained to restrain oneself from unwilful desires and wants. The more I practised self-discipline the more I was able to find meaning in things, be it in business dealings or personal development. My relation to my own being was thus established.*

As alluded to by Hazrat Inayat Khan (The Soul Whence and Whither, 1977), 'every being whether a human being, an animal or a plant, is destined for one great climactic transcendental experience of unveiling – it must come – it will come, yet, it's coming is unpredictable'.

*Thus, it came for one of us (Aneeqa). After being on a spiritual quest and soul-journey of finding my soul purpose and my true self, that moment came when I met with my spiritual guide, Naila Hayat Noon, also known as Shaykha Amat-un-Nur by her spiritual name, for the first time in Lahore. It was a case of instant heart-to-heart connection. My soul's quest came full circle, as this was how I was able to quench my soul's thirst of 'knowing myself', and then to find my soul's purpose of migrating from one place to another. Having a spiritual guide was important for me to translate my soul experiences. It was this trans-migration of the soul that changed the course of my life, as it opened an inner dimension, never explored before, giving me a whole new perspective on my understanding of religion and my connection with the Divine. Once initiated, this soul-wisdom was channeled through my work. It was through my spiritual training that I started questioning the purpose of work in my life and how transcending the self and/or employing the self (Lessem Bradley, 2018) gives a whole new meaning to being spiritually enterprising. The whole experience transformed my outlook on life and living; eventually this was what set me off on a quest to explore whether we can incorporate this layer of soul-wisdom into practice, from education to enterprise and economics, which took me to Lessem and Schieffer and TRANS4M, and on to our collective quest of sketching an integral model of finance and economics.*

*My individualistic pursuits were to find a middle way for enterprise (physical/material) and soul (spiritual/sacred) to form an integral-spiritual discipline which could effectively make work/entrepreneurial endeavours soulful for individuals, communities and societies.*

*Hence the guiding question for my SOUL-idarity postulation which I explore throughout the course of this book is: If disciplining our SELF could help us in mastering our lust for money, which is considered the main ill in our existing societal framework, what effect could this bring to our physical and soul's wellbeing?*

Thus, the first round of our solidarity impulse GENE-alogy originates from the holistic East, Pakistan in our case.

### *3.2 Round I: Pakistan's spirit and culture – Eastern orientation – the philosophy*

> 'Eastern' emergence 'lifts' the issue and the people involved to deeper insights into the unfolding nature of the issue. Here the people and issue engage in dialectic processes with others, thereby co-evolving to new insights. Such a

> process always includes a 'stepping into the unknown' and 'letting go' of some of the previous assumptions... . 'Eastern' emergence is about 'becoming'. It deals with 'intuiting' and 'imagining' the new form that is emerging. Here the 'local' perspective of the Southern grounds evolves to 'local global' viewpoints. This is the 'reformative' part of the transformation process. Here, we seek to activate 'inspiration' or the 'spirit'-level of a human system (Schieffer & Lessem, 2014b).

As both of our (Amjad and Aneeqa's) stories originated from the Pakistani soil, thus, staying true to our realities, we start our journey from the East (Pakistan). For both of us, East (holistic) holds the natural orientation of our souls. For Akhuwat's first **I** is **Iman** (faith).

Furthermore, building on TRANS4M's 'Care-4-Society' process developed by Lessem and Schieffer and also drawing on their 'releasing the GENE-IUS of a society' (Schieffer & Lessem, 2014b), our aim is to illustrate how societies conceived on faith-bases, which is true in Pakistan's case, need to develop an economic system which closely matches their ideals, e.g., spiritually based, as in Akhuwat's case, built on brotherhood, yet is aligned with the global worldview, specifically aligned, in this case with Rudolf Steiner's 'Economics of Association' (Lessem & Schieffer, 2010) or 'the Economics of Love', as defined by (the late) Ibrahim Abouleish, Founder of Sekem.

For Abouleish (Lessem, Abouleish & Herman, 2016); the term 'Economy of Love' expresses *that it is not only about gaining the highest possible profit when cooperating with business partners, but more about a social and respectful dealing with each other.*

*Something Amjad has stressed ever since his conception of Akhuwat's philosophy is the need to fight Pakistan's most pressing societal challenges, poverty being the highest priority for him. For he sees poverty as the root cause of moral decay of any particular society, i.e., Pakistan in our case. The same echoes in the words of Hazrat Inayat Khan, the Indian Sufi mystic and originator of the sufi order in the West,* 'Many evils are born of riches, but still more are bred in poverty' (Khan, 1914).

*The paradox of (artificial) scarcity amidst abundance, created by humans within urban spaces or cities – the 'us' against 'them' and the 'rich' vs the 'poor' catchphrase – is breeding resentment against social classes, yet the concept sells very well within the development sector. For we believe it is one thing to face scarcity when everyone suffers, as in a famine or a drought. Those are natural disasters, and they do not produce abundance for anyone else. But it is quite another to face scarcity when there is plenty. A living example is seen within the Pakistani society and was felt by Amjad, wherein the social class divide is conspicuously dividing the Pakistani society further, owing to a feudal mindset reminiscent of British colonisation. Those who 'have' are ranked higher than those who 'have not'.*

*Thus, in Part I we aim to explore Akhuwat's solidarity impulse, specifically set in a Pakistani society (spiritual/local), being activated by a collective trauma of this division amongst communities, i.e., the poorest of the poor (have-nots) and the richest of the rich (haves).*

Taking mystic wisdom from Hazrat Inayat Khan's words of wisdom in Gayan (Khan, 2007), '*The whole of life is a chemical process; and the knowledge of its chemistry helps man to make life happy.*'

*Combining the Sufi wisdom with the integral GENE rhythm (Grounding, Emerging, Navigating and Effecting), I was able to recognise a similar pattern through Akhuwat's 'solidarity impulse', that is, a multiplier effect of chemical and biological process doing rounds through their community of Muhsineen (those who embody Ihsan) and Mukhliseen (those who observe Ikhlas).* ***Ikhlas and Ihsan****, being two of the most effective constituents of Akhuwat's 4 I's (Iman, Ikhlas, Ihsan and Ikhuwah) genealogy (Chapter 4).*

### *3.3 4C-ing an integral Pakistan through CARE-4-Society model*

*Throughout the course of our book we will be journeying through Pakistan's socio-economic terrain, further demonstrating this by taking Akhuwat's role in Pakistani society as a case study. The idea of solidarity is intrinsic to a society standing on the verge of developmental crisis and in need of one such model of solidarity emerging from within its own soil and as per the nature and stipulation of its people.*

As such, TRANS4M's CARE-4-Society is an 'alternating rhythm', comprised of the 4 C's (Call, Context, Co-creation and Contribution), '4C'-ing singular development and the four institutionalising functions underpinning 'CARE' (following the sequence of Community activation, raising Awareness, Research-to-innovation and Embodied action).

This will be further elaborated on through TRANS4M's CARE-4-Society model in our next chapter (Chapter 2).

Chapter 2, then, '4Cs' Pakistan's societal challenges through this model, thereby exploring Pakistan's CARE model in Chapter 4 through Akhuwat's 4C postulation.

Pakistan, officially the Islamic Republic of Pakistan, is the sixth-most-populous country, with a population exceeding 201 million people. It is a state founded on an ideological basis and not on territorial grounds. As such, Pakistan is unique among Muslim countries, as it is the only country created in the name of Islam. Evidentially Pakistan, being purely an ideological state whose foundations were laid on Islamic ideology based on the Quranic teachings and Sunnah, has failed to keep up with its primary 'Islamic' focus as such, and with an amalgamated terrain of various faiths and diverse cultures is in need of finding a system which works for its multi-dimensional societal challenges and rising secular notions often understood as 'Westernisation'.

Notwithstanding Pakistan being conceived as an Islamic republic, the Indian subcontinent has also been historically acclaimed as a region of centuries-old mystical traditions, from Buddhism to Vedantic traditions to Islamic Sufism. The amalgamated soil of Pakistan is still moist with some such traditions and a culture of Sufi karamat (miracles) which reflects intrinsically through Akhuwat's philosophy of ishq/love. Whereas the religious beliefs form the globality of Pakistani society amongst the Muslim ummah, the mystical traditions of the region form the pre-emptive culture of locality for the Pakistani nation. Epistemologically, these traditions ordain an Islamic semblance, yet, ontologically, the social behaviour has a deeper wisdom locked inside the daily habits of the society which comes directly from the soil and has semblance to the ancestral history of Persian and Indian spiritual traditions of the region.

### *3.3.1 My spiritual quest continues*

*As Akhuwat's philosophy of Mawakhat (solidarity) was born of hijrah (migration) to another land, this was the main theme of my transformational journey too. In his Urdu book* Kamyab Loug *(successful people of Chiniot)*, (Saqib, 2016) *Amjad writes about migration as an imperative to finding one's livelihood after travelling to another land. There is a spiritual semblance to every travel one takes, leaving one's comfort zone behind.*

*As per Islamic religious tradition, making one's halal (rightful) living is considered as an ibadah (worship) too, and travelling to another land (hijrah) to find one's livelihood is also termed as ibadah – the same holds true for me. With my spiritual needs addressed with practices and guidance from my teacher, there came, for me, a total emancipation from reliance on how businesses were conducted in a conventional way, so divorced from real purposefulness, especially for those who are engaged with socially enterprising work. Notwithstanding the fact, being self-employed gave me the freedom to practise spirituality within my own work sphere and the freedom to be engaged with the community in a more unconventionally caring way. For example, time and again I was questioned by my fellow associates as to why I invest my heart in my public, and particularly in my business dealings. The total redundancy of spirituality within work spheres in particular, and the public domain in general, became my call to look for models, if any, that are soul-fully bringing soul-prosperity (sakinah) and sacred purpose into practice. Could there be such sacred spaces within enterprise and economics?*

*As fate would have it, one day, on this journey of travelling between East and West, I was to discover an unconventional (Islamic) spiritual-financial model: Akhuwat Foundation, which I was soon to find was quite unique in the way it has incorporated the spirit of giving interest-free loans and sharing one's abundance with the needy ones, inspired by the philosophy of Mawakhat. As it happened after having a few sittings with its founder and CEO, Dr. Amjad Saqib, a new chapter of my journey was to begin, that is, of writing this book, presenting a unique model of Qard-e-Hasan to the wider world outside of Pakistan. Whereas before I used to go to Pakistan to spend time in my Shaykha Amat-un-Nur's sohbet (company), with this new and shared endeavour my spiritual was to meet the social purpose of my life. The answer to my question, could the spiritual be practised in a more practical way willingly and consciously, was locked in Akhuwat's philosophy.*

*As I immersed myself deeper into the spirit of Mawakhat, what I found most rare in this micro-lending model, as it's acknowledged, was the way they have not only set an example of lending money as Qard-e-Hasan – a loan given to Allah as advised in the Holy Quran – but have also revived the Sunnah (tradition) of Prophet Muhammad's (peace be upon him) philosophy of Mawakhat – an unusual incidence of such precedence and scale to be found anywhere in the world. Although the world does know about microfinance from Dr. Muhammad Yunus's perspective and through his Grameen Bank model, but from an integral lens, as identified collectively by myself with my integral mentor, Professor Ronnie Lessem of TRANS4M, Centre for Integral Development, Akhuwat is anything but a microfinance organisation. Therefore, I aim to take my readers on a stage-by-stage journey of unfoldment from micro to the integral finance model of SOUL-idarity as contemplated by my deeper integral-spiritual orientation.*

*Incidentally, through my regular traveling, owing to my work, between the UK and Pakistan, soon I was to arrive at a new kind of awareness of how the two countries I consider my homes are centuries apart – wherein within the first world social is the new hype and way to a communal survival, the other (third world) is still immersed in and practices spirituality in whatever people do, be it conducting businesses or giving alms and sadaqah jariyah (perpertual charity).*

*This called for my pursuit to explore further, as part of my work involves engaging with diaspora communities, to see how the knowledge gap and cultural migration, which has resulted in their recoiling from the mainstream socio-economic scene, could be patched by considering a model from their country which could help in lifting them from a state of social despondency and economical or entrepreneurial passivity, particularly in faith-based, i.e., Muslim communities.*

*We explore this further.*

### *3.3.2 Being Muslim in Britain*

*Another exposed realisation that came after emigrating to a non-Muslim country was my sense of being preservative towards my own faith, Islam, which to me and every Muslim is inherently a peaceful way of life and living. Islam, originating from the triliteral root S-L-M, means peace and surrendering, yet all I saw was Islam and Muslims being portrayed in the news, mostly for anything other than being peaceful! As I engaged more with my Pakistani Muslim communities, I realised the insecurities of these communities; safeguarding and practising their deen (faith) has further widened the divide between themselves and other communities. Although the space they are residing in, i.e., the UK, is rather secular and immigrant-friendly, still the knowledge gap that exists between communities is a hindrance for communities to co-exist in unison. As a result, making the migrant communities recoil and huddle together in their own self-selected community repositorie, has rendered them socially isolated and, in some cases, economically inactive too.*

*However, it was surprisingto note that, in an era of confounded globalisation e.g. Brexit & Trumpism, and with scientific and technological advancements, a secular society still has pockets of groups and sub-communities that are totally detached from the concept of globalisation per se and rather follow their own values, traditions and culturesso religiously which clashes idealogically with what is in practice externally. Equally interesting is to note people's reliance on their own clans and communities whilst still living in a relatively individualistic society like the UK.*

Now with the global mass migration of communities moving to alien lands and expatriation becoming a prominent feature of our global reality, how communities will co-exist is becoming a mass challenge for many governments and a major concern for social as well as cultural anthropologists around the world.

*With the recent globalisation fiasco of Syrian and Mexican refugees denied access to European and American borderswhat hope do we have for a pluralistic existence? Could solidarity with universality be our new hope for a harmonious 21st century global co-existence in a very divided world?*

We now explore the nature of co-existence amongst communities who principally differ in their beliefs in a shared modern secular space.

### *3.3.3 Augmented human realities: co-existence in an age of virtual existence*

Although the idea of co-existence is not new, the term came into common usage during the Cold War. According to Angela Nyawira Khaminwa a researcher in dispute resolution from the University of Massachusetts;"the Coexistence Continuum is not static.

> Like all social environments, it fluctuates, depending on the level of social interaction. Coexistence exists in situations where individuals and communities actively accept and embrace diversity (active coexistence) and where individuals and communities merely tolerate other groups (passive coexistence).
>
> (Khaminwa, 2003)

In my UK context, this theory applies to racial co-existence, but in the same vein this passive co-existence is a challenge within the Pakistani context too. The ever-widening social class divide between the rich and poor was what prompted Amjad to come up with Akhuwat's solidarity proposition.

**Populist Belief**: The year is 2017, after the Brexit referendum and the election of Trump, the populist era, or to borrow the term from Ziauddin Sardar as:

> post-truth/*postnormal times*, an era of 'declining value of truth as society's reserve currency'. Whereas social media is providing a platform for insignificant groups to connect globally and create chaos the world over, we are nudged towards accepting the fallacy that all truths are relative. The consensual definition of populism, coming from political scientists Cas Mudde and Cristobal Rovira Kaltwasser, is a two-sided equation. Populism, they suggest, is a form of politics that pits 'a morally virtuous people against a corrupt elite'. Whilst the Muslim world is in the grip of a triple plague: populism, corrupt despotism and terrorism, each is its own worst enemy. The evil alliance between terrorists, Islamophobic populism and despotism will usher in a dark age of experimentation with old-style colonialism, as Europe goes back home to its Islamophobic dark ages.
>
> The other side of the equation is all about hope. Often the 'morally virtuous' find themselves in a position where they have nothing – not even hope.
>
> The problem is not so much populism per se but the subject of hope – what exactly the populist movements desire. The populist movements led by Jeremy Corbyn in Britain and Bernie Sanders in the US place their faith in accountability and democratic reform – the hope is that this would lead to a more *just and equitable society.*
>
> (Sardar, 2017)

Whilst there are reasons to be pessimistic, for some of us the deeper call to action is to challenge our biases and assumptions about each other. This calls for a collaborative enquiry and systems that could provide a middle ground for communities to cross-pollinate and co-exist integrally whilst holding true to their own moral cores, as suggested by Lessem and Schieffer (Schieffer & Lessem, 2014) in their seminal work on releasing the GENE of a particular community and society.

We now explore the impulse of solidarity and what compels it.

## *3.4 The impulse of solidarity*

For us, the wayfarers on the *wisdom of the soul* path, we believe what lies at the core of a community's well-being (*SOUL-idarity*) is the well-being of the SOUL. It is the awakening to the true identity of the SELF. The true Self has been patiently awaiting our attention, but we have been so occupied with the drama of the little self that we have not even noticed that there is something far greater which is our true nature. The superficial aspect of each of us, which is the cause of divisive ideas such as I, me, mine, yours, is the source of all of our pain and confusion. When we venture beyond our little self, we discover something far greater, something that has been given names such as Self, God, Allah, Brahma, Atman, Tao, or Buddha-nature. But no matter what we choose to call it, this is our true home, the source of the greatest bliss, the greatest peace, the greatest understanding.

According to Liaquat Ali Khan, professor of Law at Washburn Law School,

> Humanity is taking a quantum leap beyond the religions of the world. Emerging from this quantum leap is a universal spirituality (USP) that removes ideological, gnostic, denominational, and sectarian borders within and across religions. Universal spirituality does not nullify the teachings of" any religion, nor does it denigrate any faith or creed. The USP incorporates the morals derived from religions into shared consciousness. It respects the practices of each creed.
>
> (Khan, 2017)

Khan terms the USP "a non-excluding phenomenon, with any religion, faith or creed from the realm of truth or authenticity. Consistent with the moral evolution of the human species, the USP interfuses the human psyche with cosmic intelligence, promoting the free flow of spirituality in and beyond space and time. His USP paradigm defines spirituality as goodness to oneself and to others. As per his belief, economic systems that promote material acquisitiveness and egotistical self-assertions may produce wealth but bring no spiritual joy for the participants". (Khan, 2017)

From a layman's perspective, spirituality, thus, as generally perceived, is what binds people together by 'being good' to each other as per Khan's above definition.

*For us, it is about co-existing SOUL-fully and purposefully with the Self to let the light of divine wisdom shine through: the main call of my philosophical quest. But what maintains it and how long it takes to travel to reach that apex is what I intend to investigate through the course of this book and, consequently, in the concluding chapter, where I expand on this concept further.*

For this purpose, let us now connect the spiritual to integral GENE rhythm and see how it helps in its transformational journey from East (sanctuary) to South (community).

### *3.5 The transformational GENE*

For Amjad, this transformation in (any) society, Pakistan in his context, comes by extending Mawakhat to one's community. Akhuwat, for him, is a message of equal partnership – a vision of an ideal society, where there exists no divide between the wealthy (haves) and the poor (have-nots).

*Ever since my engagement with inter and intra-communal work, what I'd find most interesting and often fascinating is the microbial nature of human communities, similar to the concept of community ecology in plant and animal ecology. Although our thicker communal concentration in urban spaces now has detached us from the ecology of nature. If anything, this whole trans-migration has made us human beings more brazen than mineral; hence, the chemical imbalance has rendered us barren from the inside.*

*Now deeply immersed in the spirit of Mawakhat – a spiritual paradigm of solidarity – I can name this solidarity impulse which is the transcendental spiritual alchemy human ecology creates through SOUL-idarity amongst their communities, thereby borrowing from TRANS4M's integral terminology, this impulse is transformational, doing its rounds from one community to another, generating virtuous circles. This is apparent in Amjad's archetypal paradigm of Mawakhat, whereby this solidarity impulse originating from the holy city of Medina is now doing rounds in Akhuwat's Pakistani community of Akhuwateers (its family of borrowers, donors, volunteers and institutional ecosystem).*

According to scientists, microbial communities are defined as multi-species assemblages, in which organisms live together in a contiguous environment and interact with each other. *Microbes strongly interacting with each other in a microenvironment comprise a local community.* As such the complex nature of microbes affects the biogeochemical transformation of communities and how energy flows through them. Now, because microbes possess mechanisms for the horizontal transfer of genetic information, the *metagenome* may also be considered as a community property (Konopka, 06 August 2009)

This also resonates deeply with Ibrahim Abouleish's (Lessem, Abouleish & Herman, 2016) SEKEM vision of sustainability of an 'Economy of Love', by developing a community in the desert. According to him, 'The biological organic principle is based on the existing symbiosis between all living things, that means – on the earth, above the earth – also plants, animals, birds and all the way to above stellar constellation.'

For us, this *metagenome* represents the GENE-IUS (Schieffer & Ronnie, 2014), the integral moral core of Being (Self), or as per Tony Bradley (Lessem & Bradley, 2018) this is the God-Gene that is present at the heart of a community's transformational activation.

This is the 'TRANS4M Gene' of any particular self, organisation, community and the society which represents the integral worlds approach developed by Lessem and Schieffer (2014).

It is also the Ubuntu spirit of '*I am because WE are.*'

This *Transformational GENE* thus,merged with the *solidarity impulse*, creating further rounds of benevolence, in Amjad's terminology, reversing the effect of vicious circles of social isolation (poverty) to create '*virtuous circles*' of solidarity/Mawakhat amongst community members: that which Father Anselm Adodo (Schieffer & Lessem, 2014a), Founder of Paxherbals in Edo State of Nigeria terms 'Communitalism'. Communitalism demonstrates that an institutionalised model of business and enterprise based on nature, community, spirituality and humanism is a better driver of social and technological innovation in Africa.

*We now evaluate the emergent quality of Akhuwat's solidarity impulse by creating virtuous circles of benevolence, what I term as the 'barakah rounds', further explained in Chapter 6. The guiding question which persuaded me to do a further (deeper) exploration is my fascination with Akhuwat's initiation of 'reciprocal endowment' – transforming borrowers into donors, a paradigm of Ikhlas – the second I of Akhuwat's 4I genealogy (Iman, Ikhlas, Ihsan and Ikhuwah) – emerging from the integral Northern realm of knowledge creation, of Integral Dynamics Theory, developed by Lessem and Schieffer.*

### *3.6 Emergent properties – Akhuwat's virtuous circles*

The concept of emergence was first explained by the philosopher John Stuart Mill in the year 1843. The term 'emergent' was, however, coined by G. H. Lewes.

The definition of *Emergent Properties* by Stanford Encyclopaedia of Philosophy states:

> A variety of theorists have appropriated *Emergence* for their purposes ever since George Henry Lewes gave it a philosophical sense in his 1875 *Problems of Life and Mind.* We might roughly characterise the shared meaning thus: emergent entities (properties or substances) 'arise' out of more fundamental entities and yet are 'novel' or 'irreducible' with respect to them. (For example, it is sometimes said that consciousness is an emergent property of the brain.) There has been renewed interest in emergence within discussions of the behaviour of complex systems and debates over the reconcilability of mental causation, intentionality, or consciousness with physicalism.
>
> (O'Connor, et al., Summer 2015 Edition)

In arts, science, and philosophy, emergence is defined as a process where smaller entities and patterns combine together to form a larger entity that is unique from its constituents.

Thus, holds true for Akhuwat, as per our barakah rounds postulation, subsequently emerging through Akhuwat's virtuous circles of benevolence and reciprocity, transforming its borrowers into donors, we aim to delve deeper into the spirit of this *communal solidarity* (Mawakhat). This is further elaborated in Chapters 6 and 8.

Consequently and as could be explicitly seen in Akhuwat's case, the emergent virtousity from these rounds of benevolence have gathered momentum amongst their community of Akhuwateers.

This has a clear resonance with the Islamic philosophy of solidarity amongst the community of believers (ummah), as reported by An-Nu'man ibn Basheer in Ṣaḥiḥ al-Bukhari 5665, Ṣaḥiḥ Muslim 2586: The Messenger of Allah, peace and blessings be upon him, said, 'The parable of the believers in their affection, mercy, and compassion for each other is that of a body. When any limb aches, the whole body reacts with sleeplessness and fever'.

We now come to the next section of this chapter, which aims to integrate the spiritual (soul) with integral (transformational) Hikma (wisdom) to indicate the activation process of a community.

## 4 Section 2: soul-wisdom to trans4mational GENE activation

In this section, as a continuation from the previous section, we examine the effect of the coming of soul-wisdom paired with integral *Trans4mation* of the GENE. This we do by drawing a parallel to Akhuwat's 4 I's doing trans4mational rounds with integral's four rounds, inspecting the pulse of Oriental soul-wisdom submerged with the integral GENE rhythm. Thus, putting our SOUL-idarity GENE into an Akhuwat (brotherhood) activation, or rhythm.

*This is when the soul (philosophy) is set into motion (practices), flowing through the genealogy of the 4 I's (principles), thereby rounding off the integral SOUL-idarity paradigm. Thereafter,Chapter 4 further deepens Akhuwat's 4 I's elaboration.*

According to (Schieffer & Ronnie, 2014):

> With every human system being in continuous evolution, so do integral worlds incorporate an inbuilt transformational rhythm, which makes the entire approach dynamic.
>
> It is a rhythm that we could equally trace back to natural and cultural systems and their respective evolution. We call this rhythm the **GENE** (an acronym for Grounding, Emerging, Navigating, Effecting), representing a fourfold spiralling force, activating the entire Integral Worlds model.
>
> The *GENE rhythm* is embedded in the diverse reality views and knowledge realms of the Integral Worlds, bringing them all together in transformative interaction. While we see the GENE as a spiralling, iterative, ever-unfolding force, we nevertheless start most of our transformational processes in the South, thereby beginning with a conscious grounding in a given context and issue, before we then engage in its transformation. Drawing on Integral Dynamics, and the resultant 'four worlds' integral orientation and overall cultural transformation, through a new 'genealogical combination' of *community, sanctuary, university and laboratory.*

### *4.1 The fourfold of solidarity (Akhuwat): 4 I's genealogy*

Thus, elaborating the *four worlds* further, Lessem and Schieffer (2014) specifically draw the 'four worlds' theory as ***pragmatic*** (Western), ***rational*** (Northern), ***holistic*** (Eastern), and ***humanistic*** (Southern), that is, in their respectively positive, or functional, manifestations. Each has its under-developed or dysfunctional mode of expression, and its developed, or functional, one. The more connected with the other three worlds, the more dynamically integral any one world will be; the more disconnected, the more dysfunctionally disintegrated.

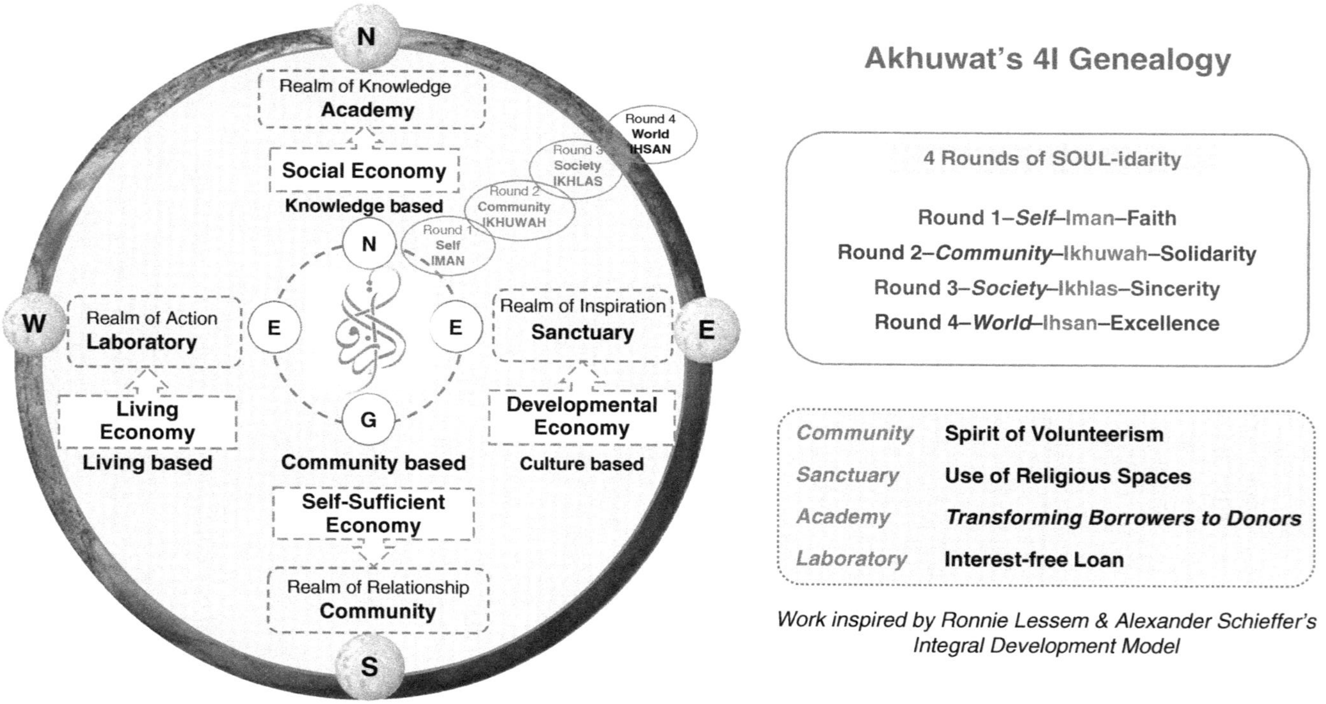


*Figure 1.1* Akhuwat's 4I genealogy

Drawing from their methodology of the integral four worlds theory, throughout the course of this book, we will be examining Akhuwat's under-developed or disconnected orientation, thus proposing a more integrally aligned SOUL-idarity noesis.

The figure (Figure 1.1) is one such endeavour to align Akhuwat's 4 I's (philosophy) through an integral four worlds compass.

As such, the ontological orientations of Akhuwat's 4 I's, or 4 Alifs, respectively in Urdu and Arabic, are:

- *Iman (Faith) – Utilising Religious Spaces*
- *Ikhlas (Sincerity) – Reciprocal Endowment*
- *Ihsan (Excellence) – Qard-e-Hasan*
- *Ikhuwah (Solidarity) – Volunteerism*

The 4I postulation came as a reflection of Islam's three fundamental principles: Islam, Iman and Ihsan, as shown in the introduction of Part I. This is further elaborated on in Chapter 5.

This 4I praxis as drawn in Figure I.1 is a parallel articulation of integral dynamics' four *transdisciplinary realms*, as conceived by Lessem & Schieffer:

- *Southern Realm of Relationship: Nature and Community*
- *Eastern Realm of Inspiration: Culture and Spirituality*
- *Northern Realm of Knowledge: Science, Systems and Technology*
- *Western Realm of Action: Enterprise and Economics*

**'Southern' Grounding – Community**: The issue at hand and the people involved are grounded in a particular nature and community, which need to be fully understood. For any living system, the southern grounds represent its '*local identity'* and its connection to a common source of life.

**'Eastern' Emergence – Sanctuary**: is hence about '*becoming'*. It deals with 'intuiting' and 'imagining' the new form that is emerging. Here the 'local' perspective of the southern grounds evolves to 'local-global' viewpoints.

**'Northern' Navigation – Academy**: The move to 'northern' navigation requires that the new insights (images, visions) gained are translated – in a structured and systematic manner – into new concepts, new knowledge. 'Northern' navigation is hence about 'knowing' and about 'making explicit' what hitherto had been rather implicit.

**'Western' Effect – Laboratory**: Moving to 'western' effect is now requiring us to put all prior three levels into integrated action. It is about pragmatically applying the new knowledge that has been developed, thereby actualising the innovation that it contains. 'Western' effect is hence about 'doing' and 'making it happen' (2014b).

According to their model, each *transcultural reality* viewpoint has a different emphasis, which leads to four different knowledge fields or realms, each providing a particular perspective. For any given development calling and challenge requires the transdisciplinary engagement with all realms.

We now arrive at our second round of *solidarity impulse*, navigating our readers through the Akhuwat paradigm – and its fundamental principles of solidarity. Akhuwat, through their many operations and initiatives, have been successfully raising awareness of social challenges of Pakistani society, thereby creating knowledge of how these issues could be tackled systemically by employing local knowledge to Islamic (global) philosophy of sociology.

## *4.2 Round II – the Akhuwat paradigm – Northern orientation – the principles*

**1.2 Extreme poverty is a crime, and extreme wealth is oppression – both must be eradicated**

In his Urdu book *Akhuwat ka Safar* (A Journey of Hope), Amjad recalls a prayer his father taught him which touched my heart deeply: 'O Lord, save me from poverty' – to that, he added, 'Lord, save me from wealth'. In his words:

*Akhuwat* is no longer a dream but has now become a social movement. It is no longer a passion limited to a few, but an institution for all. Society cannot be left at the mercy of a capitalistic and feudalistic financial system, a system mostly founded on the basis of exploitation. Banks lend to those who are already wealthy, while the poor and indigent are treated like untouchables. This divide in the 21st century is the worst form of financial apartheid. A few people have appropriated the treasures of the world for their own use. If they had their way, they would even put a price on the sunshine and the moonlight. Perhaps they have not understood the purpose of creation. 'Might is right' is not a rule that can be imposed upon humanity. Whatever belongs to the Lord, belongs to all.

The equitable distribution of resources must take place according to effort and skill. The poor are needy not of alms, but of cooperation. We give charity to the poor and make them dependent upon it. They are deprived of wealth and assets, but not of ego and pride and, through charity, we deprive them of those.

Akhuwat has done nothing new, but by institutionalising Islam's basic system of interest-free loans, the rule of solidarity and mutual support can become the norm of a just and fair society.

For him to then humbly claim that Akhuwat hasn't initiated a new discipline of reciprocity shows the purity of his heart and intention. In fact, thus became my call, as the vision I was perceiving with the inner eye of my spiritual heart is what I am endeavouring to translate here by using my Sufi knowledge and integral terminology as a tool to then contemplate a New Age Hikma (wisdom) of SOUL-idarity.

Thus, Part II of the book translates Akhuwat's Mawakhat paradigm as an indigenous model of *solidarity economy*, emerging out of Pakistan (East), integrally creating a social knowledge base for its community of Akhuwateers.

Based on Lessem and Schieffer's analysis; "the world is undergoing a profound civilisational crisis in an attempt to outgrow the existing, modernist worldview and form a new, more sustainable paradigm: what they term 'alternative to modernity". As such, this book aims to explore whether 'liberation' from the dominant Western worldview is really an answer to developmental problems for a faith-based country like Pakistan, withholding the fact that the spiritual-financial solution Akhuwat came up with has proven to be successful in its local albeit spiritual context. Basing our conclusion on Akhuwat's success due to its founder's vision and leadership qualities emulating from the Prophet's Tradition (Sunnah) and taking Iqbal's wisdom, as the philosopher and Muslim visionary of the East.

Or as Sardar (1986) sees it, "*Muslim intellectuals have two types of knowledge, operational and non-operational.* The 'operational' knowledge is that of the Occidental sciences – physical, technological, and social – acquired either in the Occident or in the Occidental type of educational establishment in their own countries. As Muslims, however, they also have some knowledge of Islam. That is their 'non-operational' knowledge. Islam, for Sardar, is either entirely unoperational in daily life, or its operational forms are confined to prayers, fasting and other rituals at birth, marriage and death.

No operational and functional social order of Islam exists in its entirety today or has existed, for Sardar, in recent history. The model social, economic and political order of Islam in fact existed so long ago that, for minds immersed in modern Occidental disciplines and philosophies, it is difficult to comprehend how socio-economic and political problems of today could be solved along those lines. Islam can certainly solve all problems, but the Muslim intellectuals of today cannot. He then goes on, proposing the need for well-articulated models of *Islamic economic theory* that clearly define the relationship between land, labor and capital, *economic growth and resource consumption, based on social justice and brotherhood"*. (Sardar, 1986)

In the light of Sardar's above propositions, we aim to build a case through Akhuwat's consonant successive micro-lending mechanism, which is borrowed from the Quranic prescription of *Qard-e-Hasan* (a virtuous loan), an operational model of Islamic economic theory. As understood by modern Occidental disciplines, the current Crowdfunding practices could also be seen as the revival of Qard-e-Hasan, *interest-free loans*, as Akhuwat's micro-lending methodology.

## 5 Section 3 – from solidarity impulse to generating a bond of solidarity

### 1.3 The regime of selfish wealth must now be razed

According to Oxfam's 'An Economy for the 99%' report (AN ECONOMY FOR THE 99%, 2017):

New estimates show that just eight men own the same wealth as the poorest half of the world. As growth benefits the richest, the rest of society – especially the poorest – suffers. The very design of our economies and the principles of our economics have taken us to this extreme, unsustainable and unjust point. The impact of this gap between the fortunate few and the rest of us is felt everywhere, but especially by the forgotten poorest. While eight men's wealth is today the equivalent to that of 3.6 billion people, one in nine go to bed hungry every night. The super-rich are accumulating wealth at such a rapid rate that the world could see its first trillionaire in a mere 25 years, yet 1 in 10 of us still earns less than $2 a day (Anon., 2017).

We believe poverty is not limited to the definitions furnished by the World Bank and the United Nations; far murkier is the narrative of poverty. Deprivation of basic amenities is poverty, but so is the lack of education, health and clean water. The privation of political and social justice, and the paucity of morals and values is also poverty. In order to combat poverty, it is important to be aware of statistics. However, the stark reality of poverty, in all its wretchedness, often renders these figures insignificant. The fact is that as long as even a single fellow citizen remains impoverished, we are all poor. The worst poverty, however, is the bankruptcy of hope. If hope no longer exists among people, what recourse is left to them?

Economists in the 21st century are suggesting that "to transform today's divisive economies, we need to create economies that are *distributive* by design – ones that share value far more equitably amongst all those who help to generate it".

According to Kate Raworth (Raworth, n.d.) economist at Oxford University's Environmental Change Institute: Old economics is based on false 'laws of physics' – new economics can save us. According to her, an economy is not best thought of as a mechanism that returns to equilibrium and follows fixed laws of motion. It should be thought of as the living world: it's complex, dynamic and ever-evolving. For economists, it's time for a metaphorical career change: from engineer to gardener. It calls for getting stuck in, digging, pruning, weeding and watering the plants as they grow and mature. It's time to nurture a thriving economy, one that is inclusive and sustainable, and this could be done by following two core principles: make it regenerative and distributive by design.

Distributive economic design, for Kate Raworth, in turn ensures "that the value created is spread far more equitably among those who helped to generate it" (Raworth, n.d.)

We now turn to Akhuwat's model of re-distirbution amongst its Paksitani communities.

### *5.2 Akhuwat's re-distributive model*

In his poem 'Muslim' (Bang-e-Dara 117 June 1912), Iqbal asserts that for the sake of attaining the national entity the glories of the past should not be forgotten. To borrow from Iqbal's moving sentiment, Akhuwat traces the relics of long-forsaken flames and endeavours to rediscover the glory of the values of faith. This institution, founded on the philosophy of solidarity, has four fundamental principles.

*First, avoid interest; second, work from within a house of worship; third, promote the ethos of service; fourth, ensure that the borrowers of today turn into tomorrow's donors by awakening the spirit of Mawakhat.*

Notwithstanding its spiritual postulation, Akhuwat, as a philosophically conceived spiritual model of finance, belongs to Muslims, as much as it does to Christians, Hindus, Sikhs and every other individual who believes in social justice.

#### 1.4 A new discipline

After affirming Akhuwat's global philosophy, the question about the institution's practical shape arose. Following considerable deliberation, we concluded that an affluent household in Pakistan could help a weak one in two ways – either in the form of charity, or in the shape of a loan. We were aware of the consequences of charity – the creation of disincentives and further incapacitation. That is why we turned to loans as our choice. From there, we became inclined towards Qard-e-Hasan – a loan upon which there is no condition of any kind of interest or profit. Moreover, Akhuwat's loans are not intended for individuals but for families. We held that the basic unit of society is the family and it is the family that should be strengthened going forward.

Among Akhuwat's initial loans, one was granted to a widow from Rasool Park, Lahore, whose story was to become an integral part of our history. With tears in her eyes, each one of which mirrored years of tribulation, this woman related that, after her husband's death, her circumstances had worsened considerably, and all the household responsibility had fallen onto her shoulders. She was not averse to fulfilling these responsibilities, but begging appeared unacceptable to her. Once her situation was confirmed, she was presented with Rs. 10,000 ($100) in the form of an interest-free loan. She bought herself two modern sewing machines with this. During the next six months, she toiled and sweat day and night. With the help of the income obtained from these two sewing machines, this determined woman was able not only to meet the expenses of her house, but later married off one of her daughters and eventually repaid the whole loan. Neither she nor her daughters picked up the begging bowl nor sought charity but, against all odds, preserved their dignity.

This loan was the first drop of rain that intensified our confidence that thousands of respectable households could be helped in a similar way.

### *5.3.1 Round III – a fourfold Islamic perspective of solidarity – Western orientation – the practices*

In his recent book, A World of Three Zeroes (, Dr. Muhammad Yunus suggests:

> a citizens' movement can make the world ready to overcome an ever-impending disaster of poverty and dangers of wealth concentration. He further suggests, extreme wealth concentration is not an unalterable fate that humankind was born with. Since it is our own creation, we can solve it through our own efforts. Our collective *blocked mind* prevents us from seeing the forces that are pushing us toward the inevitable social explosion.
>
> (Yunus, 2017)

In this Round, we explore and elaborate on the 'Trans4mational GENE',of any particular self, organisation, community and the society which represents the integral worlds approach developed by Lessem and Schieffer (2014). Thereby, proposing a unique Islamic fourfold quaternity and the GENE rhythm of Akhuwat's solidarity rhythm, all through practical examples of how it activates a community of Akhuwateers – a community of 21,000 Akhuwat volunteers – to offer their support and services in the spirit of khidmet-e-khalq (service to humanity).

Delving deeper into the psyche and chemistry of communitas and inquiring the nature of co-existence, we will further explore what holds communities together in times of trauma and disaster, or veritably in economic calamity, i.e., abject poverty in the Pakistani community's case.

*Could opening our 'spiritual hearts' be the way to deal with our communal traumas which are induced by our 'blocked minds', as suggested by Dr. Muhammad Yunus, the social business guru of the 21st century, in his recent book?*

We now turn to the integral impulse of our solidarity GENE to look for an answer.

### *5.3.2 Integral impulse of solidarity GENE*

In the case that we are presenting here, Akhuwat, or rather Amjad Saqib, has not only taken it upon himself to devise an excellent method of helping the very poor and destitute strata of the society, but in doing so, he has also revived the spirit of Qard-e-Hasan (benevolent loan) by initiating a regenerative model of finance, fostering a culture of sharing and caring.

Thus, corresponding to Lessem and Scieffer's approach to integral development, geared towards understanding pervasive imbalances in a particular context, thereby catalysing research and development with a view to alleviating them. (Schieffer & Lessem, 2014)

> By deeply understanding those imbalances, we tend to find that the monocultural influence of the 'West' on the rest is all-consuming; that the hidden cultural and spiritual depths of a particular society are all too seldom tapped, and interlinked with the economic and political surface; that a uni-disciplinary focus on politics, economics, business studies or information technology belies a more trans-disciplinary orientation; and that all too often development of self and community, organization and society, takes place in isolation, leaving different development impulses disconnected.
>
> Integral worlds initiates processes of healing and holistic realignment by activating all the complementary parts of any human system, such as the *realms* of nature and community; culture and consciousness; science, systems and technology; as well as enterprise, economics and politics. Starting off and acting as a continuous focal point of any transformation process within an integral worlds perspective is the *inner core* of the individual or collective entity, its deepest value base, spiritual and moral source.
>
> It is here, at the core of an individual, organisation, community, or society, that the impulse for transformation or development is initiated – be it through a perceived imbalance of the overall system, that becomes an objective concern, be it through a particular, subjective evolutionary calling. This inner personal core and the outer, global circle are then connected through the '4Rs' of Integral Worlds: Realities (worldviews), Realms (Knowledge Fields), Rounds (different levels, from self to world) and Rhythms (transformative rhythms, applied to all of them).

Amjad, having a deep understanding of his society's needs and challenges, and being a devout believer in his faith and its obligation of turning to the Sunnah, the Prophetic Traditions, in times of societal needs bestowed upon those who cultivate a deep sense of compassion in their hearts for their community well-being and welfare, draws inspiration from the Islamic history of Mawakhat-e-Medina, the migration of Prophet Muhammad (peace be upon him) and his companions from Mecca to Medina.

This brings us to the core philosophy of Akhuwat as an institution as well as Akhuwat as brotherhood with one's fellow community members, as a result of deprivation and land-migration.

*Hijrah* (migration) is a cumbersome course, as it takes a heavy emotional, or might I say spiritual, toll on one's soul. Feeling at home away from home as in Rumi's words, *I was at home wherever I am*, only happens when the journey is transcended with an openness, placing full trust in the divine order of things by bowing down to HIS Divine intellect, knowing HE/SHE is the best of carers and the Judge of our destiny.

The story of Akhuwat started 1400 years ago in another land: in Arabia, the heart of Islam.

### *5.3.3 Hijrat-e-Nabwi: solidarity with migrant community*

The calendar year of Islam begins not with the birthday of Prophet Muhammad (peace be on him), nor from the time that the revelation came to him, nor from the time of his ascension to Heaven, but with the migration (hijrah) from an undesirable environment to a desirable place to fulfil Allah's command. It was migration from a plot that was set by the leaders of the Quraysh to kill Prophet Muhammad and to destroy the truth that today is being conveyed to mankind everywhere against tyranny and injustice.

The migration of the Prophet (peace be upon him) illustrates the principle that; "everything, howsoever coveted by one, ought to be sacrificed for the sake of one's faith or ideal. A worldly estate and effects, or any other thing that a man is disposed to value, can never take the place of his faith, nor can the faith be bartered away for the entire world. For what does it profit a man if he gains the whole world but suffers the loss of his own soul? (Anon., n.d.)

The Prophet loved Mecca, but he valued his faith more. One was a natural feeling of affection and the other an insatiable thirst of soul. We find the two tenderest feelings of human nature articulately expressed by the Prophet while leaving Mecca emigrating to Medina.

*Commit no excess, God's earth is spacious – Migrate if required.*

From a Quranic perspective, one cannot plead that the pressure of adverse circumstances forced one to endure difficulties, or that in one's lack of action they allowed injustices to afflict them and others. If the conditions do not allow one to act in accordance with our faith, then we must be prepared to suffer exile and ostracism.

It may be that we will have to change our homes, jobs, towns or cities, or even migrate to other lands. We may have to change our positions in life or, indeed, the nature of our social relationships. It is ultimately God's pleasure we seek and our integrity before our Creator is **more** important than any of the factors considered.

Believers should always endeavour to speak the truth and must never inflict or tolerate injustices. However, if all reasonable attempts to resolve a situation fail and life or property are at risk under sustained oppression, believers should be prepared to emigrate to different lands by putting complete faith and trust in God (tawakul-Allah).

It was this context of *self-sacrifice (hijrah)* in Prophet Muhammed (peace be upon him) and his companions' case which gave birth to a unique model of solidarity (brotherhood) borne out of sharing what one has in *abundance* for the sake of Allah, bringing *prosperity* to others and maintaining peace and equity on earth.

How does this establish a SOUL-idarity (Mawakhat) between various community members? We explore further here.

#### 5.3.3.1 MAWAKHAT (BROTHERHOOD) ESTABLISHED BETWEEN MIGRANTS AND THE ANSAR

It was thus in this context that the hijrah of the Prophet (peace be upon him) gave birth to a communal sharing and caring between two tribes after one had left their homes (comfort zone), making a sacrifice in the name of faith. Thus, throughout the course of our journey of this book, we will be referring to migration as *taking leave from one's Self* or what one holds as too valuable and dear.

Muslims of Medina (the Ansar) embraced with love and sincerity the Muslim migrants (Muhajiroun) who settled in Medina, leaving everything they had behind for the sake of God. They (the Ansar) did not and would not begrudge any kind of help they could offer to them.

However, the migrants were not familiar with Medina's climate, customs and working conditions. They did not bring anything with them when leaving Mecca. For this reason, they needed to be familiarised with Medina's working conditions and with the Muslims of Medina, who came to be called the Ansar (the helpers) because they offered all kinds of help to them.

Therefore, the Messenger of God gathered the Ansar and the migrants together five months after migrating to Medina. He appointed 90 Muslims, 45 of whom were from the Ansar and the other 45 from the migrants, as brothers. And this is the spirit and philosophy of Mawakhat.

The foundation of *brotherhood* established by the Prophet was based on mutual economic and psychological support and the principle of being inheritors to each other, which in turn aimed to provide migrants with support to get over the sorrow and misery they felt because of homesickness. This proves the point Dr. Amjad Saqib often emphasises and is Akhuwat's fundamental tenant: that giving is not always about giving your money to the poor and needy, but it's also about sharing your time with those who are in need of some moral support too.

According to this foundation of *brotherhood* that was established, leaders of each family in Medina would provide a Muslim family from Mecca with accommodation and share their belongings with them, and they would work together. Through this brotherhood, the life expenses and accommodation problems of immigrants, who left everything behind except for their love for God and His Messenger, were solved. Each person from the Ansar put one migrant up, and they worked together, sharing what they earned. This was a brotherhood that outpaced biological brotherhood. Through this bond of brotherhood, a large social charity was established. Muslim migrants were saved from economic problems. *Each Muslim of Medina would give half of their belongings to their brother from the Muslims of Mecca.* The Ansar (helpers) showed the zenith of hospitability, generosity, gratitude and humanity to their migrant brothers. This spiritual brotherhood yielded positive outcomes in a short time. Various strata of society got closer to each other with the help of this brotherhood, and tribalistic pride and enmity were also abolished. As a result, a society with divine aims, supreme goals, and virtuous souls emerged.

Drawing from this unique story of Mawakhat, and referring to the SOUL-idarity GENE model, we now draw upon the chemistry between a community or a group of people working towards a common goal, which activates a certain alchemy of the communal soul of communitas.

From transmutation to transformation, this soul alchemy is implicitly flowing through individuals to communities. In this next section, we will be exploring the attributes of the SOUL-idarity dynamics and see how this process activates the collective GENE rhythm of a particular community in a faith-based society, i.e., Pakistan.

## 6 Section 4: the Hikma of integral SOUL-idarity rhythm

> On the surface, each of us is separate and we have our own individual way of life. But, in the depth of being, we are One. The goal of spiritual practices is to move beyond the surface, and to discover the depth
>
> (Khan, 1977)

*Conclusively, we are proposing a reawakened lexicon for Hikma of an Islamic archetypal community, emerging as an (after) 'effect' of completing the four rounds of solidarity rhythm. As identified in Akhuwat's case, there emerges from the 4I genealogy of Iman (faith), Ihsan (excellence), Ikhlas (sincerity) and Ikhuwah (solidarity), an integral Hikma noesis of* ***ishq, ilm, akhuwat and amal****, containing the root letters for Hikma (wisdom) in Arabic and Urdu.*

'Remember God's blessings upon you, and what He has brought down upon you of the "al-kitab" (the Book/Scripture) and "al-hikmah" (the wisdom) to enlighten you "bihi" (with it)'. 2:231

In the Quranic context, the word 'al-kitab' means the book, in this case it is the Quran. The word 'al-hikmah' means 'the wisdom'. This is the meaning of Hikma that is found in every Arabic dictionary in print (due to the different alphabet, Arabic words are spelled many different ways in English). Nevertheless, in an attempt to create a reference to the Sunnah of Muhammad (peace be upon him) in the Quran when there is none, it is claimed that the word 'al-hikmah' in such verses as 2:231 refers to the Sunnah of Prophet Muhammad!

Fundamentally, in an Islamic setting, the four rounds of this rhythm circumambulate the Kabah (the *God-GENE)*, manifesting itself through *ishq (divine love), ilm (universal knowledge), amal (communal action and/or good deeds) and finally, akhuwat, (universal soulidarity).*

The underlying circular design, inspired by Lessem and Schieffer's GENE model, acknowledges that since time immemorial the circular shape has been a symbol for the totality. It also symbolises the cycle of life that each living system undergoes.

In integral worlds, the outer globe marks a worldly, holistic perspective. Embedded in the outer global circle is the local context. At the very centre of such a globally embedded context is what they call the inner core.

Additionally, drawing from the integral dynamics of the GENE rhythm flowing through the core of a community, we aim to draw a parallel between the GENE (Grounding, Emergence, Navigation and Effect) and its reiteration from an Islamic and mystical perspective, yet through a Pakistani community to delve deeper into how the alchemy between the GENE elements takes effect in a fourfold spiralling force as is shown in Figure 1.2.

We aim to elaborate on these four rounds further in the conclusive Part IV of our book. For now, we turn to the alchemical nature of SOUL-idarity amongst community.

### *6.1 The alchemy of SOUL-idarity*

Alchemy, as maintained by Jung, is a process of separation, transformation and integration.

In the 20th Century, Carl Jung described alchemy "in terms of depth psychology and shed new light on an old science. Contemporary 21st Century alchemy can be viewed as a dynamic process in terms of Chaos Theory and its related sciences" (C.G.Jung, 1980)According to Jung, a Swiss psychiatrist and psychoanalyst who founded analytical psychology, alchemy is central to the Jungian hypothesis of the collective unconscious. Introducing the basic concepts of alchemy, Jung reminds us of the dual nature of alchemy, comprising both the chemical process and a parallel mystical component. He

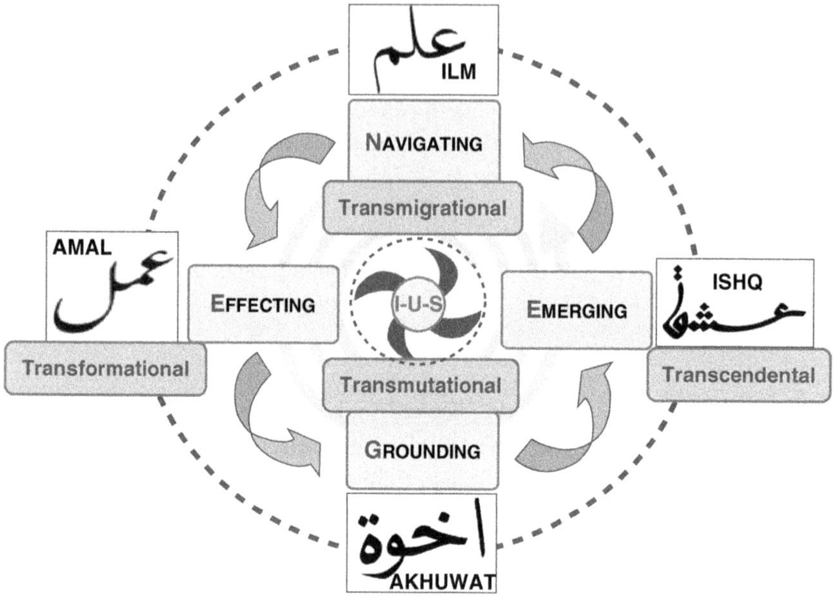


*Figure 1.2* The Hikma of SOUL-idarity

also discusses the seemingly deliberate mystification of the alchemists. Finally, in using the alchemical process to provide insights into individuation, Jung emphasises the importance of alchemy in relating to us the transcendent nature of the psyche.

Whereas the alchemy that results in virtuosity, from an Islamic philosophical perspective, for Al-Farabi (c.870–950), is an association of human beings collaborating 'in order to preserve [themselves] and to attain [their] highest perfections', as he writes in his book Kitab ara' ahl Al-Madinah al-Faḍilah (The Virtuous City).

According to him, in a society without collaboration, he insists, 'Man cannot attain the perfection, for the sake of which his inborn nature [*fitra*] has been given to him' (Perfect State V, 15, 1: 229).

Al-Farabi, also known in the West as Alpharabius, was a renowned Persian philosopher and jurist who wrote in the fields of political philosophy, metaphysics, ethics and logic. In Arabic philosophical tradition, he is known with the honorific 'the Second Master', after Aristotle.

Moreover, just like Aristotle, Al-Farabi is convinced that:

> attaining the highest possible degree of perfection entails happiness, a key concept of his thought. He further elaborates on the concept of human perfection: first, he links it with the notion that people live in societies and, second, draws the conclusion that these societies serve a specific purpose,

> beyond the mere allocation of daily needs, such as food, shelter, and protection. Societies have their own 'natural telos' which consists, according to al-Farabi, in guiding their members towards their end: true felicity.
>
> (Anon., 2016)

Hazrat Inayat Khan (1914) echoes Al-Farabi's definition of true felicity as the soul happiness.

> THE SOUL in Sanskrit, in the terms of the Vedanta, is called Atman, which means happiness or bliss itself. It is not that happiness belongs to the soul; it is that the soul itself is happiness. Today we often confuse happiness with pleasure; but pleasure is only an illusion, a shadow of happiness. The man who does not know the secret of happiness often develops avarice. He wants thousands, and when he gets them they do not satisfy him, and he wants millions and still he is not satisfied; he wants more and more.
>
> (Khan, 1914)

This soul distillation, in the light of the wise words spoken by the sages of the past, and as mentioned above, comes through muhasabah (retrospection), as a fundamental tenet of Tasawwuf, and one of the most important practices on the Sufi Path. As alluded to by Al-Farabi, and so we believe, 'true felicity' could only be achieved by going through the process of an inward reflection (muhasabah); in integral language, this is what we call the *inner calling* of an individual, matching it with the *outer calling* (societal), thereby giving birth to a '*virtuous society*', a vision, travelling through this chain (silsilah) was reawakened in Amjad's soul.

Perhaps this is best explained in Jung's words:

*Who looks outside, dreams; who looks inside, awakes.*
*Everything that irritates us about others can lead us to an understanding of ourselves.*
*In all chaos there is a cosmos, in all disorder a secret order.*

### *6.1.1 Round IV – caring 4 the society – integral finance – Southern orientation – the integral Hikma process*

Remember God's blessings upon you, and what He has brought down upon you of the 'al-kitab' (the Book/Scripture) and 'al-hikmah' (the wisdom) to enlighten you 'bihi' (with it) (Quran 2:231).

*As we round off in the concluding part, we aim to establish, drawing from Akhuwat's financial model, a new language for an integral finance, as identified by us, emerging from the Hikma (wisdom) of SOUL-idarity realms. All this was catalysed by Amjad Saqib, in the form of a social integrator, successfully activating a large community of micro-entrepreneurs and Akhuwat volunteers, also through reviving a Prophetic spiritual tradition.*

*Could Akhuwat, then, take the lead by institutionalising one such language which could be spoken and understood globally, if not only, within the Muslim world?*

> As observed by Lessem and Schieffer (ibid), "for the past 150 years, and most particularly during the course of the twentieth century, global politics and economics has been marked by two sets of politically and economically divisive, rather than culturally and psychologically integrative, forces – the 'East/West' mutually antagonistic divide of communism/capitalism, and the North/South chasm of wealth and poverty. Indeed, such an ideological divide is a gross misinterpretation of the ideas of both lead protagonists, Smith and Marx. The result, worldwide, has been, to a considerable degree, stasis and disintegration, in recent years, in the global 'south', but now also in the global 'north' (the Euro/zone) and so called 'west' (United States of America)". (Schieffer & Lessem, 2014)

Having successfully sustained itself for the past 17 years through its distinctive model of *interest-free loans* in a local setting, the call for Akhuwat now is to expand their *solidarity paradigm* globally.

As posited by Lessem and Schieffer, their *local identity* is in need of co-evolving towards *global integrity*, thus aligning the soul of *solidarity* with *universality*. This poses the question of whether the world, outside of Pakistan, will welcome an alternative model of finance in such a philosophical setting borne out of the need to combat their local poverty defiance.

*How can we bridge this gap between solidarity and universality?*
*Could a new Theory of Knowledge (TOK) be developed using the Hikma locked in this model for a communal conceptualisation of an integral-spiritual finance model for communities to generate their own micro-self-sustained economies, banking on its benevolent members to share their abundance (barakah) with the less fortunate ones amongst them?*

## 7 Conclusion

*Through an alchemy of soul happiness and opening our hearts to the Hikmah (wisdom) of SOUL-idarity, we are arriving at the juncture, whereby our aim is to investigate this interplay of archaic wisdom (Mawakhat), especially doing Rounds through Akhuwat's community GENE rhythm.*

*We aim to explore whether the innovatory evolution of the Mawakhat paradigm as proposed by us, in fact emanating from Akhuwat's practically observed model, could act as a catalyst to provide a SOUL-idarity roadmap. Thereby, engaging the 'inner' (batin) with the 'outer' (zahir) calling of a community. Could this be the new age dictum for an integral Pakistan as an emerging 'solidarity economy' generated by the poor (borrowers of Akhuwat)?*

*This sets the scene for our next chapter, which takes us on a journey through Akhuwat's Pakistan. Throughout our journey, we will aim to establish how Pakistan could genealogically lead the way for other microfinance institutions, through Akhuwat's practical example of a fourfold model, parallel to the integral CARE model, to do away with the micro-ness of microfinance, if not throughout the Islamic world. Thereby benefiting from an integral finance model, as proposed in this book, and eventually by conceptualising this SOUL-idarity Hikma in an Akhuwat (comm)University context, hence, institutionalising the Mawakhat philosophy for future generations to take guidance from.*

## Note

1 **Ubuntu** is an ancient African word **meaning** 'humanity to others'. It also **means** 'I am what I am because of who we all are'.

## Bibliography

Adodo, A., 2017. *Integral Community Enterprise in Africa. Communitalism as an Alternative to Capitalism*. London: Routledge.

Anon., 2016. *Al-Farabi's Philosophy of Society and Religion*. Available at: https://plato.stanford.edu/entries/al-farabi-soc-rel/

Anon., 2017. *An Economy for the 99%*. UK: Oxfam.

Anon., n.d. *The Prophet's Migration to Medina*. Available at: http://seerah.net/the-prophets-migration-to-medina/

Jung, C. G., 1980. *Psychology and Alchemy (Collected Works of C.G. Jung)*. London: Routledge.

Khaminwa, A. N., 2003. Coexistence. *Beyond Intractability*, July.

Khan, H. I., 1914. Love, Human and Divine. In: *Spiritual Liberty*. Delhi: Motilal Banarsidass Publishers Pvt. Ltd.

Khan, H. I., 1977. *The Soul Whence and Whither*. s.l.: Omega Press.

Khan, H. I., 2007. *The Gayan: Notes from the Unstruck Music*. New York: Omega Publications.

Khan, L. A., 2017. *A Quantum Leap Toward Universal Spirituality*. Available at: https://www.huffingtonpost.com/liaquat-ali-khan/quantum-leap-toward-unive_b_5348034.html

Konopka, A., 06 August 2009. What is Microbial Community Ecology? *The ISME Journal*, 3, pp. 1223–1230.

Kumar, S., 2013. *Soil Soul Society: A New Trinity for Our Time*. Brighton: Ivy Press.

Lessem, R., & Bradley, T., 2018. *Evolving Work*. Abingdon: Routledge.

Lessem, R., Abouleish, I., & Herman, L., 2016. *Integral Polity: Integrating Nature, Culture, Society and Economy*. Abingdon: Routledge.

O'Connor, T., & Wong, H. Y., Summer 2015 Edition. *Emergent Properties*. Available at: https://plato.stanford.edu/archives/sum2015/entries/properties-emergent [Accessed 2018].

Raworth, K., n.d. *Global Development Professionals Network Development 2030*. Available at: https://www.theguardian.com/global-development-professionals-network/2017/apr/06/kate-raworth-doughnut-economics-new-economics

Rumi, 1995. Mathnawi, I. In: *The Essential Rumi*. San Francisco: Harper.

Saeed, J., 1994. *Islam and Modernization: A Comparative Analysis of Pakistan, Egypt, and Turkey*. London: Praeger.

Saqib, A., 2016. *Kamyab Loug*. Lahore: Sang-e-Meel Publications.

Sardar, Z., 1986. *Islamic Futures: The Shape of Ideas to Come (Islamic futures & policy studies)*. London: Mansell Publishing.

Sardar, Z., 2017. Populism: Fibs and Fibbers. In: *Critical Muslim Edition 24*. October–December, pp. 7–13.

Schieffer, A., & Lessem, R., 2010. *Integral Economics: Releasing the Economic Genius of your Society*. Farnham: Gower Publishing Ltd.

Schieffer, A., & Lessem, R., 2014a. *Integral Development: Releasing the Transformative Potential of Individuals, Organisations and Societies*. Farnham: Gower Publishing Ltd.

Uzdavinys, A., 2011. *Ascent to Heaven in Islamic and Jewish Mysticism*. United Kingdom: The Matheson Trust.

Yunus, M., 2003. *Banker to the Poor: The Story of the Grameen Bank*. London: Aurum Press Ltd.

Yunus, M., 2017. *A World of Three Zeroes*. London: Scribe Publications.

# 2 Pakistan's cultural genealogy

## Through integral 4 C's

### 1 Preamble

*Transforming the notion of a conventional PhD, and as part of my PHD (Personal Holistic Development) process, in this chapter we engage in a dual rhythm:* ***4C rhythm and CARE*** *process, developed by* Lessem and Schieffer (2013), *investigating how Akhuwat is 'CARE-ing 4 Pakistani SOCIETY' through the integral development lens.*

> *With the GENE-process as their overarching transformational rhythm, they developed two further parallel trajectories that assist each agent of transformation to successfully undertake the transformation journey and to transcend the individual contribution towards a collective embodiment of an integral innovation. The ultimate objective is to go beyond a singular and individual impulse of renewal, but rather arrive at collective and, ideally, institutionalised action to sustain this impulse on a long-term basis.*
>
> *The initial trajectory with a focus on a personal contribution follows the 4 C's, which we will be using as a process to probe Pakistan's 4 C's in this chapter.*
>
> *The 4C process is, as such: Call, Context, Co-creation, Contribution.*
>
> *In parallel, the transformational GENE works towards 'full C+A+R+E' – a process and acronym representing Community activation, raising Awareness, Research-to-innovation and Embodied action.*

*On the one hand, following a '4C' trajectory – including* ***Call, Context, Co-Creation and Contribution*** *– equipped us to examine Pakistan's existing challenges, as our collective call for integral development. On the other hand, amplifying Akhuwat's particular impulse with an institutionalised one thereby sustained and evolved our original contribution.*

*As such, the 'CARE' rhythm institutionally involves us in Community activation; Awakening individual and collective consciousness, institutionalising innovative Research, and Embodying transformation in the final phase.*

*Within the Muslim world, Pakistan is a heartland of Islamic mysticism where the 'path of love' (Ishq), as posited in the previous chapter, is distinctive and especially alive in its popular manifestations. Steeped in centuries of subcontinental folklore, poetry and spiritualism, Sufism reflects the mystical side of Islam in most areas of Pakistan, pre-eminently in the Punjab region, home to Akhuwat and its Founder, Dr. Amjad Saqib.*

*Lodged in the local culture of the region, plus emanating from the Prophetic Tradition (Sunnah), the Akhuwat/Mawakhat integrative model required a CARE-like process as developed by* Lessem and Schieffer (2013) *to examine it from this dual, corresponding rhythm of 4 C's and CARE-4-Society.*

*I start this journey by retracing my steps back home – Pakistan and the way I remember it after my migration.*

## 2 Introduction: home coming – the Islamic Republic of Pakistan story

*Pakistan represents a place of love and reverence for the simple reason of being our shared birthplace. Indeed, the attachment to the land and its soil stirs a soul-striking awakening wherever we are. Thus, this chapter aims to depict Pakistan and its diverse communal culture with such affinity. For me, it serves the purpose of projecting the soil that birthed me with sincerity – an almost romanticised representation of my soul-soil impact, for what I term Soil Soulidarity.*

### *2.1 Topophilia of Maqam*

The word topophilia, which literally means love of place, was popularised by Yi-fu Tuan, a human geographer, in his book *Topophilia: A Study of Environmental Perception, Attitudes and Values*, published in 1974.

For Tuan, topophilia is 'the affective bond between people and place or setting. It is a familiar sentiment, a word that encapsulates the pleasantly varied relationships we have with particular bits of the world both as individuals and as participants in cultures with long histories' (Tuan, 1974).

The word *Maqam* in Urdu denotes just that, as also 'locality'. The meaning of its Arabic equivalent is 'station'. Its plural, *Maqamat*, refers to 'stations' in Sufi traditions.

Per Murshid F.A. Ali ElSenossi in an online dictionary of *The Language of the Future: Sufi Terminology*; 'These stations are the necessary foundation for actualizing human perfection and must be passed through on the Journey of Return to Allah. Maqamat are earnings which have been acquired through spiritual struggle. The People of Perfection have passed beyond the stations to the most exalted station of 'no station' (la maqam) (ElSenossi, n.d.).

*And thus it is for me: every visit to Pakistan would strike a chord and arouse a new emotion. The smell of the soil suddenly feeling familiar. Making me ponder the relationship between my soil and soul. Migration, I now believe, is less of the soil (body) than the soul, as the soil (the seed) remains planted in the ground.*

*This must be the reason why the folklore, tales and fables of one's particular soil echo inside them wherever they might travel to, East or West.*

*And as fate had it, after meeting Amjad, I also found him to be a 'son of the soil', deeply rooted in his own cultural* being *and immersed in its Soil-idarity. A man of high ideals and Sufistic nature and with a strong affinity to the land (soil) and its people. The simplicity of his heart (nature) yet the firmness of his faith is transmissible. Such simplicity of thought process is hard to find in the Western cultures where I had come from. His answer to every complex question that I posed to him was a simple benediction of faith and tawakul (reliance) on Allah or, quite often, a verse of Iqbal's poetry, or a quote from a Sufiana kalam (verse from Sufi poetry) of Baba Bulley Shah or Sultan Bahu – a message of love and reverence for land (soil) and its local culture and wisdom. His mantra was* My message is love wherever it reaches.

*In the previous chapter, we alluded to the SOUL-idarity GENE rhythm flowing through the inner core of communitas. Yet, this GENE transmutation emanates from an individual's inner being and translates into 'effect' for transformation, communal or societal. The alchemy of soil/soul connection sets the Hikma GENE (soul-wisdom) in motion.*

For the law of motion lies at the heart of Creation, which is a dynamic environment and not a static one. Planets rotate around their own centres while circumambulating around others, and the entire solar system moves harmoniously while positioned on the spires of galaxies. These, in turn, are part of bigger galactic clusters that also move together, and so on.

*In this chapter, we will revisit our Hikma GENE (soil-soul wisdom) by revisiting our roots, or connection to the soil and soul of the place/Maqam, along with Pakistan's creation to present-day challenges faced by the society, further investigating the correlation of the soil's connection to the soul reiterating through us (Amjad and Aneeqa).*

*Thus, we explore the philosophy of soil/soul connection and what constitutes particular archetypes coming out of that soil or Maqam. For this resonates so deeply with my own trans-migration of soul and physical body, the purpose of my connection with my country of origin. The more I explored the local mystical traditions, the more it resurfaced and resonated with my own reality, hence inspiring a thorough soul-full exploration of Akhuwat's embeddedness in Pakistani society and culture.*

*This is home-coming.*

## 2.2 Genealogy: cultural complexity

Mohammad Qadeer (2006), a researcher of planning for multiculturalism and professor emeritus at Queen's University, cites in his book on Pakistan Sir Mortimer Wheeler. The British archaeologist entitled his book *Five Thousand Years of Pakistan* for a country formed in 1947. Pakistan, undoubtedly, is one of the oldest inhabited regions of the world. Paralleling Mesopotamia, Egyptian, and Chinese civilisations, the Indus River Valley, the heartland of Pakistan, supported planned cities and a thriving commercial economy for millennia BCE. The country may be new in name and political organisation, but its cultural and social roots reach back to antiquity. There are parcels of land in Pakistan that have been farmed uninterrupted for thousands of years.

> This long territorial history is equally manifest in the cultural traditions and community life of Pakistan's villages and towns. The Muslim nationalism that gave birth to Pakistan as a 2th-century nation state is layered over ancient communities and territorial societies that evolved from the mingling of Aryans, Greeks, Arabs, Mongols and various tribes of Central Asia and Persia, who periodically came as invaders and migrants but settled and assimilated in the prosperous agrarian communities of the Indus Valley.
>
> (Qadeer, 2006)

Located in the ancient Indus Valley of the Middle East, the settlements in the region, among the Khyber Pass, Himalayas and Arabian Sea, are some of the oldest in the world and most heavily travelled in history.

The Indus River, like the Nile in Egypt, has not only been the lifeline for Pakistan since ancient times but also denotes the name of one of the oldest human cultures: The Indus Valley civilization.

> This civilisation evolved in the areas fed by the mighty river and its tributaries. It has symbolized the cultural history of the entire south Asian subcontinent. The ancient Indus Valley inhabitants, often known as Dravidians, established their settlements many millennia before the development of great Indian religions such as Brahmanism, Hinduism, Jainism, and Buddhism. As their ancient hymns suggest, these religions evolved in the Indus regions.
>
> (Malik, 2008)

While the history of Pakistan as an independent nation dates only to 1947, the history of the territory it encompasses dates back many thousands of years, during the period when the territory was a portion of the Indian subcontinent. In addition, the land is home to the famous Khyber Pass, which is the route that many invaders into India used. These include Mogul invaders and Alexander the Great. Many centuries ago many Buddhists also used that northern section as a route, so Pakistan today has many interesting Buddhist sites and historical notes as part of its history. Punjab is also a portion of the country; it was the home of the founder of the Sikh religion, and it continues to play a significant role in Pakistan.

In brief, the landscape of Pakistan is a tapestry of various cultures, customs and traditions that vary from province to province. These customs and traditions form the basis of how communities conduct their daily businesses, often by employing the traditional wisdom, also known as Hikma, by people who are mostly peasants and craftsmen and often not educated, relying on age-old customs and traditions and treating work or trade as a sacred act. Deeply immersed in the ancient culture of the land and soil, the people of Pakistan revere their traditions as nothing less than holy.

### *2.2.1 Holy be the land – Astana*

*Soil is the source of all life, literally and metaphorically. All life comes from the mother soil and returns to her...if my outer body is soil, then my inner being is the soul* (Kumar, 2013).

Etymologically, the name *Pakistan* literally means 'land of the pure' in Urdu and Persian. It is a play on the word Pāk, meaning *pure* in Persian and Pashto; the suffix *-stān* is a Persian word meaning place of, cognate with the Sanskrit word *sthāna*. The name of the country was coined in 1933 as Pakistan by Choudhry Rahmat Ali, a Pakistan Movement activist, who published it in his pamphlet *Now or Never* (Ali, 1933).

The *soil* is fertile with an abundance of natural minerals and gems and a total of 28% of the land under cultivation. A total of 61% of the population lives in rural areas, which indicates a majority being still connected to the *soil and land*, peasantry and the outflow of abundance propter hoc.

The 'land' in its territorial and cultural meanings is the anchor of Pakistan's national identity and society. Its centrality in defining Pakistan as a nation is expressed in Pakistan's national anthem too, which begins with a three-line ode to the land of Pakistan:

> Blessed be the sacred land,
> Happy be the bounteous realm, and
> Symbol of high resolve, land of Pakistan.

*And that's how I grew up, albeit spending more than half of my life outside of Pakistan, listening to patriotic songs renewing the pledge of giving life and blood to my country, if needed. Instilled with the 'sacred and holy' land ideal from my childhood, this national song (Milli-naghma) still echoes in my soul, as it was my father's favourite song too*:

> My heart is a clime of your love,
> My chest has strong sanctity of yours
> My beloved country, if my life is sacrificed for you,
> I will know the wealth of my body was put to good use!
> O native and beloved country!
> Holy land, O holy land!
> O my Beloved country!
> O native and beloved country!

*This is a land where people to this date believe in magic, miracles and going to shrines of the mystics to pray for prosperity and procreation. Their infinite faith in an Omnipotent and Omnipresent God and their unspoken allegiance to their tribes, clans, Biradari and land are what has been holding them together in this region, before and after the partition of Indo-Pak. Where seventy years on, people still talk about the split that divided people of two nations who had been living together in harmony for centuries. The pain of separation is often the theme of many native*

*Sufi mystic poets of the region. This same theme echoes in the verses of mystical poets of the land, where antiquity is still cherished and traditional wisdom drawn from the verses of mystical folklore is put into practice in the day-to-day work routine and in business dealings, or kar-o-baar in Urdu. And this very allegiance to the Sufi mystics of the land binds the communities together.*

The happenings of 1947 are an important part of the cultural memory of the communities in Pakistan. Additionally, partition stories are shared with the younger generation, with a renewed pledge to stay loyal to the land which was gained after many sacrifices in the name of faith. Incidentally, Pakistan has the distinction of being the only country which came into existence in the name of Islam, to provide the Indian Muslims with a country of their own where they could practise their faith freely.

*How is this faith-cultivation helping Pakistan and Akhuwat form a 'bond of solidarity'?*

> In his book *Akhuwat ka Safar*, narrating his Akhuwat journey, Amjad recounts how at a very young age he internalised the following verses of Iqbal which distinctly resonate with Akhuwat's philosophy and his veneration for the Prophet Muhammed (peace be upon him):
>
> Kheera Na Kar Saka Mujhe Jalwa e Danish e Farang Surma Hai Meri Ankh Ka Khak e Madina o Najaf No glitter of Western science could dazzle my eyes The dust of Medina stains, like collyrium, black.

### *2.3 Soil transcendence through soul cultivation: transmutation of Ishq GENE rhythm*

As propounded in the previous chapter, the alchemy of the soul sets the Transformational GENE in motion, transmutating at the Ishq/love realm in the heart of an individual (Self) to then manifest in the heart of a particular community. Throughout this chapter, we will thus explore the effects of solidarity through the faith-cultivation of a spiritual-financial model – Akhuwat – immersed in one such philosophy stemming from an Islamic faith tradition.

*I was destined to spend most of my life outside Pakistan, affixed to my soil through a soul connection, hence the GENE transmutation. Amjad, in the interim, having grown up on the 'land', has his roots genuinely planted in the soil and its culture. Whereas I was to discover Iqbal at a later stage of my life, Amjad cognates Iqbal's idealistic predisposition – to the land and its people – from a very early age. Growing up in a village in the heart of Punjab, Amjad is inherently rooted in the cultural values and traditions of the 'land and locality'.*

Thus, Iqbal's words etched onto his soul, he established the ideology of Akhuwat and a road map to establish a system which not only rings true to his nature, but also encourages others to put into practice what Islam and its Prophet have preached. The authenticity of his thoughts, Iqbal's idealism resonating in the echo of these verses, and sheer love for his land proved to be a guidance and a strong reason for him to return home whilst studying for his Master's degree in public administration and international development at an American university.

*We now turn to Punjab, the shared birthplace of Amjad and I, to briefly illustrate the spiritual resonance of the region shaping our work-life ethics. For Amjad it reflects in Akhuwat's spiritual base of its philosophy, whereas for me it came in the form of putting my spiritual into my work practices.*

*My romanticism with the place of my origin-ality, Punjab, continues.*

### *2.3.1 Fertile be my land of Punjab – of five rivers and Sufi saints*

*'Why die of thirst when the water of life is near? Drink from the source, For all things live from water.' Hafiz Shirazi*

According to the Quran, man is created from dust and water – of clay moulded integrally. Hence, water holds a vital significance in spiritual philosophies. Furthermore, Punjabi folklore is full of romantic tales of spiritual significance in Punjabi cultural heritage.

Punjab (the land of five rivers) is the biggest land area of Pakistan and is popularly known for its culture. It shares most of its cultural values and festive occasions with its neighboring Indian province. According to census 56% of the total population of the country is situated in Punjab province. It has a total of 36 districts and contributes approximately 50–60% of the economy.

The rivers dictate the rhythms of the romanticised Punjabi life. People live in villages surrounded by fields. Punjabi culture is one of the oldest in world history, dating from ancient antiquity to the modern era. The scope, history, complexity and density of the culture are vast. Some cities of Punjab have more importance for the Sikh community from India. The founder of the Sikh religion was born in Nankana Sahib, a district of Punjab, so Sikhs from different parts of the world come to visit Punjab. Most of Islamic Punjabi literature comes from this region.

This is the land of many renowned Sufi saints and their soul wisdom is still locked in the soil. People of Punjab visit the shrines of these Sufi saints to pay homage to them and derive their local wisdom from the poetry of Sultan Bahu, Baba Bulley Shah, Hazrat Data Ganj Buksh and Baba Farid, to name a few.

*For both of us, these Sufi saints merit immense reverence and are a source of Hikma (soul-wisdom).*

*Moving on with our journey around Pakistan, whilst I was to emigrate Westward (UK), Amjad's life was spent serving the people of his (Pakistani) community, exploring what was and was not working for them.*

### *2.3.2 Chinioti community*

For Amjad, the city of Chiniot holds a special place due to his time as a civil servant, serving the Chinoiti community.

His time in Chiniot, an ancient city of about 500,000 dwellers located on the bank of the river Chenab, inspired Amjad to research and then compile a book (Saqib, 2016) on the Chinioti business model. Totally fascinated by the communal impulse of Chinioti Biradari (clan), he further alludes to the distinction of this city, considering its Chinioti community as making a huge contribution to Pakistan's economy and industry. Its most prominent dwellers are known as Chiniot Shaikhs, a business community that takes pride in having produced 30 of Pakistan's richest men and prominent businesses.

Apparently, out of the 40,000 Chinioti families, as observed by Amjad, none have ever been poor or marked as living below the poverty line, unlike other smaller cities of Pakistan. This inspired Amjad to investigate the Chinioti community model as a living example for Akhuwat's solidarity paradigm contemplation, as he noted their community was thriving on reciprocity.

The business model of the Chinioti community follows a similar 4P paradigm (Philosophy, Principles, Practices and integral Paradigm) to Akhuwat's. Per Amjad's narrative of the Chinioti community in his book *Kamyab Loug*, the Chinioti people to this date value their indigenous culture dearly by putting their cultural and spiritual values in practice within their business model. This inspired Amjad to present a spiritual entrepreneurship model originating from the Chinioti business model.

For Amjad, these values are already embedded in their business model and only need to be redefined in the generic entrepreneurial terminology for the coming generations to follow as emerging from a place of love (Ishq) and compassion.

We now explore the mystical dimension of Ishq (love and compassion) as understood through Punjabi esoteric traditions.

## *2.4 Ishq – mystical love and romance of the land of Punjab*

*Punjabis, being very warm-hearted and fun-loving people, are a heterogeneous group comprising of different tribes, clans and communities, and they are known to celebrate each and every tradition of their culture. The region of Punjab has given birth to some of the subcontinent's most romantic yet mystical folklore. It is said the rivers of Punjab have many tales of lovers to tell. For both Amjad and I, having been born of this land, Punjab thus holds a mystical resonance and reverence for us. Hence, it is important for us to relate our Punjabi lineage to our distinctive journeys.*

The mystic waters of the majestic river Chenab, home to the Chinioti community, hold secrets of Punjab's famous legends. Many a writer and poet has written about Pooran-Bhagat, Heer-Ranjha, Sohni-Mahiwal and Mirza-Sabhiban and Sassi-Punnu. The most famous among them is Waris Shah, who immortalised the love story of Heer and Ranjha in his famous poetry.

*For poetry enjoys pride of place among literary and artistic forms throughout the Islamic world and especially in the region of Punjab. While this is no doubt due in part to its aesthetics, the mnemonic quality of poetry makes it easy to learn for people who cannot read and write – a significant proportion of the Pakistani population takes its inspiration and guidance from the poetry of Sufi saints of the region. One of the most satisfying marriages in world literature is the one between Islamic mystical (Sufi) experiences and teachings and poetry, which is capable of conveying these ideas in a manner that is as seductive as it is instructive. This was evident in my experience of observing Amjad and Akhuwat's idyllic lineage inspired by Iqbal's philosophical rendition of Ilm (knowledge) and Ishq (love), and the mystical tradition of Ishq tracing its roots back to Sufi saints of Punjab and beyond.*

Punjabis can literally be moved to tears and go into a deeper meditative trance, known as muraqaba, by listening to the Sufiana kalam (Sufi poetry) of Sultan Bahu or Bulley Shah.

> Sultan Bahu's mystical poetry is an expression of disillusionment with formal, legalistic, and institutionalized forms of religion, and of optimistic faith in the possibility of a personal, individual spiritual relationship with God. Bahu emphasises a central tenet of Sufism: that an absolute love for and devotion to God can result in the experience of losing oneself within the divine. Many of the themes discussed by Bahu and the metaphors he uses are drawn from the literary bank of Sufi writing and are then adapted to the Punjabi environment.
>
> (Elias, 1998)

*If anything, Punjabi Sufi poetry proffers us the negation of the (ego) Self and the taming of this false self. This concept of self-discipline ploughs and prepares the heart to observe faqr, a term used for spiritual poverty, in Tassawuf. Poverty, as I have often witnessed Amjad saying in his talks, is the badge of the saints, the adornment of the pure.*

*Faqr, from a Sufi perspective, is an absolute crop of zuhd or taqwa (cognisance) to Allah as the Sustainer. This is the moral inner core of an Islamic country or society. Ishq is a direct consequence of taqwa – our Eastern realm of our SOUL-idarity orientation as per Lessem and Schieffer's integral GENE rhythm.*

*Being born of the soil where Sufi saints took pride in their indigence, I used to struggle with explaining this to people who see no fault in decadence and extravagance, whereas faqr trains the soul to minimise the intake and maximise the output.*

Something my Canadian colleague and wellbeing guru Mark Anielski is striving to bring to our economic wellbeing and consciousness, he envisions 'an economy of "genuine wealth," a society where the core values of our hearts are aligned with the measures of our well-being. Where virtuous actions will be the measure of progress'. For Mark; The journey to genuine happiness literally means finding the source of well-being of our spirit. The journey takes us from the head to the heart; the source of love.

He goes on eploring further if we, the residents of a developed world;have enough faith and courage to BE GENUINE and act according to the four cardinal virtues defined by Plato (moderation, justice, courage and wisdom) and the three theological or holy virtues (faith, hope and charity or love)"? (Anielski, 2007)

*To our collective dismay, this concept of 'building economies based on love', as per Mark's postulation, or adopting a path of faqr (spiritual poverty) as per the propagation of Amjad and me, sounds untrue to many in the wider world, yet somehow this was instilled in me by my dear mother, who embodied these virtues by practising them as well as by teaching us the importance of such. Now, finding this conceptualised in Akhuwat's philosophy of 'solidarity/sharing' with the community members for the sake of love, be it Supreme (Divine) or communal love, is what instigated the Ishq transmutational premise of my SOUL-idarity Hikma (soul-wisdom) proposition.*

*For the land we both originated from is imbued with this tradition of mystic Akhuwat (Bhai-chara) and communal caring.*

*We now briefly encapsulate this anthropological tradition of the spirit of SOUL-idarity Hikma of ishq, ilm, amal and akhuwat.*

## *2.5 Islam and mystic lineage in the Indian subcontinent*

Akbar Salahuddin Ahmed, the Ibn Khaldun chair of Islamic Studies at American University's School of International Service in Washington, DC and a former Pakistani High Commissioner to the UK and Ireland, writes in his book *Discovering Islam*;

> Three ancient streams fed the Islamic river of learning and knowledge. These were Hellenic, Persian and Indian. The Arabic word *Falsafa* was derived from Greek Philosophy. The Persian influence was restricted to art and belles letters suffused with mysticism. Astronomy, mathematics and later the decimal system were inspired by India.
>
> (Ahmed, 2002)

According to Akbar, Islam in India presents seemingly intractable problems.

> In India alone, Islam met Hinduism, a polytheistic, ancient and sophisticated religion. The mutual stimulation and synthesis between Islam and Hinduism were most notable during Mughal rule in India.
>
> It is no accident that the early eighteen century produced one of the greatest Muslim scholars and reformers in India, Shah Waliullah, emphasizing a reversion to pristine Islam. Pointedly, he wrote his major contribution to theological dialectics, Hujjat Allah al-baligha in Arabic.
>
> (Ahmed, 2002)

Another prominent name amongst the Mughal emperors with Sufi leanings is Dara Shukoh, a story retold many times throughout the ages. Dara Shukoh remains my favourite Mughal mystic prince as he's still remembered: the prince who turned Sufi, thereby exemplifying the faqr (spiritual poverty) manifest in the Self once Ishq-e-Haqiqi (Divine/true love) has started sprouting in one's heart.

And the mystic ethicality of the region further unfolds.

## *2.6 Mystic kings of Indo-Pakistan*

Annemarie Schimmel was an influential German Orientalist and scholar who wrote extensively on Islam, Sufism in the Indo-Pakistan region, and on Muhammed Iqbal's work, which was acknowledged by the government of Pakistan as a seminal work. Schimmel explores the origin and traditions of Sufism in her magnum opus, *Mystical Dimensions of Islam*. She writes:

> The western provinces of the Indo-Pakistan Subcontinent had become part of the Muslim Empire in 711, the year in which the Arabs conquered Sind and the adjacent provinces Northward up to Multan. The Muslim pious in these areas were, in the early centuries, apparently interested mainly in the collection of hadlth and in the transmission to the central Muslim countries of scientific information from India (mathematics, the 'Arabic' numbers, Astronomy and astrology, medicine), but their religious feelings may sometimes have reached the heights of mystical experience.
>
> (Schimmel, 1978)

Per Schimmel's research,

> Spiritual contacts between the Muslims and the small Buddhist minority, as well as with the large group of Hindus (who were slightly outside the main current of orthodox Hinduism), may have existed, though earlier European theories that tried to explain Sufism as an Islamized form of Vedanta philosophy or of Yoga have now been discarded.
>
> In 905, a mystic like Hallaj travelled extensively throughout Sind and probably discussed theological problems with the sages of this country.The second wave of Muslim conquest in India, that of the Ghaznawids in about the year 1000, brought into the subcontinent not only scholars like al-Biruni (d.1048), who made a careful study of Hindu philosophy and life, but theologians and poets as well.
>
> (Schimmel, 1978)

Incidentally Lahore, my birthplace, became the first centre of Persian-inspired Muslim culture in the subcontinent. Hujwiri composed his famous Persian treatise on Sufism in this town, and his tomb still provides a place of pilgrimage for the Punjabis. The full impact of Sufism, however, began to be felt in the late twelfth and early thirteenth centuries, after the consolidation of the main Sufi orders in the central provinces of India. The most outstanding representative of this movement is Muinuddin Chishti, born in Sistan and a part-time disciple of

Abu Najib Suhrawardi. He reached Delhi in 1193, then settled in Ajmer when the Delhi kings conquered this important city in the heart of Rajputana.

> His dwelling place soon became a nucleus for the Islamisation of the central and southern parts of India. The Chishti order spread rapidly, and conversions in India during that period were due mainly to the untiring activity of the Chishti saints, whose simple and unsophisticated preaching and practice of love of God and one's neighbour impressed many Hindus, particularly those from the lower castes, and even members of the scheduled castes.
>
> The fact that the Chishti khanqahs avoided any discrimination between the disciples and practised a classless society attracted many people into their fold. Muinuddin reduced his teaching to three principles, which had been formulated first by Bayezid Bistami.
>
> (Schimmel, 1978)

*'A Sufi should possess "a generosity like that of the ocean, a mildness like that of the sun, and a modesty like that of the earth".'*

From Khawaja Muinuddin Chishti grew a silsilah (chain) of Sufi saints and mystics, highly revered in Pakistan for the miracles they performed, mobilising communities and educating them on the spiritual dimension of Islam. Their teachings are deeply embedded in the cultural traditions of this region. It is a popular belief in many cities of Pakistan that host the shrines of these mystic kings, that their barakah (grace) is what brings abundance and sustains these localities – a concept ingrained in Amjad's teachings and writings, as well as Akhuwat's philosophy and its fourfold principles of Iman, Ikhlas, Ihsan and Ikhuwah.

*We are gradually entering the age of partition which constitutes the Pakistani predominant animus – the story of Pakistan anthropologically, for most Pakistanis, starts from here. The nostalgic majesty of the shared Indian cultural space is almost forgotten now.*

## *2.7 Entering the age of colonisation – end of Mughal majesty*

Akbar, in his book, *Discovering Islam*, further states:

> that Muslims during the Mughal dynasty were on top of the social hierarchy. But by the end of the Mughal period, in the last century, the Muslims had tumbled down from the top. Their political role was terminated, their language rejected, and their very identity threatened. The trauma of this downfall lies at the heart of the Muslim problem in India today.
>
> (Ahmed, 2002)

Akbar further maintains, how the colonial rule for Muslims was an unmitigated disaster. No arguments about Europe providing railways and the telegraphs, or maintaining law and order, can conceal or assuage the fact. Colonization affected the Islamic ideal by contorting and smothering it. During the colonial century Muslims would wage a desperate battle to salvage the ideal. The costs were heavy, and Muslims are still paying them.

From the middle of the nineteenth century, when the British saw Muslims as the main culprits for the uprisings of 1857 and discriminated against them, to the middle of the twentieth century was a period of despair for Muslims in South Asia.

In 1888 Dairatul-Maarif-it-Osmania was founded, an institution which promoted the collection of rare and original Arabic manuscripts and their translation into Urdu. Famous works of literature were translated into Urdu. These translations provided a legitimate scientific and intellectual base for the language.

In the nineteenth century, Sir Sayyed Ahmad, in an attempt to rebuild Muslim society in India, established Aligarh Muslim University. The university grew out of the work of Sir Syed Ahmad Khan, the great Muslim reformer and statesman, who in the aftermath of the Indian War of Independence of 1857 felt that it was important for Muslims to gain education and become involved in the public life and government services in India.

The British decision to replace the use of Persian in 1842 for government employment and as the language of Courts of Law caused deep anxiety among Muslims of the sub-continent. Sir Syed saw a need for Muslims to acquire proficiency in the English language and Western sciences if the community were to maintain its social and political clout, particularly in Northern India. He began to prepare foundation for the formation of a Muslim University by starting schools at Moradabad (1858) and Ghazipur (1863). His purpose for the establishment of the Scientific Society in 1864, in Aligarh was to translate Western works into Indian languages as a prelude to prepare the community to accept Western education and to inculcate scientific temperament among the Muslims.

### *2.7.1 Pakistan ka Matlab kya La Ilaha Illallah*

Seventy years after independence, Pakistanis still chant on their streets, 'Pakistan ka matlab kya?' (What was the purpose of creating Pakistan?) The answer, obviously, is Islam. Pakistan was created for Islam.

Whether Pakistan was created for Islam or not is a dispute that has not been settled yet and there is no indication that it can be settled in the near future, writes Anwar Iqbal, a correspondent and political analyst, based in Washington, DC.

Pakistan was carved out of India because the Muslims of the subcontinent demanded a separate land for themselves. They did so because they felt that an early exposure to Western education and British patronage had put India's Hindu majority well ahead of them. They could not compete with them in a united India.

But the leaders of the political movement that led to the creation of Pakistan were secular Muslims, who appeared more interested in creating a British parliamentary democracy than an Islamic state.

Most of those who could have had a desire to create an Islamic state, the subcontinent's Muslim clerics, were against the creation of Pakistan. This, however, did not prevent the same clerics from trying to convert Pakistan into an Islamic state once it was created. Yet, the country is still struggling to establish a practical Islamic constitution.

### *2.7.2 Echoes of colonial mindset in the collective consciousness*

For us, it was crucial to explore the main antecedent of Pakistan's striving. To this day, the whole social/class divide – of haves and have-nots – in our view, is a colonial culmination. This is another reason for Amjad and Akhuwat to invest their time and energy in conspiring for an education system that instils the spirit of Mawakhat (solidarity) into the underprivileged class of Pakistani society.

Pakistan inherited the colonial legacy of educational policies and practices when it became independent in 1947. After establishing its political control over India, the next logical step for Britain was to create a situation in which the vanquished people should willingly accept their inferior position, whereby making the job of administration easier for the colonial power. British Imperial education policies in the Indian Subcontinent installed English language as a measure to establish British influence and control over the colony. This established the English/Western supremacy and the historical beginnings of English in Pakistan in the postcolonial context, which resulted in the loss of Persian, the end of the indigenous system of education, formation of hybrid identities, and the establishment of elite institutions. These issues are still plaguing the education as well as the social system in present day Pakistan (Waseem, 2014).

Moreover, the British education policy helped create a polarised situation in Indian society. The British educational system, based on utilitarian objectives, focused on the urban elite and the middle classes and ignored the masses. Of more significance to our context is the fact that the British education policy favoured elitist patterns that have persisted to this day.

Henceforth, in present-day Pakistan, this polarity is ever prevalent, dividing the society into two visible groups: the native-locals, aka people considered to be from the lower strata of the society, and the Western-ly educated (English medium) of the country's ruling elite.

This fascination with the Western education model inspires Pakistanis to seek knowledge in western universities. Quite often, they never return to their home country, hence, making Pakistanis the sixth-largest diaspora in the world.

### *2.7.3 Migration of separation: SOUL-idarity of Mawakhat*

*Regarding my own soul-evocatory call which keeps taking me back to my homeland and resulted in collaborating projects between UK and Pakistan, consequentially, working closely with my Pakistani diaspora community in the UK, my emigrational experience is twofold. On the one hand, it denotes my physical migration from my homeland, and on the other hand, it implies my soul's trans-migration – of now being able to perceive realities more intuitively. I could sense the deeper trauma, now locked inside the collective consciousness of the Pakistani society and diaspora, being in an existential conflict uniformly.*

*From an emigrational point of view, having lived outside of the country for most of my life and having witnessed my interaction with Pakistani diaspora in the UK – it is the collective trauma of the partition of India and Pakistan which distils a sense of conflicting identities, in addition to the challenge of spiritual crisis British Pakistani Muslims (and Muslims on the whole), face living in a Western country. In my experience of working with diaspora-led communities, especially of Pakistani origin, due to their lack of social connectivity most are quite emotionally attached to their country of origin. Their reluctance to adopt local (UK) models of finance and enterprise building methodology calls for an Akhuwat-like solidarity model of finance which, to my understanding, could help in restoring their confidence in their spiritual stature in a non-Islamic country. Notably, the Islamic Finance arena is bustling with a UK revival for its Muslim populace.*

Back home in Pakistan, the collective trauma of separation and displacement still reverberating in the subconscious of the Pakistani society needs a collective healing. Bert Hellinger's phenomenological systemic Constellation work could help maintain the 'orders of love' amongst Pakistani communities.

Bert Hellinger (1998), a German psychotherapist associated with a therapeutic method best known as Family Constellations and Systemic Constellations, identifies what he terms 'the Orders of Love'and observed that certain governing principles must be respected for the love in the family, community and society to flow in a healthy way. And when these orders are disturbed, for example, when a child tries to take on the fate of a parent, suffering and unhappiness ensue.

*Instinctively, this could also work for diaspora communities living in the UK to re-establish their flow of 'love' with Pakistan or the UK and establish a healthy non-dualistic relationship with their local-ity, which at the moment is of a misplaced identity.*

*We are now ready to move away from the past to the next section of our chapter, stepping into present-day Pakistan, in the light of the above and our shared interwoven journey of brotherhood (Bhai-chara) and SOUL-idarity.*

## 3 Pakistan's 4 C's: class conflict, colonisation, civil society, culture of giving

*We now turn to the four phases of our collective 4C rhythm, building on an Islamic society/Pakistan's 4M (Musavat, Mashawrat, Mawakhat and Maashrat) communal/solidarity GENE rhythm.*

Before we elaborate on the 4C process for Pakistan, it is relevant to give a brief account of what the whole process is about and why it is important to analyse Pakistan's social and cultural landscape as such.

As proposed by Lessem and Schieffer (2013) in their integral development Bible:

> Most developmental thinking, societally speaking, has taken place in a rather distant, intellectualised manner and much of the subsequent work has thereby proven to be out of touch with the actually experienced life worlds and cultural contexts of the people it seeks to benefit. The reason for this is that such a societal approach has not emerged out of prior individual and communal contexts. As a result, it is plucked out of societal mid-air.
>
> Among development thinkers there is only a relatively small group of primarily anthropolo-gists that have not only delved into the depth of such contexts, but also managed to understand local conditions and to see development with the eyes of those 'to be developed.

*Thus, the 4C'ing of an individual's or societal development is to pursue their inner and outer* **Call, Context, Co-creation and Contribution** *on an individual as well as on a communal level. This seemed to be the case in practice in Akhuwat's communal paradigm as I have directly observed, albeit implicitly, thus, proposing Akhuwat's 4 C's in its local context.*

*Emerging from a particular Pakistani context, i.e., the need to tackle Pakistan's growing poverty challenge, Akhuwat has contributed to the society by co-creating a model of micro-lending which has helped in transforming the lives of 2.3 million destitute families.*

*We aim to elaborate this further in Chapter 4 of the book, but firstly let us explore Pakistan's 4 C's in the same vein to understand her developmental needs to emerge as an integral CARE model from the South Asian region.*

*The initial trajectory, with a focus on our personal contribution, follows the 4 C's*:

**Call**: *Discovering our Inner Call*
**Context**: *Understanding Self-in-Society Context*
**Co-Creation**: *Transforming our Reality*
**Contribution**: *Leveraging our Transformation*

As such, the **4 M's** of a Muslim/Pakistani trajectory implicitly working through Akhuwat's organisational pattern are

**Musavat (Equality)**: *Society's inner call*
**Mashawrat (Mutual Consultation)**: *Understanding one's individual role in community's context*
**Mawakhat (Solidarity)**: *Transforming community's reality*
**Maashrat (Community Life)**: *Community building/Leveraging transformation*

The figure (Figure 2.1) shows a full CARE model, inspired by Lessem and Schieffer's (ibid) towards full CARE model as mentioned above.

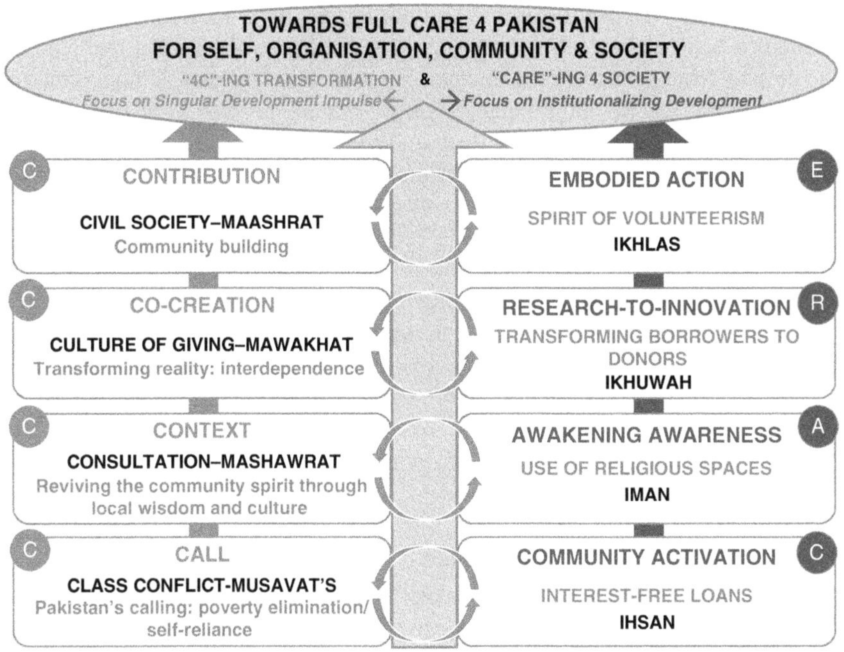


*Figure 2.1* 4 C's + CARE Model

Figure 2.1 illustrates an integral 4C (Call, Context, Co-creation and Contribution) process paired with a Pakistani 4M (Musavat, Mashawrat, Mawakhat and Maashrat) societal rhythm, proposing a CARE-ing (Community activation, raising Awareness, Research-to-innovation and Embodied action) for society model as inspired by Lessem and Schieffer's model.

This chapter will investigate Pakistani society's 4 C's, whereas Chapters 4 and 5 expand on the CARE proposition more broadly through Akhuwat's example of a solidarity economy caring for Pakistan as per its 4C-ing of 4 M's.

*We now turn to the first C of our collective Call, as well as what Pakistan is calling for.*

### *3.1 Our collective call – irtiqa: Pakistan's revival and survival*

#### *3.1.1 Musavat – equality amongst mankind*

Allah the Almighty says in Surat Al-Hujurat, verse 13, what could be translated as, 'O Mankind! We have created you from a male and a female, and made you into nations and tribes, that you may know one another. Verily, the most honourable of you in the sight of Allah is he who has most Taqwa among you. Verily, Allah is All-Knowing, All-Aware.'

With this verse, Islam declares equality among people, that is, because Islam respects a human for being a human and not for any other reason; Islam does not distinguish between two races, or two groups of people, or between two colours. The prophet Muhammad (peace be upon him addressed the people regarding that concept during the last pilgrimage, saying: *'O People! Your God is one; your father is one; no preference of an Arab neither over non-Arab nor of a non-Arab over an Arab or red over black or black over red except for the most righteous. Verily the most honoured of you is the most righteous and performs good deeds.'*

This is further emphasised in practical terms by looking at all the Islamic rituals, for example, prayers in the mosque (no class difference), pilgrimage (all dressed in one garb), fasting (practising sabr/patience) and zakat (just distribution of wealth).

Yet, there is an unmissable unjust divide within the Pakistani society. Akhuwat, in their effort to bring Musavat (equality) to the society, are challenging the status quo. They are doing this by giving access to finance to the poorest of the poor of the society. Their principle of granting Qard-e-Hasan ('interest-free benevolent loans') is one such practical example of equalising the societal divide.

## *3.2 What is Pakistan calling for?*

Pakistan is home to nearly 2.1 million souls, at only 70 years old and with a faltering infrastructure. This young nation has survived many atrocities, natural disasters and two wars with its neighbouring country, India. And with a poverty index showing four out of ten Pakistanis living in multidimensional poverty, one can't help but wonder, how is the population still multiplying with such rapid speed and what sustains them?

Pakistan's first ever official report on multidimensional poverty launched by the Ministry of Planning, Development and Reform shows that nearly 39 percent of Pakistanis live in multidimensional poverty, with the highest rates of poverty in FATA (Federally Administered Tribal Area) and Baluchistan. Pakistan's MPI (Multidimensional Poverty Index) showed a strong decline, with national poverty rates falling from 55% to 39% from 2004 to 2015. However, progress across different regions of Pakistan is uneven. Poverty in urban areas is 9.3 percent as compared to 54.6 percent in rural areas. Disparities also exist across provinces. According to the report, deprivation in education contributes the largest share of 43 percent to MPI, followed by living standards which contributes nearly 32 percent and health contributing 26 percent. These findings further confirm that social indicators are very weak in Pakistan, even where economic indicators appear healthy (UNDP in Pakistan, 2016).

### *3.2.1 Amjad's call: desire to overcome the impact of class conflict and poverty (Musavat)*

Whilst working with Punjab Rural Support Programme (PRSP), I noticed the oppressive economic system at work. A wealthy person could borrow at an interest rate of about 10–12% and a poor person at 30–40%. This was ironic because access to credit made a wealthy man wealthier, but a poor person only acquired two extra morsels and a roof over his head, or enabled his child to go to school or his elderly parents to receive medicine. This made me think, could there be an economic system where the fruit of a poor man's toil falls into his own lap? There was struggle inside me to create a society where there is no deprivation and exploitation of the poor and wherein, instead of rapacity and temptation, the ethos of benevolence and sacrifice rules.

> Ever since Pakistan's coming into existence, the social class disparity has been a serious issue. During the time of partition, many people were stripped of their lands, properties, valuables and other financial assets. The unequal distribution of income experienced today has its roots from the time of the partition of India and Pakistan. Feudalism in those days was at its peak and remnants of it can still be seen in the modern society. Many powerful feudal lords claimed lands by force from people who were financially or socially weak, thus the wealth became concentrated and its effects can be seen in today's Pakistani society, as the unequal distribution of income. Even today, many influential people such as politicians and local feudal lords all around Pakistan are in control of the major chunk of the income that is generated and flows through the economy, which is why Pakistan also faces extreme poverty. This uneven pattern of income distribution has been the root cause of the division of the population into various classes on the basis of income inequalities. The formation of these classes has led to the widening of the social gaps between the people and has also led to social exclusion of people belonging to different classes. As the general population is divided into these stratums, belief and ideals change, thus a conflict arises due to these changing ideals. Over the past years, since the birth of Pakistan, this conflict between the different classes has been slowly boiling and has erupted into a class conflict based on income disparity.
>
> (Essays, November 2013)

### *3.2.2 Eliminate wealth instead of poverty*

*The growing gap between the haves and the have-nots of the society as observed by Akhuwat's founder, Dr. Amjad Saqib, proved to be his call to action. Being the son of the soil, possessing a tender heart and sensing this constant social unrest around him was what made him experiment a new wealth 're-distributive' model.*

In his book *Akhuwat ka Safar – A Journey of Hope*, written in Urdu, he probes:

> 'Who are these people we call wealthy? Are they human too, those who have neither hearts, nor souls, but only wealth? Yet, at the same time, we also come to know of those who are affluent but also compassionate. If there exists wealth of the heart along with worldly wealth, that is the ultimate human completion. Poverty was never a misfortune, so who are these people who turned it into a crime and a source of humiliation? Once I said to a group of capital-owners, "We don't wish you to forsake all your wealth, and endow us with this wealth of yours, but at least do not snatch our poverty from us. You have oppressed us, for you have snatched our pride in our poverty from us. We used to consider our poverty our fortune. We used to live our lives with comfort and respect. Now you have made our lives a torment between shame and brutality. We cannot become brutal, so what's left for us is to become shameful. We are not alive, we are shamed of our poverty.'

As a civil servant, and having worked with marginally poor rural communities during his time at the Punjab Rural Support Programme (PRSP), he had first-hand knowledge and experience of how these communities operated. Most of them are peasants, craftsmen, greengrocers and micro-entrepreneurs selling from their small kiosks. They have limited access to funds yet take pride in their crafts and skills. Hence the reason, whilst speaking to affluent groups of people, Saqib would reinforce their self-worth and pride repeatedly. Always believing in the goodness of people, also having strong faith in Islamic values and the local culture of giving and sharing, he knew there must be an effective way of bridging the income divide and channelising the wealth accumulation in an equitable way.

Amjad, also a great Aashiq-e-Rasul (admirer of the Prophet) and inspired by Iqbal's poetry and philosophy, wanted to set a practical example of the Prophet's Sunnah. The Medina community, as the perfect model for a community, inspired him to adopt the same model of community activation. Another thing which inspired Amjad and resonates in his talks was the Chinioti community's business model and the support system they had for their own clan (Biradari). Never a supporter of charity, Amjad was keen to devise a way to provide the poor with access to funds to utilise their skills to generate an economy that works for them, rather than relying on foreign aid money which cripples creativity and claims local ownership and authority.

### *3.2.3 Aneeqa's call: Pakistan's global reimaging*

#### 3.2.3.1 FOREIGN AID DEPENDENCE VS. OWNERSHIP DEFICIT

*Pakistan's strategic geopolitical location has fostered a culture of dependence on foreign aid. Today the typical mentality at the federal level is that the international community cannot afford to allow our economy to sink, as that would severely compromise its strategy for the region. Thus, rather than developing and following through on a long-term plan for investment in human capital, infrastructure and industry and hence sustainable economic growth, Pakistan waits for a bailout and relies on short-gap measures to carry from one crisis to the next.*

*Upon my every visit to Pakistan, I am always told that Pakistan is moving up the ranks in the world. It is always the opposite case outide of Pakistan. The diaspora have little hope in Pakistan and are always worried about Pakistan's declining global image. The government, for their part, has been reassuring the global community of the upward progression in Pakistan, for example, the stocks are soaring, improved security is fuelling economic growth and the South Asian nation will be upgraded to 'emerging market' status by index provider MSCI. Yet, the country's image is hampered by its violent past; especially its allegiance with fundamentalists is what stops foreign investors from investing in Pakistan. The question that keeps coming up as the main challenge for Pakistani diaspora communities living around the world is, how can Pakistan improve its ranking and trust amongst international communities and its own diaspora, which stands at approximately 8 million?*

*According to the UN Department of Economic and Social Affairs, Pakistan has the 6th-largest diaspora in the world. In 2014–15, overseas Pakistanis sent remittances amounting to Pak Rupees 1928 billion (US$18 billion). These are the people who not only represent Pakistan to the outside world but also bring back with them a worldview which is Pakistan's window to the outside world. Also, these are the people who could bring the global to a local perspective helping Pakistan to emerge as an exemplary Islamic state with a renewed global identity.*

According to Hadia Majid, a development economy research at Ohio State University:

> The matter of ownership is fundamental to the failure of development aid in Pakistan. While the works being sponsored by bilateral and multilateral agencies have been integral in getting such efforts as those related to women's empowerment and disaster management off the ground, these projects are sustainable only so far as their funding agencies remain interested. For Pakistan to see some systematic change, there is a need for the local players to take centre stage in Pakistan's developmental work.
>
> (Majid, November 12, 2010)

*And this was the call that took me to Pakistan to explore Pakistan's socio-economic landscape and its on-the-ground realities, then bring back positive stories and models to share with the Pakistani diaspora community to bridge the knowledge gap that exists between them and Pakistan. For I strongly believe Pakistan could benefit from her diaspora talent pool that left the country in pursuit of their economic ideals.*

## 4 Context – imbalances promoted by colonisation: past and present

### *4.1 Mashawrat (mutual consultation)*

Mashawrat is an Urdu word which comes from the Arabic word shura, which literally means consultation, and as a basic Islamic principle it calls upon Muslims, usually under a system of proportional representation, to gather and, through debate, forward formed opinions to the caliph which they feel are for the betterment of the ummah (community).

When studying the life and example of the Holy Prophet, it becomes clear that consultation is an absolute must. The Holy Prophet never shied away from consulting his companions – and even the opponents of Islam – on a variety of issues.

The way Akhuwat has brought in this Prophetic (Islamic) tradition is by utilising religious spaces as communal gatherings, which is another one of Akhuwat's basic principles. In the times of the Prophet, mosques were also used to practise this exercise of Mashawrat (mutual consultation) by engaging all members of the society. Akhuwat's board of trustees is also one such example of Mashawrat; as it happens, all of their board members work on a voluntary basis to support Akhuwat's philosophy of Mawakhat. In Amjad's philosophy of reciprocity and virtuosity, this is how 'virtuous circles' of abundance and connectivity could be created.

### *4.2 Understanding the societal context*

#### *4.2.1 Demystifying the Western supremacy and decadenace*

Among those whom Pakistanis see as the founders of their country is the poet Muhammed Iqbal (1877–1938). Throughout Asia, poetry is seen as a direct expression of a person's education. As well as being a poet, Iqbal, was a prominent Muslim philosopher and deep thinker who saw the individual and their free development of personality playing a central role in Islamic philosophy. Using his poetry as a medium to engage the youth and by evoking their nationalistic pride in post-colonial Indian sub-continent era, Iqbal, constantly stressed the need to retrieve the Muslim *self* (Khudi), to rise to the occasion of a glorious past which to him was the apex of Muslims ruling over the world.

Iqbal's poetry, filled with references to the 'glorious Islamic' past, helped in reconstructing the lost Muslim dignity, boosting the newly formed Pakistani nationalist identity. It seems obvious from his poems that, to him, by rekindling the idealist flame, especially in the Muslim youth of Pakistan, was the remedy to overcome their post-colonial partition trauma. In his attempts to constantly demystifying the decadence of West, Iqbal writes in one of his poems;

> *Kheera Na Kar Saka Mujhe Jalwa e Danish e Farang*
> *Surma Hai Meri Ankh Ka Khak e Madina o Najaf*

*No glitter of Western science could dazzle my eyes*
*The dust of Medina stains, like collyrium, black*
(Iqbal, 1935).

> Amjad constantly draws his inspiration and solidarity mettle from Prophet Muhammed's model of Mawakhat and Iqbal's Muslim cultural philosophy, all this with the mystical heritage and traditions of the land, form Akhuwat's philosophy of Mawakhat.
>
> Being well aware of the social disparity, Akhuwat takes pride in being of service to the common men and women of Pakistan. In a country divided and plagued by the social class system and elite culture, Akhuwat promotes partnership with the poor, making them a direct stakeholder in Akhuwat's legacy of Bhai-chara (brotherhood).

*But do the poor really have a partnership in Akhuwat's matters? That remains to be seen.*

What Akhuwat has done is an attempt to promote an equitable social integration and to counter the colonised mindset by hiring their staff from state-run college graduates rather than hiring from private English-medium qualified staff. Hence, Akhuwat is also setting a trend of using Urdu as their official language, which is also Pakistan's national language. For example, Hassan Qadeer, divisional manager of Akhuwat's finance department, is a graduate of a local college, comes to the office wearing Pakistan's national dress, shalwar kameez, and writes reports in Urdu. All of Akhuwat's loan applications and forms are in the Urdu language, which makes it easier for the locals to read these with ease and complete them in Urdu rather than seeking professional help in getting this done. Most of Akhuwat's borrowers are not college educated, and some lack a basic-school literacy level.

Incidentally, Akhuwat's board of directors are the people who Amjad initially consulted with this innovative idea of practically applying the Qard-e-Hasan model to help the poor micro-entrepreneurs of Pakistan, thereby putting the Sunnah of Mashawrat into practice.

## 5 Co-creation: co-evolving a culture and religion of giving

### *5.1 Mawakhat (brotherhood/solidarity)*

This foundation of brotherhood was established by the Prophet, along with the Ansar, based on mutual economic and psychological support and the principle of being inheritors of each other.

## *5.2 Transforming reality – addressing our calling and challenge*

*Thereby, the third C of TRANS4M's 4C rhythm prepares the individual to engage in action-oriented research, coming up with integral theory and practice addressing an individual, organisation, community or society's calling and challenge.*

*In Amjad's context, it was clear to him that in order for Musavat (equality) to manifest in the society, Mawakhat has to be established between the haves and the have-nots of Pakistan. This to him was the best possible option, given a Muslim community's perspective and in the light of the Prophet's Mawakhat tradition, i.e., by channelising and benefiting from the culture of giving so prevalent in Pakistan.*

*Whereas in Aneeqa's context, it called for deciphering as well as showcasing this culture of giving/Mawakhat into a global language for the world outside of Pakistan to take example of.*

*This book is the culmination of our collaborative C of Co-creation, further co-evolving into the SOUL-idarity of universality research-to-innovation paradigm transpiring as Akhuwat UK.*

## *5.3 Culture of giving: Pakistan's 3rd C*

We now turn towards the Eastern philosophy of culture and heritage as per Amjad's embeddedness in Pakistan's culture and Akhuwat's distinct and unique model of 'reciprocity'. We will briefly review, in the now post-colonial Pakistan, the factors that helped in the nation building of this newly formed Muslim idealist state.

According to Iqbal, in the history of civilisation, culture and religion have always developed in close proximity to each other. Indeed, one cannot conceive of the development of religion and culture in isolation from each other. It is precisely this unity of culture and religion which was the basis of Muhammed Iqbal's views on Muslim culture. Culture, for Iqbal, is the most important factor of sociological life and the basis of its change. In explaining social change, he believed that culture plays a greater role than other factors, such as economy and politics. Although he deeply studied Western thought, Iqbal's views on culture were essentially shaped by the teachings of the Quran. A follower of mystical and Sufi traditions of Islam, Iqbal placed his hopes on the culture of the soil of the land which, to him, is moist with compassion and the culture of sharing. Thus, he writes in Bal-e-Jibril-009:

> *Nahin Hai Na-Umeed Iqbal Apni Kisht-e-Weeran Se*
> *Zara Nam Ho To Ye Mitti Bohat Zarkhaiz Hai Saqi*
> *But of his barren acres Iqbal will not despair:*
> *A little rain, and harvests shall wave at last, oh Saki!*
>
> (2000)

Added to the culture of giving is the tradition of austerity (faqr), which is locked in the collective consciousness and GENE of the Indian subcontinent. The folklore of the land is full of stories of this tradition of Sufi saints sustaining themselves on tawakul Allah (reliance on God).

Syed Ali Hujwiri was an illustrious personality of the subcontinent. A Sufi, dervish, devoted to the Lord, he was the chief of the caravan that spread light in the subcontinent's abode of darkness. He spoke of love and affection, brotherhood and altruism, human friendship and tolerance. His popular masterpiece, *Kashf al Mahjoob*, was written a thousand years ago, but it remains a source of wisdom and intellect, a bountiful treasure to this date.

People also call the shrine of Data Ganj Baksh, 'Data Darbar', the court of faith. Courts belong to kings, but the Syed of Hujwir was no king but a faqir (beggar). Kings are those who amass, whereas the faqirs distribute. It is related in *Kashf al Mahjoob* that a king once said to a faqir, 'Ask, what do you want to be granted?' The faqir replied, 'What can I ask from the slave of my slaves?' The king was enraged. Slave of your slaves? What are you talking about?' Replied the faqir, 'I have two slaves – greed and desire. Both are your lords and you are their slave. What can you give me?' To think that and to live in such proximity to that same Ali Hujwiri who had subordinated both greed and desire as his slaves is truly overwhelming and a very humbling experience.

That same Ali Hujwiri, about whom Allama Iqbal said,

Saint of Hajvair was adored by the people
And Pir-e-Sanjir paid a visit to his shrine
Punjab land was brought to life by his blessing
Our dawn was made splendid by his sunshine

One story along the same lines, as shared by Amjad in his Urdu book *Akhuwat ka Safar*, is the story of Syed Ali Hujwiri.

If anything, this story reinforces the ennoblement of the concept of faqr (austerity), which subsequently disciplines the self/individual to dissociate from accumulating dispensable amounts of wealth which per Islamic ordination should be circulating within the community and not resting with a few privileged ones.

This brings us to the core of our SOUL-idarity Hikma postulation, which suggests a praxis of self-discipline through self-actualisation by employing self-realisation (Ilm) of one's place in the divine order. The next phase after this is the transmigration from whatever holds us captive to our material desires of wants and needs.

In Amjad's words: In the sacrifice of life and wealth, the status of the offering of life is greater, but it is harder to part with wealth. Making this difficulty easier is the work of the compassionate. The compassionate seek the compassionate, and they are able to find each other.

According to Amjad, to take loans and to give loans is considered a Prophetic tradition. But those loans were Qard-e-Hasan, a virtuous loan given to Allah, for its reward is with Allah. The adoption of this interest-free system has granted Akhuwat a distinctive esteem. How great are those people, they who give a loan to Allah? For he who gave a loan to Allah's servant, it is as if he loaned to Allah. The indebted and the beloved become one and the same.

### *5.3.1 Giving of self: migration from SELF*

Compassion, in principle though all too often sadly not in practice, lies at the heart of every religious, ethical and spiritual tradition. Compassion impels us to work selflessly to alleviate the pain and sufferings of others. For it is this love (*Ishq*) and compassion that make people do things for others, be it community work or sharing their wealth with others by giving sadaqah, zakat or alms.

We have no choice over where we are born, but we have some control over what we leave behind in the world. In the United States, there are over two million NGOs. Each year, 600 billion dollars are received by philanthropic endowments. Compassion in Pakistan is also quite conspicuous, being famous for its charitable giving.

Akhuwat, Edhi Foundation, Shaukat Khanum Memorial Hospital, Al Shifa Trust, Chippa, Fatimid, Sahara Trust, Amin Maktab, Hijaz Hospital, The Citizens Foundation, Kavish, Indus Hospital, Selani Trust, and Fountain House – these are some of the names associated with the stories of altruism.

As Amjad sees it, as long as these names are alive, humanity is alive. The pleasure of giving is not in the fate of each person, and neither is this reward limited to a single nation. However, only those nations and individual names endure who have the desire to give to the less privileged.

The land of Pakistan is enriched by this culture of compassion, which is interwoven intricately through every sphere of life and living. It is out of this culture of compassion that rich families have adopted at least one poor family who, in return for their service, get food and shelter as live-in maids and servants. Though from the outside or from a Western perspective, it looks like an act of slavery, many families are really kind to these families they've adopted as their own. I always struggle with explaining this phenomenon to my non-Pakistani friends, but personally, I see this as a blessing in disguise for these poor families who are also uneducated and have no access to finances to do anything but housework.

Another phenomenal practice which is still prevalent in this region is the culture of langar at Sufi shrines. Langar is the soup kitchen, which serves food to visitors to Sufi shrines and to travellers in Central Asia. It is a Persian word, meaning a place to rest and eat. It became prominent in Turkestan around 1600 CE, as local Sufi saints established langars as a way of service both to the travellers and the needy who visit a Sufi pir's shrine.

### *5.3.2 Shared economy of giving*

*It is also a country where traders and businessmen believe that trade was the occupation of the prophets; henceforth, tijarat (trade) is practised as a Sunnah tradition too.*

> Thousands of people continue to benefit from him. Haji Inaam Elahi experienced many ups and downs, but his relationship with righteousness never faltered. All his life, he remained in search of an honourable livelihood until he began to share his wealth in the name of the Lord, while asking others to do the same. For the sake of humanity, he does not shy away from asking other philanthropists to contribute to his efforts. Hijaz Hospital in Lahore is a source of blessing for Haji Inaam Elahi Asar. Among other virtues, he has generously helped Fountain House, Chiniot Bait-al-Maal, and Islamia Hospital, Chiniot. It is said that there's not a single individual or institution that called out to Haji Sahib that he did not offer his support to. He once told me that he considered himself to be the biggest beggar of the city, for he loved to spread his hands out for the sake of Allah.
>
> Haji Sahib is a living legend. He has distributed his wealth and assets during his lifetime, some among his heirs and others in the way of Allah. People like Haji Inaam Elahi follow the traditions of Sufi saints of the region. These stories are passed around in Pakistani society, by many as folklore.

Amjad, in his book *Akhuwat ka Safar*, writes fondly about Haji Inaam Elahi, one of Akhuwat's major donors, a businessman of positive and intuitive qualities, as a singular example of altruism, benevolence and sacrifice.

From individual philanthropic acts to organisational philanthropy, Pakistan's communal sustenance thrives on the contributions given by the rich and affluent. Now Amjad, with a deep understanding of the culture and traditions prevalent in the society, through his work as a civil servant, had his finger on community's pulse. He tested the Akhuwat model, firstly on a smaller scale, which succeeded and reinforced his belief in the people's 'giving' impulse, for a religious and humanitarian basis of Mawakhat (solidarity).

This tradition of giving also extends to giving one's valuable time for community-building – Akhuwat's 4th principle of Volunteerism, which further consolidates the spirit of solidarity and Bhai-chara (brotherhood).

We now turn to our final C of Contribution in a Pakistani society setup.

## 6 Contribution – Pakistan's civil society

### *6.1 Maashrat (communal living)*

The word *Maashrat* comes from the Urdu word mwaashra, which translates as society. Epistemologically, it is related to the Arabic word mushtarik (communal) or musharakah. The literal meaning of musharakah is sharing. Another word from the same root in Arabic is shirkah, which means being a partner. It is used in the same context as the term 'shirk', meaning partner to Allah. Under Islamic jurisprudence, musharakah means a joint enterprise formed for conducting some business in which all partners share the profit according to a specific ratio, while the loss is shared according to the ratio of the contribution.

Islam emphasises the welfare and wellbeing of the community and provides a complete code of conduct when it comes to cultural and economic interdependence. More so, it promotes communal living and community spirit as opposed to nationhood or nationalism.

In Iqbal's view of a *'perfect man'* (Iqbal, 2000), man's most remarkable capacities are activity and creativity (amal). He is able to defeat his own limitations to conquer space and time. More so, he's capable of shaping his own destiny as well as that of the universe, by adjusting himself to its forces by putting the whole of his energy to mould its forces to his own ends and purposes. And in this process of progressive change, God becomes a co-worker with him, provided man takes initiative.

This forms the basis of Akhuwat's fourth principle, *spirit of volunteerism*. Akhuwat has revived the community spirit of Mawakhat/musharakah (partnership) and community building, relying on their self-sustained social capital.

### *6.2 Our collective contribution – local identity towards global integrity*

Continuing from our (Amjad and Aneeqa's) shared co-creation call, what is emerging from this shared partnership is, firstly, institutionalising the Mawakhat philosophy (local identity) to global integrity, which forms the basis of writing this book, to present Akhuwat's model to wider global circles. As assumed by Aneeqa, phenomenally, Akhuwat has worked wonders within Pakistan, in a localised manner. Within a global setting, particularly in the UK, the ever-growing ideological East/West divide is becoming a real challenge for the third generation British-Muslim youth, as observed by Aneeqa. This was one of her incentives to research, exploring how the East is coping with their socio-economic challenges and if there is an example of local (cultural) wisdom applied to solve such issues.

*Could such distinctive models emerging from within the Eastern cultures have any acceptance within the Western economic cultures? And how could these local models be adaptive to new innovative ways of thinking and application?*

Referring to the GENE-process developed by Lessem and Schieffer (2013) as an overarching transformational rhythm, they developed two further parallel trajectories that assist each agent of transformation, individually or communally, to successfully undertake the transformation journey and to transcend the individual contribution towards a collective embodiment of an integral innovation. The ultimate objective is to go beyond a singular and individual impulse of renewal and arrive at collective and, ideally, institutionalised action to sustain this impulse on a long-term basis.

### *6.2.1 Leveraging (integral) development for Pakistan – revival of Qard-e-Hasan tradition*

Per philosopher George Hegel, civil society was an inclusive concept of 'society minus the state', as cited by S.W. Dyde, Professor of Mental Philosophy, Queen's University, Kingston, Canada.

In his seminal work on the 'Philosophy of Right', he professes:

> The concrete person, who as particular is an end to himself, is a totality of wants and a mixture of necessity and caprice. As such he is one of the principles of the civic community. But the particular person is essentially connected with others. Hence each establishes and satisfies himself by means of others, and so must call in the assistance of the form of universality. This universality is another principle of the civic community. In the course of the actual attainment of selfish ends – an attainment conditioned in this way by universality – there is formed a system of complete interdependence, wherein the livelihood, happiness, and legal status of one man is interwoven with the livelihood, happiness, and rights of all. On this system, individual happiness, &c., depend, and only in this connected system are they actualised and secured. This system may be prima facie regarded as the external state, the state based on need, the state as the Understanding envisages it.
>
> (Dyde, 2001)

From our modern-day creed of civil and political philosophers Locke, Hobbes et al, all reinforced their belief in the 'bonds of a civil society' whereby humans agree to enter a 'common-wealth' for a safer, comfortable and peaceful living amongst each other.

Religious revivalists like Shah Waliullah, from Pakistan's own soil, have written extensively on the role of religion forming the basic ethics and foundations of Muslim Mashawrat (civil soicety) in the light of Quranic and Sunnah traditions.

The fact that no two social scientists agree on a common definition reflects the reality that in each culture, civil society is a reflection of the traditions, conventions and codes of behaviour outside the legal hierarchal structure of the state. Its changing meaning reflects its changing attitudes towards human behaviour and relationships among economy, society and state.

But South Asia in general, and Pakistan in particular, has followed a different evolutionary route, resisting modernity. The fact that the region has witnessed prolonged rule by invaders through loose governance helped characterise hybrid forms and multiple inheritances, giving rise to unresolved struggles between the practices and values of pre-capitalist society and new modes of social life, between authoritarian legacies and democratic aspirations.

Pakistan also has more than one historical context related to the evolution of its society, each with its effects in positive and negative. The many ancient civilisations of Pakistan were highly evolved, globally dominant and civic.

The advent of Islam and rich Sufi traditions resulted in a tolerant and progressive society.

The role of village panchaits and jirgas, particularly in rural areas of Pakistan, is to act as a *shura* [Arabic word for mutual consultation] for communal welfare and as mediators from land disputes to family disputes, is still largely practiced. With colonialism came the policy of 'divide and rule'as a new concept of government and rule of law.

A new class that emerged was feudal and opportunist in character and evolved an exclusive fiefdom of its own. Pakistani society inherited a strong tradition of progressive citizen organisations with their roots in culture, tradition and Islamic philanthropy.

Organisations that share certain characteristics, such as private, not profit distributing, self-governing and voluntary (to some extent) have been grouped as Non-Profit Organisations (NPOs). Based on a nation-wide survey, the study found about 45,000 such organisations active in Pakistan.

Civil society:

> a term much-used in current development discourse in Pakistan, but among those who consider themselves active in this arena there has been little time spent on definitional issues. As a result, the term has become a catch-all phrase by development workers within Pakistan, and possibly by policy-makers and financiers of development to refer to non-state activities and associations that serve as a bridge somehow between the largely poor masses and the ruling establishment. For the purpose of this discussion, we will define civil society in Pakistan as an arena with certain characteristics: that is, it involves citizens collectively or in organizations, it is a public space positioned somewhat outside the state institutions (but still deeply engaged with and responsive to state actions), and its activities are outside the market and private for-profit sector.
>
> (Khan & Khan, 2004)

However, there are ample stories of brave hearts too. Akhuwat, LUMS, Shaukat Khanum Memorial Trust Hospital, Orangi Pilot Project, the Edhi Trust, the Al-Shifa Trust, Sahara for Life Trust, Layton-Rahmatulla Benevolent Trust, the Citizens Foundation, Human Rights Commission of Pakistan, Riphah University, FC College, Christian missionary institutions and thousands of other smaller, little known philanthropic and public service organizations and NGOs are examples that all Pakistanis are not silent (Sharaf, 2010).

*The question then arises for us, what renewal path should an organisation like Akhuwat take in the future to sustain itself rather than depending on civil society's contribution, which is what sustains Akhuwat's solidarity economy as of now?*

*Could the new brand of Akhuwateers invent new creative models leveraging Akhuwat's 17 years of on-ground research, bearing in mind the Haji Inaams or Amjad's of the society are nearing retirement?*

## 7 The statelessness of an Islamic state

Here, in the concluding part of our chapter and in light of the above comparisons we have drawn, we briefly present an overview of current-day Pakistan and the socio-economic challenges facing it. The biggest challenge is the overpopulation of a nation that's still in its prime of youth, if not infancy, with a faltering infrastructure and regional political pressures as an outcome of constantly being at a tug of war with its neighbour (twin) country, India. Another unsurmountable challenge facing Pakistan since the last decade, is the rapid fanatic surge which has consequently alienated Pakistan globally, as well as regionally.

Pakistan is predicted to be the world's fastest-growing Muslim economy in 2017, ahead of large Muslim economies like Indonesia, Malaysia, Egypt and Turkey How is it preparing herself to maintain this title?

*Keeping true to its Islamic Republic title, is Pakistan ready for the challenge of taking the lead in the Muslim world, if not the world, to propose new innovative/integral economic models, such as Akhuwat's solidarity economy model?*

In his analysis on Pakistan as a foreign policy expert, Stephen P. Cohen suggests that when security, human services, justice, and basic necessities are not provided, states fail. 'Because these factors are man-made, diagnosing and rectifying shortcomings is theoretically possible. The case of Pakistan, however, raises very different and more difficult questions than those generated by a study of mere failure' (2002).

> Pakistan's most unique feature is not its potential as a failed state but the intricate interaction between the physical/political/legal entity known as the state of Pakistan and the idea of the Pakistani nation. Few if any other nation-states are more complex than Pakistan in this respect, with the Pakistani state often operating at cross-purposes with the Pakistani nation. The state has certainly been failing for many years, but the Pakistani nation also is a contested idea, and the tension between them is what makes Pakistan an especially important case. Pakistan has not fulfilled either its potential or the expectations of its founders, but it is too big and potentially too dangerous for the international community to allow it simply to fail.
>
> (Cohen, 2002)

*Figure 2.2* Pakistan's positioning

With each passing day, geopolitically, Pakistan becomes an even more crucial player. Globally acknowledged as the epicentre of global jihad, housing world's second-largest Muslim population, armed with nuclear weapons and planet's most dangerous borderlands. Post Afghanistan-Russia war, it has maintained a centrally strategic positioning in world politics in the South Asian region of Indian-subcontinent.

### *7.1 What is emerging for Pakistan?*

According to US News, the world's most powerful countries may not necessarily be the most well-liked, but they are the nations that consistently dominate news headlines, preoccupy policymakers and shape economic forecasts (US News, 2017).

Throughout its history of turbulent military coups and constant power struggles between politicians, Pakistan has maintained its position as a very resilient nation, with an emerging economy promised to rise by 2030.

According to a definition given by Investopedia, An emerging market economy is a nation's economy that is progressing toward becoming advanced, as shown by some liquidity in local debt and equity markets and the existence of some form of market exchange and regulatory body. Emerging markets are not as advanced as developed countries but maintain economies and infrastructures that are more advanced than frontier market countries.

The questions we would dare to pose now are, could a standard Western definition of *emergence* befit an Islamically created nation whose people still believe and practise their historic mystic traditions and values? Is it practical for an Eastern (holy-istic) economy to fashion herself through a Western-wise garb now, in the wake of internationalisation taking the place of globalisation, which dismally failed all nations?

From our spiritual-integral perspective, this could be a call for a socio-spiritually aligned economic model like Akhuwat to now take a lead in developing such 'emerging' models of integral solidarity. All this knowing the starkly disintegrated social divide within the Pakistani society, and in the light of Akhuwat's *Transformational GENE* now taking rounds in the Northern orientation (universality) as per Integral Dynamics Theory developed by Lessem and Schieffer (2013).

From our spiritual noetic orientation, Pakistan and Akhuwat are in the realm of Ilm (knowledge creation) of SOUL-idarity, with universality circumvolution. We anticipate, or so we believe, this is the time for Pakistan to shine its integral Hikma (*ishq, ilm, akhuwat and amal)* light as an (after) effect of Akhuwat's 4I genealogy of *Iman (faith), Ihsan (excellence), Ikhlas (sincerity) and Ikhuwah (solidarity).*

### *7.2 What's NEXT (Next 11) for Pak-China*

According to Goldman Sachs, the world's largest investment bank, Pakistan will be among the top 20 economies in the world by GDP (gross domestic product). Goldman Sachs is the one that coined term BRICS, followed by N-11 (Next 11). Pakistan is one of the N-11.

Pakistan has the world's 40th largest economy by gross domestic product (GDP) ranking, as ranked by an IMF (International Monetary Fund), and it is expected to become the world's 18th largest economy by 2050, according to Goldman Sachs (Zahid, 2015).

Incidentally, all the top six fastest-growing economies are in Asia. Pakistan is a full member of the Shanghai Cooperation Organisation (SCO) and is a member of international organisations including the United Nations, World Trade Organization and International Monetary Fund. It can take a lead role in the Muslim world; especially with the advent of OBOR initiative, Pakistan's economic future seems to be taking a turn for the better.

Incidentally, China and Pakistan share a longstanding bond of *friendship (*regional solidarity), an odd relationship for some. For China is atheist, Pakistan is Islamic; China is a stable communist/capitalist country, Pakistan is an unstable military junta/capitalist country; China is the world's factory, Pakistan is neither a big market nor a big supplier of resources; and as a geopolitical balance to India, China simply doesn't worry about India very much.

But if there is one international relationship that China is 'emotional' about, it's the relationship with Pakistan. China is 'Confucius' at heart. She wants to maintain friendly relationships with every country, but the word 'friend' has a special meaning in the Chinese culture. It means someone who stands by you when you are down and out. Pakistan has stood by China in many a geopolitically challenging time. Hence, if anything, China is returning the favour to Pakistan by *investing* in Pakistan economically.

The OBOR will connect 62 countries in Asia, Africa and Europe. China has already invested more than $50 billion in OBOR countries. It will have six economic corridors, the flagship $52 billion CPEC (China-Pakistan Economic Corridor) being one of the six. The OBOR will be 12 times bigger in absolute dollar terms than the Marshall Plan, says Bloomberg.

'Dubbed "One Belt, One Road", the plan to build rail, highways and ports will embolden China's soft-power status by spreading economic prosperity during a time of heightened political uncertainty in both the United States and European Union, according to Stephen L. Jen, chief executive officer at Eurizon SLJ Capital, who estimates a value of US$1.4 trillion for the project.... With the potential to touch on 64 countries, 4.4 billion people and around 40 percent of the global economy, Jen estimates that the "One Belt, One Road" project will be 12 times bigger in absolute dollar terms than the Marshall Plan. China may spend as much as 9 per cent of gross domestic product – about double the US' boost to post-war Europe in those terms'.

China's ambition to revive an ancient trading route stretching from Asia to Europe could leave an economic legacy bigger than the Marshall Plan or the European Union's enlargement, according to a new analysis (Curran, 2016).

*Could this herald another era of colonisation for Pakistan, or is Pakistan now capable of countering these invading threats of cultural dilution, albeit, in this particular case, China being an Eastern economic partner?*

The Gandhara region, which surrounds present-day Peshawar, was an important point along the Silk Road between China and the Mediterranean more than 1,500 years ago. Propelled by Alexander the Great's conquest of the Persian Empire, settlers from the West brought classical Greco-Roman influences, while traders from the East brought Buddhism. This unique cross-pollination permeated the art of the Gandhara region, which encompassed swaths of Northwest Pakistan and Eastern Afghanistan between the first century BC and the fifth century AD. The remnants of this Buddhist culture were destroyed by the fanatic extremists of the region after the Talibanist insurgency took hold of the Northwestern terrains of Pakistan.

China may not be a (practising) Buddhist society anymore, but it is still holding on to a spiritual tradition that matches Pakistan's Eastern values of SOUL-idarity. For Pakistan, this could be heralding an era of *emerging* Eastern economic renewal.

*Is there a role for an institution like Akhuwat to play in conceptualising this new model of economic corridor for its micro-borrowers, helping Pakistan emerge as a flourishing economy in the South Asian region?*

## 8 Conclusion

Lawrence Taub (2002), a futurist and the author of the book *The Spiritual Imperative: Sex, Age, and The Last Caste*, predicting future trends maintains that *humans create systems, not the other way around.*

For him; "It is not technology, economics, money, business, religion or ideology. The real drivers of history are changes in human values and world views".

We deem it as imperative for Pakistan to rise to the occasion and create systems that work in favour of Pakistani people. "With a population boom of 2.4 per cent per annum, the country's population is around 208 million. That marks an increase of more than 57pc since the last population census in 1998 and is higher than what had been projected. With abysmal human development indicators, this population explosion presents a most serious challenge to the socioeconomic stability and security of this country. With 60pc of the population under the age of 30 and fewer job opportunities, it is a disaster in the making", writes Zahid Hussain, an author and a journalist (Hussain, 2017).

What Pakistan is calling for are home-grown localised solutions to its overly complex multidimensional problems. Incidentally, poverty is a relative outcome of all the other issues facing Pakistanis, e.g., scarce resources, and the lack of infrastructure and an uncontrollable population explosion have resulted in a state of chaos. Additionally, with nearly a third of Pakistanis living in poverty and only 58 percent literate, the immediate step that needs to be taken, as per Akhuwat's approach, is to provide access to finance to very poor micro-entrepreneurs to sustain themselves through their Qard-e-Hasan (benevolent interest-free loans). Evidently, and as will be demonstrated throughout the course of this book, their philosophy has been practically successful. What remains to be done is to develop a localised knowledge solution by applying the TOK (Theory of Knowledge) for the poor micro-entrepreneurs capable of generating and managing their own micro-economies that work in their favour and not against them as per the prevailing systemic feudalistic post-colonial dictum and aggrandisement of Northern and Western educational and power structures.

With all her cultural complexity and colonial baggage, will Pakistan rise to the occasion and prove its mettle as a resilient nation having survived many calamities?

What role could organisations like Akhuwat play in instituionalising an integral CARE (Community activation, raising Awareness, Research-to-innovation and Embodied action) model as designed by Lessem and Schieffer through their integral dynamics theory?

Chapter 4 thereupon explores how Akhuwat has been CARE-ing for Pakistani society in light of its four principles as shown in Figure 2.2, all this through its philosophical 4I postulation.

For our next chapter, we revert back to exploring the ontological phenomenon of 'solidarity replication' as the subsequent activation of the impulse of solidarity from our integral-spiritual mutation.

## Bibliography

Ahmed, A., 2002. *Discovering Islam: Making Sense of Muslim History and Society.* Abingdon: Routledge.

Ali, C. R., 1933. *NOW OR NEVER*. Available at: http://www.columbia.edu/itc/mealac/pritchett/00islamlinks/txt_rahmatali_1933.html

Anielski, M., 2007. Building an Economy of Love Based on Genuine Wealth. *Celebrate*, 11, 11, pp. 6–7.
Anon., 2016. *UNDP in Pakistan*. Available at: http://www.pk.undp.org/content/pakistan/en/home/presscenter/pressreleases/2016/06/20/pakistan-s-new-poverty-index-reveals-that-4-out-of-10-pakistanis-live-in-multidimensional-poverty.html
Askari, H., & Rehman S. S., 2010. How Islamic are Islamic Countries? *Global Economy Journal*, 10, article 2.
Cohen, S. P., 2002. *The Nation and the State of Pakistan*. Available at: https://www.brookings.edu/articles/the-nation-and-the-state-of-pakistan/
Curran, E., 2016. *China's Marshall Plan*. Available at: https://www.bloombergquint.com/china/2016/08/07/china-s-marshall-plan
Dyde, S. W., 2001. *Hegel's Philosophy of Right*. Kitchener: Batoche Books Limited.
Elias, J. J., 1998. *Death Before Dying*. Oakland: University of California Press.
ElSenossi, M. F. A., n.d. *The Language of the Future Sufi Terminology*. Available at: http://www.almirajsuficentre.org.au/qamus/app/single/921
Essays, U., November 2013. *The Elements of Class Conflict in Pakistan*. Available at: https://www.ukessays.com/essays/sociology/the-elements-of-class-conflict-in-pakistan-sociology-essay.php?vref=1
Federici, M. P., 2011. *Custom*. Available at: http://www.firstprinciplesjournal.com/articles.aspx?article=589&theme=home&page=2&loc=b&type=ctbf
Hellinger, B., 1998. *Love's Hidden Symmetry: What Makes Love Work in Relationships*. Phoenix: Zeig, Tucker & Co
Hussain, Z., 2017. *Exploding Population Bomb*. Available at: https://www.dawn.com/news/1354793/exploding-population-bomb[Accessed 2017].
Iqbal, M., 1924. *Bang-e-Dra-072 (Chand Aur Tare)*. Available at: http://iqbalurdu.blogspot.co.uk/2011/04/bang-e-dra-072-chand-aur-tare.html
Iqbal, M. (2000). Reconstruction of Religious. Lahore: Sang-e-Meel Publications.
Iqbal, M., 1935. Mir-e-Sipah. In: *Bal-e-Jibril* (Bal-e-Jibril-036). http://iqbalurdu.blogspot.com/2011/04/bal-e-jibril-036-mir-e-sipah-na-saza.html.
Khan, A. & Khan, R., 2004. *Drivers of Change Pakistan: Civil Society and Social Change in Pakistan*. Islamabad: IDS-Collective-DFID.
Khan, H. I., 1914. Love, Human and Divine. In: *Spiritual Liberty*. Delhi: Motilal Banarsidass Publishers Pvt. Ltd.
Kumar, S., 2013. *Soil Soul Society: A New Trinity for Our Time*. Brighton: Ivy Press.
Lessem, R., & Bradley, T., 2018. *Evolving Work*. Abingdon: Routledge.
Lessem, R., & Schieffer, A., 2013. *Integral Dynamics*. Abingdon: Routledge.
Majid, H., November 12, 2010. *Development Aid Failure*. Lahore: Dawn Newspaper.
Malik, I. H., 2008. *The History of Pakistan*. Westport: Greenwood Press.
O'Neill, J., 2007. *Brics and Beyond*. s.l.: Goldman Sachs.
Qadeer, M., 2006. *Pakistan: Social and Cultural Transformations in a Muslim Nation*. Abingdon: Routledge.
Saqib, A., 2016. *Kamyab Loug*. Lahore: Sang-e-Meel Publications.
Schimmel, A., 1978. *Mystical Dimensions of Islam*. Chapel Hill: The University of North Carolina Press.
Schieffer, A., & Lessem, R., 2014. *Integral Development*. Farnham: Gower Publishing Ltd.
Sharaf, S. S., 2010. *Civil Society in Pakistan*. s.l.: s.n.
Taub, L., 2002. *The Spiritual Imperative: Sex, Age, and The Last Caste*. Tokyo: Clear Glass Press.

Tuan, Y.-F., 1974. *Topophilia: Study of Environmental Perception, Attitudes and Values*. 1st ed. New Jersey: Prentice Hall.

US News., 2017. *Overall Best Countries Ranking*. Available at: https://www.usnews.com/news/best-countries/overall-full-list.

Waseem, F., October 2014. The Legacy of the Colonial Project of English Education in Pakistan. *International Journal of Business and Social Science*, 5, 11(1) Query page number.

Zahid, W., 2015. *Pakistan at $300B is World's 40th Largest Economy*. Available at: https://walizahid.com/2015/07/pakistan-at-300b-is-worlds-40th-largest-economy/

# 3 The SOUL-idarity impulse

## 1 Preamble

In the previous chapter, we narrated Pakistan's story in our personal contexts, as well as closely examining Pakistan's existing challenges through a '4C' trajectory – including *Call, Context, Co-creation and Contribution* – as per our collective call for Integral Development. The Transformational GENE, in parallel with the 4C process, works towards 'full C+A+R+E' – a process and acronym representing Community activation, raising Awareness, Research-to-innovation and Embodied action.

Now, before we move on to a full CARE process in conjunction with Akhuwat's four principles, starting with Community activation as the first step, we intend to explore the impulse that pulsates at the core (heart) of a community and how it aids in building communities and solidarity between them. In Chapter 1, we elaborated on the transmutation of the Transformational GENE in a similar light. This is particularly set in an Islamic/spiritual grounding, as is the case with Akhuwat and Pakistan as per our exploration.

We now move on to community-building from nation-building, as explored in our previous chapter on Pakistan.

## 2 Creating virtuous circles: community building through IHSAN (compassion) and Mawakhat (solidarity)

As proposed by Lessem and Schieffer in their Integral Development Bible:

> The natural starting point for working with society is the immediate community of the Integral Developer. Starting there, rather than with society as a whole, helps us to bring things back to human scale, back into a sphere were interaction is possible and tangible.... Focusing in this realm on restoring natural and community life, we clearly promote a developmental attitude that simply recognises the natural and social realities on the ground and subsequently contributes to reactivating the restorative potential that can be found in each physical nature and human community, as well as in each individual and organisation of which such is constituted (2014).

As per Lessem and Schieffer's postulation, developmental studies have failed to deliver the purpose they were conceived for. Typically, such studies have developed top-down, with theories born and bred in the 'West' affecting, or maligning, practices in the 'rest'.

What they have evolved in their CARE (Community activation, Awakening of integral consciousness, innovation-driven institutionalised Research and Embodied action) model is a 'middle-up-down-across' with approaches to what they term as **community activation**, born and bred locally, in particular societies, with a view to their being further evolved, locally-globally, in developing societies at large.

For them, communities hold the key and lead the way to societal development on a larger scale. And this is what we are postulating through our SOUL-idarity Hikma (wisdom) contemplation, set in an Islamic (Pakistani) society's context. By presenting Akhuwat's community of Akhuwateers as a prime example at hand for such, taking Lessem and Schieffer's 'middle-up-down-across' approach of community activation, we are thus proposing in this chapter a soulful cognisance of one such 'impulse' that is present in a particular community, Pakistan, in our case.

In the previous chapter we briefly explored the 4 C's (Call, Context, Co-creation and Contribution) of Pakistani society and the *'impulse of solidarity'* as an aftermath of partition from India and then in the absence of an equable stately infrastructure. The benevolence of Pakistan's civil society and voluntary, charitable giving is what sustains not only Pakistani underpriveleged communities but is also what is fostering Akhuwat's 'reciprocal endowment'.

Thus, throughout this chapter, we aim to delve deeper into the communal impulse of 'solidarity' with Akhuwat's brotherhood paradigm. They have auspiciously generated pools of benevolence (barakah) spiralling out of the 'virtuous circles' as an aftereffect of SOUL-idarity with the Supreme Self, community and society.

*What role then does community play in such a process?*

We first turn to an ontological phenomenology of communitas in various societal settings.

### *2.1 Community – a place to serve and be served*

There is a story in the biblical book of John (John 13:1–10, New International Version [NIV]) that inspires me, which narrates an instance of Jesus washing his disciples' feet.

> It was just before the Passover festival. Jesus knew that the hour had come for him to leave this world and go to the Father. Having loved his own who were in the world, he loved them to the end.
>
> The evening meal was in progress, and the devil had already prompted Judas, the son of Simon Iscariot, to betray Jesus. Jesus knew that the Father

> had put all things under his power, and that he had come from God and was returning to God; so, he got up from the meal, took off his outer clothing, and wrapped a towel around his waist. After that, he poured water into a basin and began to wash his disciples' feet, drying them with the towel that was wrapped around him.
>
> He came to Simon Peter, who said to him, 'Lord, are you going to wash my feet?'
>
> Jesus replied, 'You do not realize now what I am doing, but later you will understand.'
>
> 'No,' said Peter, 'you shall never wash my feet.'
>
> Jesus answered, 'Unless I wash you, you have no part with me'
>
> (New International Version, n.d.)

Per Howard Macy, Professor Emeritus at George Fox University, also the author of Rhythms of the Inner Life:

> Communities are the places where we learn to strip away our self-interest in order to serve others. It is here that we learn to share what God has given us, whether it be goods or spiritual gifts. It is also here that we learn to be served, though we are sometimes prideful and reluctant like Peter, who balked at Jesus washing his feet.
>
> (Macy, May 29th 2011)

Sometimes we are the washers and sometimes the washees, but in many ordinary ways we can learn what submission and service mean.

Another inspiring story is of Umar ibn al Khattab (may Allah be pleased with him). Umar succeeded Abu Bakr as the second caliph of Islam in 634 AD. Umar ibn al Khattab was the first ruler in world history who introduced the system of social security into his government.

Islamic law provides an advanced and comprehensive vision of effective, efficient and good governance. The principles of *amanah* (accountability), *akhlaq* (morality), *shura* (mutual consultation) and *ijtihad* (respect for opinions) form the basis of Islamic administration. These principles were effectively implemented under the rule of Umar ibn al Khattab, as the second caliph of Islam.

> During the time of Caliph 'Umar ibn al-Khattab (634–44 AH/1237–47 CE), (May Allah be pleased with him), the Muslims ruled from Tripoli (Libya) to Balkh (Afghanistan), from Armenia to Sindh (Pakistan) and Gujrat (India), and over the countries lying in between such as Syria, Iraq and Iran etc. The reign of 'Umar ibn al-Khattab is considered to be the brightest period in the history of the Islamic system of social security. The social and economic justice prevailed, and every citizen of the state was given his due share.
>
> (Nadvi, 2012)

Once when a famine hit areas of North Arabia and Syria, Umar sent food grains from Egypt and Medina. He visited the affected areas personally, distributed the grains, and avoided meals most of the time. When Umar was asked to take care of his health, he replied, 'If I don't taste suffering, how can I know the suffering of others?'

In Pakistan, Amjad fosters a similar sentiment. He narrates in his book *Akhuwat ka Safar*:

> 'Once, I tried washing a Khwaja-sira's[1] wound asking her to put her foot on my lap, by washing her wound, it felt like my own soul was being cleansed.'

*By tasting the sufferings of others (community) outside our own Self (individual), the collective alchemy of communal survival – the 'impulse of solidarity' as we term it – starts pulsating, setting it in a circumvolutory motion.*

*And this is what I call the 'SOUL-idarity' impulse iteration, the common thread that runs between humans. It transmutates, in times of suffering originating in the Ishq/love realm, thereby horizontally taking effect as communal Ihsan (perfection of beauty).*

*For what is Ihsan after all? It is a matter of taking one's inner faith (Iman) and showing it in both good deeds and action (amal), and a sense of social responsibility (Akhuwat) borne from religious or spiritual convictions.*

We now turn towards **Ihsan** as the primal force driving this 'impulse of solidarity' between communities of people.

### *2.2 The Ihsan emergence*

Per Al-Jayyousi (2012), Professor of Technology and Innovation Management at Arabian Gulf University, Bahrain, *Ihsan* is an Arabic word with many meanings, such as excellence and beauty. It also refers to a higher level of evolving consciousness. Arabesque art illustrates how an individual element contributes to the whole, and to the community (*ummah*). It – ihsan – also involves *the awareness of the Divine in every act, leading to the realisation of inner beauty and insight.*

> Hence, through this inner renewable consciousness, human actions are regulated to protect the freedom of the community. True individual value and freedom is found in doing what is good and beautiful for the community. The unveiling of beauty in the human, in nature, and in the cosmos, provides an inspiration for 'Ihsan', which is doing what is good and beautiful for all the community of life. Excellence (*ihsan*) also means inner beauty, and conscious evolution of individuals, organizations and

> society (*ummah*). This also entails continuous improvement and value and knowledge creation for all humanity.
>
> (Al-Jayyousi, 2012)

Incidentally, Ihsan in Urdu means 'an act of kindness' – 'a benediction'. From a cultural Pakistani backdrop, this is a tradition of 'favour' petitions – an act of kindness in return for the favour given. Hence, the 'reciprocity' of Akhuwat's MDP (members donation program) – the customary reciprocal endowment which I term the 'multiplier-effect of the barakah rounds'. Chapter 6 submits this mediation further.

We now deliberate the pervasive 'effect' of 'Ihsan' manifestations in the communitas.

### *2.2.1 Communal excellence through Ihsan: community (Biradari)*

*The Ihsan emergence takes effect by spreading horizontally [middle-up-down-across] benefitting the society at large – South dominant.*

> From an integral perspective then, for any living system, the Southern grounds represent its '*local identity*' and its connection to a common source of life.
>
> 'It is seeking to activate the relational "feeling" or "heart"-level of a human system as well as participation and engagement' (Lessem & Schieffer, 2013).

For any society to sustain itself, engaging its 'heart' faculty is vital for its survival. Islam advocates a virtue-based approach for a communal sustainability. And it continuously emphasises the need for a just and equitable society through this approach.

Per Muhammad Asad, a Muslim scholar and political theorist; in the saying of the Prophet:

> Asabiyyah was explained by him as "helping your own people in an unjust cause", where the Prophet says, "He is not of us who proclaims the cause of tribal partisanship and he is not of us who fights in the cause of tribal partisanship; and he is not of us who dies in the cause of tribal partisanship". When the Prophet was asked by the Companions about the meaning of 'Asabiyyah (tribal partisanship), he explained: "(It means) your helping your own people in an unjust cause".
>
> (Asad, 1961)

> The term asabiyah has been variously translated as "solidarity," "group feeling," "social cohesion," and even "clannishness." Ibn Khaldun did not invent the term, but he did retool it for his own purposes. The meaning he imparted to it is

> largely what it means today". (Anon., 2015) According to the Arab-English Lexicon; the term 'Asabiyyah emerged from the word 'ta'asub' which literally means '...bounding the turban round (his own) head'. Thus, 'Asabiyyah is explained as the "...quality of an individual who is possessing 'Asabiyyah which refers to the action of ones in helping his people or his group against any aggressive action.
>
> (Halim, Nor, Ibrahim & Hamid, 2012)

Al-Jayyousi proposed something similar in his book on Islam and Sustainable Development. Per Al-Jayyousi:

> the third component of the sustainability model, after social justice and the pursuit of beauty, is social capital (arham). The Islamic social order can be viewed at three levels: the community (*ummah*), the family, and the individual. The value-based community, or what is called 'median community' (*ummah wassat*) provides the common ground and the common world for all people.
>
> (Al-Jayyousi, 2012)

In a Pakistani context, as previously mentioned in Chapter 2, the Biradari system is one thread (silsilah/chain) that binds people together in a sense of community and 'spirit of solidarity'. Still prevalent, more so in the rural areas now, the tribal allegiance fosters a communal sense of ownership – similar to the 'asabiyyah' philosophy, as above.

We will now further explore the 'nature' of the Ihsan effect and how it helps in spreading the effect by creating circles of 'virtuous' asabiyyah in a 'median community', as proposed by Al-Jayyousi.

*Could this model of 'median community', as per his postulation, sustain itself through a process of creating 'virtuous circles' as underlined by Amjad Saqib?*

First off, let us now explore how these virtuous circles are created through Ihsan, which in conjunction with Akhuwat's 4I genealogy, forms the third tenet of its philosophy.

## 3 Creating virtuous circles through Ihsan

*Akhuwat's term 'virtuous circle' was introduced to me for the first time when I met Amjad in 2016 to share the idea of translating Akhuwat's philosophy (work) into an integral (global) language. My fascination with the concept to this date remains ever abounding. In fact, the more I contemplated it, the more it unwrapped itself – making me wonder more deeply. How could this concept which is implicatively embedded in Akhuwat's philosophy – more so, through Amjad's idealistic inception – be made a persistent phenomenon in communal co-existence?*

Reverting back to Amjad, his expression deeply resonates with this Quranic verse:

> Hal Jaza ul Ihsan Illal Ihsan; *'Is the reward of goodness (ihsan) anything but goodness (ihsan)?'* (Al-Rahman, 55:60)
> For the key to strengthening a beneficial love – for something that is good – is to perform righteous deeds (amal) and, hence, to behave virtuously (Akhuwah). As per Amjad, Virtue (or goodness – ihsan) is truly its own reward.
> Truly those who believe and perform righteous deeds – for them the Compassionate One shall appoint love (ishq)
> (Surah Maryam, 19:96).

*This all sounds very simple. Yet, in the profitability-centric societies we have all formed and live in, this could be the most challenging task albeit the most pressing need for our communal co-existence. For those of us avid dream-activists, this is the legacy we are all working on: to leave behind a world that is not damaged by our own material pursuits.*

*From an initial stage, and from my standpoint of perceiving Akhuwat as not 'just' a microfinance organisation, this was my enthrallment with Amjad's 'virtuosity' and Mawakhat social movement.*

*By and by, as I immersed myself deeper into its philosophy, it started unfolding all the hidden layers of its Ihsan/virtuous paradigm – the virtuous circle (silsilah) in motion, creating other virtuous circles (reciprocal endowment) for what we call barakah rounds that keep on replicating naturally. Chapter 6 elaborates more on this postulation.*

*For now, it comes as no surprise to note that Akhuwat has a long list of accomplishments to its credit, for the reward of goodness (Ihsan) could only be goodness.*

We now turn to the impact this virtuosity generates as a community's 'solidarity capital'.

### *3.1 Solidarity capital – the Ihsan advantage*

Amjad's words explain it better:

> Much like the spiral of downfall and degeneracy, known as a vicious cycle, there is also a spiral of ascent and accomplishment, known as a virtuous cycle. This is exactly the philosophy of forbiddance of evil and exhortation of good. It is the Will of the Lord which cycle He grants to whomever He pleases. No responsibility is given beyond one's capacity. And then, there is also the intoxication of uprightness, which the virtuous keep yearning after. Nobody has monopoly over righteousness (Ihsan); nobody has privilege over divine graciousness. It is He who selects whomever He wills for His blessings and mercy. What Allah grants is from His Will and Mercy.Akhuwat was the first blessing on my journey of hope. Then countless avenues began opening up (virtuous circles). The journey led to more journeys, some due to the grace of a generous grant, some as a result

of a prayer. Many initiatives seemed to enter the list of deeds on their own. Punjab Endowment Fund, Punjab Welfare Trust for the Disabled, and Fountain House are all part of Akhuwat Biradari. Their stories progress hand in hand with that of Akhuwat.

Through 17 years of existence, besides generating its own 'solidarity/circular economy' (Chapter 6), by rekindling the spirit of Ihsan, Akhuwat has successively created its own 'community of Akhuwateers', that is, multiple virtuous circles.

For Amjad, brotherhood (Bhai-chara/Akhuwat) is an unmatchable feeling of compassion that promises to empower people. By virtue of solidarity, the cyclic reverberation has spiralled through their many community initiatives as shown in Figure 3.1.

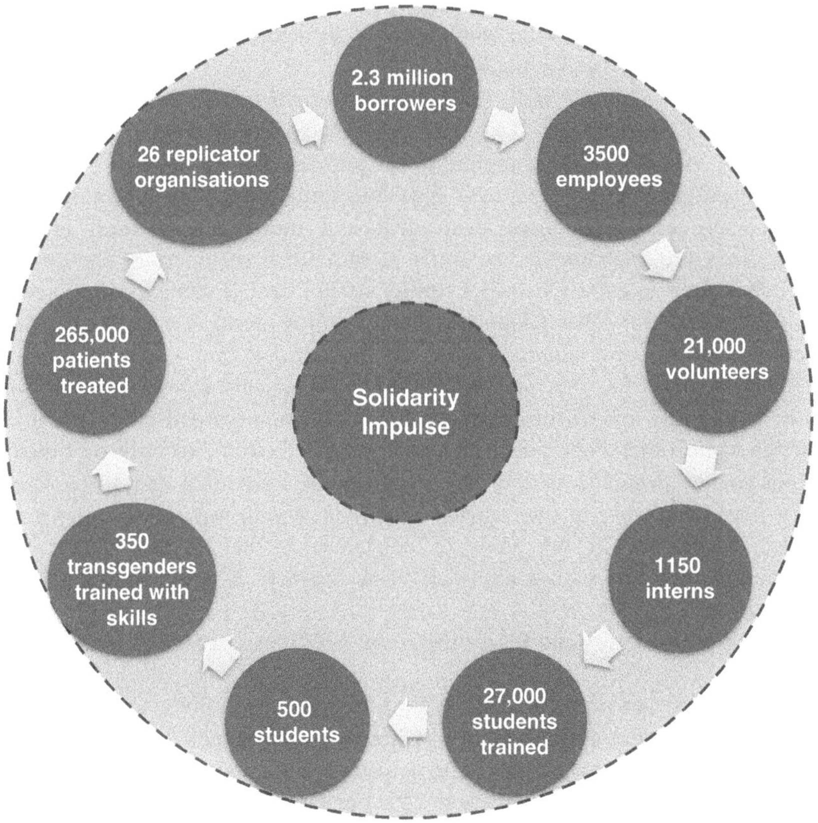


*Figure 3.1* The Virtuosity Wheel

Figure 3.1 gives an overview of Akhuwat's virtuous circles growing by way of emulating its Mawakhat philosophy, something which Amjad prophesied years ago and which is now taking effect. For example, the 26 organisations adopting Akhuwat's model of Qard-e-Hasan are now the multipliers of these virtuous circles, thus reflecting the Ihsan advantage. This is further elaborated in Chapter 8.

We will further elaborate on the replication process through the course of this chapter. Let us now answer the question, how is this culture of virtuosity and solidarity cultivated in a community of Akhuwateers?

## 4 Virtuous communities and solidarity cultivators

According to Al-Jayyousi (2012), one of the three fundamentals of Islamic faith is Trusteeship – Khalifa: the human being as viceregent on earth has been endowed with all the spiritual and mental characteristics, as well as material resources, to enable him or her to live up to their mission. Since the human is good by nature, he or she feels psychologically happy so long as (s)he stays in, or moves closer to, his or her inner nature. The resources with which God has endowed the world are not unlimited but are sufficient to cater for the needs of all, if used efficiently and equitably.

In the same vein, Al-Farabi thought of a perfect human being (al-insan al-kamil) in his virtuous city (Al-Farabi, 1959) as the one who has obtained theoretical virtue – thus completing his intellectual knowledge – and has acquired practical moral virtues – thus becoming perfect in his moral behaviour. Then, crowning these theoretical and moral virtues with effective power, they are anchored in the souls of individual members of the community when they assume the responsibility of political leadership, thus becoming role models for other people. Al-Farabi unites moral and aesthetic values: good is beautiful, and beauty is good; the beautiful is that which is valued by the intelligentsia. So, this perfection which he expects from education combines knowledge and virtuous behaviour; it is happiness and goodness at one and the same time. Theoretical and practical perfection can only be obtained within society, for it is society that nurtures the individual and prepares him to be free. If he were to live outside society, he might only learn to be a wild animal. Then, one of the goals of education is the creation of the ideal community, 'the one whose cities all work together in order to attain happiness' (al-Talbi, 2000).

Per Spinosa, Dreyfus and Flores (Spinosa, 1997), as cited by Lessem (2017):

> community activism, in their civic terms, is the joining together of all, individually and collectively, to promote diverse goods... A civic activist looks for fair distribution of participation and participatory skills, acting skilfully in concert with others to effect change.
>
> Overall, Spinoza and his colleagues have argued for the importance of history-making skills. As such they have cited three history makers – the

> entrepreneur, the virtuous citizen and the orchestrator of cultural solidarity – altogether providing meaningful lives for citizens by disclosing new worlds.
>
> The three modes of innovative activity each have the same structure. The entrepreneur, virtuous citizen and orchestrator of cultural solidarity each find in their lives something disharmonious that common sense overlooks or denies. They then hold onto this disharmony, between past and future, individual and community, East and West or North and South, and live with intensity until it reveals how the common-sense way of acting fails. As the source of disharmony became clearer, each of our history makers became a puzzle solver.
>
> (Lessem, 2017)

And this stands true for our solidarity cultivator, Dr. Amjad Saqib who, being embedded in the community in a socio-economic context, experienced the pain and sufferings of poor people. And through applying his participatory action research knowledge, he devised a way to tackle the problem by activating a community of micro-entrepreneurs, consequently building a community of people who believe in the same philosophy.

As cited by (Lessem, 2017), 'Participatory Action Research (PAR) implies participatory, democratic process concerned with developing practical knowing in the pursuit of worthwhile human purposes, grounded in a participatory worldview which is believed to be emerging at this historical moment. It seeks to bring together action and reflection, theory and practice, in participation with others, in the pursuit of practical solutions to issues of pressing concern to people, and more generally the flourishing of individual persons and their communities.' (Reason & Bradbury, 2004)

We can see in Akhuwat's case how cultivating the seeds of solidarity created a ripple effect of 'goodness as a reward for goodness', thus, practically reflecting virtues of Ihsan being cultivated in the community of Akhuwat partners, i.e., borrowers, replicators, partners et al.

We now move on to the concluding part of this chapter, analysing the multiplier effect of Ihsan in Akhuwat's community of solidarity cultivators.

## 5 The solidarity multipliers

> Every time somebody expresses an interest in our work and wishes to embark on the same path, it is music to our ears.
>
> The kindling of any spark in the darkness bears evidence that darkness will inevitably come to an end. However, there are some conditions that must be honoured before embarking on this path. Whoever wishes to do this work, must first surrender their being (ego). It is this surrender that

stands as the greatest manifestation of his devotion. After this sacrifice, each hindrance falls flat.

As *Maulana* Rumi said, 'There are seven cities of love and each city contains seventy thousand streets. Right now, I am standing at the first street of the first city. Heaven knows when the destiny will arrive.'

### *5.1 The borrowers*

Over the period of one decade, Akhuwat has grown from a small initiative to large movement fighting against usury and exploitation of the poor. The trust and honour of the borrowers has helped them with their members donation program (MDP). It is a program that relies entirely on the philanthropic spirit within their borrowers. Their eagerness to donate for the cause of Akhuwat along with their monthly payments increased their confidence as it developed a new foundation within the organisation which is supporting Akhuwat's operations and expanding to create more virtuous circles.

### *5.2 The partners*

Akhuwat's message of Mawakhat and its approach to alleviate poverty is known as 'the Akhuwat Model'. Through various interactions and interventions, the organisation trains and speaks about 'the Akhuwat Model' with all relevant and interested stakeholders in order to promote its replication and for better understanding of the Islamic principles in general. The benefits are two: Firstly, it helps to broaden the Islamic microfinance industry within the country, which helps immensely to reach more beneficiaries time efficiently, and to create more jobs. Secondly, it creates a parallel microfinance industry that produces a Shariah-compliant finance system tailored on the religious and cultural practices of the region that aims to use the tool of microfinance as a charitable service.

Akhuwat supports all organisations engaging in this worthy endeavour and makes all resources available for interested stakeholders in order to facilitate their transition or the first step into this field. This includes providing training to the affiliate staff in interest free non-profit microfinance (Qard-e-Hasan) by lending their loan methodology literature to all those that require it to ensure the establishment and sustainability of all desiring ventures. Their support for replications is purely based on Amjad's dream of building an interest-free Mawakhat community throughout Pakistan and hopefully the world, thus without any interest in capitalising on market shares, they invest their energy and resources into helping develop other organisations without detracting from their objective. It contributes to Amjad's ultimate vision of a poverty-free society. In a period of over a decade, several organisations have implemented 'The Akhuwat Model' and added Qard-e-Hasan as one of the tools for their community services.

After achieving successful results on local grounds, Akhuwat also saw the replication of their model at a global level. International Muslim charities like Helping Hands and Muslim Aid UK also implemented microfinance on the lines of 'The Akhuwat Model'.

## 6 The orders of love – silsilah – the solidarity chain

We have thus far briefly explored Akhuwat's community-building Ihsan (excellence) multiplier in the form of creating a chain (silsilah) that emanates from love for humanity and one's community. This love originates in the form of universal love, i.e., love for the Creator and consequently HIS creation, which forms the basis of Mawakhat (solidarity) in our case.

*Silsilah, an Arabic word, also used in Persian, Malay and Urdu, means chain, link, connection, and is often used in various senses of lineage. In particular, it may be translated as '(religious) order' or 'spiritual genealogy'.*

For mystics, the state of ecstasy (perfect happiness) is reached after losing one's 'self' and ascending vertically to the state of *la maqam*, the 'I am not only YOU are' state! This is where the 'Ishq/love' orientation reaches its highest pitch, that is, union with the God-reality. The journey back from that state is the purified state of God-realisation in all one does afterwards.

For Amjad, prayer is a form of love too, as it is surrendering one's will to Allah and then HIS Rasool's[2] will. He strongly believes that the power of prayers coming from an indigent heart could move the earth beyond. He usually gives the credit of Akhuwat's success to the prayers of these indigent hearts and, of course, from his ancestors. Another widespread cultural tradition and belief practised and acknowledged in the land of the pure, Pakistan.

Thus, he writes, in his book *Akhuwat ka Safar*:

> In the calendar of *ishq (love)* and impassioned ardour, there are many ages other than the prevailing one – which refers to the life hereafter.

For him, it was the love of Allah and his profound love and reverence for the Prophet (may peace be upon him) that transcended into love (Ishq) and compassion for the people of his land, which made him travel beyond the age he is living in – the soul resonance of Mawakhat.

For he relates it to predestination, which in Iqbal's work is a succession to 'free will' which is directly attached to action: the amal orientation of our SOUL-idarity GENE.

This brings us to the conclusion of this chapter and Part I of our book, which deals with the Mawakhat (solidarity) paradigm from a transcendental phenomenological lens.

*Table 3.1* Akhuwat Model Replication Process

| *The Eight Strides to Akhuwat (Solidarity) Replication Process* | |
|---|---|
| Training of Staff | The staff of the replicating organisation is trained through different sessions by senior management professionals at operations and branch level from Akhuwat on the principle of Islamic microfinance and modalities related to the implementation of the program. This process also includes field visits to Akhuwat branches. |
| Provision of requisite materials | Akhuwat provides requisite training material to the replicating organisation. Moreover, it provides the manuals and documentation related to the management of an Islamic microfinance system to the replicating organisation. |
| Standard Operating Procedures Manual | A standard operating procedures manual customised to the objectives of the program is prepared in close association between Akhuwat professionals and the replicating organisation. |
| Credit documentation | The process of credit and documenting the transaction is brought into practice. Credit documentation is the key to transparency and accountability; moreover, it helps in protecting the rights of the lender and the borrower as per the principles. |
| M & E systems replication | The monitoring and evaluation procedures are implemented at the management section overviewing this key task. The roles of regional manager and area managers, the steering committee and the loan approval committee are thoroughly explained. Moreover, the use of certain software used at Akhuwat is also provided for the purpose of achieving effective and up-to-date monitoring and evaluation system. |
| Institutional Development | The institutional capacity building is the foremost objective. The capacities of the management at the replicating organisation are built in order to achieve key fundamentals and principles of management required to run the organisation the way an ideal publicly administrated organization should be run. Apart from management trainings, Akhuwat also helps the replicating organisations on the principles of resource mobilisations, mass communication and The Akhuwat Model in general; in totality. |
| Audit Mechanisms | Akhuwat helps the replicating organisation to put in place audit mechanisms which include monthly reviews, internal audit twice a year and an external audit. Akhuwat also provides third-party evaluation services to its replicators in order to provide policy recommendations and to increase the credibility of its replicators. |
| Financial Management | Akhuwat helps in teaching the key financial management rules that help in analysis (for example, operational self sufficiency %) and the account system the organisation would have to manage with its bank, preferably an Islamic bank. The replicator has to manage the following three accounts: credit pool, disbursement account and operations. |

## 7 Conclusion

*With our modern-day world going virtual by the minute, whereby AI (Artificial Intelligence) is commanding our intelligible knowledge, we see the need for creating such virtuous spaces as vital to keeping the human(e) tradition alive.*

*For humans can feel compassion for those people who are not in our virtual space, whereas machines/Blockchain technological environment cannot feel the pain and sufferings of the ones left behind due to our own misgivings.*

*In the light of the above proposition, we would like to say that Ishq (universal love) breeds Ihsan (communal and societal excellence), and all in the process comes from it. It might sound too parochial to believe that some such process could exist and also be self-sustaining through Akhuwat's practical (living) example. Thus, my fascination with it too. Whereas, in Western societies of debt economies, it is believed that debt is the way to create more money. Akhuwat is doing exactly the reverse by lending and creating a massive impact when it comes to growth. The wealthier a country, the more difficult it is to maintain the necessary growth rate. Thus, while developing countries can grow at rates of 5 to 10 percent a year, developed countries struggle to maintain the minimum rate of 3 to 5 percent.*

*Notwithstanding the fact, the Western financial system that had its origin in the financial innovations of the 16th and 17th centuries has clearly produced dramatic increases in some people's standards of living. But it may now threaten to environmentally and socially bankrupt us.*

*For the most current debate in the global West revolves around constructing a financial system that can create money where it is needed without requiring environmentally and socially unsustainable capital accumulation. The Akhuwat Model demonstrates one such model, as is evident from their philosophy of creating virtuous models. This is done by simply channelising wealth accumulation with an innovative manipulation of an archaic social system working for a faith-based community. For in Pakistan, it all seems doable through a simple philosophy of 'giving' or parting with your excess money in exchange for winning divine consent through khidmet-e-khalq (service to humanity). But is such an idealistically compassionate model of Akhuwat-ness acceptable where the sustainability denominator is not God-reliance (tawakul-Allah) but individualistic self-reliance and self-survival?*

*Through the course of this book, we aim to investigate this inquiry further, as per my own call-to-action, working with the deprived migrant communities within the UK, I tend to explore this self-sufficient model of virtuosity generated through Mawakhat being beneficial to these (often-neglected) communities.*

*For now, we have set the scene for our solidarity impulse to take effect by CARE-ing-4-Society (Community activation, raising Awareness, Research-to-innovation and Embodied action) in a Pakistani/Islamic context.*

*The next chapter, then, is a promulgation of such, with further elaboration of Akhuwat's four principles in the light of Transformational GENE rhythm, that which makes it a unique phenomenon.*

## Notes

1 Transgender person
2 Messenger

## Bibliography

Al-Farabi, A. N., 1959. Mabadi' ahl al-madina al-fadila. In: *On the Perfect State: Mabadi Ara Ahl Al-Madinat Al-Fadilah*. Beirut: Imprimerie catholique, p. 97.

Al-Jayyousi, O. R., 2012. *Islam and Sustainable Development*. Farnham: Gower.

al-Talbi, A., 2000. Al-Farabi's Doctrine of Education: Between Philosophy and Sociological Theory. *Prospects: The Quarterly Review of Comparative Education (Paris)*, 23, 1/2, 1993, pp. 353–372.

Anon., 2015. *Introducing: Asabiyah*. Available at: http://scholars-stage.blogspot.com/2015/05/introducing-asabiyah.html [Accessed 2018].

Asad, M., 1961. *The Principles of State and Government in Islam*. California: University of California Press.

Halim, A. A., Nor, M. R. M., Ibrahim, A. Z. B., & Hamid, F. A. F. A., 2012. Ibn Khaldun's Theory of 'Asabiyyah and its Application in Modern Muslim Society. *Middle-East Journal of Scientific Research*, 9, 11, p. 1233.

Lessem, R., 2017a. *Community Activation for Integral Development*. Abingdon: Routledge.

Lessem, R., 2017b. Integral Awakening of Community Activation. In: *Community Activation for Integral Development*. Abingdon: Routledge, p. 53.

Lessem, R., 2017c. Participatory Action Research. In: *Community Activation for Integral Development*. Abingdon: Routledge, p. 60.

Lessem, R., 2017d. The Virtuous Citizen. In: *Community Activation for Integral Development*. Abingdon: Routledge, p. 53.

Lessem, R., & Schieffer, A., 2013. *Integral Dynamics*. Abingdon: Routledge.

Macy, H., May 29, 2011. *Community: God's Design For Growth*. Available at: https://bible.org/article/community-god%E2%80%99s-design-growth [Accessed March 2018].

Nadvi, M. J., January–June 2012. Social Security During the Reign of Caliph 'Umar Ibn Al-Khattab. *Ma'arif Research Journal*, 3, pp. 33–40.

New International Version., n.d. *Jesus Washes His Disciples' Feet*. Available at: http://biblehub.com/niv/john/13.htm [Accessed 2017].

Schieffer, A., & Lessem, R., 2014. *Integral Development*. Farnham: Gower Publishing Ltd.

# Part II
# The Mawakhat paradigm

## 1 Introduction: the Akhuwat (brotherhood) paradigm

> 'The Akhuwat Model' is based on two pillars of strength: first and foremost, the philosophy and, secondly, the model itself and its modalities. The philosophy of Akhuwat is based on four principles: importance of Qard-e-Hasan (benevolent loan), Mawakhat (solidarity), role of religious places and volunteerism. The strength of the model lies in its methodology, of first going through a loan-approving committee and second by taking inspiration from the borrower. These two pillars, along with a pure intention to serve the community, have proven sufficiently self-reliant to serve hundreds of thousands of families in Pakistan; it's enough to change the way microfinance is inferred.

This brings us to the most important part of the book, as what genuinely sets Akhuwat apart as an integrally unique phenomenon from other such organisations operating in Pakistan – or, in fact, anywhere around the world – are Akhuwat's fourfold principles of Mawakhat.

*For me, this was the main instigation, as I could instantaneously spot the similarity between Akhuwat's fourfold principles and integral four worlds and their Transformation GENE rhythm as developed by Lessem and Schieffer; particularly their 'CARE-4-Society' fourfold process* (Lessem & Schieffer, 2013).

*The world sees Akhuwat as yet another microfinance provider, albeit Islamic in its approach and practices. In the presence of microfinance pioneer Grameen and Dr. Muhammad Yunus, and other such microfinance giants, Akhuwat doesn't compete. Moreover, what Akhuwat has been doing for their community of Akhuwateers (donors, borrowers, volunteers and third-sector organisations) by raising awareness of Qard-e-Hasan (interest-free loans) and now providing free education is a job outside the domain of microfinance. By constantly educating people against the ills of riba (usury and debt-slavery), they are doing a huge service to the spirit of 'solidarity'.*

*This inspired me to establish the fact that Akhuwat is not 'a microfinance organisation' only, as it is characterised within Pakistan and globally. Notwithstanding the fact that Akhuwat's philosophy originates from within the Islamic fold, it should, by no means, be referred to as an Islamic microfinance organisation. For me, as well as my TRANS4M colleagues, it qualifies as an alternative model of integral-spiritual finance, coming out of an Islamic philosophy – a financial model that not only provides people loans, but also helps them in their development of becoming a community of Akhuwateers through a solidarity regime, by educating them to play an active role in a process of societal transformation. For example, they help borrowers transform into donors of Akhuwat, thus, CARE-ing- 4-their society (Community activation, raising Awareness, Researching-to-innovation and Embodying action through transformative education) integrally and through their local (Islamic, in their case) traditions and value system.*

For all that, microfinance is not a recent phenomenon. One earlier and longer-lived micro-credit organisation providing small loans to rural poor with no collateral was the Irish Loan Fund system, initiated in the early 1700s by the author and nationalist Jonathan Swift.

*Incidentally, this part of the book does not deal with whether Akhuwat is a microfinance organisation or not. What surprises me about Akhuwat is its minimal global visibility as an alternative to microfinance – something that is globally enjoyed, for example, by Grameen and Muhammad Yunus as their widespread recognition throughout the world. I particularly felt at loss, as being a Pakistani by origin it strengthened me to know this model is coming out of Pakistan, yet it deserves more recognition on a global level and definitely outside the academic echelons.*

What sets Akhuwat apart from other microfinance organisations, in addition to its *interest-free loans* model of Qard-e-Hasan – a Quranic ordination – is its model of 'reciprocal endowment', that is, transforming borrowers into donors, thereby producing further rounds of benevolence (barakah rounds), along with its process of community building through emphasising the philosophy of Mawakhat and volunteerism. Thereby, working on a societal transformation trajectory to find solutions for Pakistan's burning issue of poverty and social injustice.

### *1.1 The story*

The concept materialised in 2001 with the first interest-free loan to a widow, who returned it after six months with a message to give it to someone needier than she initially was. Since that day, the core program of *Qard-e-Hasan* (benevolent loan) kept on expanding. As the demand for Akhuwat's products grew, Akhuwat adopted a dual-track approach to growth, one that is not driven by the need to maximise earnings but rather focuses on spreading the message of Mawakhat to as many people as possible within our resources. On one hand, Akhuwat continues to expand its operation in a traditional manner, by opening up new branches in different cities and towns across Pakistan. On the other hand, it invites others to replicate the Akhuwat model, with Akhuwat training the staff of other organisations and assisting them with the initial setup. These replications are urged to strive to become local successes through local support and resources. Akhuwat has now disbursed more than 500 billion rupees ($500 million) to over 2.3 million families around Pakistan through more than 600 branches in more than 300 cities. It plans to open more branches, as Akhuwat intends to further expand in areas where the poorest of the poor do not have access to credit and are therefore deprived of respectable livelihood. For the past 17 years, Akhuwat has not only consolidated its financial services but also ventured into the arena of health services and educational services.

This is our attempt to present Akhuwat through a different lens, i.e., a spiritual-integral lens, and establish it as one such model of integral finance emerging through the spirit of SOUL-idarity.

## 2 Section 1: the GENE-alogy of solidarity

Moving on from our previous chapter on *The Solidarity Impulse*, we will expand more on our solidarity GENE in this section through an Islamic-integral-Akhuwat perspective. This is aligned with our SOUL-idarity premise and the process it encompasses, which translates into Akhuwat's solidarity paradigm definitively.

This is to *root* ourselves in the philosophy and spirit of solidarity through its multiplier effect, i.e., the impulse, its impact and the advantage of solidarity, thereafter serving to illustrate how Akhuwat, as a community of donors, borrowers and volunteers, banks on this solidarity bond. This altogether turns the whole process into an integral rhythm of solidarity:

*Table II.1* Integral Solidarity Rhythm

| *Solidarity-GENE* | *Integral-GENE* | *SOUL-idarity Hikma* | *Integral Realms* |
|---|---|---|---|
| Impulse (Iman) | Emergence | Awakening (Ishq) | Sanctuary |
| Employ (Ikhlas) | Navigation | Conceptualisation (Ilm) | Academy |
| Bond (Ihsan) | Effect | Application (Amal) | Social Laboratory |
| Impact (Ikhuwah) | Grounding | Advantage (Akhuwat) | Community |

This section will take you into the deeper realms of Akhuwat's solidarity/ Mawakhat rhythm to then explore Akhuwat's fourfold solidarity paradigm, before we move on to explain how all of this is put into practice through Akhuwat's various initiatives.

## 3 Section 2: the four principles

> 'We did many things at *Akhuwat* that had not been previously done in the field of microfinance. We wanted a system that would be simple, straightforward and transparent. Instead of profit, altruism and volunteerism would prevail. None of us favour interest, but there is hardly anyone out there who opposes it systematically and also presents an alternate solution or system. We wanted to go beyond sermons and advice and into the thicket of the thorns of practice. For, if vehemence does not pick the plough, then it is a mere claim. If passion does not mould, it is merely a claim.'

Akhuwat is a beacon of hope, a virtuous cycle of caring for the society and sharing happiness with others – which in turn takes people out of isolation and engages them to think about others too. It binds them with a sense of ownership and solidarity within their particular societies.

*Could this be true for marginalised and disadvantaged communities anywhere in the world adopting the Akhuwat model of Mawakhat (solidarity)?*

*We will explore this further in Chapter 5, albeit in a Pakistani society's context – through a South-Eastern integral orientation as postulated by Lessem and Schieffer (ibid), whereby these communities are (still) holding on to their cultural and spiritual moral values occupying a central place in their socio-economic spheres, unlike other North-Western societies that consider such values as 'ancient' and 'primitive'.*

Incidentally, the *Akhuwat Philosophy* is based on the following four principles:

### *3.1 Qard-e-Hasan – interest-free loans*

Microfinance is the provision of capital in small amounts to those who do not offer physical capital as a security for the return of borrower capital. Conventional microfinance is the circulation of that capital in such a way that it earns a financial return for the lender. Islamic microfinance is a form of non-conventional microfinance that is in keeping with the principles of Islam, i.e., interest is not involved. Akhuwat is a practitioner of the latter and is based on the principle of Qard-e-Hasan, the provision of interest-free loans to those in need.

### *3.2 Mawakhat: compassion and social justice*

Akhuwat derives its name from 'Mawakhat' or brotherhood; the earliest illustration of it was seen in the network formed by the citizens of Medina and the Muhajiroun (or Meccans who had migrated to Medina to escape persecution). Inspired by the idea which induced the Medinites (Ansar) to share half of their wealth with outsiders, with the two groups declared brethren by Holy Prophet (peace be upon him), Akhuwat seeks to diffuse this brotherly spirit through its operations.

### *3.3 Central role of religious spaces*

For Muslims, the mosque occupies a central place in the social, political, and economic activities of the community. Most certainly, the mosque is first and foremost a place for remembering and worshipping the Almighty. The fact that Akhuwat has been able to achieve awe-inspiring success in meeting its goals is the natural consequence of the earnest application of its policy of abolishing *riba*,[1] honourably helping the poor, and giving the mosque a significant role in the implementation of its objectives, i.e., the loans are always disbursed from the premises of the mosque (the church in the case of Christians and temples for Hindu clients). The disbursement event symbolises the communal harmony which Akhuwat propagates, and is attended by both borrowers and guarantors, where they become members of the Akhuwat family and its torchbearers – the mosque is transformed into a centre of social and economic development.

### *3.4 Khidmet-e-khalq – role of volunteerism*

One very important contributor to the success of Akhuwat is volunteerism. According to Amjad Saqib, the founder and executive director of Akhuwat:

> 'We expect people to give their time and their abilities in the spirit of Khidmet-e-Khalq (community service); the spirit of the entire organisation is based on volunteerism. This is also derived from our faith, in which the principle of volunteerism is the most important part of our tradition. Every prophet is a volunteer, right from Abraham, Moses, Jesus and the Holy Prophet (PBUH). The Prophets always looked beyond themselves to help the community socially, morally, economically, and politically. We wanted to follow the footsteps of these great prophets and adopt their methods of bringing change to the community through participation".

This section of the book, thus, unfolds Akhuwat's multi-layered societal initiatives, taking a philosophical approach – applying the transcendental phenomenological methodology developed by Edmund Gustav Albrecht Husserl, a German

Philosopher, who established the school of phenomenology. For Husserl's 'intentionality' based the 'intent' of human consciousness being interconnected to all things around us. As such, through this method, we look at the 'essential qualities', or essence, of a phenomenon. In Akhuwat's case, we will delve deeper into its intentionality of 'Mawakhat/solidarity', which goes over and beyond the call of microfinance as the term is understood in the world.

For Akhuwat's call is much bigger than simply eradicating poverty from the society, as per my integral-spiritual postulation and the phenomenological intentionality of their fourfold principles as above. This will be further explored in Chapter 4 – thereafter presenting an integral Akhuwat (solidarity) model CARE-ing *(Community activation, raising Awareness, Research-to-innovation and Embodying action through transformative education)* for the Pakistani society, as developed by Lessem and Schieffer through their 4C *(Call, Context, Co-creation, Contribution)* to CARE-4-Society model for an integral development.

## References

Lessem, R., & Schieffer, A., 2013. *Integral Dynamics*. Abingdon: Routledge.

# 4 The GENE-alogy of Mawakhat/solidarity

## Integral solidarity rhythm through Akhuwat's 4 I's

### 1 Preamble

In the previous chapter, we set our solidarity impulse into motion, that which lies at the core of Akhuwat's Mawakhat philosophy. In our opening chapter we introduced a new assimilation of Hikma (wisdom) orientation borne out of Akhuwat's 4 I's: Iman, Ikhlas, Ihsan and Ikhuwah.

As has been previously communicated, this part of the book establishes the philosophical elements of Akhuwat's solidarity phenomenon. Therefore, this chapter aims to establish a link between Akhuwat's 4 I's in a GENE-alogical order of its solidarity impulse.

### 2 Introduction: the soul of solidarity spirit

In Pakistan, Amjad takes to the path of solidarity with 'passion' (Ishq), as he writes in his book *Akhuwat ka Safar* (A Journey of Hope), with these opening words:

> ***Ishq key Durdmund ka Tarz-e-Kalam aur hai***
> ***Distinct is the timbre of those tempered by love***
>
> I remember the furniture that was placed in *Akhuwat's* first office – it was at least two decades old. When I borrowed a ragged chair, sofa and table from home, doubts crept into my mother's eyes. 'You have left your job; now is this the chair you will sit on?' For her son to leave his high-raking civil service and do 'something unusual' was distressing. Gradually, that chair also seemed to take up too much space, as people found it hard to find a place to sit in that small room. Also, the chair represented indulgence and paramountcy, whilst *Akhuwat* was an aspirant for sacrifice and simplicity.
>
> When someone pointed out that work could go ahead just as well without the chair, the custom of sitting on the floor was adopted – floor mats, rugs, cushions and pillows were brought in. As the dilapidated state of lime walls painted a gloomy picture, we put up screens of reed to cover the walls.

In another part of the world, writes Eric Butterworth, a Canadian minister, author and presenter of universal spiritual ideas, in his book *The Universe is Calling*:

> The call of the universe is like the pull of the sun on the sunflower, which causes the blossoms to open up and face the sun continuously as it crosses the sky. It is the pull of life upward and outward on all growing things. It is the healing activity in which life is always biased on the side of health. “Many are called, but few are chosen”, said Jesus (Matt.22:14) This is not stating discrimination. It is the universe calling, and it is a continuum, innate in all persons. It is the call to come up higher, to take charge of your life, to release your imprisoned splendour. The universe is calling, but sadly, few persons respond with a commitment to make progressive changes in their lives
>
> (Butterworth, 1994).

*The year is 2018*: Whilst in Davos, Alibaba founder and Executive Chairman Jack Ma spoke openly and at length about some of the key challenges facing the world, delivering a stream of perspectives and guidance. Alibaba is a chinese multinational e-commerce, retail and internet, consumer-to-consumer, business-to-consumer and business-to-business sales services web portal.

According to Jack Ma;

> To gain success, a person will need high EQ (Emotional Quotient); if you don’t want to lose quickly you will need a high IQ (Intelligence Quotient), and if you want to be respected you need high LQ – the IQ of love.

Or as per Ronnie Lessem, co-founder of TRANS4M movement, that chosen one must be an ‘integrator’, a term coined by Lessem for 21st century social integrators and leaders:

> As such, we give rise to a new notion of ‘integrator’ in the twenty-first century. Such an integrator, emerges as a further evolution of personal entrepreneurship (or ‘intrapreneurship’) in the nineteenth century, management in the twentieth, and leadership, in the twenty-first, centuries. Moreover, such an *integrator*, in each particular part of the world, only becomes fully such, by virtue of such differentiation and *integration*, to the extent that he or she gives rise to a newly evolved form of enterprise . . . that arises out of both a personal *individuation*, that is self-actualization, and of societal *acculturation*, or organizational-and-cultural evolution (Lessem, 2016).

For that ‘chosen one’, taking Akhuwat’s founder, Amjad Saqib as an example, has to be an integrator of love (Ishq), harmony (Ikhuwah) and beauty (Ihsan) to borrow the words from the mystic saint and founder of the Inayati Sufi order, Hazrat Inayat Khan's opening invocation.

The need for us in the 21st century is for those leaders who can transcend the soul of solidarity amongst communities – for their timbre is distinct and tempered by divine love, as per Amjad's words above, and they must integrate this trait amongst whoever comes in contact with them.

*In Pakistan, I noticed this distinctive trait in Amjad and his Akhuwat colleagues. He is not only a pioneer of a social innovative enterprise, but also fits the definition of Lessem's social 'integrator'. In my personal experience of working with him, I found him an exemplar of such an integrator – full of compassion and love for his people. For who else would go around the community gathering funds for the needy ones? From a Sufi perspective, living a purposeful life for others trains the ego to be less demanding (of material wants and needs). Personally, I feel that asking for money from other people, not for your own personal needs but for others, tames and disciplines the ego-self. I experienced this whilst running a crowdfunding campaign for Akhuwat University's Buy-a-Brick; Build-a-University initiative, here in London in 2017. The whole experience was self-rewarding to say the least, as the sense of achievement it gave me is hard to articulate. In my personal experience working with disadvantaged communities and, to be part of a social movement for an altruistic purpose invokes a communal solidarity impulse, as was displayed by people living in the UK or around the world contributing to a cause/call which wasn't their own. For this is the splendour of 'SOUL-idarity' gene transmutation with a horizontal effect, as also noticed in Akhuwat's fourth principle of volunteerism – khidmet-e-khalq, an Urdu term which literally translated means service (khidmet) to community (khalq).*

*From a Sadarain* (Shirazi, 2010) *school of thought, khalq means creation, whereby certain attributes of the Creator are manifested in the creation (khalq). Furthermore, serving the community is premeditated as a divine call, or duty.*

We now explore the trans-migrational gene which runs as a common thread between communities of human-kind.

## *2.1 The common thread – continuum of the spirit of solidarity*

Over the centuries and across continents, the common thread of solidarity is what has kept us linked together in human bonds. A message of love-reverence from China with a call for self-sacrifice (compassion) from Pakistan, and the continuum of the 'spirit of solidarity' keeps recurring to sustain our planetary ecology.

*What does it mean to be in solidarity?*

Solidarity might be conceived and defined in various ways within various faiths, communities and societies, yet the common thread that runs through has the ultimate intent of sustenance – sustaining the Self, environment, planet, people and/or our existential purpose. For some it is ethical or spiritual – related to conscience and godliness – whilst for others it's *just* – humanistic and justifiable.

In recent times solidarity is an idea – a parlance, something to imitate, which defines itself in the course of realisation and which we must continuously redefine. It is not connected with any complete theory.

From a Christian viewpoint, the meaning is defined by Christ as 'Bear ye one another's burdens: and so, you shall fulfil the law of God' (paraphrase of Gal. 6:2).

It means to carry another's burden. No man is an island. We are united even when we do not know it. The landscape binds us, flesh and blood bind us, work and speech bind us. However, we are not always aware of these bonds and the common thread that is running through us.

It is, thus, our attempt to delve deeper into the spirit and phenomenon of solidarity through our understanding and conviction which comes through a deeper study of Akhuwat's Mawakhat-e-Medina phenomenon, eventuated more than 1400 years ago, in another time and space, yet its recursive iteration is visibly creating virtuous circles – that which we are calling barakah circles (rounds) as a progression of their 'virtuous circles'.

In Amjad's words, the multiplier effect of bhalai (beneficiation) is sequential and keeps multiplying with divine grace and barakah (divine bounty).

## *2.2 The solidarity eminence*

In his seminal work, *The Reconstruction of Religious Thought in Islam* (Iqbal, 2000), Iqbal asks us to remember that the universe we belong to is yet to be completed and perfected. It is neither a blocked nor a locked universe because according to Iqbal:

*'Every moment things are being ordered to "become" and they are becoming.'*

What this means, from an Iqbalian viewpoint, is that the process of creation is still going on. To him it is an organic world. He substantiates the process of recurrent creation and an ever-expanding universe by arguing from the Quran:

'*Every day is He (God Almighty) engaged in some new work.*'

Through his poetic expression, he further elucidates man's position in divine order by invoking a spirit of solidarity between man and God to shake him (the Muslim) off his callousness and take ownership of his place in the divine scheme of Being and thus Becoming.

For Iqbal, man (the Self) plays an important role in delivering God's work on earth:

> The spark within you contains the brightness of the world-illumining sun. A new universe flourishes in your skill. It does not behove you to accept Paradise in charity. Your Paradise lies hidden in your capacity to be engaged in blood-consuming exertions and foils. *O you, who are an embodiment of dust, look for the reward of incessant toil.*
>
> (Gabriel's Wing; published in Urdu, 1935).

This elucidates Iqbal's concept of 'khudi' (ego-self), the discipling of man's ego by striving to excel and claim his rightful ownership of Paradise by performing good deeds (amal) on Earth.

In the divine order of *Kun fa Yakun*, therein lies the eminence of solidarity reiteration between God and HIS creation.

'Kun fa Yakun' is a phrase repeated five times in the Quran. It symbolises God's creative power. It is about God's will and absolute control over all creation (khalq). 'Kun (كُنْ)' means 'be' or 'exist'.

'*When He decrees a thing, He says to it only: "Be!" And it is*' (Surah al-Baqarah 2:117).

Through this divine eminence, the solidarity effect, once transcended, manifests in human beings, consequently instilling a sense of compassion and responsibility for his/her earthly duties. Contrary to this, on the ethereal sphere, the spirit of solidarity (with HIS creation) keeps reiterating itself in a circular motion (the arc of descent and ascent) until it reaches perfection.

Iqbal, being a spiritual visionary and thinker, had a deep understanding of this phenomenon, hence, his poetic enunciate was rife with the provocation of man's perfect Self (khudi) and ego and the divine secrets it holds within.

Therefore, Iqbal invariably underlined this in his poetry and writings, in his concept of the perfect man (Sheikh, 1972); the self in man, his I–am-ness, has specifically earthly antecedents, yet sparkles with ambient divine attributes. Man alone has been described as the bearer of the Divine Trust which was granted to him by God and which the heavens and the Earth had earlier refused to accept.

*So, when I have made him (i.e., man) complete and breathed into him of my spirit... (Al-Quran: Verse 15:29).*

The verse really relates an incident of a man–God encounter as the surest mode of delivering faith (Iman) in the godhead of Allah to the primordial nature of man.

From an Iqbalian postulation then, matter is 'spirit in space-time reference'. It is

> a colony of egos of a low order out of which emerges the ego of a higher order. It is in this higher order that the spirit of Divine solidarity starts emanating in man to reciprocate the act on a physical (earthly) plane
> (Sheikh, 1972).

The above from a scientific standpoint is what Jeremy Lent (2017), founder of the Liology Institute in California, which integrates systems science with traditional wisdoms, has propounded upon in his new book. Per Lent, "as opposed to the Darwinian approach to evolution which was based on a one-way flow, there is a two-way evolutionary flow going on – a process known as gene-culture coevolution, which they call 'niche construction', thereby suggesting the culture has shaped the human niche so profoundly that it has caused changes in the human genome, affecting the very direction of human evolution".

Jozef Tischner (1984), an eminent Polish priest and philosopher and the first chaplain of the trade union 'Solidarity', maintained in his seminal work on 'The Spirit of Solidarity' that the virtue of solidarity is an expression of a person's goodwill. This virtue is born all by itself, spontaneously, from the heart (Ishq/love).

*And so we believe, the concurrence of this two-way flow, what we are terming the SOUL-idarity [the spirit of solidarity] corollary of the godly (spiritual) with man (material), is what sustains the solidarity equilibrium between communities.*

*Is there a cognitive process that prepares us to be aware of this sustainability cycle of solidarity between them?*

## 2.3 The virtues of solidarity dynamics in Islam

As observed in Akhuwat's case, and by virtue of its essence and nature of solidarity, this chapter thus traverses through four stages of the spirit of solidarity: *impulse, employ-ability, bond (silsilah) and effect*. In correspondence to this, we will also be prospectively illustrating attributes of Akhuwat's 4I GENE-alogy (Iman, Ikhlas, Ihsan and Ikhuwah) along with integral four realms of sanctuary, academy, laboratory and community (Lessem & Schieffer, 2013) as illustrated below (Table 4.1), of a threefold integral genealogy.

First, let us explore the 4 I's (or Alifs) of Akhuwat's genealogical order from an Islamic context, albeit Akhuwat being a non-religious and non-discriminatory organisation based on the humanistic values of Mawakhat (solidarity), which originated from Islamic philosophy and takes its inspiration from these fundamental (universal) Islamic tenets:

*Iman (Faith) – Impulse – Sanctuary*
*Ikhlas (Sincerity) – Employ – Academy*
*Ihsan (Excellence) – Bond – Laboratory*
*Ikhuwat (Solidarity) – Effect – Community*

In Islam, there are three levels of faith a person can attain: **Islam, Iman and Ihsan**.

The first level is Islam: Prophet Muhammad (pbuh) explained it as observing the five major ways of worship (ibadat) or duties (the adhering to which creates an Islamic structure, as these duties constitute the pillars of Islam).

The second level is Iman: By properly practising the five ways of worshipping, Muslims as individuals and as communities benefit from the rewards Allah has promised to them. Yet, there are some who are more ambitious to be closer to God, to gain a higher level of his rewards, and to enjoy more intellectual happiness, and they need to reach a higher level of faith than Islam, *which is Iman*, as we are told in verse 14 of Surah Al-'Hujurat of the Holy Quran:

The Arab said, 'We have believed'. Say: 'You have not believed', but say 'We have submitted', for faith has not yet entered your hearts (Al-'Hujurat, 49: 14).

For unless the faith enters the deeper recesses of one's heart, it is not completed or sanctioned by God. Incidentally, this is the stage of Ikhlas – Akhuwat's second I.

The third level is Ihsan: This is higher than both levels of faith, and the closest to God. It is to worship Allah as if you are seeing Him. While you do not see Him, He truly sees you, which relates to feeling God's presence everywhere. The word 'Ihsan' in Arabic is a derivative of the verb 'ahsana', which means doing things better. Thus, the literal linguistic meaning of Ihsan is doing the best, which is doing what God commanded us to do. Ihsan petitions us to feel responsible for others as God's viceregent (caliph) on Earth.

Figure 4.1 presents our solidarity emergence derived from the above three levels of faith, according to Islamic doctrine; this further branches out from two of the main criterions that perfect the religion (Islam) – **Iman** and **Ihsan** (two of our I's).

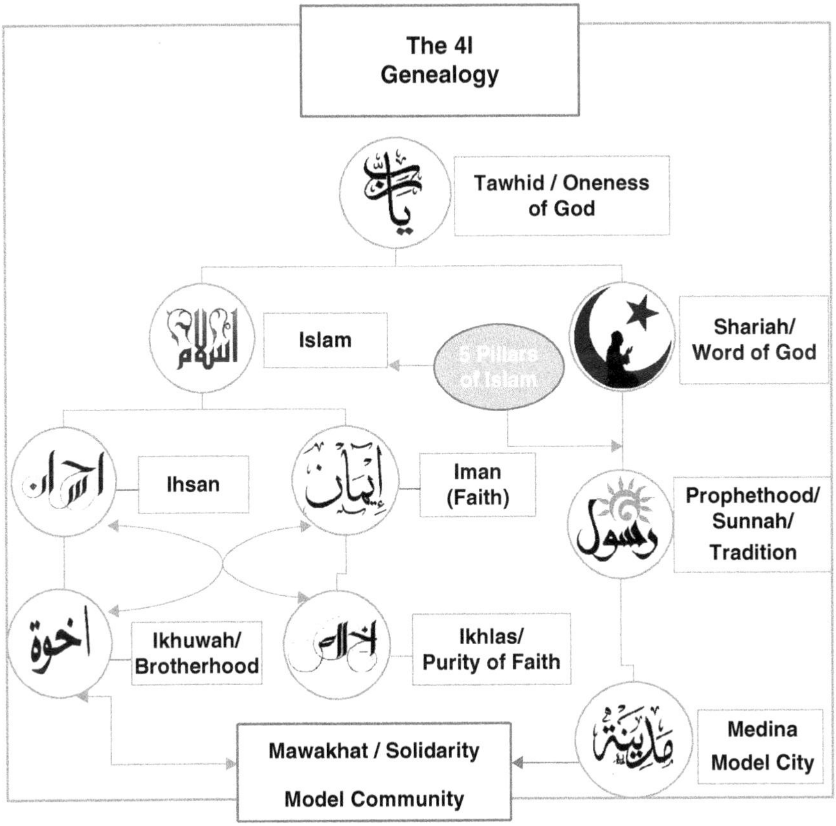


*Figure 4.1* Islamic 4I Genealogy

***Ikhlas** (Akhuwat's second I), stems from Iman*:

The person whose heart reaches an ideal degree or level of Iman – called a *Mu'min* – not only believes in divine destiny but also practises Iman through his/her own good deeds and actions. That belief is borne out of Ikhlas/purity of the heart and Iman/ shahada. Shahada is bearing witness by placing one's full faith in tawhid (Oneness of God) and the finality of Prophet Muhammad (may peace be upon him).

Consequently, Akhuwat's fourth I, **Ikhuwah** (Mawakhat /brotherhood), flows through all the aforementioned three I's, that is, *Belief in God's Unity/Iman, with the purity and sincerity (Ikhlas) of heart/intention, and doing good/spreading beauty around (Ihsan) for the wellbeing of community and society.*

The next section positions our 4I postulation, aligned with Akhuwat's four principles (utilising religious spaces, Qard-e-Hasan (interest-free loans), transforming borrowers into donors and regenerating the spirit of volunteerism) to elucidate our solidarity impulse in the light of these principles.

## *2.4 The 4 I's of Akhuwat paradigm*

We have thus contemplated the 4 I's rooted in Akhuwat's four principles – transpiring from the three levels of faith as above.

Akhuwat's four principles are:

- *Role of Religious Spaces – Iman – Faith: being a higher degree of Islam, Iman covers all faiths on a non-discriminatory basis as per Akhuwat's policy of non-discrimination by religion, race, class and gender.*
- *Interest-Free Loans (Qard-e-Hasan) – Ikhlas – Sincerity: a derivative of tawhid (Oneness of God).*
- *Transforming Borrowers into Donors – Ihsan – (spreading) Excellence: the multiplier effect of virtue/barakah, further forming a solidarity bond amongst the community of Akhuwateers.*
- *Volunteerism – Ikhuwah – Brotherhood: the eventual effect of the solidarity GENE rhythm – transforming the spirit of solidarity into SOUL-idarity.*

This contemplation came after delving deeper into the heart and soul of Akhuwat and after many interactions with Amjad. As reflected in Akhuwat's philosophy and conceptualised by Amjad, who along with being a true devotee of Prophet of Islam (peace be upon him) is also an ardent disciple of Iqbal's philosophy of ummah (community) and brotherhood.

Iqbal (2000) was a firm believer in religion, without which the social system cannot work properly. This was the reason he focussed his efforts on the revival of Islam and the protection of Islamic society. He believed Islam to be the most valuable contribution to world thought. For him, Islamic society has a permanent element in its structure of thought, such as the unity of God, the finality of prophethood, the Shariah (scripture/text), the Islamic code of law and Ikhuwah.

For Iqbal, the stable character of a society directly depends upon the essential regard for the ultimate realities that govern life. Iqbal defined tawhid (oneness), risalah (prophethood), and Akhuwat (brotherhood) as the foundational and basic principles of ummah (Muslim community). According to him, if a community deviates from any of these principles, it will deviate from the actual goals.

In a relative manner, Iqbal's characterisation of a perfect ummah reinforces our 4I positioning as per Akhuwat's solidarity philosophy. The love and sacrifice of the Ansar of Medina for the Muhajiroun from Mecca are the proverbial instances of brotherhood (Ikhuwah) in human history to encourage a genuine brotherhood.

As emphasised in the Quran and underlined by Iqbal in his poetic expositions, one cannot be a Mu'min unless he/she likes for the brother that which he/she likes for himself. The integrity of the ummah has been compared to a human body: the entire Muslim society is considered as one body and if any one part becomes diseased the other parts shall feel the agony.

We now turn to our own postulation of an integral GENE-alogical order of solidarity and as we go, it is important to recall the 4 R's of integral development first.

## *2.5 The integral development model: the 4 R's of integral development*

The four main elements of the integral development (Lessem & Schieffer, 2013) approach, drawn from Lessem & Schieffer's overall 'integral worlds', are what they called the 4 R's: **Realities, Realms, Rounds and Rhythms**. These four constituents are dynamically and interactively interwoven to bring the desired transformational development of any Self (individual), organisation (management), community (local) and society (global).

### *2.5.1 Transcultural realms*

Integral development acknowledges diverse reality viewpoints within each context and across the world. It captures this diversity by differentiating and integrating four archetypal worldviews or realities, related in turn to an Inter-Institutional Genealogy (Lessem & Schieffer, 2013):

- **Southern** - *Relationship*-based Viewpoint on Reality - Community
- **Eastern** - *Inspiration*-based Viewpoint on Reality - Sanctuary
- **Northern** - *Knowledge*-based Viewpoint on Reality - Academy
- **Western** - *Action*-based Viewpoint on Reality - Laboratory

Altogether these realities relate to a rich variety of typological and structural patterns across civilisations.

### 2.5.2 Transdisciplinary realms

Each reality viewpoint has a different emphasis, which leads to four different knowledge fields or **realms**, each providing a particular perspective. Any given development calling and challenge requires the transdisciplinary engagement with all realms:

- *Southern Realm of Relationship*: **Nature & Community** (Ikhuwah)
- *Eastern Realm of Inspiration*: **Culture & Spirituality** (Iman)
- *Northern Realm of Knowledge*: **Science, Systems & Technology** (Ikhlas)
- *Western Realm of Action*:**Enterprise & Economics** (Ihsan)

### 2.5.3 From genealogy to institutional genealogy

For Lessem & Schieffer (2013), in order to particularise the identity of specific groups of people in the institutional genealogical case, innovation-driven institutional research is aligned with Community, Sanctuary, Academy, and Laboratory, connecting and renewing oral, scriptural, textual and digital forms. Such interactive linkages lead to states that release GENE-IUS (of a society) and recognise GENE-alogy; problems are thereby tackled genealogically, going back to the roots, incorporating as such the universal future of the particular past. This lies at the heart of their functional, dynamic CARE and structural, stabilising CARE.

Table 4.1 demonstrates a threefold GENE-alogy of spiritual-integral solidarity rhythm with a focus on CARE-ing-4-society through four stages of transformational development through Self (Iman), organisation (Ikhlas), community (Ikhuwah) and society (Ihsan).

We now take you on to our journey of a solidarity round which starts its reiteration with the impulse of Mawakhat in the *Eastern Realm of Culture and Spirituality* and takes full effect in the *Southern Realm of Community*.

## 3 The emergence of solidarity impulse – Iman

Per Amjad, solidarity (Ikhuwah) is a derivative of Iman (faith).

Prayer, for him, is a form of love too, as it is surrendering one's will to Allah and HIS Rasool's will. He strongly believes that the power of prayers coming from an indigent heart could move the earth beyond. He usually places the credit of Akhuwat's success as coming from the prayers of these indigent hearts and of course, from his ancestors. Another widespread cultural tradition and belief practised and acknowledged in the land of the pure, Pakistan.

Thus, he writes, in his book *Akhuwat ka Safar*;

*In the calendar of ishq (love) and impassioned ardour, there are many ages other than the prevailing one* – which refers to the life hereafter.

For him, it was the love of Allah and his profound love and reverence for the Prophet (may peace be upon him) that transcended into love and compassion for the people of his land, which made him travel beyond the age he is living in.

*Table 4.1* GENE-alogy of Spiritual-Integral Solidarity Rhythm

| *INTEGRAL REALM* | *CARE ROUND* | *SOLIDARITY RHYTHM* |
|---|---|---|
| **Eastern**<br>**Culture & Spirituality**<br>Theme: Regenerating Meaning via Culture and Spirituality<br>Core Value: Balanced & Peaceful Co-Evolution | **Sanctuary: Awakening**<br>**Awakening Integral Consciousness**<br>Main Focus: Societal Learning and Consciousness Raising<br>Key Terms: Catalysation, Consciousness, Conscientisation | **Iman**<br>Emergence<br>**Heart Dimension/Ishq**<br>Theme: Invoking Solidarity Impulse<br>Relation with Self & Society<br>Sensory/Feelings |
| **Northern**<br>**Science, Systems & Technology**<br>Theme: Reframing Knowledge via Science, Systems and Technology<br>Core Value: Open & Transparent Knowledge Creation | **Research Academy: Liberating**<br>**Innovation driven, institutionalised Research**<br>Main Focus: Scholarship, Research and Knowledge Creation<br>Key Terms: Content, Concepts, Complexity | **Ikhlas**<br>Realisation<br>**Aql (intellect) Knowledge Dimension/Ilm**<br>Theme: Engaging Solidarity<br>Husn-e-Ikhlaq (Compliance)<br>Purity of Soul/Cognisance |
| **Western**<br>**Enterprise & Economics**<br>Theme: Rebuilding Infrastructure and Institutions via Enterprise and Economics<br>Core Value: Equitable & Sustainable Livelihoods | **Social Laboratory: Democratising**<br>**Embodying Integral Development**<br>Main Focus: Capacity Building and Individual Realisation<br>Key Terms: Capacity, Co-Creation, Contribution | **Ihsan**<br>Application<br>**Amal (Action)Dimension**<br>Theme: Solidarity Bond<br>Husn-e-Suluk (Noble)<br>Associative/Cooperative Virtuous Circles |
| **Southern**<br>**Nature & Community**<br>Theme: Restoring Life in Nature and Community<br>Core Value: Healthy & Participatory Co-Existence | **Community: Healing**<br>**Community activation**<br>Main Focus: Community-based Learning and Development<br>Key Terms: Context, Community, Care | **Ikhuwah**<br>*Manifestation*<br>**Mawakhat(Kinship) Dimension**<br>Theme: Solidarity Effect<br>Bhai-chara (Communal)<br>Developmental/ Transformational |

We thus start by rooting ourselves in the 'heart' dimension of 'Solidarity with Self'. For we believe, this is where the impulse of solidarity is invoked and roots itself, i.e., starting with the existential relationship of self with the universe and the Divine.

Islamic scholars have defined Iman as 'to believe with one's heart (grounding), to confess with one's tongue (emergence) and to demonstrate in one's physical actions (effect)'.

In the opening chapter, we postulated the idea of communities being organisms pulsating with an impulse for a communal renewal and survival. This impulse; Transformational GENE, in integral terminology, is at the heart (centre) of every community – for it to take effect on a societal level, it vanquishes through an individual. That which we call the Iman (faith) impulse.

The following extract from Iqbal's second lecture elucidates this point:

> It (the universe) is present in its nature as an open possibility. It is time regarded as an organic whole that the Qur'an describes as *taqdir*, or destiny – a word which had been so much misunderstood both in and outside the world of Islam. Destiny is time regarded as prior to the disclosure of its possibilities.
>
> (Iqbal, 2000)

Now, as communicated above and suggested by Eric Butterworth, only a 'few chosen ones', such as Iqbal's perfect man (mu'min), amongst the community are attuned to this impulse pulsating at the centre. As observed in Akhuwat and Amjad's case, in a particular Pakistani, Islamic country's context, this 'chosen one', being aware of the process, has to be an awakened being with this realisation which comes directly from faith/Iman.

Now Iman, being a higher state of Islam, opens the heart dimension to receive a deeper understanding, the source of which is divine. It is with this awareness that I position Iman in the Impulse block, which is also the realm of Ishq (universal love).

According to Brené Brown (2017), a research professor at the University of Houston, human connection is the spirit that flows between us. She writes in her new book that when our belief that there's something greater than us, something rooted in love and compassion, breaks, we are more likely to retreat to our bunkers and disassociate ourselves from our human reality. This interrupts society's equilibrium, resulting in a spiritual crisis, thus, eventuating a societal (alkimiya) chemical imbalance.

*And thus, we suggest that this solidarity impulse is a result of our human connection with each other, without which the society becomes bereft of its soul and impulse to sustain. Veritably, the spirit of this impulse is love and compassion between our fellow-beings, which connects and binds us all together, and this transpires after the Iman (faith) transcendence in Self, in an Islamic and Akhuwatistic way.*

### *3.1 Solidarity eminence: Ishq*

#### *3.1.1 Akhuwat's 1st principle – engagement of religious spaces – sanctuary*

In his book *Ahuwat ka Safar* (Journey of Hope), Amjad writes about his reverence for Sufi mystics of Punjab, in this instance, the shrine of Ali Hujwiri in Lahore:

> *Akhuwat's* third branch was established at the esteemed mosque/tomb of Hazrat Ali al-Hujwiri (c. 1009-1072/77), a renowned Sufi saint, aka Data Ganj Baksh in Punjab. He was also the author of Kashf al Mahjoob (Unveiling of the hidden), which is one of the most ancient and revered Persian treatises on Sufism, as it contains a complete system of Sufism with its doctrines and practices.
>
> This was the site where the most venerated mystics of South Asia resided: the likes of Nizamuddin Aulia, Qutbuddin Bakhtiar, Khwaja Muinuddin Chishti, and Fariduddin Masood Ganjbaksh. It is here they retreated for penance and spiritual solitude and beseeched their Lord. This was the third stop of *Akhuwat's* caravan in 2005. Under the tomb in the hall, there is a large room. We attained this room. When the auqaf (religious affairs) Secretary Javed Iqbal Awan presented the key to this room, my eyes began to dampen in gratitude. After some time, he handed three more keys – those of the mosques/tombs of all of the most revered Sufi saints of Punjab: Baba Shah Jamal, Hazrat Mian Mir, and Madhulal Hassan. I asked him the reason for his generosity. '*Such is the nature of solidarity*', he replied. '*For as long as you evoke this sentiment, I will continue to comply with whatever you say.*'
>
> People also call the shrine of *Data* Ganj Baksh '*Data Darbar*' – the court of faith.

For Amjad and Akhuwat, having Akhuwat's offices and disbursement ceremonies in places of worship hold a significant resonance to divine blessings in the form of these mystics being present at their mausoleums. As believed in the Sufi traditions, the soul of a Wali-Allah (Friend of God) is ever-present at the resting place and is a source of a interconnection between God and the devotees.

The next phase, then, is the phase of practising Ikhlas (sincerity) with faith (Iman).

## 4 Employing solidarity with Ikhlas

From God-radiance of solidarity to the purity of human action and intention, our solidarity impulse now enters into the realm of realisation, i.e., employing the knowledge of intangible (impulse/ethereal) to tangible (corporeal).

There is a story about some travellers who passed through a dark tunnel during their journey. It was pitch dark at that time of night, and wherever they stepped, the sharp stones and gravel scattered all over the path pierced their feet. They could have just carried on, but the thought of those who would come after them and encounter the stones halted them. Some of them started picking up the stones to clear the path as they went along. The tunnel ended, and they came out into the brightness. As they were about to throw away the stones they had gathered, they realised that what they had picked up were no ordinary stones but diamonds and pearls.

*'Those who had picked up the most were the happiest; those who had picked up fewer, less so. Those who had not picked up any were the most rueful.'*

This world is no different. There are those who see the stones of sorrow and desolation around them and start gathering them, oblivious to the fact that on the Day of Judgment, these very stones will turn into diamonds and gems.

On the Day of Turmoil, a voice will be raised. The people who removed the pain of My people; today, on this day, I will take their pain away.

This story reminded me of the many gems and diamonds within Akhuwat's cadre. These gems and diamonds are the nameless volunteers of Akhuwat. There is no medal adorning their chests, no story commemorating them, no book lauding them. Morning and evening, day and night, oblivious to the harshness of the weather, they remain riveted to their work. Work is no less than worship for them. They care not for fame or name; their zeal, hard work and loyalty all belong to another realm.

The story above relays this in an intricate and indistinctive way, i.e., in a metaphysical (Sufistic) way. For the Sufi heritage is suffused with metaphorical parables along with the Punjabi culture of dastangoi (storytelling). Often these tales full of allegorical folklore are a source of local wisdom traditions of the Punjab province. These stories have been transmitted from one generation to the next as a sacred legacy.

### *4.1 Intention of sincerity (Ikhlas)*

Islam places a lot of importance on a personal intention (niyya), for the vital element that gives importance to a person's action is his intention, motive or objective. In Quranic verses, the phrase 'in the way of Allah' (fisabilillah) is often used (seventy times), thus, a warning for people to ensure that their actions and intentions are in the way of God, and not for the sake of other than God or their own carnal desires.

This is where Ikhlas (purity/sincerity) steps in. This is the stage where the impulse (metaphysical) engages with the physical (material world). In integral terms (Lessem, 2017), our Eastern reality (realm of inspiration) of faith (Iman) advances towards the Northern reality (realm of knowledge) of Ikhlas (purity).

Prophet Muhammad (peace be upon him) said: 'Certainly there is a reality of every truth and a servant cannot reach the reality of Ikhlas unless he doesn't like people to praise him for the actions he has done (only) for the sake of God' (Al-Majlisi, Bihar al-Anwar, vol. 72, p.304, hadith # 51).

And this is how we could best employ the spirit of Ikhlas in the case of Akhuwat's camaraderie of volunteers, from its board members to a community of volunteers who have been serving the cause (philosophy) selflessly for 17 years now. The Quran refers to their cadre as ***mukhliseen***; "*Mukhlisun* are those who worship God in such a way that they don't see themselves in service nor do they take notice of the world or its people, Thus they and their actions totally belong to Lord.

The great gnostic al-Shaykh al-Muhaqqiq Muhyi al-Din Ibn al-Arabi (c 1165–1240), an Arab mystic, philosopher, poet, sage, and one of the world's great spiritual teachers, has also stressed purity of intention to the highest degree as ordained in the Quran: Lo, to God belongs sincere allegiance (al-din al-khalis) (39:3).

Shaykh Ibn al-Arabi deciphers the message as such: 'Lo, to God belongs sincere allegiance, free from the taints of otherness and egoism. And that your extinction in Him should be total, the Essence; the Attributes, the Acts and the din should cease to be relevant for you. Lo, until the allegiance is not purified by reality, it will not belong to God'.

The Quranic Surah Al-Ikhlas, usually translated as the surah of purity, fidelity, or sincerity, holds a very special place in the metaphysics of Ibn al-Arabi. It is also known as the Surah al-Tawhid (Oneness), referring to the absolute unity of God, and was related when Muhammad (peace be upon him) was asked by the polytheists to explain the lineage of his Lord.

*Metaphysically and according to Sufi traditions, the first step in the journey towards God is the abandonment of self-love and crushing the head of egoism by submitting one's self to the service of fellow humankind, i.e., employing solidarity in whatever one does. To the extent that one succeeds in purging his or her heart of self-love, the love of God shall enter it to the same extent and it shall also be purified of latent shirk (egoism).*

*Thus, we have placed Akhuwat's second principle of reciprocal endowment (transforming borrowers into donors) in the Ikhlas bracket.*

### *4.2 Solidarity of sincerity – Ilm*

*Akhuwat and Amjad employ this sincerity (Ikhlas) by employing mukhliseen – people who employ the same degree of selflessness to stretch it diagonally: from Self to organisational employability of purity of intention. And this does not only apply to Akhuwat's volunteers but also to its 3,500 employees. I remember having a dialogue with Akhuwat's CFO, Shahzad Akram, whose modesty and genteelness has always inspired me. Shahzad comes from the first crop of Akhuwat office-bearers who joined the ranks as 'just an employee' until the spirit of solidarity (Mawakhat) befell him. In Shahzad's words (unbeknownst of Akhuwat's spirit and philosophy), listening to stories of the destitution and indigence of people opened up a heart dimension which, according to his professional disposition, transcended to surprise, a revelation to him. For him, that was the turning point – of employing solidarity in his work. Fourteen years on, there has been no turning back for him. He has found 'meaning' and purpose in his work, knowing Akhuwat and its community need his sincerity (Ikhlas) to fulfil its purpose.*

### *4.2.1 Akhuwat's 2nd principle – Mawakhat: reciprocal endowment – academy*

Waqf – endowment – is an Arabic word which epistemologically means to set aside. In Urdu, it also means to nominate or assign for a cause or purpose. The one who looks over a waqf is known as a mut'wali, a carer or a trustee, as of an estate – a viceregent. He is someone people have full faith and trust in because of his sincerity (Ikhlas) and because he is mukhalis (one who practices Ikhlas) with the cause.

*Reading through Amjad's words and compassionate dream, it is but obvious that he's assigned (waqf) his life for a cause which he holds very dear, and this is also spread to others via Akhuwat's many initiatives, above and beyond its board members, Akhuwat employees, volunteers and community of borrowers.*

Historically, from an Islamic perspective, waqf is used to indicate an endowment fund. Waqf, or 'endowment', is a long-standing Islamic tradition. As such it refers to the dedication of valuable goods or assests, e.g., land, a building, or even money which longer belongs to anybody and cannot be bought or sold. The profits which are then generated from this endowment are given away for the welfare of the society. Mosques are such buildings that come under this provision.

> When Umar ibn al Khattab acquired a piece of land and asked the Prophet, peace be upon him, how best to use it, the Prophet advised him to establish it as a waqf: 'make the land inalienable (unable to be sold or given away) and give its profit away as charity'. The harvest and profits of this land were then donated to the poor, travellers through the land and others who were in need. Over the centuries, this tradition was continued – land and buildings have frequently been given as waqf, and used to build schools, hospitals and mosques, amongst other functions to benefit the community.
>
> (Anon., n.d.)

With reference to Akhuwat as an organisation, in keeping with the Islamic tradition, it is established as a waqf, a trust, and not as a charity and certainly not as a microfinance organisation. Although it is delivering more than intended from a waqf, as is recounted here through our contemplation of solidarity impulsive effect, its second principle is a testament to this Islamic tradition.

The MDP (members donation program) was introduced when a successful borrower asked for ways in which to contribute to the organisation that was responsible for his upliftment. His spirit and tenacity struck the staff of Akhuwat as an exemplary realisation of the culture (Mawakhat) which it had been trying to promote. The board immediately decided to set up a fund that borrowers could contribute to, with the explicit instruction that donations would NOT be compulsory.

In doing so, the whole philosophy of Akhuwat's Mawakhat paradigm is conceptualised by their community of borrowers – by employing their communal spirit of solidarity, they have become an integral part of Akhuwat's community of micro-entrepreneurs making an impact on Pakistan's economy, however micro it may be at this time. We believe this impact is gaining eminence, as is apparent through Akhuwat's 26 replicator organisations.

Our solidarity compass is now pointing towards the next stage of Ikhlas (purity), which is Ihsan – spreading excellence on Earth.

## 5 The solidarity bond of Ihsan

Moving forward with Amjad's sentiment, 'Love is the beginning of this journey and beauty its quest', let us decode *Ihsan* and its vertical effect.

> Everything in this universe is marked by a sense of restlessness – the stars, the stones, the trees and man; all are in motion. Love is the beginning of this journey and beauty its quest. Those who live by this rule are the ones who succeed; those who are indifferent remain at a loss.
>
> Akhuwat's greatest accomplishment is that it pieced together the frayed promise of hope. It strove, and repeatedly succeeded, to give many the confidence that they are not alone. Amidst the inclemency of life, it endeavoured to affirm that there are those who extend their hands and open their hearts.
>
> How many people are plagued by poverty? In order to combat poverty, it is important to be aware of statistics. However, the stark reality of poverty, in all its wretchedness, often renders these figures insignificant. The fact is that as long as even one person remains impoverished, we are all poor. Regardless of how many flames of joy have been lit, how many havens of contentment have been built, even if one among us suffers, we cannot sleep in peace. As long as even one neighbour of ours remains hungry, one home is deprived of a hot meal, one child is out of school, one ailing citizen is unable to afford medicine, we cannot claim to have conquered despondency.

Ihsan, an Arabic term, means 'perfection' or 'excellence' (root word husn). It is a matter of taking one's inner faith (Iman) and showing it in both deeds and action (amal), a sense of social responsibility borne of religious convictions.

Some of Ihsan's many attributes are:

- *Attaining perfection or excellence*
- *Performance of righteous deeds on Earth*
- *Doing good to people to benefit them*
- *Advocating for the oppressed and vulnerable*

A few of my favourite verses from the Quran are:

So, give good tidings to My servants, those who listen to the saying and follow the fairest of it. They are those whom God has guided, and they are those who have intuition (Quran 39:17–18).

The people who are the fairest and extend *good tidings* are termed as *muhsineen* [those who do good (to others)]; who spend (benevolently) in the cause of Allah (2:195) in favourable as well as in adverse circumstances; who divert and sublimate their anger and potentially virulent emotions to creative energy and become a source of tranquillity and comfort to people; who sleep but little at night (reflecting on His Commands and on ways to implement His Commands) and heartily seek to be guarded against imperfections (51:16–18).

## *5.1 The bond (silsilah) of solidarity – amal*

### *5.1.1 Akhuwat's 3rd principle – Qard-e-Hasan (interest-free loans) – laboratory*

These are the people who carry the beauty of their inner faith (Iman) to further God's love for HIS creation, binding it into a chain (silsilah) of solidarity. For after the stages of inner faith, which invokes Ishq/love for creation and embodying pure intention (Ikhlas), the third stage is to practically disperse its effect (Ihsan) Earth-wide (horizontally).

Subsequently for Akhuwat, as a result of the solidarity impulse unravelling, the call for sustainability beckoned. The benevolent of the society became its *muhsineen*. In the wake, the spirit of Qard-e-Hasan (benevolent loan) was revived. Thus, rather than depending on a charity bond, a *solidarity bond* was created, its sustainability solely dependent on societal Ihsan (benevolence) and Mawakhat (solidarity). Those who 'have' and can share, look after those who cannot – the have-nots of the society.

*In Amjad's book of Ihsan, this process is what he calls creating 'virtuous circles' impeding the effects of the 'vicious cycle' of despondency.*

A charity bond, as per Big Society Capital's definition, is an independent financial institution with a social mission, set up to help grow social investment in the UK; it is a tradable loan between a charity or social enterprise and a group of social investors.

> It offers investors a fixed rate of interest. In return the charity borrows the investor's money for a fixed period of time. The charities issuing the bond also commit to report on the social impact created through their work to investors. For investors wishing to incorporate their social or ethical goals within their investment portfolios, Charity Bonds are often a preferred method for investment because they are simple, transparent and recognisable (Charity Bonds, n.d.)

A *solidarity bond*, on the other hand, has no investors or stakeholders, rather *muhsineen* (those who embody Ihsan) and *mukhliseen* (those who observe Ikhlas). The borrower has no obligation to pay them any fixed interest on their investment; rather they become part of a virtuous circle which is ever-evolving and pays back by way of Mawakhat (brotherhood).

As time stands witness, Akhuwat has transformed this idealistic concept into reality. For in its 17 years of existence and from a personal contribution of $100, Akhuwat now stands at $500 million in its loan circulation. All this through banking on the benevolence of society members for no ROI (return on investment).

Thus far, this pool of abundance is spinning ever more – churning out spiritual investment rather than social investment, as the collective intent is to gain Allah's compliance, communal wellbeing and societal welfare.

We now arrive at the last stage of the solidarity impulse manifesting in the community by passing through the above prescribed stages of Iman, Ikhlas and Ihsan to finally reach the Akhuwat (Ikhuwah) effect or expansion.

## 6 The Akhuwat/solidarity effect – Ikhuwah

As Amjad puts it:

> Akhuwat is a dream of the times to come that is envisioned by truly the ardent ones. Great dreams, after all, always gleam in the eyes of passionate souls. It is not the dominion of the highly intellectuals. Whenever there is the mention of a great dream, I remember Allama Muhammed Iqbal and Mohammed Ali Jinnah's dream of Pakistan – and I remember Sir Syed Ahmad Khan's dream of Aligarh University in India.
>
> I also dreamt of Akhuwat, as a social movement that could end man-made caustic divide between the haves and the have-nots of the society. A society where everyone can live by their own realities. This dream has become the first phase of the first destination of love, the beginning of the arduous paths of passion and compassion (Ihsan) – the desire to return to people the respect taken away from them, and a struggle to revive their self-honour. Akhuwat, veritably, is a common man's legacy.

*As we are concluding our solidarity eminence – we started our journey from (holistic) East/Iman (faith), navigating through Ikhlas (purity) awareness and transferring the solidarity effect into a solidarity bond (silsilah) – we have now arrived at the final stage of transforming (grounding) it into communal solidarity, Mawakhat. Where (God) eminence – the solidarity impulse – permeates (God) presence, that which we are calling the Hikma of SOUL-idarity (Chapter 1). The soul of solidarity; the presence of divine illumination within us.*

We intend to establish the interrelation between eminence and presence through Suhrawardi's Illuminationist epistemology of Philosophy of Illumination, which revolves around his theory of 'presential' (huduri) knowledge that one is able to achieve through intuitive apprehension or contemplative vision (mushahada). Shihab al-Din al-Suhrawardi (1154–1191) became the founder of an Illuminationist (ishraqi) philosophical tradition in the Islamic East.

In Suhrawardi's 'science of lights', the object of perception – light – cannot be known discursively, but only through an immediate presence or awareness of its luminosity. For Suhrawardi, intuitive knowledge thus constitutes a superior means of accessing the luminous reality and the divine realm of metaphysical truths.

> The vertical hierarchy of lights interacts with a horizontal hierarchy of lights. Out of the interaction of the vertical and the horizontal lights, the bodies of the lower world are generated. These horizontal or vertical lights are all structurally interrelated through the principle of love that the lower lights have for the higher lights and the principle of domination that the higher lights have over the lower ones. The two-dimensional hierarchy of lights introduces a new non-linear notion of metaphysical causation.
>
> For Suhrawardi, true vision does not require the presence and transmission of forms but occurs through the soul's ability to be aware of the essential light-reality of the object. Physics and metaphysics thus merge, as objects have the ability to receive and emit light, though only in an accidental manner, light being precisely what the light-soul, the Isfahbad-light, is able to perceive, whether it be through the senses, the intellect, intuition, or dreams
>
> (Marcotte, 2016).

This sets Akhuwat's fourth principle: regenerating the spirit of volunteerism – a solidarity bond of Mawakhat through brotherhood.

## *6.1 Eminence in presence – the solidarity effect*

### *6.1.1 Akhuwat's 4th principle – regenerating the spirit of volunteerism – community*

Thus, the spirit of solidarity manifests in a communal spirit of volunteerism (khidmet-e-khalq) in the final stage of our solidarity impulse iteration through Akhuwat's community of donors, borrowers, volunteers and its replicators. Akhuwat is fortunate to entertain a regiment of volunteers who willingly designate their time and services for Akhuwat's many operations, from helping at loan disbursement ceremonies to volunteering at Akhuwat's schools and colleges. This also includes internship with Akhuwat's internal research to offer their skills for its communication and media purposes.

As of now, 21,000 people have volunteered with Akhuwat Foundation – another mulitiplier-effect of the solidarity effect.

## 7 Conclusion

Conclusively, and for the ease of our readers, what we are establishing here is a link between the solidarity impulse and impact orientation – Eminence to Presence, through Suhrawardi's postulation of the 'Philosophy of Illumination', i.e., two-dimensional hierarchy of light (presence and transmission). We will expand on this further in our final chapter (Chapter 9).

Furthermore, this is supported by Iqbal's definition of brotherhood through tawhid (Oneness), risalah (prophethood), and Akhuwat (brotherhood) as the foundational and basic principles of ummah (Muslim community).

All this in the light of Islam's basic principles of faith: Islam, Iman and Ihsan, following through Akhuwat's 4I GENE-alogy positing an integral GENE rhythm dynamic.

This emerges as an awareness, in the case of Akhuwat and Amjad, from an intuitive heart through emanation (Iman in our case) – East dominant, and remains present (effect) – West dominant, in the form of a soul consciousness – North dominant, thus homogenising a solidarity impact – South dominant. The whole GENE iteration is recursive, through Self/individual (Amjad), to orgnaisational (Akhuwat), community (Akhuwat's employees, borrowers and volunteers) and society (Akhuwat's donors-base, replicators etc.).

The next chapter, whilst elaborating on Akhuwat's fourfold principles philosophically, completes Part II of the book, supported with integral CARE function through a spiritual-integral lens, before we move on to the next part (Round III), which showcases Akhuwat's solidarity paradigm (Mawakhat) in a practical way, as observed through Akhuwat's various initiatives.

## Note

1 Usury

## Bibliography

Anon., n.d. *Charity Bonds*. Available at: https://www.bigsocietycapital.com/about-us/previous-projects/charity-bonds

Anon., n.d. *Waqf*. Available at: https://www.islamic-relief.org.uk/resources/charity-in-islam/waqf/ [Accessed 2018].

Brown, B., 2017. *Braving the Wilderness: The Quest for True Belonging and the Courage to Stand Alone*. New York: Random House.
Butterworth, E., 1994. *The Universe is Calling: Opening to the Divine Through Prayer*. New York: Harper Collins.
Iqbal, M. (2000). Reconstruction of Religious. Lahore: Sang-e-Meel Publications.
Lent, J., 2017. *The Patterning Instinct: A Cultural History of Humanity's Search for Meaning*. New York: Prometheus Books.
Lessem, R., 2016. *The Integrators: The Next Evolution in Leadership, Knowledge and Value Creation (Routledge Focus)*. 1st ed. Abingdon: Routledge.
Lessem, R., 2017. *Awakening Integral Consciousness: A Developmental Perspective (Transformation and Innovation)*. Abingdon: Routledge.
Lessem, R., & Schieffer, A., 2013. *Integral Dynamics*. Abingdon: Routledge.
Marcotte, R., Fall 2016 Edition. *Suhrawardi*. Available at: https://plato.stanford.edu/entries/suhrawardi/
McNeely, I. F., & Wolverton, L., 2009. *Reinventing Knowledge: From Alexandria to the Internet*. New York and London: W. W. Norton & Company.
Sheikh, M. S., 1972. *Art, Studies in Iqbal's Thought and Art*. Lahore: Bazm-i-Iqbal.
Shirazi, M. S., 2010. *Divine Manifestations: Concerning the Secrets of the Perfecting Sciences*. London: Islamic College for Advanced Studies Publications; UK ed.
Tischner, J., 1984. *The Spirit of Solidarity*. New York: Harper & Row.

# 5 Akhuwat CARE-ing 4 Pakistan

## 1 Preamble

In the previous chapter, our solidarity impulse (emanation) completed its full effect, that which lies at the core of Akhuwat's Mawakhat (brotherhood) philosophy, consequently activating the Hikma of SOUL-idarity.

In our opening chapter, we introduced a new assimilation of Hikma (wisdom) (ishq, ilm, akhuwat and amal) orientation borne out of Akhuwat's 4 I's: Iman, Ihsan, Ikhlas & Ikhuwah. Sequentially, the previous chapter characterised the 4 I's elaboration in this light.

As has been previously communicated, this part of the book establishes the philosophical elements of Akhuwat's solidarity phenomenon. This chapter aims to establish a link between Akhuwat's 4 I's, comprehended with awareness and integrally aiding in CARE-ing 4 (Pakistani) Society, that is Community activation, raising Awareness, Research-to-innovation and Embodied action in a transformational way, as contemplated by Lessem and Schieffer through their 4 C's (Call, Context, Co-creation and Contribution) to a fully institutionalised CARE process.

## 2 Section 1: The GENE-alogy of solidarity – Akhuwat's 4I genealogy

### *2.1 Introduction: The 4 C's to CARE-ing-4-Society*

Per Lessem & Schieffer (2014), by engaging the institutionalising *CARE* rhythm in parallel to the *4 C's*, the institutionalising, collective activities are geared to gradually building up communities and organisational structures that can sustain and further evolve the particular integral development impulse and give rise to new ones.

> **The 4C Process** (Chapter 2) supports the integral researcher and developer as an individual in an interconnected trajectory from Call to Context to Co-creation to the final Contribution. The 4 C's enable him or her to '4C' a particular integral development. The second part of the alternating rhythm leverages the particular development by serving to institutionalise it.

**CARE** is the acronym for this second part of the dual rhythm towards full-fledged integral development, and consists of Community activation, raising Awareness, Research-to-innovation and Embodied action.

Together, the four *CARE* functions enable us to fully '*CARE-4-Society*'. Whereby CARE, as a whole, is one of the key transformative trajectories of TRANS4M, enabling the gradual actualisation of a social innovation in real-life context.

*As part of my PHD project (Acronym for Process of Holistic Development), I have adopted this method to investigate Pakistan and Akhuwat's collective 4 C's to probe into their collective call to contribution, which has been explained in Chapter 2 of Part One.*

*In this chapter we further elaborate a dual rhythm of Akhuwat's 4 I's (Iman, Ikhlas, Ihsan and Ikhuwah) with the CARE process, also proposing the institutionalisation of such a process. As the E in CARE also stands for Embodying the integral, we believe that for Akhuwat to now complete the full CARE-ing-4-Society rhythm, there's a pressing need for them to institutionalise their Mawakhat philosophy through the integral Research-to-innovation process as contemplated by* Lessem & Schieffer (2014).

*Incidentally, with their recent endeavour to build a university under Akhuwat's leadership, it becomes ever more pertinent for their community of employees, volunteers and board members to discern Akhuwat's Mawakhat philosophy in an integrally fourfold way, as contemplated in our previous chapter through their 4 I's and building on the institutional research through their many operations. Subsequently, upholding their position in the region through transforming and innovating the knowledge of microfinance, as understood and existent presently, to an integral finance and SOUL-idarity economy institution, having emerged from an indigenous Islamic model of 'reciprocal endowment' in the form of a solidarity bond, for the coming generations to take as precedent.*

### *2.1.1 From microfinance to reciprocal endowment*

For Akhuwat to ascertain its position through its compassionate spiritual finance model, there needs to be a successive emphasis on long-term evolution, through innovative models of institutional research to discern its philosophy.

After keenly searching over the length and breadth of South Asia, trying to find a similar model that embodies societal transformation to the same level Akhuwat has been engaged with over a period of 17 years, we have found Akhuwat to be quite unique on this account, as compared to, for example, Grameen in its neighbouring country of Bangladesh, pioneer of microfinance in the South Asian region, or Sarvodaya Development Finance in Sri Lanka.

Whereas both these organisations offer micro-loans to small and medium-sized enterprises and entertain a portfolio similar to Akhuwat's loan portfolio, i.e., SME loans, housing loans etc., none of them offer an interest-free facility as Akhuwat does, as well as the other community-based initiatives Akhuwat is involved in. Essentially, these organisations have not come from a spiritual philosophy like Akhuwat has, though Sarvodaya does follow the Gandhian principle of political economy as a social movement of 'progress of all' or 'universal uplift', which is the meaning of Sarvodaya.

Closer to home, as per a study by ACCA Global (2018), Pakistan's microfinance institutions – serving 5.2 million borrowers with a loan portfolio of PKR184bn (US$1.6bn) as of September 2017 – range widely in strategy, capacity and outreach. In late 2017, Pakistan's microfinance sector had more than 40 accredited institutions operating in 106 districts.

Furthermore, these organisations depend on funds from foreign development funds rather than generating their own self-sufficient solidarity economies – something Akhuwat champions on the local ground.

### *2.1.2 Solidarity Bayt-al-Hikma (house of wisdom)*

Consequently, we sincerely believe, being immersed in its local culture, Akhuwat's philosophy could take a centre-stage role as a spiritu-socio-economic community, to play a catalytic role in the South Asian region in particular, and the Muslim world in general, by grounding itself as an innovative Bayt-al-Hikma (house of wisdom) archetype.

After the decline of Muslim intellectual and learned culture in the 10th century, the tide is finally turning for Muslims for a 21st century social renaissance and a perennial call for knowledge creation for the globalised Muslim communities living in non-Muslim countries.

Additionally, Muslim intellectual growth stalled in Pakistan, or rather the Indo-Pak region, after the Aligarh University movement, envisioned by Sir Syed Ahmad, an Indian Muslim pragmatist, Islamic reformist and philosopher of nineteenth century British India. Notwithstanding the fact that the region boasts of having seen many philosophers and intellectual heavyweights born out of its soil, the impact of British invasion and colonisation had an irrevocable impact on the authenticity of its indigenous culture and tradition of archetypal theosophical, mystic and spiritual values. Thereafter, the outbreak of the fanatic and fundamentalist surge after the Soviet-Afghanistan War divided Pakistani society into two distinct social classes: an affluent and powerfully resourceful Western-educated class against a majority class of proletariats who happen to be more attached to their indigenous and spiritual culture and traditions.

As a model, Akhuwat, being immersed in the local culture and infused with a spiritual philosophy, gives them a sense of ownership and national dignity. Its principles are borne out of the local phenomenon and speak to people in their language. Its methodology and practices are not alien or foreign to poor people from grassroots communities.

Furthermore, the local tradition of Bhai-chara (brotherhood), husn-e-saluk (nobility of conduct) and husn-e-Ikhlak (ethical compliance) has revitalised the spirit of self-reliance and self-sufficiency of CARE-ing and sharing. It almost resembles Ibn Khaldun's concept of asabiyyah, a social bond that can be used to measure the strength and stability of social groupings.

As one of the most important concepts in Ibn Khaldun's writings, asabiyyah (esprit de corps or social solidarity) is seen by Fuad Baali (1988), professor of Sociology at University of Western Kentucky, as the seed of the Khaldunian cyclical theory of human history. It is derived, as such, from the Arabic verb asab (to bind), thereby binding individuals in a group (asabtun). In fact, the term has been translated as 'esprit de corps', tribal consciousness, vitality, group mind, collective consciousness, feeling of solidarity and social solidarity.

Akhuwat, persistently endorsing its philosophy of Mawakhat, is reviving the spirit of solidarity amongst communities. Also, by granting Qard-e-Hasan (benevolent loan) as its capital source of loan or grant money, it is reinforcing the Islamic philosophy of economics and a just society without any social classifications and divide.

Subsequently, Akhuwat has been successful in renewing the anomalous culture of dependency on charity (sadaqah money) and/or reliance on a foreign concept of debt (microfinance).

Mawakhat (solidarity with your needy brothers), a new discipline, has emerged from the land of the pure, Pakistan, which harkens a new age – Bayt-al-Hikma of SOUL-idarity, the multiplier-effect of barakah.

## *2.2 Releasing the Mawakhat (solidarity) GENE-ius of Pakistani society*

Borrowing from the Khaldunian concept of asabiyyah, Pakistan's rural communities – much more than the urban communities – bank on their social capital of Bhai-chara. In the spirit of this Bhai-chara, people are often familiar with the Mawakhat concept from Prophetic tradition. Ever since Pakistan's partitioning from India, this spirit of social solidarity has sustained migrant communities, thriving on their tribal (Biradari) system.

The figure 5.1, thus, maps out Akhuwat's solidarity paradigm, in an integral four-dimensional process of Akhuwat's Mawakhat philosophy, corresponding with the integral CARE process, thereby releasing Pakistani society's GENE-IUS (Grounding, Emergence, Navigation and Effect), as per Lessem and Schieffer's (ibid) postulation.

This descriptive positioning allows the readers to navigate through what might seem like an over-espousal of three disciplines merged together to counsel a new way forward in the age of integrality.

*Whereby,*

- *The Eastern – Path of Renewal, aids in a conscious co-evolution of Iman (faith). In Akhuwat's example, this is done by engaging the religious spaces as places of community activation.*

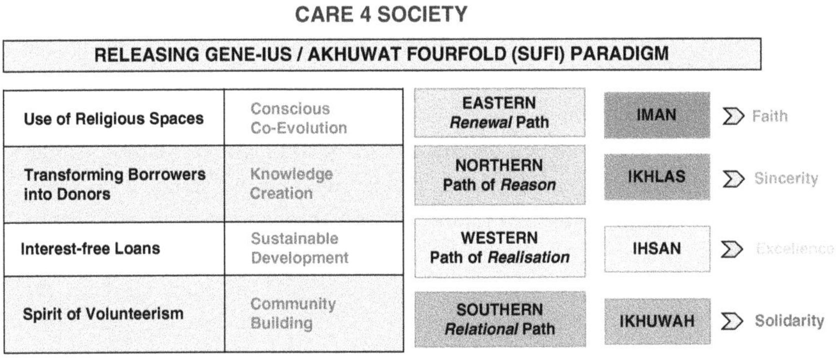


*Figure 5.1* CARE 4 Society – Akhuwat's Fourfold Paradigm

- *The Northern – Path of Reason, aids in knowledge-creation through Ikhlas (purity of intention). In Akhuwat's example, this is done by innovating a new paradigm of 'reciprocal endowment', i.e., transforming the borrowers into donors.*
- *The Western – Path of Realisation, equips one with sustainable development of enterprise and economic models, spreading the Ihsan (beauty and excellence) in a horizontal effect. In Akhuwat's case, this was done by granting Qard-e-Hasan to micro-entrepreneurs to sustain a respectful livelihood for themselves.*
- *The Southern – Relational Path, helps in community building through the spirit of Ikhuwah (solidarity and brotherhood). In Akhuwat's case, it is regenerating the 'spirit of volunteerism' amongst a community of Akhuwateers.*

We now move on to our CARE-ing process through Akhuwat's fourfold principles, elaborating its fourfold dimension. We start with Catalysation (C) as the first step towards a full C+A+R+E process.

## 3 Raising awareness (catalysation) – use of religious spaces

In the early days, Akhuwat did not even have an office, and the squalid streets and alleys of an urban slum at the rear of Lahore General Hospital named Rasool Park served as our 'headquarters'. It is hard to forget the minuscule wooden cabin on the PRSP premises where Akhuwat's staff worked for eighteen months. Then there was the day when we entered a mosque to shade ourselves from the scorching sun, and it opened a door that has never been shut.

This opened a new door for Akhuwat's solidarity (Bhai-chara) endeavour. 'This act of community service must take place from inside a house of worship'. The imam of the mosque welcomed our resolve. Thus, the mosque became an integral part of the milieu and character of what Akhuwat was to become.

'Akhuwat is not governed by any sect or denomination. We believe that the mosque is a house of the Lord, a place without prejudice. The offices of Akhuwat are situated within mosques of every denomination – a sign of historical solidarity, pure from any form of discrimination. Other than mosques, we also utilise churches, Hindu temples, and gurdwaras for the service of humanity. A famous church in Lahore is used by us. Our belief, based on firm evidence, is that women and members of other religions can enter the mosque provided that the requisites of *Shariah* are respected. If women and persons of other faiths visited Masjid-e-Nabwi, what could hinder them from entering other mosques? Tradition dictates that, under special conditions, the Prophet (pbuh) even allowed Christians to pray in the mosque. By shutting the doors to our heart, can we ever open the doors to other people's hearts?

The philosophy of *Akhuwat* has been adopted from Islamic principles, but clearly no religion or tradition can ever claim a monopoly over the principles of solidarity. The very concept of solidarity leaves no room for exclusion. Akhuwat belongs to Muslims, as much as it does to Christians, Hindus, Sikhs and every other individual who believes in social justice.

The guiding collective activity for **Catalysation**, or Community activation, is to '*build up an interdependent innovation ecosystem to support your integral development with a view to alleviate imbalances*'.

- *Focus*: Catalysing self and communal, organisational and societal renewal and consciousness raising with a view to alleviate imbalances within a particular context.
- *Integral Four Worlds* Orientation: **Holistic – Eastern – Sanctuary**; The belief that the determining features in nature are wholes, that organisms progressively develop, are irreducible to the sums of their parts, but function in relationship to them.
- *Progression towards*: **Conscious Evolution**

### *3.1 Catalysation builds on context*

In Chapter 2, examining Pakistan's call to context, we propounded the need for revival of community spirit through local traditions after colonisation and Westernisation. The stark disparity between social classes has resulted in a social divide, with poor getting poorer in the absence of ample support and resources and infrastructure from the state. A benevolent, compassionate and holistic process of development is what could 'heal' the communal trauma and build a just society. Akhuwat took it as their religious as well as their societal responsibility to fill that gap. And what better place to start this than a holy place – a sanctuary – to renew the pledge of solidarity, but to start from a faith institute (inner) to heal outer collective trauma and social divide?

For Pakistan, being an Islamic republic, religious spaces serve as centralised spaces for religious and communal and often times political activities. Mosques are frequented by men of all classes and status, five times a day, which cultivates a sense of fraternity amongst the mosque-goers.

Per Ibrahim Madkour, president of the Academy of Arabic Language in Cairo, in any society, culture is the offspring of many factors: human potential, creative consciousness, intellectual and spiritual vitality, real achievement and progress, and freedom, among others. In the Arab society of the early eighth century, the potential for extraordinary cultural achievement clearly existed. The introduction of Islam into Arab societies generated creative activity within the Arab consciousness. By providing new purpose and a sense of direction, it unified a loose assemblage of tribes, inspired leadership, and unleashed collective and individual GENE-IUS.

Conversely, the Indian subcontinent was an amalgamation of many religious traditions before the first Arab Muslims captured the lower Indus Valley and opened the way for Umayyad caliphs to penetrate the region. For that region, culture (saqafut), means cultural traditions practised between various ethnic groups and tribes. The role of village panchaits, jirgas, barter, care of widows and orphans, and collective participation in celebrations and mourning are aspects that are still practised. In this spirit of communalism, Akhuwat and Amjad played the role of a catalyst, reinforcing the sanctity of religious places as a central communal gathering place.

### *3.2 Sanctuary – a place of awakening higher consciousness*

The Benedictines were pioneers in agricultural techniques all over Europe. They developed Sweden's corn trade, Ireland's salmon business and Italy's cheese-making factories. While some tend to think of monasteries as being shut away from the world, that is a narrow view of monastic life. Benedictine monasteries were, and still are, places of beauty, hospitality and learning: models of a caring community. The root cause of the lack of identity and chaos in the world today is the banishing of the 'sanctuary' from social life. While the separation of state and church in the so-called age of renaissance helps to set the stage for rapid economic and scientific growth, it also set the scene for a dichotomy between the holy and the profane, the sacred and the secular, nature and science, economics and politics.

The associative economics of Rudolf Steiner (1977), a German-Austrian philosopher and social reformer, build upon culture and spirituality. Steiner was not often referred to as an economist, at least not in the Anglo-Saxon world where much of modern economics has its locus, but his 1922 lectures on economics are surely paradigmatic in that Steiner's primary concern is with the need to think economically.

With his threefold commonwealth, Rudolf Steiner offered a fundamental reinterpretation of a developmental economy and society, distinguishing three independent as well as interdependent (co-evolving) societal parts: economics, politics *and* culture. He saw culture as the rightful place for competition in order to achieve personal freedom and liberation. Economics, in contrast, is about fraternity, and politics is about equality, according to Steiner. In this combination, an individual strives to fully actualise his or her personal skills in the field of culture which, in turn, informs his or her unique and knowledgeable contribution to economic life. The focus of economics, then, is on the real needs of society, and its organising form is the association.

In contrast, Lessem (2017) places emphasis on awakening integral consciousness in a functional, dynamic way, and on actualising an innovation ecosystem in a structural and stabilizing manner. Awakening integral or holistic consciousness is conventionally associated with Eastern philosophy, which in Akhuwat and Amjad's case was the revival of the prophetic tradition of using religious places for communal catalysation. In doing so, they managed to not only renew the tradition but also to 'think economically', as per Steiner's insinuation, thereby (re)awakening the collective consciousness of their community.

### *3.3 Congregational solidarity*

Islam is one of the finest examples of a religion in which brotherhood and unity act as pillars for a Muslim community.

Humans as social beings have always been interested in social activities and communication with others, and they fear seclusion and isolation to such an extent that exile is considered to be a very severe penalty for criminals. It seems this principal quality is applied to most aspects of human life, e.g., business, study, entertainment and decision making. Indeed, to bring different arguments and examples regarding human social life is to utter an obvious truth, in fact a tautology. The importance of this natural quality becomes more obvious when we realise that the messengers of God and founders of religions placed emphasis on social aspects of life to remind people of their social, God-given nature and of the fact that all humans are in need of one another. This emphasis on congregation was also meant to strengthen the foundation of religion and to increase public trends towards religious life. This was because intercultural and interethnic conflicts and enmities had caused considerable loss and hatred among people; hence, it seems that unity and congregation are influential factors in reinforcing adherents' tendency towards religiosity (Monib & Din, 2013).

For Monib and Din (2013), some of the main features in Islamic communal rituals are as follows:

- Unity of language
- Unity of direction
- Various occasions, for example, Eid, breaking of fast etc., and places and numerous functions of congregational rituals.
- Good governance

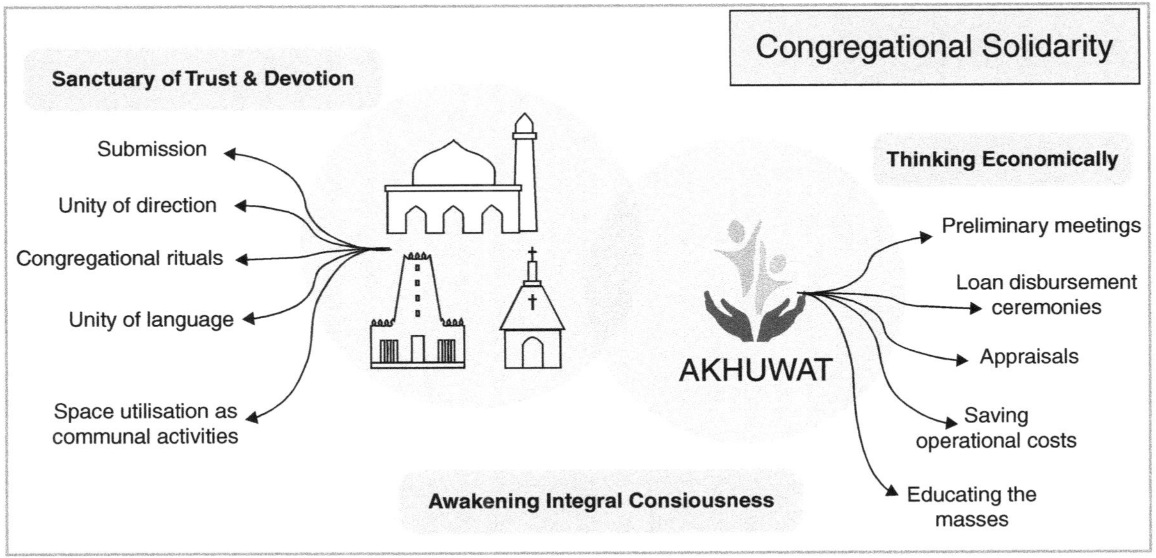


*Figure 5.2* Congregational Solidarity

### *3.4 Submission and devotion*

Although the mosque plays different vital roles to maintain the identity of the Muslim community, the Quranic verses explicitly introduce the devotional expression, connection and submission to God the Almighty as the main element for the validity of the mosque, without which there is no mosque worthy of name (The Holy Quran, 24:36, 2:114, 7:29).

*The Urdu term that denotes holiness or sacredness of a sanctuary is muqaddas, coming from the root word quds (q-d-s). Al-Quddus is one of the 99 Divine names of Allah.*

Knowing the devotional reality of a sanctuary and the reverence people show towards these spaces, Akhuwat seized this opportunity of utilising religious places for their operational purposes, which also include loan disbursement ceremonies. For a house of worship is the best place to enter into a contract as a divine pact of submission. Akhuwat entertains a recovery rate of 99.9% on its interest-free loans and credits this to the reverence of the sanctuary as a place for entering into a binding contract on trust and faith.

Furthermore, one of the most significant functions of the early mosques was education. Teaching Islam was the main goal of the prophetic mission; the Prophet Muhammad (pbuh) said, I surely have been sent to fulfil moral values.

The Prophet once entered the mosque and saw two circles of Muslims. One circle was worshipping God and the other was studying. He said, both circles are on the right path, but the second gathering is more meritorious, and I actually have been sent as a Prophet to teach. He then joined the second. The Prophet used to sit in the mosque at different times, chiefly after morning and night prayers to answer Muslims' questions and to preach to them. He would sit beside one of the columns in the mosque and the representatives of different tribes and religions came to ask him about the new religion. The Prophet prioritised education over other recommended deeds and he declared, 'Whoever enters the mosque for teaching or learning is identically rewarded as one who fights in the path of God' (Monib & Din, 2013).

Most of Akhuwat's loan disbursement rituals take place after some preliminary sessions of educating the borrowers about Akhuwat's philosophy and code of conduct.

Some examples are as follows:

- The loan money will not be used on gambling, trading alcohol or any illegal activities prohibited by faith traditions and rule of law.
- Why is the loan given to them free of any mark-up?
- Gratitude towards God and the donors who have lent their money for the financial upliftment of the borrowers.
- Invoking a spirit of community (bahami Bhai-chara) and volunteerism (khidmet-e-khalq).

With some beautiful words of wisdom from Amjad, establishing the position of the sanctuary in Akhuwat's scheme of things, we now continue to our next

CARE function and Akhuwat's next and most vital principle of interest-free micro-lending.

## 4 Activation: activating community – spirit of volunteerism

In his book *Akhuwat ka Safar*, Amjad pays a heartful tribute to his board members who have been extending their services on a voluntary basis since Akhuwat's inception days, by fully supporting Amjad's call and helping to fully transform it into a social movement.

> 'The true beauty of any society is its volunteers – people who rise above themselves and embrace humanity. For, *volunteerism* is a Sufi attribute, a habit of the *dervish.* It is also a tradition of prophets. If there is no volunteerism in acts of service, they begin to reek of business. The employees of Akhuwat are also volunteers, for they receive a salary for eight hours and work for twelve. Day or night, heat or cold, they transcend the march of hours, along with hundreds of volunteer students, teachers and social workers.
>
> Akhuwat is like an abode of fragrances. From here, there is no turning back and anyone who agrees with the ethos of equality and solidarity can become its part. Our board members joined Akhuwat's board of directors with the same fervour. The decision to include is based on longing, endeavour, commitment and devotion. Akhuwat belongs to those who are ready to belong to it. It was our good fortune that, from day one, Akhuwat found exemplary supporters: Dr. Kamran Shams, Dr. Izhar ul Haq Hashmi, Dr. Humayoun Ihsan, and Saleem Ahmad Ranjha – keen, like-minded and compassionate. They are all truly great people. Then Khawar Rafiq, Zahid Khokhar, Fazal Yazdani, Dr. Muhammad Saeed and Ali Arshad Hakeem joined them. Akhuwat is the result of the sincerity of all these people. If their help was not forthcoming, perhaps Akhuwat would not have become Akhuwat.

From an integral CARE-4-Society process, per Lessem & Schieffer (2014), the guiding collective activity for **Community activation** is to:

'*form an inner circle and start building an outer community*'. Activation builds on Call, seeking to connect a growing community to the initial 'inner calling' and 'outer challenge'.

- *Focus*: Self-and-community development; tap purposefully into inner calling and respond to outer challenge
- *Integral Four Worlds* Orientation: **Humanistic: Southern: Community**, Asserts the dignity of (wo)man, promoting human and social welfare,

incorporating the arts and humanities, fostering self-fulfilment in the context of collective and community relations.

- *Progression towards*: **Community Building**

As contemplated by Lessem and Schieffer, at the heart of the activation of one's community is a '*healing component*' to restore the relational fabric within a particular person-and-community, required to release participatory potential, and of the community to its natural environment. For Lessem and Schieffer, activation of community contributes to healthy and participatory co-existence.

Akhuwat's fourth principle played a vital role in the regeneration of community spirit through volunteerism. The word *Akhuwat* became synonymous with volunteerism – their volunteers introduce themselves as '*Akhuwateers'*. People associated with Akhuwat did not volunteer their time to gain any kind of material benefit nor view the betterment of humanity through the lens of political or personal benefit. As Amjad once stated, the one who dedicates him/herself to service does not belong to the tribe or faith their beneficiary belongs to, but rises above their discrimination of colour, caste and creed. The spirit of service derives from many ideals – from the vision of such a society where each individual has access to social and economic justice, and the basic amenities of life. Most of all, it is the creation of a society where each person thinks for him/herself, and also for others.

Akhuwat's message of brotherhood is often communicated as *the Mawakhat Model*. By adopting this approach, they have not only been successful in alleviating poverty but also in mobilising a large community of volunteers to virtually adopt their philosophy of Mawakhat. Having activated their internal organisational and/or external societal community, in keeping with the inner/outer calling, and after establishing an appropriate structure and processes to go with it, the next step for Akhuwat was to build a more wide-ranging, catalysing development ecosystem.

Through various interactions and interventions, Akhuwat trains and speaks about 'the Mawakhat Model' with all relevant and interested stakeholders in order to promote its replication and for better understanding of the Islamic principles in general. The benefits are two: Firstly, it helps to broaden the Islamic microfinance industry within the country, which helps immensely in reaching more beneficiaries, timing the work efficiently, and bettering more livelihoods. Secondly, it creates a parallel microfinance industry that produces a Shariah-compliant finance system tailored to the religious and cultural practices of the region, and which aims to use the tool of microfinance as a charitable service.

Moreover, Akhuwat supports all organisations engaging in this worthy endeavour and makes all resources available for interested stakeholders in order to facilitate their transition or the first step into this field. This includes providing training to the affiliate staff in interest-free non-profit microfinance and lending our loan methodology literature to all those that require it to ensure the establishment and sustainability of all desiring ventures. Our support for replications is based out of our desire to expand the horizons and scope of pure interest-free microfinance throughout Pakistan and hopefully the world; thus without any interest in capitalising on market shares, we can invest our energy and resources into helping develop other organisations without detracting from our objective and actually significantly contribute to our ultimate vision of a poverty-free society.

We now move to the next step of the CARE function and Akhuwat's third notable principle of transfiguring the once-borrowers to now-contributors to Akhuwat's solidarity bond of Mawakhat.

## 5 Institutionalising socio-economic R & D – transforming borrowers into donors

> The philosophy of Akhuwat, and its rules and methods were a learning practice, like an island on which new shoots and new buds blossom each day. Akhuwat's philosophy was not adopted from the capitalistic system but from the sentiments of solidarity and compassion. The source of this vision can be traced back to Mawakhat-e-Medina more than 1400 years ago – a historical display of solidarity that changed the course of history. After being banished from Mecca, Muslims sought refuge in Medina. Braving the perils and hardships that accompanied the exodus, these people reached Medina in destitution. The people of Medina welcomed them into their homes with the pledge that, from then onwards, they would share half of whatever they owned with the refugees. This bond of fellowship formed the seed of an exceptional tradition. Considered to be an isolated incident, this event has been confined to the pages of history books. Through Akhuwat, the same pledge of solidarity was reignited: if you have one loaf of bread, half of it ought to be given to the person who has none. It was this conscientiousness that formed the basis of the Akhuwat foundation.
>
> Among Akhuwat's initial loans, one was granted to a widow, Hakim Bibi, from Rasool Park, Lahore, whose story was to become part of our history. Once her situation was confirmed, she was presented with Rupees 10,000 ($100) in the form of an interest-free loan. She bought herself two modern sewing machines with this. I had almost forgotten about her when after six months she turned up at my house to return her loan and advised me to lend this money to someone else in need. Yet another borrower insisted he would like to donate some money to Akhuwat from the money he'd made from Akhuwat's loan.
>
> This to me is the true partnership of solidarity with the poor – making them part of the movement. And the chain (silsilah) kept on multiplying, showing us new ways of expanding beyond our own belief.
>
> Akhuwat is dynamic in its nature, as the multiplier effect of solidarity bond has expanded our comprehension of the phenomenon. Every instance brought a new lesson in its folds.

The guiding collective activity for **Research-to-innovation** is to '*newly evolve a – or link up with an existing – centre (organisation) to institutionalise, sustain and further leverage your research-and-innovation*'.

- *Focus*: focused on institutionalised research and knowledge creation, along one research path and trajectory or another, altogether combining research methodology and knowledge fields.
- *Integral Four Worlds* Orientation: **Rational: Northern: Academy**; The power to make logical inferences, whereby reason is a source of power independent of sense perceptions, based on deduction through a priori concepts rather than via empiricism.
- *Progression towards*: **Knowledge Creation**

Over a period of 17 years, Akhuwat has grown from a small initiative to a large movement fighting against usury and exploitation of the poor. The trust and honour of the borrowers has helped Akhuwat to develop their members donation program (MDP). It is a program that relies entirely on the philanthropic spirit within their borrowers. Their eagerness to donate for the cause of Akhuwat, above their monthly payments, increased their confidence, and they saw it as a development of a new foundation within the organisation which is going to support and expand the work of Akhuwat.

The third principal of Akhuwat is to turn the beneficiary into a donor – the hand that receives into the hand that gives.

*How can those who accepted loans become those who give loans?*

We learned this when people who had borrowed from Akhuwat began to earn a sufficient income themselves and approached us. They reported with pride, and with tears of gratitude in their eyes, that their children now have enough to eat and were enrolled in schools. They insisted that they now wished to donate to Akhuwat. As Akhuwat had allowed them to stand on their own feet, they considered it their imperative to do something in return. These people often became donors with a contribution of just one or two rupees. Many of them kept an Akhuwat donation box in their kiosk or vending cart and would place two, four or five rupees in it each evening. Some of their customers also began to contribute. Thus, every month, one or two hundred rupees were collected in each box and this donation became a part of Akhuwat's interest-free loan fund.

An unbelievable and unprecedented phenomenon was witnessed. It illustrated that the appreciation of good is not only goodness, but something much beyond that. It was at this point, the board decided to adopt this principle and spread the message to other borrowers – if they so desired, they could become benefactors with just one rupee. However, this wasn't a prerequisite to be a borrower. The aim was not to coerce, but only to communicate that 'the status of he who gives is much higher than that of he who receives'. For Amjad, in a virtuous society, the number of benefactors must be far greater than the number of beneficiaries. After all, Akhuwat envisions such a society where every individual is familiar with the pleasure of giving, and in striving for his own welfare, never forgets the welfare of those around him.

To this end, Akhuwat established its distinction by achieving this monumental feat of being a one-of-its-kind micro-lending institution, innovating an old tradition of Mawakhat – sharing with others from one's wealth. Through this, the idea of institutionalising and inculcating the spirit of Mawakhat took root in Amjad's heart, giving birth to Akhuwat University, which will start operating by August 2018. Conforming to its tradition of extending a helping hand to the underprivileged segment of the society, Akhuwat has focused on making education accessible to the poorest of the poor by offering free higher education to deserving students. The university aims to not only promote learning in terms of the regular curriculum; it also aims to fine-tune its students to become productive and efficient human beings in all walks of life by teaching them the spirit of Mawakhat (solidarity).

For Amjad, institutionalising Akhuwat's many social experiments could be the only way of inculcating the spirit of Mawakhat into the coming generations. His dream is to produce an institution which brings back the lost glory of the land that produced intellectuals and philosophers like Shah Waliullah and Allama Mohammed Iqbal – and innovators like Dr. Tariq Mustafa, the first Pakistani rocket scientist and Nobel Laureate Dr. Abdus Salam.

### *5.1 Aligarh Muslim University*

Historically, it is the re-emergence of a dream Sir Syed Ahmed Khan had around the time of the Indian subcontinent's colonisation. Khan was a Muslim educator, jurist, and author, and the founder of the Anglo-Mohammedan Oriental College at Aligarh, Uttar Pradesh, India, He was the principal motivating force behind the revival of Indian Islam in the late 19th century. His works, in Urdu, include Essays on the Life of Mohammed (1870) and commentaries on the Bible and on the Quran. In 1888 he was made a Knight Commander of the Star of India.

The role of Aligarh Muslim University in its role of uplifting and improving the wellbeing of the Muslims of the subcontinent stands in bold relief in the annals of history.

This university worked in accordance with a philosophy that was the driving force for Aligarh Movement. This philosophy was Initiated by Sir Syed Ahmad Khan and developed by relentless work by his associates and followers. The Movement was remarkably universal and abiding in its appeal and applicability. Its essence was education as the prime mover of modernisation, progress and development. It put great emphasis on keeping intact the community's own distinctive cultural identity and base. The Movement gave equal importance to character building along with scholastic instruction. The real outcome of Aligarh movement was the *Aligarh Spirit*, which was being inculcated in every student, through the special pedagogy and instructional methods.

The 1857 revolt was one of the turning points in Syed Ahmed's life. He clearly foresaw the imperative need for the Muslims to acquire proficiency in the

English language and modern sciences, if the community were to maintain its social and political clout, particularly in Northern India. He was one of those early pioneers who recognized the critical role of education in the empowerment of the poor and backward Muslim community. In more than one way, Sir Syed was one of the greatest social reformers and a great national builder of modern India. He began to prepare the road map for the formation of a Muslim university by starting various schools. He instituted Scientific Society in 1863 to instil a scientific temperament into the Muslims and to make the Western knowledge available to Indians in their own language. The Aligarh Institute Gazette, an organ of the Scientific Society, was launched in March 1866 and succeeded in agitating the minds in the traditional Muslim society.

After the partition of India and Pakistan, the *Aligarh Spirit* remained in India, with no replication of some such spirit in Pakistan and in the same context.

As for Amjad's aspiration of inculcating the Mawakhat spirit, could Akhuwat University invoke the same spirit in Pakistan? Consequently, could this pave the way for Pakistan in establishing her as a beacon of contemporary Muslim knowledge in Southeast Asia?

For the re-emergence of the Transformational GENE after a century must hold some meaning.

## 6 Embodied action: interest-free loans

'We studied Comilla Model, Orangi Pilot Project, Rural Support Program, Grameen Bank, BRAC, ASA Initiative, Foundation for International Community Development (FINCA), Proshika – institutions from all over the world and then, in accordance with the local needs, carried out all sorts of new experiments. When one has to work with people, one learns best not from books, but from the people.'

Once the main functions of delivery were established, those eager to help from within the community came forward. When we received two initial grants of Rs. 200,000 ($200) each, there was no limit to our joy. It seemed as if all the treasures of the world had been found. The years 2001–2002 were pivotal. In these two years, Akhuwat had only two employees – Rehana and Tabassum. Then came Shehzad, Tayyab, Aftab, Shahid and Sajjad. Sohail Awan and Saeed, some experienced employees of PRSP, also became volunteers at Akhuwat. Muhammad Saeed, who came from Peshawar, took care of the finances.

The guiding collective activity for this final CARE function is to '*develop a transformative educational program delivered by the center you created or have become affiliated with*'. Educational transformation and transformative education builds on contribution, seeking to deepen and leverage, through fundamentally transformed education, the original development impulse.

This involves institutionalising research and knowledge creation with a view to developing self and community, organisation and society. Such an institutionalisation consciously includes the prior CARE functions and is designed to 'deliver' the fourth and final one – 'Embodying action'.

- *Focus*: Embodiment as a laboratory for creative experimentation; an innovative, conducive space in which new theories and practices can be individually conceived of, tested and implemented through action learning and action research addressing burning issues
- *Integral Four Worlds* Orientation: **Pragmatic: Western: Laboratory**; The practical treatment of things, emphasising the application of ideas, whereby thought is a guide to action, and the truth is empirically tested by the practical consequences of belief.
- *Progression towards*: **Sustainable Development**

For Amjad, the metaphor of brotherhood entails the creation of a system based on mutual support in society. To this end, microfinance was only one of the tools, albeit a powerful one, employed by Akhuwat. One of Akhuwat's primary deviations from conventional microfinance is that it charges no interest. Akhuwat has sought to base its movement on the principles of Qard-e-Hasan found in the Islamic tradition, which entails helping someone in need with interest-free loans, a practice favoured over charity and dole. While drawing on the tradition of Qard-e-Hasan, Akhuwat has over time incorporated many of the best practices and lessons learnt from conventional microfinance movements from across the globe as well. In the absence of interest and with a minimal registration fee (Rs. 200), every effort is made to ensure operating costs are kept very low. Extreme simplicity in operational activities, plain offices, use of religious places and high levels of volunteerism in the workforce ensure that Akhuwat realises its aim of minimal operational costs, making it possible for them not to overburden the poor people. After much contemplation, Amjad realised that the only way of breaking the poverty vicious circle was to turn it around by forming virtuous circles of solidarity/Bhai-chara.

In doing so, Amjad and his associates had to judiciously manipulate a method which could work in the context of Pakistani society's social class system, wherein one section of the society is impoverished and the other section enjoys abundance of wealth and influence. The call for Amjad was to bridge this gap of wealth imbalance in the cultural context of Islamic and Pakistani tradition and belief system.

Akhuwat's message of brotherhood, often communicated as the Mawakhat Model, has been successful in alleviating poverty using this approach. The common belief is that a microfinance organisation only works towards a common goal of providing loans to the section of the society which banks consider an un-bankable group of people in the community. As written above and as per Amjad's sentiment of 'going beyond the sermons of doable', Akhuwat and Amjad have achieved the undoable task assigned to a conventional microfinance organisation, starting with bringing the focus back to mosques as communal hubs for raising the collective consciousness of the community of worshippers, borrowers and donors in Akhuwat's case, and progressing to implementing an avant-garde model of loans (interest-free), and at the same time mobilising the borrower community to be part of their solidarity movement. Akhuwat have achieved the overall integral mark of CARE-ing for the society in an integral way as communicated by Lessem and Schieffer in their CARE model.

For Lessem and Schieffer then (Lessem & Schieffer, 2014), the final function of transforming the society through embodying development of individual, organisation and society

based on all that has come before – the renewed approach to education – addresses the burning socio-economic issues in society. It is geared to alleviate imbalances in a particular context, and thereby also for a particular person and community; it is underpinned by a research-to-innovation process that includes nature and community, culture and spirituality, science and technology, as well as economics and enterprise. Such education is therefore inherently trans-disciplinary. At the same time, true to integral forms, it is experiential and imaginative, conceptual and practical.

## 7 Akhuwat: from local-identity to emergent global integrity for Pakistan

Given that the combined, alternating '4C' CARE rhythm strengthens existing institutions and gives rise to new ones, building an integral green society requires both our local and global selves. We are called to reaffirm our 'local identity' and to connect such, in a contributing manner, to 'global integrity'.

For us, this posits a question for Akhuwat: After sustaining its local identity as an alternative model of microfinance, is Akhuwat ready to dissipate its solidarity effect globally and how?

### *7.1 The model: ingenuity of solidarity*

Could an idealistic model of institutional solidarity work for Pakistan, then?

Idealism is the name of the unyielding passion one adopts in life'. Akhuwat University is just such a passion, such stubbornness. How will this stubbornness come to bear fruit? Had somebody asked me this question 17 years ago, I would perhaps not have been able to answer. However, the story of Akhuwat has now become the answer to many such questions. If loans without interest can triumph, then so can education without huge fees. The model of solidarity is before us; it just needs to be repeated.

> For Amjad, those who have come to do business are those who have financial concerns. For some, idealism is the name of relentless passion.
>
> For the passion merchants, what fear do they have of financial statements? People are surprised by Akhuwat University's financial model, but for those who believe in solidarity, there is nothing astonishing about it.

Similarly, in another part of the world, according to Moroccan-American anthropologist extraordinaire Apffel-Marglin (Apffel-Marglin & (PRATEC), 1998), in citing the experiences of Peruvian indigenous peasants, PRATEC (Andean Project of Peasant Technologies), development itself is the problem because its epistemologies and practices are alien to the indigenous peasantry. Their knowledge of the Andean worldview helped them to utilise their innate knowledge of the landscape. The realisation was not simply that development had failed, but that development consisted of a package of practices, ideas, epistemologies and ontologies that came from the modern West and were profoundly alien to the native peasantry.

Apffel-Marglin further writes in her book *The Spirit of Regeneration* that the professionalisation of knowledge has made knowledge a commodity as well as an individual pursuit. What is bought on the market – the academic market as well as the *industrial*, military and government markets – is an individual's ability to produce knowledge, and in order for this to be bought and sold on the market, it has to be indivisibly held by an individual for it to become a commodity. Conversely, in the collective action way of making knowledge, emotional bonding with particular others is what generates new insights and knowledge. Furthermore, those others need not be only human, but any aspect of the environment that becomes part of the collective action. In fact, it is the individual, passionless, factual expert professional knowledge that reproduces the existing social, political and economic orders (Apffel-Marglin, & (PRATEC),1998).

This seems to be the case with Akhuwat University, for the knowledge 'regenerated' by their community of borrowers, donors, stakeholders and beneficiaries could form a new curriculum for solidarity traditions to be taught (academy) and consequently applied (social laboratory), to their wider community's welfare (community).

For Amjad, this could be Pakistan's first institution built in partnership with local and common people, and to their advantage as the hub of local knowledge generated through their social experimentation and communal learning.

## 8 Conclusion

### *8.1 Great is what remains to be done*

We have now come to the end of Section 1 of this part of the book, which has mapped Akhuwat's foundational guidelines to set off their solidarity impulse, which over the years has turned into a phenomenon. It is time for us to now scope the solidarity impulse through Akhuwat's 4I Genealogy before we move on to examine these principles in practice.

To sum up our journey through this chapter in the words of Amjad, many lamps could be seen lit on the horizon of Akhuwat, but the completion of these tasks is possible only when there is inclusion of the individual in the development process. One path to this inclusion is solidarity, the name of making the joys of others one with our own. In order to embark on the road to development, the first role is not of institutions, but that of individuals. The change in the individual becomes the backdrop of the change in society.

Akhuwat is a knock on the door of exactly this change – giving the individual the realisation that if he changes, so will the times, and then telling him that he is not alone and that a few others also think of his welfare. When he is convinced of this, transforming him from beneficiary to benefactor and urging him to coexist with others is not hard. As the wave of change gains momentum, institutions should be established that carry this change forward – not one or two, but hundreds of thousands. All this cannot be accomplished in a single day. This is a process approach, for which much time is needed.

From our integral quadrifocal approach, we could see that for the transformation happening through a community to take effect on a societal level, Akhuwat might have to take the Comm-university approach as cited by Lessem & Schieffer in their seminal work on Institutional Genealogy (Lessem & Schieffer, 2012).

According to American cultural historians McNeely & Wolverton (2009), today's epochal historical events, most recently climate change and economic crises, have determined that *the laboratory, not the university – or what we call the academy – will continue to exercise a strong influence on learning and knowledge creation, especially in the natural sciences.*

For McNeely and Wolverton, laboratory, then, is the most evolved form of knowledge-based, or indeed knowledge-creating, institution, whereas for us at TRANS4M, in GENE-alogical terms, it is the community (nature reserve), sanctuary (future redemption), academy ('mode 2') and laboratory (knowledge-creating enterprise), altogether genealogically constituted in a particular communiversity-and-society, that marks the next evolution of pre-school, school and university.

*We now move on to our next part of the book, which aims to determine this through Akhuwat's social laboratory, that is, its organisational methodology and practices, and we will ask, how does solidarity work as a knowledge-creating enterprise in an Islamic/Pakistani setting?*

## Bibliography

Apffel-Marglin, F., & PRATEC., 1998. *The Spirit of Regeneration: Andean Culture Confronting Western Notions of Development (Spirit Regeneration).* London: Zed Books.

Baali, F., 1988. *Society, State and Urbanism.* Albany: State University of New York.

Ikram, S. M., n.d. *Sir Sayyid Ahmad Khan*. Available at: Encyclopedia Britannica: https://www.britannica.com/biography/Sayyid-Ahmad-Khan

Klasra, K., 2018. Microfinance is a growing business in Pakistan. [Online] Available at: http://www.accaglobal.com/in/en/member/member/accounting-business/2018/03/insights/microfinance-pakistan.html

Lessem, R., 2017. *Awakening Integral Consciousness: A Developmental Perspective (Transformation and Innovation)*. Abingdon: Routledge.

Lessem, R., & Schieffer, A., 2010. *Integral Research and Innovation: Transforming Enterprise and Society*. Abingdon: Routledge.

Lessem, R., & Schieffer, A., 2012. *Integral Community: Political Economy to Social Commons (Transformation and Innovation)*. Abingdon: Routledge.

Lessem, R., & Schieffer, A., 2014. CARE 4 Zimbabwe: Towards a Pundusto Centre for Integral Development. In: A. Schieffer, & R. Lessem, eds. *Integral Development: Realising the Transformative Potential of Individuals, Organisations and Societies*. Farnham: Gower Publishing Ltd.

McNeely, I. F., & Wolverton, L., 2009. *Reinventing Knowledge: From Alexandria to the Internet*. New York: W. W. Norton & Company.

Monib, M., & Din, M. S., October 2013. The Role of Congregational Rituals in Islamic Pattern of Life. *Academic Journal of Interdisciplinary Studies*, 2, p. 8.

Steiner, R., 1977. *Towards Social Renewal*. Edinburgh: Rudolf Steiner Press.

## Part III

# The Mawakhat effect – employing solidarity

## 1 Introduction: the practices – the 3rd P

By adopting the Mawakhat philosophy of brotherhood, Akhuwat has affirmed that solidarity is the name of a living, vibrant philosophy. There is no justice in the concentration of wealth, and neither is success based only on monetary acquisition. People do wish to help others and are sated with the zeal of volunteerism. The poor are reliable and giving out loans without interest is a potent possibility indeed. Further, the mosque or the church can be made the axis of social activities. All these things are worthy of importance in their own place, but the real achievement of Akhuwat is that it gave the poor the confidence that they are not alone. There are others who feel their pain and deprivation and are happily shouldering their burdens and standing by them in their strife against poverty. Poverty is not just the name of deprivation of wealth; it is the name of being alone and social alienation too. A person is poor when he has no well-wisher left. This world has become the centre of social and economic injustice – there are people who enjoy an abundance of wealth, while others do not even have a claim over three full meals a day. No civilised society should allow such disparity.

I do not wish to conceive of such a world where a child is unable to find his way to school, where his parents become desperate for medicine, where each door of justice is shut upon them, where people are deprived of even the glimmer of hope.

Akhuwat's second-most cherished acquisition is the transformation of its beneficiaries into benefactors, with a 100% rate of return for loans, and in addition to that, donations also received from them. What's more, this dream was not borrowed from the vestige of any capitalistic and pragmatic culture. Rather, we have envisioned these dreams sitting in the shade of our own traditions. We found guidance for our future by following in the footprints of our beloved Prophet Muhammad (pbuh).

We have now come to the most practical part of our book, which demonstrates the practicality of Akhuwat's solidarity paradigm in a Pakistani and Islamic society setting. Whereas the philosophical guidance came from the prophetic tradition of Mawakhat, Amjad, being the son of the soil – deeply rooted in his societal and cultural backdrop – felt compelled to devise a practical yet localised solution to some of the most pressing needs of his community. Many solutions emerged by applying the knowledge he acquired whilst working on-the-ground and hands-on with his local community. And this is what sets Akhuwat distinctively apart from other paradigmatic microfinance organisations that have seized the opportunity as a 'business' opportunity. For Amjad, the solution should work in favour of the poor people and not against them, and most importantly it should not go against people's faith beliefs – for riba (usury) is considered a sin in Islamic and other Abrahamic faiths.

*From a personal standpoint, as per my own call, working with disadvantaged migrant communities within the UK after studying Akhuwat's model of reciprocity which generates self-sufficiency for their community of borrowers, I am becoming ever more aware of the whole 'process', as observed in this case, helping to release the GENE-IUS of their particular community, as postulated by Lessem and Schieffer.*

*Could a similar process work to help the marginalised communities in the UK find their communal impulse working through a similar 4P process to create their own solidarity economy? We will further investigate this in our final part of the book.*

Ronnie Lessem and Alexander Schieffer, in their seminal work on *Integral Economics* (Schieffer & Lessem, 2010), make a strong case for a new approach to an integral economy by taking an explicit account of the natural and cultural – including psychological heritages of diverse societies – around the world. In their book they presented Chinyika, Zimbabwe as a model integral community that originated its own local and natural form of communal self-sufficiency by uniquely establishing a culturally laden local-global Zimbabwean foundation as a developmental economy. It prospectively emancipates itself globally, navigating a path through a knowledge-based, social economy and ultimately transforming lives, globally as well as locally, as a living economy. In each case, moreover, there is a dual rhythm, a dual trajectory if you like, structure building and structure changing. That is the position they have taken for an integral economy emerging from a culturally rooted integral community. As per their contemplation, an evolving individual and community, enterprise and society, via origination, foundation, emancipation and transformation, needs to alternate between continuity and change in each case, thereby releasing its GENE-IUS.

Steiner (1977) also regarded it as necessary to take the relationship of the social organism to its natural base into consideration, just as it is important to take the relationship of the individual to his aptitudes into account. 'In the autonomous economic sector therefore, through the forces of economic life, people will develop faculties which best serve the production and interchange of commodities.'

Steiner (1861–1925), an Austrian philosopher, educator, architect and social innovator, was the founder of a new spiritual movement: Anthroposophy, often described as a 'spiritual science'. According to Steiner, human cooperation in economic life must be based on the 'fraternity' (Bhai-chara), which is inherent in associations.

As per Steiner's 'Associative economics'; capital arises not out of any single person's intellectual effort alone, but out of the accumulated capacities of previous generations, and also out of other men and women at any one time.

> Therefore, capital is neither by origin nor destination the property of any one individual. The continual inventiveness of human beings is ultimately the only source of capital. In that context, capital is an intellectual, cultural, even 'spiritual' force. Associative economics, thus, is about making the invisible hand visible. It is about making clear that we will not achieve a healthy economic life unless we deliberately cooperate to that end, transcending the automaticity that market forces imply, and making ourselves the agents for the many processes that we normally want to place outside ourselves.
>
> (Schieffer & Lessem, 2010)

This part of the book thus explores such processes that make Akhuwat a dynamic social organism, continuously evolving through its many operations and through its associative culture of Mawakhat, generating an economy of solidarity for which the source is coming from an integral finance theory as postulated by Basheer Oshodi and Jubril Adeojo, co-founders of CISER (Centre for Integral Social & Economic Research, Nigeria) through their integral banking model. For CISER, banking and finance are the pivotal enablers of community building and sustainable development in any given society. However, as realised by them, the founding principles and ideologies of banking and finance as a theory and practice are not adequately suitable for, and compatible with, the peculiarities of different communities and societies. From their standpoint, is the incompatibility of widespread modern banking and finance with the peculiarities of indigenous rural communities (in Nigeria and the rest of Africa), hence, impeding development in those communities.

Therefore, this part of the book firstly examines Akhuwat's operations and practices in the above light, and secondly presents Akhuwat's 'solidarity bond' as substantiated through our Integral Theory lens – that is, a circular solidarity economy model of integral finance.

This is structured through the following two sections, wherein:

**Section one** exhibits Akhuwat's various initiatives as a consequence of its fourfold philosophy of solidarity. From loan disbursement to replication of the 'Mawakhat Model', developing their social capital of employees and volunteers, Akhuwat's processes run in parallel to CARE-ing 4 Pakistan integrally as asserted in the previous chapter (Chapter 5).

**Section two** then reviews Akhuwat's local-global positioning as a distinctive model of finance by a brief comparison of other such models. As a matter of fact,

Akhuwat is admittedly acknowledged as an Islamic microfinance organisation. Whereas, throughout the course of this book, we have taken an antithetical viewpoint originated through an integral dynamics (Lessem & Schieffer, 2013) perception of Akhuwat being one such dynamic model of Eastern (holistic) model of finance.

The method adopted comes through applying critical realism, a method developed by Roy Bhaskar (1944–2014), a British philosopher best known as the initiator of the philosophical movement of critical realism. Bhaskar's critical realism emerged from the vision of realising an adequate realist philosophy of science, of social science, and of explanatory critique.

In short, critical realism argues for ontology, and for a new ontology. In this sense it is an heir to the Enlightenment. It is much more like a series of family resemblances in which there are various commonalities that exist between the members of a family, but these commonalities overlap and criss cross in different ways. There is not one common feature that defines a family, instead it is a heterogeneous assemblage of elements drawn from a relatively common 'genetic' pool (Bhaskar, 2008).

To this end, we perceive Akhuwat to be a unique model of Islamic finance and economics, yet sharing the same 'GENE' pool with other microfinance models extant regionally or globally, yet with a distinction at par with none, by nature of its processes of community building, knowledge creation and transformative action.

This is the third P of our 4P process: the Mawakhat paradigm in practice.

## References

Bhaskar, R., 2008. *A Realist Theory of Science (Radical Thinkers)*. London: Verso.

Lessem, R., & Schieffer, A., 2010. *Integral Economics: Releasing the Economic Genius of your Society*. Farnham: Gower Publishing Ltd.

Lessem, R., & Schieffer, A., 2013. *Integral Dynamics*. Abingdon: Routledge.

Steiner, R., 1977. *Towards Social Renewal*. Edinburgh: Rudolf Steiner Press.

# 6 Embodying action

## Akhuwat's bond of solidarity

We start with Amjad's visit to Harvard Business School.

### 1 Preamble

*My Visit to Harvard Business School in 2012 – A Dialogue with a Professor*

The interviewee is a professor of Business Administration at Harvard Business School. He was born in China, grew up in Uruguay, and settled in the United States. Harvard Business School is like home to him. It was here that he acquired his education and it is here that he now teaches. He is a virtuoso in conversation; his words knock at the heart. He smiled as I shared the Akhuwat Model with him.

'You have accomplished something wonderful. It is always difficult to tread new paths. However, you still have a long way to go.' When I prodded further, he asked, 'How many people have you facilitated with loans so far?'

'Two hundred thousand,' I replied.

'How many more people in Pakistan need such a service?' he asked again.

'Ten million.'

'When will you reach these ten million people?'

For a moment, I was lost for words. The message behind that question was that the path that Akhuwat has adopted in order to reach those ten million people is fraught with difficulties. Altruism, sacrifice and compassion – the lover does not endure for the beloved's requital. Running microfinance as a business would have been so much easier than exhorting solidarity to people. Take money from the market, apply service charges and shell it out to the poor – you will get your profit and the poor will get what they need.

He spoke of microfinance institutions around the world, especially in Latin America, that had reached millions of poor. Their rapid expansion and outreach could be traced to the 70–80% interest they charged on their loans. He, perhaps, wished that the journey towards alleviating poverty be traversed at a much more rapid pace. This is perhaps the tragedy of capitalism; impatience and insatiability pervade even the noblest of pursuits. What is left behind is a preoccupation with the end and little regard of the journey.

How could I have told him, if the destination is important for us, then the path to reach that destination is equally important? We cannot charge interest to gain self-sufficiency; no moral system makes concessions for this.

His question, however, reverberated with me: when will you reach ten million people? Was this a question, an opinion or a challenge? It seemed like a challenge to me. Beyond myself, it was a challenge to each ruler, each thinker, each proprietor of power and affluence in Pakistan.

Are the poor not part of our national entity? There are two possible courses to adopt – either we leave them at the mercy of capitalism, or else spread the lesson of solidarity and begin by claiming them. Business or altruism, alienation or solidarity – the decision lies not with these professors of our world, but with our conscience.

*Sharing Amjad's sentiments, I can imagine how tough it must be at times for him to convince people of the intangible benedictions overlapped in Akhuwat's altruistic endeavours. To our materialistic minds, any mutual transaction should provide a tangible benefit – altruistic models of living and being are beyond us, or we have shut the doors to Hikma (our inner wisdom) of SOUL-idarity, of co-existence and co-generating 'real' wealth that genuinely benefits us all in equal measure and does not divide us into classes of the 'haves', i.e., privileged ones and the 'have-nots' – the less fortunate amongst us.*

*Thus, we start off by defining what is considered to be 'genuine wealth' after many conversations with my colleague Mark Anielski, who follows the same path of love (Ishq) and compassion in seeking the wellbeing and genuine happiness of communities as Amjad and I do.*

Mark Anielski (2007), an economist and adjunct professor at the University of Alberta, in his book *An Economy of Well-being*, writes: *too often we know the cost of everything and the value of nothing.*

He further writes in his *Genuine Wealth* treatise:

> The world is limited by its current system of measurement; most of the real wealth of communities is being wasted, ignored or under-valued. According to Mark, measuring what matters to the wellbeing of an organisation or

> community should be at the core of wellbeing of wealth. For what gets measured gets managed. Thus, measuring the wellbeing impacts of all decisions and actions matters. He also exhibits his belief in virtuous actions as the key to genuine happiness; this requires the alignment of one's actions to the desired end, which is flourishing wellbeing conditions for the greatest number of people and the planet.
>
> (Anielski, 2007)

On the point of measuring what should be managed, in an impact report measuring Akhuwat's solidarity impact on its borrowers prepared by Joana S. Afonso for Portsmouth University in partnership with Lendwithcare, Akhuwat's UK partner, Joana writes:

> A final remark would be to call attention to the overall positive evaluation made by the clients regarding the changes in their lives – 68% declared having a better quality of life in 2017. It is also interesting to note that 93% of these clients have since become Akhuwat donors, with 66% reporting making regular donations to the institution.
>
> (Afonso, 2017)

*'For the reward of goodness is only goodness', the Quranic verse echoes in my ear. Could this be the reciprocal effect of the bond of solidarity, which can perhaps only be measured through the anthropological wellbeing of human intention (niyya) and love for one's fellow-beings?*

*This is the reverberation of our 'solidarity bond' iteration as stipulated through our integral GENE rhythm in one of the previous chapters (Chapter 4).*

*What is presented below is one such resonance – of a financial model of solidarity and reciprocity amongst Akhuwat's community of donors, borrowers and volunteers – created with such an intention (niyya) of communal welfare and wellbeing.*

*This cyclical iteration arises through an anticipated spiritual integration of our solidarity GENE rhythm – with Ibn Khaldun's asabiyyah (esprit de corps or social solidarity) as the seed of the Khaldunian cyclical theory of human history.*

*This might seem strange to some of my readers, but this articulation truly came through a deeper initiative reflection of Akhuwat's fourfold philosophy, which is not perceptible as such, although postulated as such by Amjad, i.e., through his intuitive reflection on Quranic (Qard-e-Hasan) and prophetic emulation (Mawakhat) and Iqbalian perception of compassion (ishq and amal) and universal Akhuwat.*

Table 6.1 illustrates this universal brotherhood concept.

*Why is Akhuwat, then, referred to as a microfinance organisation, locally and globally? What hinders Akhuwat from communicating itself as one such distinctive model that banks on a unique 'bond of solidarity' that sustains itself through virtuosity of barakah (divine as well as communal)?*

*Table 6.1* Concept of Universal Brotherhood

| *Quran* | *Iman, Ihsan, Ikhlas, Infaq* | *Ikhuwah* | *Global* |
|---|---|---|---|
| Holy Prophet of Islam | Embodiment of all the above Quranic virtues into his Sunnah (Prophetic Tradition) | Mawakhat | Local-global |
| Iqbal | Ishq-Ilm-Amal | Action | Local |

*This is my call-to-contribution to Akhuwat's remarkable pursuit of communal solidarity and integrity for others to follow. Indeed, it is our collective attempt on behalf of my research fellow members in the TRANS4M community around the world to illustrate such models, for example, Akhuwat's solidarity economic model from Pakistan, CISER's integral banking system from Nigeria, CIFE (Centre for Integral Finance & Economics) from the UK and Tanweer Project & Medlabs from Jordan, all this in our own distinctive style to initiate what we term a knowledge-based research umma-versity or communi-versity that forms a cluster of integral finance and enterprise building.*

For Islam places a huge emphasis on the achievement of human welfare, which is more comprehensive than economic welfare. Umer Chapra a Pakistani-born, Saudi Arabian economist, also explains that while economic development is indispensable, it is not sufficient to realise overall human wellbeing by default. Humans have other needs besides satiating their economic securities or insecurities.

Additionally, as maintained by Oshodi and Adeojo (2018), achieving communal good-life and human wellbeing is the foundation of the Maqasid al Shariah. It further seeks to safeguard and enrich the human self, which further achieves dynamic balance. Furthermore, it promotes anything that safeguards and enriches the human self (nafs), faith (deen), prosperity (nasl), wealth (mal) and intellect (aql).

*Taking into account the multi-faceted approach to communal/societal welfare as proposed by our colleagues above, whilst taking this into consideration through a humanistic as well as a faith-based approach, what we are proposing here and through Akhuwat's live example is a 'middle-way' – an integral-spiritual-financial paradigm, which we will present in our concluding chapter. Standing at the cusp of two civilisations (East and West) and looking around, all I see is an errant divide between the spiritual (our integral Eastern orientation) and the financial (our integral Western orientation), whereas the spiritual practices are kept partitioned (or often undercover) when it comes to business dealings. Conversely, the spiritual disciplines, regardless of the fact, rightfully place emphasis on disciplining the Self and refraining from exorbitance and decadence, but they lack the inclination to advocate any such financial models emerging from their midst.*

*This makes me wonder if there could be a golden mean where the two could reconcile and re-think the epistemology of finance through a Hikma of reciprocity/solidarity, as is conceptualised in Akhuwat's case.*

As stated by McGoun,'By the traditionally rigorous standards of the natural sciences, financial economics has been a failure. It simply cannot predict anything with equivalent accuracy or reliability' (Scheemaekere, 2009).

Could financial models like Akhuwat, which is the simplest in its approach as stated by Dr. Ajaz Khan (Harper & Khan, 2017), thus fill this gap and start a new-age discipline of SOUL-idarity with Akhuwat – a culture of sharing one's (excess) barakah with others for a reward in the hereafter or simply for anthropomorphic resolution?

To explore this further, we now turn to Akhuwat's epistemology of solidarity and bonds of reciprocity and compassion, illustrating in depth its methodology of practising Mawakhat, a Prophetic tradition of brotherhood – of sharing and CARE-ing 4 its society.

## 2 Origination: a new discipline – a new expression of a solidarity bond of reciprocity and compassion (Ihsan)

*Amjad or I could be at loss for words distilling the message of intangible reciprocity between Akhuwat's community of beneficiaries and benefactors (borrowers-donors and volunteers, for the lack of mark-up in such transactions) but for the words of Pakistan's national poet and renowned Muslim thinker Iqbal, which deliver the message with such perceptibility that conveys the Eastern intellection of transactions of benevolence through the exchequer of Ishq/love – a sublime state known as 'Metta' in the Buddhist tradition. Love (Metta) without desire to possess, knowing well that in the ultimate sense there is no possession and no possessor, is the highest love – a divinely supreme love known as Ishq in the Sufi tradition. A love embracing all beings, knowing well that we all are fellow wayfarers through this round of existence – that we all are overcome by the same law of suffering.*

*Iqbal writes in his poem 'The Decline of Muslim':*

*Sabab Kuch Aur Hai, Tu Jis Ko Khud Samajhta Hai*
*Zawal Banda-e-Momin Ka Be-Zarri Se Nahi*

*Agar Jahan Mein Jouhar Aashkara Huwa*
*Qalandari Se Huwa Hai, Toungari Se Nahin*

*With ease you can divine to something else is due:*
*Penury cannot cause decline of Muslims True*

*Wealth has played no part to bring my worth to light*
*My faqr this spell has cast; the share of wealth is slight*
*(Zarb-e-Kaleem-010).*

*In a country like Pakistan where Iqbal's words still ring true and where an altruistic model of reciprocal endowment emerged from the teachings of a prophetic philosophy of Mawakhat, Akhuwat thrives on this Iqbalian vision of dignity and self-constraint. In a world of factitious scarcity, we certainly need to invent a new definition of economic and finance discipline which could fit in well with the definition of faqr (penury – a faqir/derwish is a person who is self-sufficient and only possesses the spiritual need for God) and be-zarri (penury), dearth of empathy rather than penury of wealth and abundance.*

*For Iqbal, the decline of a Muslim was not due to dearth of wealth possession, but rather his inadequacy of eternalising his proprietorship of faqr (penury and spiritual neediness of qalandari (renunciation). Though wealth and gold provide the worldly needs of man, per Iqbal, what faqr can bestow no wealth or gold ever can.*

*If there's any explanation for such compassionate exchange, this must be it.*

*Similarly, this also rings true in Steiner's words, the 'spiritual scientist' of the 20th century.*

## *2.1 The integrality of a solidarity economy*

*In Chapter 4, we identified the solidarity impulse/GENE reiterating through integral four realms. Thereafter, we spoke about the bond of solidarity as it emerges 'four-worldly', and how it binds communities together through this common thread of benefaction. In this chapter we explore Akhuwat's procedural structure to fully understand the 'Akhuwat Model' in its practical form, but before we do that, let us examine from our integral perspective and see what our transformation gurus say about this.*

*Per Schieffer and Lessem* (2010):

> After touring the world's economic theory and practice in an integral manner, we found that if we applied the four integral realms to map economic theory and practice we could clearly see that there was profound economic thinking in each of them. We also noticed that there was an overriding economic theme in each of the four realms, which led us to the following classification:
>
> - The 'Southern' natural and communal realm promotes the *self-sufficient community-based* economy.
> - The 'Eastern' cultural and spiritual realm promotes a *developmental culture-based* economy.
> - The 'Northern' scientific and technological realm promotes a *social knowledge-based* economy.
> - The 'Western' realm was promoted in the past through a neoliberal market economy, but below the surface we can recognise the gradual emergence of what we called a *living life-based economic* realm – which is basically a creative revisiting of the Anglo-Saxon economic model with a strong focus on ecology and sustainability.

In view of the above integral orientations proposed by Lessem and Schieffer, we thus group Akhuwat's four principles into two groups, whereby the Northern – *social knowledge-based* and Western – *living life-based* realms are grouped together in this chapter as per their operational methodology, i.e., loan disbursement with reciprocal endowment (converting borrowers to donors), consequently expounding on Akhuwat's 4 C's (Call, Context, Co-creation, Contribution) as an effect of this combination.

The Northern realm of Lessem and Schieffer's integral economics model presents:

> **North**: Working through the gene-ius of the Northern realm of a knowledge-based social economy, we evolve '*from hierarchy to democracy*', and we actively revisit the extent to which our community or enterprise responds to continuous technological change and social challenges in a cooperative and democratic manner.
>
> The role model we surfaced in the Northern realm is the *cooperative enterprise*, embodied by Mondragon in Spain, the world's largest workers' cooperative and a leader in the social-economic cooperative movement.

Their Western realm of a life-based economy presents as such:

> **West**: Working through the gene-ius of the Western realm of a life-based living economy we evolve '*from growth to sustainability*', and we actively revisit the extent to which our community or enterprise is modelled upon nature, thereby sustainable and restorative, building up human, natural and financial capital in parallel. The role model we surfaced in the Western realm is the '*sustainable enterprise*', embodied in the case of Interface in the USA, a corporate leader within the sustainability movement.

Figure 6.1 thus shows a roadmap of Akhuwat's reciprocal economy, inspired by the integral economics model articulated by Schieffer and Lessem (2010). This postulation came after closely studying Akhuwat's distinctive paradigm of reciprocity and solidarity, which has generated this most unusual model of economy which spirals from one realm to another initiating a new process every time.

The below figure illustrates the roadmap of Akhuwat's solidarity economy through an integral economics perspective, wherein the centre is occupied by the moral core of an Islamic society. In Akhuwat and Pakistan's case, we have placed Divine Sustenance in the middle as the moral core value of Mawakhat – sharing one's abundance (barakah) with others by placing full reliance on Al-Razzaq.

For, Al-Razzaq, one of the 99 names of Allah, is what pulsates in the centre of our solidarity cyclical Northwestern (reason-to-realisation) orientation.

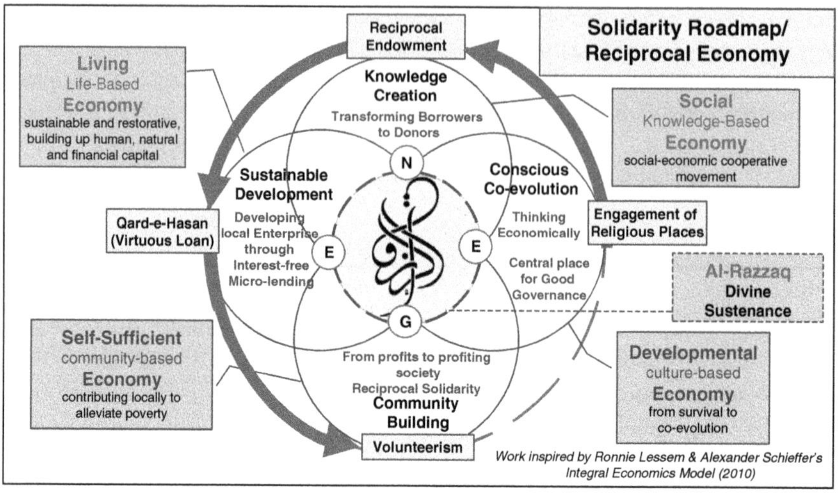


*Figure 6.1* Akhuwat's Solidarity Economy

Whereby, Al-Razzaq – a Divine attribute – is associated with being: The Bestower of Sustenance, and The Provider, The One who creates all means of nourishment and subsistence. The One who is the giver of all things beneficial, both physical and spiritual. The One who provides everything that is needed.

For in a Muslim society, rizq [God's bounty] is the root word of Al-Razzaq, and this lies at the centre, the pulsating rhythm of life sustenance. This forms the foundation of Akhuwat's 'reciprocal endowment'. In Amjad's words, *All that is from Rabb (Lord Sustainer) belongs to all (of HIS creation)*. There is no distinction or classification.

Benjamin Z. Kedar (1938), professor emeritus of History at the Hebrew University of Jerusalem and president of the International Society for the Study of the Crusades and the Latin East, in his seminal work regarding the Crusades, drew a comparison between the Arabic word *rizq* and Latin word *risicum*.

Kedar believes that; "the origin of the word risk is either the Arabic word *rizq* or Latin word *risicum*. The Arabic *rizq* has a positive connotation, signifying anything that has been given to a person (by God) and from which this person can draw profit or *satisfaction*. The Latin word, *risicum*, on the other hand, implies an unfavourable event, as it originally referred to the challenge that a barrier reef presents to a sailor. The Greek derivative of the Arabic word rizq, which was used in the twelfth century, relates to chance outcome in general. It may not be clear that what is given by God according to the Arabic *rizq*, which is always good, relates to risk, a situation that is typically understood to imply the potential of something bad (or something good) happening. However, what rizq and risk have in common is uncertainty of the outcome. There is no guarantee that *rizq* will come, and if it does there is no guarantee how much it will be". (Kedar, 1969)

By placing Al-Razzaq, the provider of *rizq*, at the centre, it on the one hand completes one's faith (Iman) in the Almighty, and on the other emancipates us from worrying about carrying the divine responsibility of providing for ourselves on our shoulders.

In Akhuwat's case, this realisation came as direct intuitive knowledge (Ilm), navigating through the integral Northern realm, thus creating Akhuwat's 'knowledge-based economy', e.g., Akhuwat's borrowers becoming Akhuwat's donors or partners. This knowledge was co-created between Akhuwat and its beneficiaries through a mutual consent which we have termed a 'reciprocal endowment'. The main idea came from the Islamic ordination of Qard-e-Hasan, wherein the debtor could voluntarily contribute any amount, at times as small as $1, with their repayments. We will further expand on this in the section below.

The stage that comes after navigating through the integral Northern realm is the Western realm of 'sustaining' development – human as well as financial. This forms Akhuwat's core principle of Qard-e-Hasan, facilitating micro-entrepreneurs to sustain a respectable livelihood for their families.

This divine quality plays a major role in sustaining a Muslim on a micro level, i.e., as an individual, at writ large, the reliance on divine sustenance (rizq) holds the central moral plane in a Muslim society and reflects in Amjad and Akhuwat's practice of Qard-e-Hasan (interest-free loans).

We now proceed to demonstrate Akhuwat's process of reciprocity and the methodology it has adopted to generate its own solidarity capital, which sustains its many operations.

## 3 The solidarity capital: reciprocity of Ikhuwah (Bhai-chara)

### *3.1 The process*

We are aware of the concerns raised by many regarding the sustainability and scalability of an organisation working on donations, voluntary contributions and voluntary efforts. We do not view Akhuwat as a short-term experiment, nor are we interested in gaining some sort of permanence through profit alone. Instead, through a spirit of volunteerism, the principle of low operational cost and dependence on generosity of the community, the Akhuwat Model has not only sustained itself but is also expanding and being replicated by others. With a recovery rate of 99.85%, Akhuwat is a challenge to conventional MFIs, to high interest rates, and traditional practices – despite which recoveries are failing. It might be a model worth considering, for there is no doubt that there is something wrong with MFIs at large. In the words of Malcolm Harper, my English colleague and expert on enterprise development and microfinance, 'Akhuwat takes us back to the early days of innocence, when poverty alleviation was what microfinance was for, and this reminder is healthy, and necessary'. For a program that originates in the philosophy of brotherhood, generosity and goodwill could not be less sustainable than any such that depends on purely financial incentives.

First off, we start with familiarising ourselves with the process by starting off from the core – Akhuwat's loans formulation and the approach applied to gather capital, thereafter the methodology used to circulate and disperse the effect.

Schieffer and Lessem (2010) place 'religion and humanity' in the centre of their integral economic model, as it provides something like a moral core of economic thought and practice.

In a relative manner, Akhuwat places the Islamic and prophetic precept of Mawakhat – solidarity with one's community – as the moral core value which stems from reliance on *divine bounty (rizq) and divine sustenance (tawakal Allah)* as shown in Figure 6.2 below.

As Akhuwat's essential mandate, this is done by sharing one's abundance with others/needy ones, by subscribing to the divine ordination of Qard-e-Hasan.

Akhuwat's philosophy is based on the premise that poverty can only be eliminated if the society is willing to share its resources with the poor/needy and less fortunate amongst the society. For Akhuwat, Qard-e-Hasan is a means to an end and not an end in itself. The end is a vibrant, economically strong society, based on sharing resources, which is an idealist approach in itself. Their aim is to

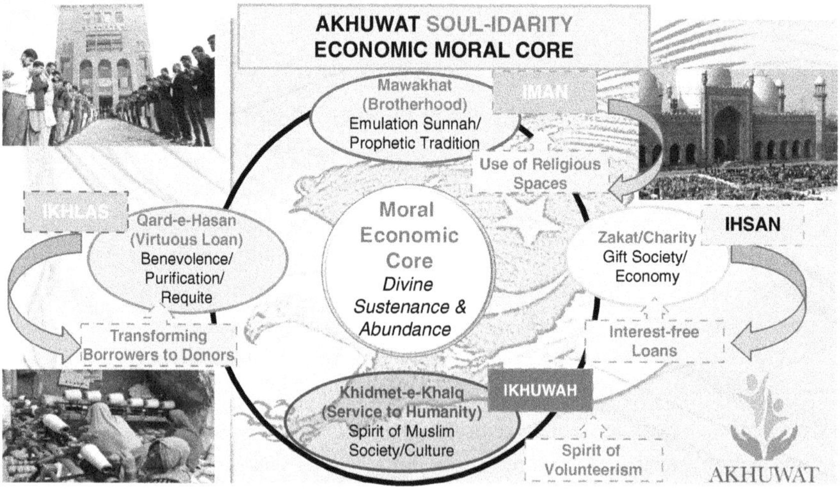


*Figure 6.2* Akhuwat's Economic Moral Core

develop and sustain a social system based on compassion, solidarity and mutual support.

Amjad's articulation of establishing one such society is what sets Akhuwat apart, particularly from other microfinance organisations operating in Pakistan and around the world in general. Microfinance organisations are considered as the most effective tool to reducing poverty, whereas Amjad appears to be more concerned about the decline in societal bonds of solidarity in comparison to other microfinance organisations that certainly lack that passion of community development through awakening the collective consciousness of communities to form a solidarity bond, something which has been Akhuwat's core principal, philosophy and practice.

That solidarity bond, as per Amjad's contemplation, was in following a faith-based prescription, that which has been ordained by Allah and not dictated by the pandemic rules of microfinance. The name of that divine remedy according to Amjad is Qard-e-Hasan – a loan given with the intent of *benefiting* the needy and not to make business out of someone's needs.

We now explore this further in the light of Akhuwat's methodology and practices.

### *3.1.1 Qard-e-Hasan – Akhuwat's interest-free loans*

Akhuwat is known definitively in the public domain as a microfinance institute (MFI). Its primary objective was to relieve people of the destitution and despondency of poverty. But all this, for Amjad, had to come from the rich customs of Islamic faith and beliefs. Inherently, for Islamic societies, the main philanthropic acts are done as a religious obligation of giving zakat and sadaqah.

Sadaqah is the charity money given to people in need. For Amjad, giving charity money (occasionally) was not the solution he had in mind, as he does not believe in creating permanent dependence, but rather he believes in sustainable growth in partnership with the poor and needy – as per the integral Western orientation of integral economics.

For this purpose, Akhuwat adopted the interest-free loan model as prescribed in Quran as its operational strategy. Interest-free small loans are given to the economically active poor of the society for establishing a new business or expanding an existing one. Such loans offer pragmatic solutions to the many hurdles that are now emerging in the field of microfinance practices. These loans aim at poverty alleviation – not as a business enterprise for the organisation, but to enable the lowest income classes and those who previously did not have a source of income to become economically independent and contributing citizens. Most importantly, it serves on humanitarian grounds without any discrimination.

Amjad firmly believes and often propagates that poverty is not about being poor in wealth; rather, poverty is when one loses self-pride and dignity by being dependent on others financially.

We now explore the nature of 'virtuous loan', as per Amjad's translation of Qard-e-Hasan, an Arabic term which, if broken down epistemologically, means a beautiful (hasan) loan (qard). For as per his apotheosis of a quintessentially virtuous society, loans given should also be none other than virtuous and benevolent.

### 3.1.2 Qard-e-Hasan: a virtuous loan

Akhuwat's interest-free loan model is inspired by the philosophy of Qard-e-Hasan, a Quranic ordination.

According to the Institute of Islamic Banking and Insurance's definition, a virtuous loan is interest-free and extended on a goodwill basis, mainly for welfare purposes, and the borrower is only required to pay back the borrowed amount. The loan is payable on demand and repayment is obligatory. But if a debtor is in difficulty, the lender/creditor is expected to extend the time or even voluntarily waive repayment of the whole or a part of the loan amount. Islam allows loan as a form of social service among the rich, to help the poor and those who are in need of financial assistance. Qard-e-Hasan may be viewed as something between giving charity or a gift and giving a loan (qard). A debtor may voluntarily choose to pay an extra amount to the lender/creditor over the principal amount borrowed (without promising it) as a token of appreciation. And this forms Akhuwat's theory of '*borrowers becoming donors*'. This type of loan does not violate the prohibition on riba since it is the only type of loan that does not compensate the creditor for the time value of money. Such loans have not been uncommon in human history among peers, friends, family and relatives, but no other organisation has been able to come up to Akhuwat's scale of channelising philanthropic funds so effectively with a recovery rate of 99.9%.

We now exemplify two of Akhuwat's main funds that continuously spiral out of each other, that is, its interest-free loans and its reciprocal endowment (members donation program).

### 3.1.3 Two principles: interest-free loans and reciprocal endowment

*Why interest-free?*

According to Financial Encyclopaedia, the Arabic term riba-al-qard is associated with lending and borrowing (i.e., received in lending or paid in borrowing). It is a type of riba that constitutes an excess amount, pecuniary or non-pecuniary, over and above the principal (asl al-qard) in a loan (qard) that a borrower pays to the lender along with principal based on a precondition in the contract (aqd) or customary practices (urf). Riba-al-qard also constitutes any excess amount paid for the extension of a loan's maturity date. The majority of fuqaha' (religious scholars) reached a consensus that riba in this sense holds the same meaning and import as the conventional notion of interest.

How does Akhuwat, then, justify this?

*Borrowers Becoming Donors*

However, any excess amount or consideration (iwadh) given by a debtor out of his/her own accord, and without the compulsion of a contractual stipulation or custom is not tantamount to riba but is rather attributed to husnul-qadhaa – i.e., willingly offered by the borrower. Riba al-qard is also known as riba al-Quran as it is mentioned in the Quran. In conventional finance, it is interest on loans.

### *The Mawakhat Model*

The seed philosophy for both above principles originates from the prophetic tradition of Mawakhat right after the migration of the Prophet of Islam to Medina from Mecca. The source of this vision can be traced back 1400 years to Mawakhat-e-Medina; a historical display of solidarity that changed the course of history. After being banished from Mecca, Muslims sought refuge in Medina. Braving the perils and hardships that accompanied the exodus, these people reached Medina in destitution. The people of Medina welcomed them into their homes with the pledge that, from then onwards, they would share half of whatever they owned with the refugees. This bond of fellowship (solidarity) formed the seed of an exceptional tradition – Mawakhat.

**Ansar -The Givers; Helpers**

- who gave asylum to their Muhajirin brethren in their own homes and comforted them with their wealth. In doing so, they aid Allah and His Messenger by fighting alongside the Muhajirun for their hardships.

**Muhajirin -The Takers; Emigrants or Followers**

- who left their homes and estates, emigrating to give support to Allah and His Messenger to establish His religion. They gave up their wealth and themselves in this cause.

The Quran calls them allies to one another – for each one of them has more right to the other than anyone else. Therefore, Allah's Messenger forged ties of brotherhood between the Muhajiroun (Followers) and Ansar (Helpers). In doing so, the Prophet demonstrated the practical example of real management, as real wealth is yielded through real management of people.

According to Agha Hasan Abedi, another Pakistani and a banking genius of his time, and president and founder of BCCI (Bank of Credit and Commerce International), "real management models itself on the laws of nature – a management ecosystem. For Abedi, the concept of *giving* permeates all aspects of real management. More than a banker, Abedi was a visionary with a clear perception of the future – a divine gift. He believed that mankind could achieve far more if only it understood the divine scheme – that we all have a purpose in life and we must feel honoured to be chosen for the task of building the future using our abilities and capacities.

Abedi, with an unconventional approach to banking, was the first person who took it upon himself to institutionalise a 'spirit of giving and sharing' amongst his employees. "In 1980, Abedi addressed a letter to all BCCI employees emphasising their obligation to share the benefits accruing to them with the less unfortunate. In his letter, he also emphasised the fact that, while extending financial help is one way of sharing, the ultimate form thereof is giving of yourself, i.e., offering your time, energies and abilities with humility for the salvation of the less fortunate. As a start, employees were offered a sum along with their monthly salaries for this purpose." (Shahid, 2016).

This is the same concept of giving that Amjad has been persistently trying to instil into his society's psyche for years now. Similarly, Abedi professed that *giving* instils a sense of acquisition in people, which eventually creates a tradition of purposeful living and co-existence. Akhuwat has been successful in cultivating the same culture of giving amongst its borrowers by becoming its donors, as well as through its employees, who are paid for 40 hours yet work for 60 hours a week, hence 'giving' 20 hours of their time as their contribution.

Per Amjad's presumption, albeit learning from the historic example of Medina and Mawakhat, he religiously believes in the above categorisation of Ansar (helpers) and Muhajroun (takers or followers) – that in any given society, there will always be Ansar, those who are always willing to give of themselves (volunteer) and from their abundance; they act as anchors for every society. Then there are Muhajroun, those who are always in need of Ansar. It is Amjad's conviction that those who are helped have also a giver or donor hidden in themselves as they are helped out of their destitute situation.

Such wisdom of cooperation (Al-Hikmat al-Ta'awuniyah) and solidarity existent in Akhuwat's case is a reflection of Shah Waliullah's fifth wisdom in the second stage of socio-economic development, which relates to cooperation among the members of the society on economic issues. Quṭb ad-Din Aḥmad Wali Allah Dihlawi, an eighteen-century prominent Sufi philosopher and scholar of Delhi, was known as Shah Waliullah (Allah's friend/ally) because of his piety.

Per Shah Waliullah:

> This cooperation necessitates itself as people in the society are not equally good for all things. Some of them have good intelligence while some others are imbecile. Some of them have capital, while some others are empty-handed but can work hard. Some people hate to do petty works, while some other do not, and so on. Thus, their mundane life would have become very difficult, had they not sought the cooperation of each other. Take the example of Mudarabah (profit-sharing), a person might have capital, but he cannot persuade himself for trade and travelling or any other such kind of job. Thus, they need cooperation and help of each other. Some people cannot do that directly, so they resort to power of attorney, sponsorship and middleman ship.
>
> (Dehlawi, 1945)

Incidentally, Akhuwat as a trust or waqf takes the position of that middleman-ship for the less-privileged strata of Pakistani society.

On another occasion in his treatsie on 'Stages of socio-economic development: Shah Wali-Allah's concept of *Irtifaqat', one of the fivekinds of wisdom,* Al-Hikmat al-ta'amuliyah, is what he termed as the wisdom of mutual dealings. Shah Waliullah mentions:

> some more institutions of mutual dealings based on virtue and benevolence, such as sadaqah (charity), wasiyah (will) and waqf (religious endowment and trusts). He maintains that "the idea of waqf was unknown to the people before Islam. This institution was established by Prophet Muhammad (peace be upon him) for different welfare considerations. The merit of waqf is that the needy people benefit from this source of income generation while its ownership remains with the endowment maker. Hundreds of such waqf (trusts) were established in Muslim societies during the Ottoman Caliphate for supporting education, health and other causes.
>
> (Aislahi, 1989)

*This is the Mawakhat paradigm of SOUL-idarity between communities. And what lies in the nature of solidarity? For too much decadence eludes the spirit of solidarity and Iqbal's exigency of faqr (spiritual poverty).*

We now access the impact of this solidarity through the methodology Akhuwat has adopted to this effect.

## 4 The solidarity impact – methodology

### *4.1 The practice*

Akhuwat's strength lies in its congregational solidarity and a unique articulation of funnelling through the benevolence of Pakistani/Islamic society in such a way that it reaches its rightful earner.

To date, Akhuwat has provided micro-credit to more than 2.6 million families and disbursed $650 million among these families. It has 780 branches in 350 cities of Pakistan with a remarkable recovery rate of 99.93%. The desire to repay the loans is not motivated by fear or insecurity but rather the knowledge that the repaid amounts will be 'recycled' to others in need. The most visible manifestation of Akhuwat's efforts is the transformation of its beneficiaries (borrowers) into donors. Most of the beneficiaries voluntarily give back to the organisation once they have achieved a sufficient degree of financial sustainability and awareness of the vision of the program.

Another common practice that has evolved in communities where Akhuwat operates has been Akhuwat's borrowers offering 'internships' to new beneficiaries to assist them in setting up their own enterprises, thus, spreading the solidarity effect of Ihsan.

Akhuwat's other remarkable local achievements have been to inspire state institutions to replicate this model on a wider scale. Effectively, Akhuwat's model is also taught at many local as well as global universities, including Harvard Business School, Stanford Business School, Cambridge Judge Business School and more.

This thereby forms the fundamental reinterpretation of a developmental economy and society as per Steiner's threefold commonwealth articulation of associative economics. He distinguished three independent, as well as interdependent (co-evolving), societal parts, economics, politics and culture.

Steiner sees culture as the rightful place for competition, in order to achieve personal freedom and liberation. Economics, in contrast, is about fraternity, and politics is about equality. In this combination, an individual strives to fully actualise his or her personal skills in the field of culture, which, in turn, informs his or her unique and knowledgeable contribution to economic life. The focus of economics, then, is on the real needs of society, and its organizing form is the association. Consequently, capital is seen in a new light. As articulated by Steiner's followers Folkert Wilken and Christopher Houghton Budd, capital becomes a means of self-expression, individual evolution and knowledge creation. Wilken was among the first to recognise the intellectual, cultural, even spiritual dimension of capital and its rootedness in accumulative capacities of previous generations (Schieffer & Lessem, 2010).

Similarly, for Amjad, knowledge creation takes a central position for the sustainability of Akhuwat's *Mawakhat paradigm.* To this effect, Akhuwat is doing a great service to Pakistan (locally) and other institutions (globally), by transmitting the effect of its solidarity capital, generated through its multiple initiatives.

For instance, in January 2018 Akhuwat organised the biggest loan disbursement ceremony ever enumerated in Pakistan's history. A total number of 25,000 families were gathered in Lahore's historic mosque built by the Mughul Emperor Aurangzeb. The ceremony was a spectacle to behold and exemplifies Steiner's threefold commonwealth of culture, politics and economy. This disbursement was a joint partnership, with the Punjab government employing Akhuwat's solidarity paradigm – a factual display of solidarity bond.

Akhuwat thrives on this interdependence and co-involvement of its Ansar (donors) and Muhajroun (borrowers), but how does it sustain this equity of solidarity bond?

We will now explore this, by virtue of what we term as Akhuwat's *sustainability paradigm.*

### 4.1.1 *The Mawakhat sustainability paradigm*

#### WHAT SUSTAINS AKHUWAT?

Inherently, most Islamic societies have four streams of money allocated for charitable purposes, whereby zakat is obligatory for every Muslim to pay. Table 6.2 illustrates the structural definition of charity/alms distribution within a Muslim society.

In a related manner, Pakistan, like any other vibrant and compassionate society, is blessed with a rich and kind-hearted civil society as well as individuals who have always placed the country's welfare and development first and foremost in their hearts. For any philanthropic act, communities bank on the benevolence of its civil society. There are some 45,000 active non-profit organisations in Pakistan.

For Amjad, the spirit of fraternity and brotherhood is what inhabits the very core of Akhuwat. Rather than relying on institutional loans and grants, Amjad has set his heart on channelling through the above-mentioned four streams of philanthropy installed within Pakistan's Islamic society. Pakistan, relatively a young nation in subsistence and in the absence of a reliable state welfare system in place, relies on the philanthropic deeds of its affluent class. As a recent study by the Stanford Social Innovation Review reports that when it comes to charitable giving, Pakistan is a generous country, and it contributes more than 1% of its GDP to charity. Indeed, the word charity here should be understood in terms of beneficence rather than of giving alms.

Amjad, after some in-depth manoeuvring of the prevailing social class system and being perceptive of the above categorisations, was aware that after paying zakat, which is obligatory on every Muslim, some kind-hearted individuals pay large sums as sadaqah for societal welfare, seeing it as their humane duty to share from their abundance with the less privileged in the society. Some other institutions like Shaukat Khanum Cancer Hospital, Indus Hospital, Edhi Trust and many others are the biggest recipients of such donations.

After zakat comes *sadaqah*, which is a virtuous deed in Islam and is considered as an integral part of one's Iman (faith) and tawakkul (reliance) on God. This also comes under discipling one's soul or what we termed the soul's trans-migrational journey, i.e., parting from one's valued possessions.

*Table 6.2* The Structural Definition of Charity/Alms Distribution

| *Zakat* | *Sadaqah* | *Saqaqah Jariyah* | *Qard-e-Hasan* |
|---|---|---|---|
| Means Purification | Means Charity | Means Perpetual (ongoing) Charity | Goodly Loan |
| Obligatory | Voluntary | Alms | Interest-free Loan |
| one of the five pillars of Islam;<br>2.5% paid annually on wealth/assets | voluntary offering at the will of the benefactor | remains active even after one's death | given with sincerity and not asked back if the borrower fails to pay |

As an act of charity (sadaqah) is not confined to giving from one's wealth, all good deeds performed with the intention of earning God's favour for the welfare of the society and wellbeing of fellow human beings are considered as a sacred duty by Muslims. In this spirit, Akhuwat's volunteerism comes under the act of sadqah jariyah (perpetual charity).

Paying tribute to all the stakeholders and volunteers, in his book *Akhuwat Ka Safar*, Amjad mentioned the names of each and every individual who contributed to Akhuwat's initial call by putting hefty amounts of money into its Mawakhat fund. Some are notable industrialists of Pakistan's most affluent class, and others are people who felt the pull towards Amjad's holy call to build an equitable society by freeing it from the shackles of poverty.

The fourth option, as illustrated above, is Qard-e-Hasan – giving a loan to someone in need. This ranked as the most appropriate and practical option for Amjad, as it encourages people to earn their own livelihoods rather than relying on state dole or societal charity monies.

Therefore, for Akhuwat, it was a case of channelling these voluntary streams (zakat, sadaqah, Qard-e-Hasan), as illustrated in the above table, in a more effective way so that the most vulnerable of the society could benefit from a pool of funds, readily available and flowing out of the font of the benevolence of a society that believes in sharing their abundance as a religious and moral duty.

Furthermore, as per the poverty scorecard of Pakistan (Poverty Survey, 2010), through the application of a proxy means test (PMT) that determines the welfare status of the household on a scale between 0 and 100, Akhuwat further sectioned various characteristics of the household as well as its assets into four parts shown in Figure 6.3 below:

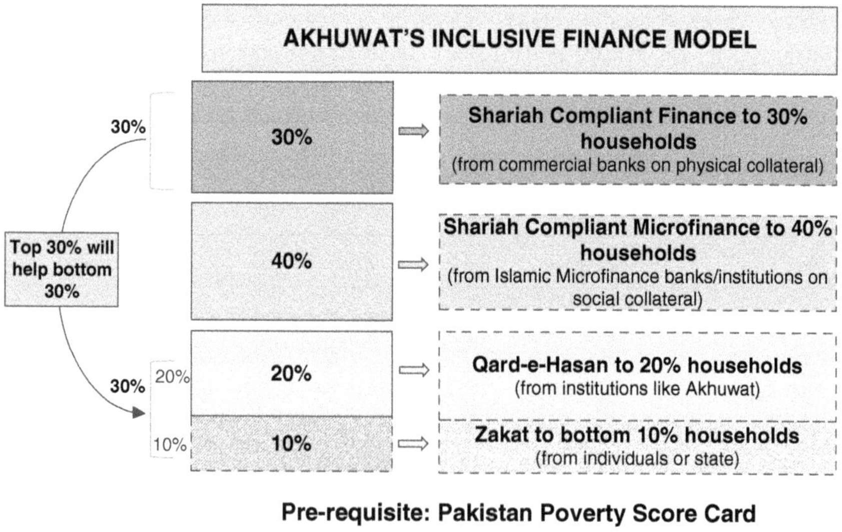


*Figure 6.3* Akhuwat's Model of Islamic Finance

The figure above draws on Akhuwat's conception of the upper 30% helping the lower 30% of the society.

Forthwith, Akhuwat, drawing from their years of excessive on-ground work, knowledge and experience, realised that the 20% were an economically active but relatively poor section of the society that had no access to micro-loans which could help them in either starting or growing their micro-businesses. These ranged from setting up a small cycle puncture repair kiosk to a fruit and veg kiosk to relatively bigger loans to buy machinery for scaling up an existing business.

In accordance with Islamic guidance, people categorised as either too old, destitute or widowed qualify for the zakat stream which, as Akhuwat identified, make 10% of the society. The 30% who are economically active and have the capability of making their own livelihoods were given access to guilt-free (interest-free) micro-loans. Akhuwat sees them as the ones qualifying for Qard-e-Hasan, an interest-free loan process encouraged and ordained by Allah and the Quran.

Akhuwat, therefore, aims to help that lower 30% portion of the society, to emancipate them from their entrapment in a vicious circle of indigence. Thus, the concept of creating 'virtuous circles' was born. For Amjad heartily believes in the perpetuation of such virtuous circles, that is, by reversing the effect of destitution. As he writes in his book, being poor equals being isolated from society. And this isolation could only be countered by forming bonds of solidarity between those who have and are capable of giving (Ansar) and those who are in need of our help (Muhajroun).

*And this is what I identify as creating 'barakah rounds', working implicitly through Akhuwat's members donation program or the reciprocal endowment as illustrated in Figure 6.4 and further explained in the concluding chapter of the book.*

Furthermore, Akhuwat's method of sustainability, after relying on the above four voluntary streams, also banks on the benevolence of individual and institutional philanthropists both local and international and civil society for its main pool of revolving funds.

This includes:

- Individual donors > contribute to Akhuwat's pool of funds through their zakat, sadaqah and charity money.
- Institutional donors > contribute through Qard-e-Hasan (interest-free benevolent loan), Punjab Government Revolving Fund, high net-worth individuals and organizations both local and international.
- Borrowers – reciprocal endowment fund > after gaining economic stability through Akhuwat's lending schemes.

### *4.1.2 Collaborations with government institutions*

Akhuwat works closely with the following government organisations, advising them to utilise their resources better by adopting Akhuwat's model. By far, this accounts for Akhuwat's biggest achievement, as by adopting this method and institutionalising the Mawakhat (brotherhood and solidarity) model, we believe the ripple effect of a solidarity movement could be far reaching by renewing a collective pledge of not making business off of the needy ones and ridding the financial system of malignancy of debt-slavery.

As of now, Akhuwat has a partnership with the following government schemes:

- Govt of Punjab (Chief Minister's Self Employment Scheme-CMSES)
- Govt of Azad Kashmir (Prime Minister Azad Kashmir Loan Scheme)
- Govt of Gilgit Baltistan (CMSES-GB)
- Federal Govt (Prime Minister Interest Free Loan Scheme- PMIFL)
- Govt of FATA (Governor KP Interest Free Loan Scheme)
- TEVTA (Technical Educational Vocational Training Authority)
- Agriculture Loans: A unique initiative for agriculture lending in Punjab. This scheme is for the entire province, however, Akhuwat provides loans in selected districts to farmers having land holdings of up to 2.5 acres, with preference to the landless. Loans are awarded on social collateral or personal guarantees.

#### 4.1.2.1 CHIEF MINISTER'S SELF EMPLOYMENT SCHEME-CMSES

Amjad enjoys a credible reputation within the third sector, owing to his previous engagement with the government as a civil servant, and he also had good relationships with many senior government officials including the Punjab Chief Minister, Shahbaz Sharif. Thus, the chief minister engaged Amjad for two major provincial social welfare initiatives. During a presentation on Akhuwat, the CM asked Amjad if he could double its reach with double the amount of funds coming to Akhuwat through its donors. Upon an affirmative response, in 2011, the CM announced that CMSES was to replicate the Akhuwat model. An interest-free loan of Rupees 12 billion (US$ 120million) was provisioned for this scheme. This was the first time Akhuwat entered into a public-private partnership contract, whereas before Akhuwat only relied on its own funds generated through civil society. CMSES remains the first organisation to give interest-free loans on a large scale – loans ranging up to Rupees 50,000 ($450).

The same model was then replicated by the governments of Gilgit Baltistan, the federal government and FATA (Federally Administered Tribal Areas) and the Government of Azad Kashmir.

Owing to the nature of politics in the local regions, Amjad's biggest achievement was to maintain Akhuwat's position as a non-party/non-political organisation. According to him, 'in developing countries like Pakistan, it's hard to reach an impactful stage of such non-profit entities without local politicians' patronage yet without indulging in the sectoral politics'.

These partnerships helped spread Akhuwat's solidarity effect manifold by bridging the provincial/political divide by bringing people from different communities together, joined by one spirit of Mawakhat and Bhai-chara – as per Steiner's fraternity of associative economy.

##### 4.1.2.2 AGRICULTURE LOANS – INTEREST-FREE AGRICULTURE E-CREDIT SCHEME

Agriculture constitutes the largest sector of Pakistan's economy. The majority of the population, directly or indirectly, depends on this sector. It contributes about 24% of the gross domestic product (GDP) and accounts for half of the employed labour force and is the largest source of foreign exchange earnings. Through this partnership, Akhuwat aims to resolve the dependency of poor farmers from the shackles of their feudal lords who have been appropriating the fruit of their toil for generations.

The Government of Punjab (GoPb) has taken an initiative in promoting the wellbeing of small farmers through the provision of interest-free loans and easy access to finances in Punjab. The objective of the Interest Free Agri. E-Credit Scheme is to reduce the cost of production for these marginalised farmers and to increase the outreach of formal and digital financial services to meet the agenda of financial inclusion. Akhuwat has been selected as one of the participating financial institutions (PFIs) to implement the scheme with small holding farmers and tenants and sharecroppers with landholding up to 2.5 acres in Punjab.

The project is running under a revolving fund of Rs. 2 billion ($1.7 million) in the credit pool, and as of February 28th, 2018, over 80,000 loans, while an amount of Rs. 4.12 billion ($3.5 million) has been disbursed among land owners and tenant farmers.

## 5 Member donation program – Mawakhat – bond of solidarity

Through Akhuwat's members donation program (MDP), Akhuwat has successfully created a unique phenomenon which emerged from its speculation in creating '*Virtuous Circles*'. This cyclical process keeps doing its rounds, starting from the civil society of Pakistan to Akhuwat's borrowers becoming donors – contributing to the main pool of fund which we term the benevolence pool of a circular economy.

For this stands true for Akhuwat's model of regenerative economy, which keeps creating opportunities for all to benefit from a benevolent pool that is ever-flowing; in this sense, their solidarity economy model defies a debt economy, by funnelling through a natural cycle of take-make-reuse, contrary to a linear economy system of take-make-dispose.

Figure 6.4 shows the natural flow of Akhuwat's solidarity rhythm.

### *5.1 Benevolence pool – the main fund*

The figure (Figure 6.4) below illustrates the main pool of funds on the right hand corner. The main pool is the revolving fund which keeps flowing through a cyclical motion as the funds funnel in through the philanthropic

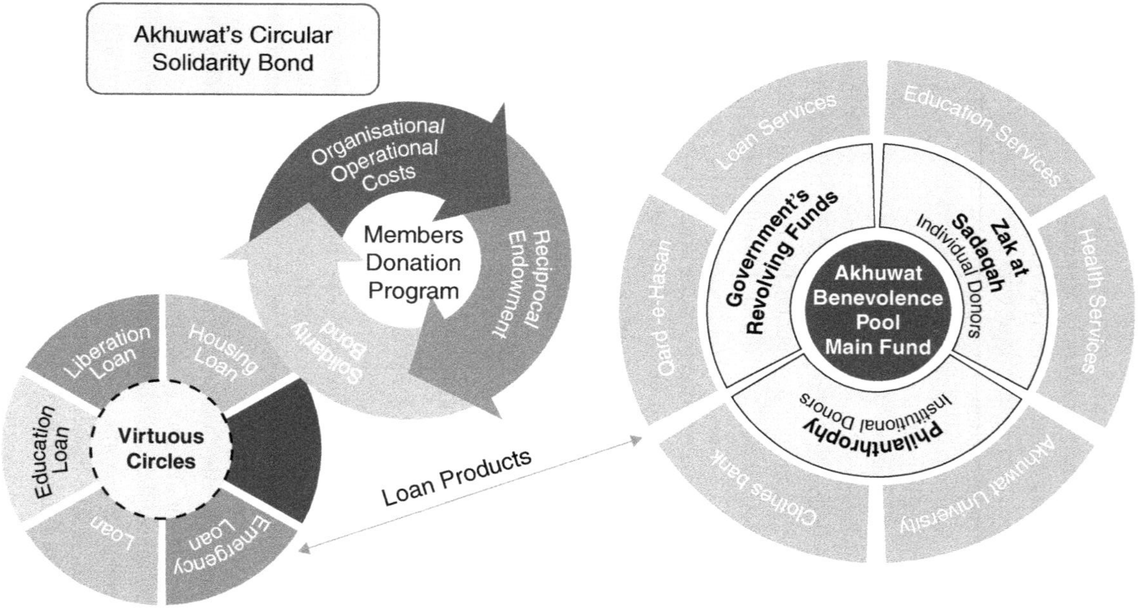


*Figure 6.4* Akhuwat's Circular Benevolence Cycle

streams. Akhuwat's main operations, i.e., Qard-e-Hasan (interest-free loans), free education and health services, as well as other activities are supported through this revolving fund. According to Amjad, providing free education is also a form of Qard-e-Hasan – a long-standing benevolent loan. The deserving students will study now but will repay once they are able to, be it after five or ten years, whereas the private educational institutions and universities ask for the fee first and then let students enter the classroom.

The various loan categories are:

i Family Enterprise Loan
ii Liberation Loan
iii Emergency Loan
iv Marriage Loan
v Housing Loan
vi Education Loan

In the next chapter we will elaborate further on the above-mentioned loans services and explain what the different loans are for.

We now turn to the other cyclical rotation of the smaller fund, which originates as an effect of the main pool of fund.

## 5.2 Members donation program – the Barakah Rounds

The Arabic word barakah is often used for blessings or the divine bounty continuously running as a current all around us. I have instinctively chosen the word barakah for this round, as it originates from the abundance which is ever-present yet unbeknownst to us. Thoroughly studying Akhuwat's members donation program (MDP), its third core principle of transforming borrowers into donors has practically proven that this divine abundance is ever-present. Once we open up to receiving this barakah in a more receptive and grateful way, it keeps overflowing throughout. We will be exploring this dimension further in our next chapter.

And the story goes, according to Amjad, that this fund came into existence when one of their borrowers insisted on repaying Akhuwat by making a small contribution as he came to pay off his loan. Upon his insistence, Amjad accepted his contribution, only to put it aside, which gave birth to the idea of this 'reciprocal endowment' pool of funds, which became the source of Akhuwat's sustainability. Small donation boxes were placed at workplaces, homes, carts and kiosks. Borrowers added a meagre amount, from Rs. 2 to Rs. 5 ($ 0.05) daily, as a contribution to Akhuwat's revolving solidarity (Mawakhat) fund, which runs in parallel to Akhuwat's main fund. Some of Akhuwat's operational costs, e.g., employees' payments, and other expenses at times come out of this pool, but most of the time, this amount is used for further lending or provision of education and health services to other needy people.

Not only does this fund sustain Akhuwat's solidarity mission, but it also generates a spirit of communitalism – of community wellbeing and togetherness, as per Father Anselm Adodo, a Nigerian scholar and my TRANS4M colleague, who is a pioneer of alternative medicine in Africa.

> For Father Anselm Adodo the relational term *communitalism*, related to a civil economy, is functionally different from communalism or, indeed, communism.
>
> "Communitalism affirms that some aspects of capitalism, such as individual inventiveness, are worth pursuing and supporting, but such inventiveness must be put to the service of the community, so that both the individual and the community prosper. The key philosophy of communitalism is 'we are either happy together as a prosperous community or unhappy together', and thereby unprosperous". (Lessem & Muchineripi, 2013)

In doing so, Akhuwat has revived the communal spirit of caring for each other and, most importantly, giving poor people the self-dignity and confidence that they are playing their role in community building and solidarity. For this remains Akhuwat's robust distinction compared to any microfinance organisation around the world or in Pakistan – especially in a country like Pakistan, where poverty is considered to be a curse. By making them a part of their solidarity circle, Akhuwat has set yet another example for others to follow.

This brings us to the conclusion of this chapter, as by now our readers will have a clear picture of the way the whole Akhuwat phenomenon operates, that is, from employing the soul-wisdom and creating Barakah Rounds to completing the solidarity (Ikhuwah) round by sharing abundance with each other. The next chapter expands on Akhuwat's loan portfolio and the categorisation in a Pakistani context.

## 6 Conclusion

I start by quoting an incident Amjad has narrated in his book:

> In Baltimore's Islamic centre, whilst speaking to a gathering, I was asked a question which was distinctive in its nature: *'What is the purpose of all this effort of yours and what have you achieved, to date?'* asked a gentleman who had been listening to our discussion.
>
> I replied after some consideration,
>
>> The purpose is righteousness and piety. I can't say much about the results that we have attained but piety by itself is a reward. After planting the seed, is it really necessary to make sure whether the flower has blossomed? Isn't the sowing of the seed itself sufficient an effort?

I wished to repeat the words of the famous Sufi poet Mian Muhammad Baksh;

*The gardener's job is to water the plants with skin-bags full of water,It is up to the Lord to allow fruits and flowers to grow.*

The curiosity of the gentleman who had asked the question seemed to linger, but he did not dwell on the issue. Perhaps he was satisfied, or perhaps he also realised the scarcity of time.

My eyes were heavy with fatigue while Imtiaz and Qadeer remained engrossed in conversation returning from the Islamic centre. I ruminated on the questions asked.

Did we embark upon this and continue to strive because we believed poverty would be eliminated? Or is it because this is what has been ordained; the path has been chosen for us and we are urged to tread on this path?

It seemed to me that both were interlinked. We will be judged by the results but *Akhuwat's* primary relation is with the calling. This is an obligation whose struggle is its own reward. Iqbal's words from Bal-e-Jibril-025 echoed in my ears;

*For selfless deeds of men rewards are less mundane;Transcend the houris' glances, the pure, celestial wine.*

*The question asked by the gentleman and Amjad's introspection in response to the question, as narrated above, also echo deeply within me – in fact it resonates with my calling as I started exploring the Akhuwat model and its altruistic philosophy of Mawakhat to pursue a deeper intuitive calling to instil Sufistic values into our enterprise and economic pursuits. Truly believing that injustice will prevail in this world and we might fail to eradicate poverty from our societies in our lifetimes, nonetheless the legacy of solidarity that Akhuwat is will live on for generations.*

*The question that arises then, for me and indeed for Amjad, is: how is this legacy passed on to the next generations? For Akhuwat, undoubtedly, is not only a legacy of granting loans and poverty elimination. It is doing much more for the Pakistani community than granting funds to the poor. For me, Akhuwat's main strength is activating the community to be self-sufficient and sustainable through generating and distributing from their own pool of abundance whilst holding on to its moral core value of tawakul (reliance) on Allah. The barakah that emanates from this unified communal way of thinking is the legacy Akhuwat needs to conceptualise more explicitly. The torch that was lit 1400 years ago in Medina has been rekindled by Amjad and his colleagues, in Pakistan. Could this spirit be rekindled in other parts of the world and with the same impulse of creating solidarity bonds and barakah circles of reciprocity, of Ishq/love and Ilm/knowledge?*

*How can the younger generation be prepared for such divine responsibility? Could a new integral universal language of SOUL-idarity help in reviving the spirit of Prophetic Mawakhat globally as envisioned by Amjad?*

As cited by Lessem and Muchineripi in their *Integral Community* bible:

For Basil Davidson, the renowned African historian, *the history of Africans, generally*, our overall source of communal ORIGINATION, *is nothing if not the 'handing on the torch' from generation to generation*. It is the appointed ancestors who have given peoples their identity and guaranteed the onward movement of life (2013).

*In Amjad and Akhuwat's case, the communal Mawakhat and virtuous circles that have been generated should be passed on with such an obligation for the next generations to carry the torch on. How Akhuwat is taking this responsibility further is what we will be discussing in our concluding chapter.*

The next chapter thus communicates Akhuwat's loan disbursement methodology and its distribution as such, in a localised Pakistani societal context.

## Bibliography


Adams, J. D., 2005. *Transforming Leadership*. 2nd ed. New York: Cosimo Books.

Afonso, J. S., 2017. *Lendwithcare Assessment Project Akhuwat Report*, Portsmouth: UoP – Portsmouth Business School.

Aislahi, A. A., 1989a. Stages of Socio-economic Development: Shah Wali-Allah's Concept of al-Irtifaqat. *Munich Personal RePEc Archive*, Issue MPRA Paper No. 29628.

Aislahi, A. A., 1989b. Stages of Socio-economic Development: Shah Wali-Allah's Concept of al-Irtifaqat. *Journal of Objective Studies*, 1, 1–2, pp. 46–63.

Anielski, M., 2007. *The Economics of Happiness: Building Genuine Wealth*. Gabriola Island: New Society Publishers.

Dehlawi, S. W.-A., 1945. *Hujjat-Allah al-Balighah*. Beirut: Dar al-Fikr, pp. 114–116.

Harper, M., & Khan, A. A., 2017. *Islamic Microfinance: Shariah Compliant and Sustainable?* Rugby: Practical Action Publishing Ltd.

Kedar, B. Z., 1969 [1938]. Again: Arabic Rizq, Medieval Latin Risicum. *Studi Medievali*, pp. 255–259.

Lessem, R., & Bradley, T., 2018. *Evolving Work*. Abingdon: Routledge.

Lessem, R., & Muchineripi, P. C., 2013. *Integral Community: Political Economy to Social Commons*. Abingdon: Routledge.

Oshodi, B., & Adeojo, J., 2018. Work democracy: Integral Banking/Communipreneurship: CISER's Perspective, a Nigerian Context. In: *Integrity at Work: (Self) Employment to Employing Self-&-Community*. Abingdon: Routledge.

*Poverty Survey.*, October 2010. Available at: http://bisp.gov.pk/poverty-scorecard/#

Scheemaekere, X. D., 2009. The Epistemology of Modern Finance. *The Journal of Philosophical Economics*, II, 2, pp. 99–120.

Schieffer, A., & Lessem, R., 2010. *Integral Economics: Releasing the Economic Genius of Your Society (Transformation and Innovation)*. 1st ed. Abingdon: Routledge.

Shahid, A. B., 2016. *Remembering Agha Hassan Abedi*. [Online] Available at: http://fp.brecorder.com/2015/05/201505161186840/

# 7 Akhuwat's lending methodology

## 1 Preamble

*In the previous chapter we elaborated on Akhuwat's sustainability paradigm, that is, from where and how the funds are acquired for their revolving fund pool.*

*We have also demonstrated the continuous overflow of their 'reciprocal endowment' (barakah circles) generated by a cyclical circumvolution, as per my postulation, all the while revolving through their main pool of funds as a subsequent progression of communal benevolence. This main fund, generated through various gratuitous streams of zakat, sadaqah and Qard-e-Hasan, sustains Akhuwat's lending operations, whereas the funds generated through its reciprocal endowment impulse (borrowers becoming Akhuwat's donors) sustain Akhuwat's operational costs and initiatives.*

*In this chapter, we aim to further illustrate Akhuwat's loan approval and disbursement methodology for our readers' discernment.*

*Incidentally, this chapter also entertains some critique regarding their sustainability and dependency on the benevolent streams, as this is one major concern/critique generally. The reason for that, I believe, is the elementary ontological misinterpretation of their 'solidarity' paradigm (Qard-e-Hasan and Mawakhat). To this extent, Akhuwat have to explicitly define and propagate their Hikma (wisdom) in communal solidarity and reciprocity as such and not appear as (yet another) microfinance organisation, albeit Islamic, constitutionally.*

*Keeping in mind the uniqueness and ingenuity of Akhuwat's funds-pool, from compilation to disbursement, the approach adopted instinctively for our book is through narrative inquiry. Therefore, this book does not compare or contrast Akhuwat with other microfinance organisations working in the same field in Pakistan or around the world.*

*If anything, this book is a call-to-action inviting our readers to transcend microfinance with a new perspective, through an alternative, i.e., the SOUL-idarity noesis, which involves firstly being aware of the abundance present all around us and secondly, being open to employ our inner wisdom (Hikma), which disciplines (and liberates) the 'self' to be more compassionate and benevolent – for that is what Akhuwat stands for: solidarity with Self (Being/Creator) and community (khalq/creation).*

## 2 Mawakhat loan portfolio

Previously, we shared the 'reciprocal' methodology adopted by Akhuwat to gather funds through the four voluntary streams flowing through an Islamic society. Akhuwat, then, categories these streams into four classifications, whereby it establishes, in Pakistani society's context, that 30% of the population could make their livelihood and meet their existential challenges if they were granted micro-loans from the main pool (the barakah pool) of Pakistan's civil and benevolent society.

In the absence of a state apparatus to make good use of these voluntary barakah streams, Akhuwat – through Amjad and his colleagues, and through an inventive manoeuvring of their society's reality – has set a new precedent in the history of Qard-e-Hasan (benevolent loans) in Pakistan, and globally to *think 'microfinance' through*.

The most laudable feature from an integral perspective is Akhuwat's methodology of loan appraisal and disbursement mechanism, which is fully embedded in the local community as per the nature of local communities. This applies on a locality-to-locality basis, as Pakistan has a diverse culture in all the four provinces, which differ in some ways from the others. For example, in the Northwestern areas of Pakistan, the jirga system is still prevalent, whereby the community-heads or elders make decisions for the whole community and, thus, vouch for each other, whereas in the rural areas in the province of Punjab, the panchayat system serves a similar purpose.

Akhuwat chooses local staff from within these communities who are not only familiar with the local traditions and sensitives but also have a mastery of the local language, which helps them communicate on a common ground.

As proffered by Lessem and Schieffer, 'It is time for development economists and modernising sociologists to shift perspective and to evolve organistaional forms that befit local nature and communities' (2014a).

By employing a local tradition of communal Bhai-chara (brotherhood) and 'mohaladari', an Urdu term for 'neighbourhood system', one of the salient features of this part of the world used not only to share sorrows and joys but also to bail one out in difficulty or distress, Akhuwat borrowers are encouraged to bring two guarantors from their neighbourhood who can vouch for that person's financial commitments, i.e., repayment of the loan money.

This practice is unthinkable in the Northern and Western individualistic societies we live in, where the communal spirit of neighbourhood is a dying trait.

By adopting this indigenous tradition, Akhuwat further promotes the spirit of Bhai-chara/Akhuwat and masawat (equality) amongst all tiers of the community.

As such, Akhuwat's loan portfolio contains the following six categories (Figure 7.1):

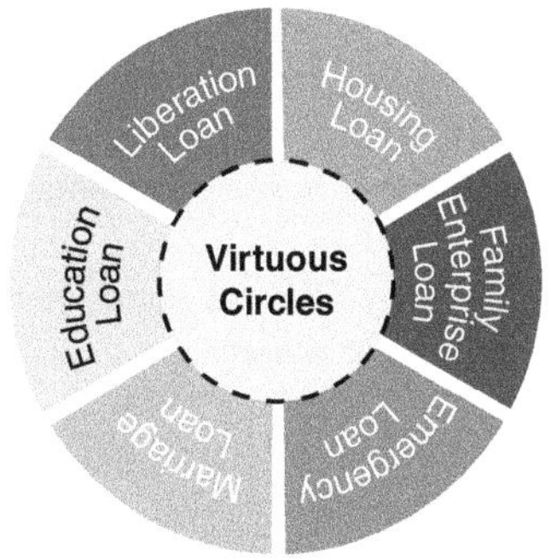


*Figure 7.1* Loan Circles

### *2.1 Family enterprise loan*

This is sanctioned for establishing a new business or expanding an existing one. The family enterprise loan is the most commonly used loan offered by Akhuwat. It comprises 91% of Akhuwat's loan portfolio. The family enterprise loan ranges from Rupees 10,000 to 50,000 ($180 to $450); however, the most common amount for the first loan is Rupees 15,000 ($135).

The enterprise loan is also known as the *family enterprise loan*, as during the period of appraisal and lending, the entire family is involved in the process, with the view of making it a family venture instead of an individual effort. The loan is granted after the applicant comes up with a viable business plan and qualifies as eligible for the loan.

Akhuwat sees family as a unit of trust and takes a family's prosperity interest as a way forward for a prosperous society. So unlike other microfinance organisations that focus on or promote women's empowerment by allocating funds to women entrepreneurs, Akhuwat sees family as a unit to that prosperity. Given the fact that Pakistan is predominantly a very patriarchal society, Akhuwat respects the local cultural values by keeping men as the head of their families involved in all matters, even if the loan is granted to a woman for her business or enterprise.

Amjad also believes in the unity of the family as the custodians of trust and faith when it comes to timely repayments – as the loans are interest-free, the risk involved of people misusing the loan for their own personal luxuries is always high. Akhuwat believes, by involving the whole family unit, it places a sense of responsibility on every member of the family to treat the loan as a sacred pact. For Akhuwat, a prosperous family reflects a prosperous community and society.

### *2.2 Liberation loan*

As well as providing loans to people wanting to establish or develop their micro-enterprises, Akhuwat provides 'liberation loans' to people who are struggling to repay debt that has been taken from local moneylenders. In most instances, borrowers took out small loans at interest rates of up to 20% per month and the debt has spiralled out of control. Sometimes borrowers have already sold what few assets they own, yet they still struggle to keep up with repayments. Shahzad Akram, Akhuwat's chief credit officer, recalls instances where young borrowers have even committed suicide and some moneylenders demanded that borrowers sell their daughters to repay the debt. In parts of Southern Punjab and Sindh it is not uncommon to find borrowers and their children who have been forced to become indentured labourers for feudal landlords as they struggle to repay debts that were often taken out many years ago.

Akhuwat calls them liberation loans because they free the borrower from the seemingly never-ending cycle of increasing debt. Each request is carefully considered on an individual basis to ensure that the application is genuine. There is a maximum loan size of 100,000 rupees or about $1,000, although most loans are smaller, typically around 35,000 rupees or $350. Akhuwat does not charge any interest and borrowers are asked to simply repay the loan in monthly instalments over a period of up to 18 months. Each year Akhuwat makes several thousand liberation loans to clear the debts of heavily indebted borrowers.

Rather than providing the borrower with the cash, Akhuwat instead directly repays the whole amount owed to the moneylender in the presence of the borrower and often other witnesses as well. It then asks the moneylender to sign a contract stating that the loan has been settled in full and that he/she will not demand anything further from the borrower. The organisation also educates borrowers on the dangers associated with taking out short-term high-interest loans to ensure that they do not fall into the same debt traps again.

### *2.3 Education loan*

This is an interest-free student loan offered to needy students so they do not drop out of college. An average loan of Rs. 50,000 ($450) is paid to help the students to complete their education.

According to a UNESCO report, Pakistan has the second-highest rate of out-of-school youth in the world. The main reason for this is poverty amongst the lower-middle working classes.

After working with the underprivileged class, which often gets neglected, Amjad believes that, to fulfil the dream of a poverty-free society, helping people with their education is the first step in this direction. With utmost faith in humanity and Pakistani civil society, Amjad proposes free quality education for children of poor households whose talent is wasted for the lack of funds and resources.

Per Amjad, 'If loans can be provided without interest, so can education be provided without charges.'

The Akhuwat University project is one such step towards making education accessible to talented yet often deprived young students who fail to continue their higher education.

As maintined by Amjad, the student loans methodology, adopted for this initiative aims to inculcate the spirit of 'Mawakhat/solidarity' in the students. In doing so, those who are taking today will be returning the same favour – further strengthening the 'reciprocal endowment' paradigm in the society.

### 2.4 Marriage loan

A marriage loan is given for dowry of bride (daughter) or marriage ceremony arrangements. This loan helps in meeting the marriage expenses of a girl from a poor family. Many girls in Pakistan remain unmarried because of dowry, a tradition which goes back many centuries. The range of this loan is up to Rupees 50,000 ($450). Boys are not entitled to this loan type.

### 2.5 Emergency loan

This type of loan is given to meet emergency situations such as school admission fee, medical treatment, purchase of medicine, etc. These loans are given to prevent the poor from major setbacks. The amount loaned to the poorest of the poor is generally Rupees 50,000 ($450). This has to be repaid within one year.

### 2.6 Housing loan

In Akhuwat's philosophy, a house means more than just a place to live. It is a place for sheltering oneself (and family) from harsh weather and predators. It is an emotional experience – a sanctuary of love and union. In material terms, it is also something to fall back upon – an asset. Yet, Pakistan has the second-worst housing requirements in South Asia, as in Figure 7.2.

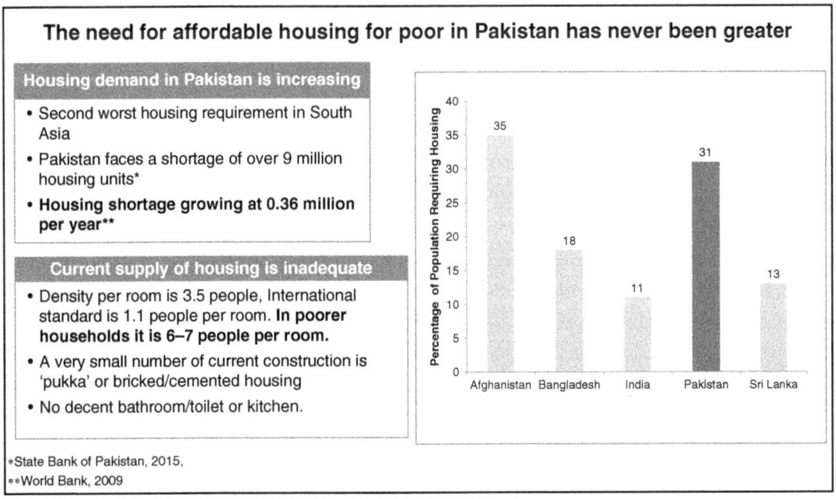


*Figure 7.2* Housing Needs in Pakistan

Akhuwat has been supporting low-income households (extreme poor) for the last five years:

- For constructing one to two-room houses
- Home improvement/addition of a room/kitchen/toilet
- Incremental construction and
- Repair

Akhuwat's housing loans are typically used for construction of one or two-room housing improvement – a roof, walls, floors, water, sewage or kitchen, latrine, or an additional room – rather than to purchase or build a new home. Akhuwat also provides housing loans for renovating a house or construction of a room. The range of this loan varies between Rupees 30,000 and Rupees 100,000 ($270 – $900). The loan must be repaid within two to three years' time (Table 7.1).

What has been termed their 'loan' portfolio is, in reality, an extension of Akhuwat's wide-scope services to lend a solidarity hand in liberating people from the shackles of destitution and debt-slavery by facilitating them with free healthcare and education and their housing needs. Whereas, conventional microfinancers, and especially local area loan sharks would, without a doubt, take advantage of poor people's afflictions with no help from anywhere else. In such times of desperation, an institution that does not only provide monetary support but also educates and develops people to be self-sustained is no less a blessing for these unfortunate people.

Particularly, the solidarity impulse that throbs at the heart of their organisation marks compassion and Ihsan as their most integral attribute, as well as their love for human dignity and SOUL-idarity with the deprived community.

We now explore their loan approval process from a customary organisational manner.

## 3 Loan approval – methodology

Akhuwat's loan approval methodology is simple and straightforward without the tedious organisational procedures. The whole structure bases decision-making on pure trust and the goodwill of a borrower. Here again, the whole emphasis is placed on solidarity amongst communities, as the local community members are contacted to act as witnesses and guarantors, which includes consulting the local area mosque and church fraternity – an age-old cultural and religious tradition within South Asia.

The borrower is able to receive a loan in a period of 21 days from applying for the loan and, in emergency cases, the loan amount is released three days from application. An application fee of Rupees 100 ($1) up front is charged in order to encourage serious borrowers only. Moreover, 1% for the purposes of 'takaful' (Islamic insurance) is charged so that, in case of disability, the borrower is provided a relief fund of Rupees 5,000 ($45), and in the case of untimely death the expenditure for burial is also provided by the organisation. In short, the loan methodology ensures that the rights of borrowers are covered and they are provided a safe environment to excel – the success of the borrower is what will make him/her a donor/lender one day.

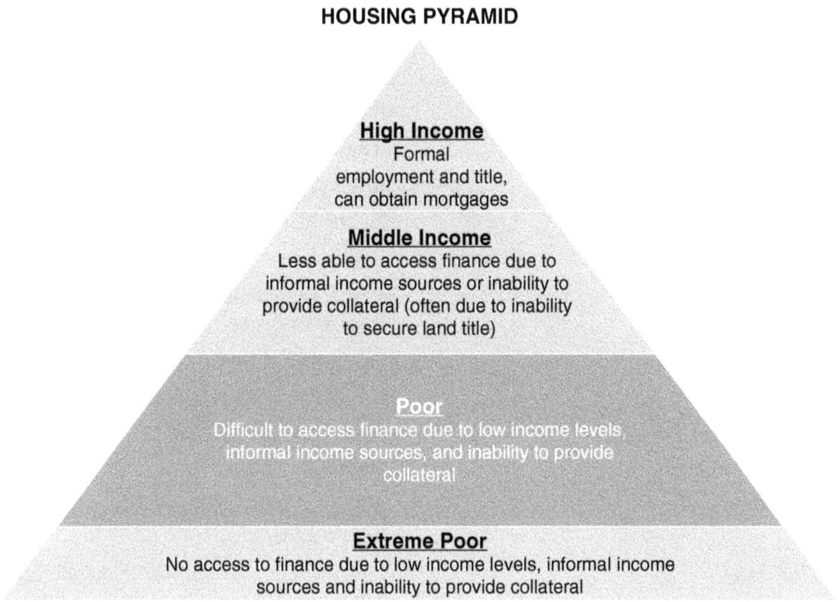


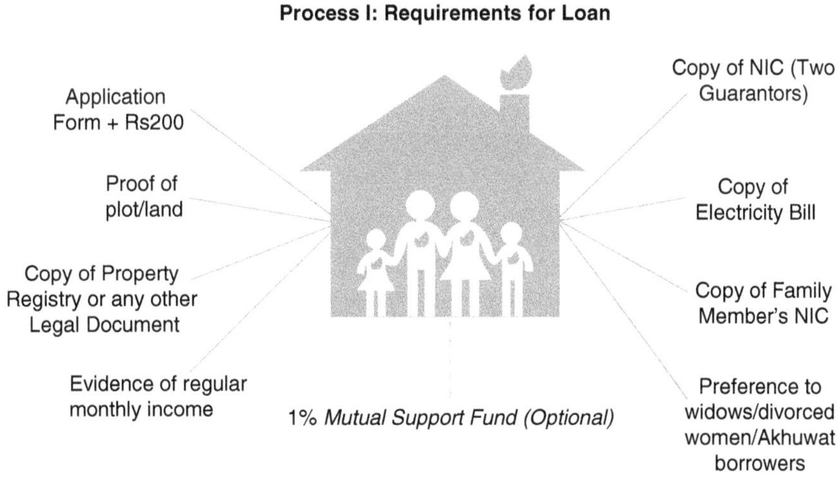


*Figure 7.3* Housing Loans Scheme

*Table 7.1* Salient Features

| *Salient features* | |
|---|---|
| • Revolving Fund: | **Rupees 14 Million ($ 1.2 million)** |
| • First Loan Disbursed on: | **August 20, 2005** |
| • Type of Loan: | **Interest-Free** |
| • Processing Fees: | **Rs.200 ($ 1.70)** |
| • Operational Area: | **Lahore** |
| • Purpose of Loan : | **New Construction of a room/Addition/ Repair/Improve Incremental** |
| • Nature: | **1st, 2nd, 3rd Loans to complete House** |
| • Amount: | **Rs. 30,000 – Rs 100,000/- ($270 - $900)** |
| • Monthly Installment: | **Rs.1,500 – Rs. 3,000 ($13 - $25)** |
| • Size of Plot: | **Marlas 1 – 3** |
| • Legal Status | **Registry in the name of owner or any legal evidence** |
| • Target: | Low Income poor household that do not have access to traditional housing finance |
| • Repayment Period: | **2 to 3 years** |

Progress of housing loans as of 31 March 2018:

Total loans: **1,117**
Total loans disbursed to males: (804) **72%**
Total loans disbursed to females: (313) **28%**
Total amount disbursed: **Rupees 82.47 million ($7.1 million)**
Outstanding loans: **Rupees 9.77 million ($85,000)** Active loans: **230**
Recovery percentage: **99.99%**

Table 7.2 charts their loan appraisal process step by step.

## 4 Loan approval committee

The committee – comprising unit, branch and area managers, along with members of the steering committee – reviews the credit cases in their totality. The approval of this committee endorses disbursements to be released to the applying borrowers. A period of 1–21 days is utilised to complete the process in order to ensure thorough appraisal and survey.

## 5 Loan disbursement ceremony

Loan disbursement ceremonies are held in local religious places, e.g., mosques, churches and temples. In a mosque, the ceremony is conducted right after a ritual prayer, giving members of the congregation a chance to be part of the ceremony.

*Table 7.2* Loan Appraisal Process

| | |
|---|---|
| **Social and Economic Appraisal of the Borrower** | The appraisal of the borrower is done by the unit manager/loan officer in order to ascertain the income of the household and client background check. |
| **Submission of Business Plan/Feasibilities to the Borrower** | The borrower provides details of his/her experience and skill set in respect to the plan proposed. The unit managers, through their expertise, help the borrowers to channel their energies in the right direction through counselling and capacity-building initiatives. |
| **Nomination of Two Guarantors** | Every borrower also provides two guarantors who vouch for his/her credentials. |
| **Forwarding of the Appraisal and Business Plan to the Loan Approval Committee** | The loan approval committee includes the unit manager, branch manager, area manager, regional manager and a member of the steering committee of that city in order to review the credit case in totality. |
| **Approved Loans are finalised in a period of two weeks and loans are disbursed in a local mosque** | The borrowers and guarantors are invited to the mosque and, in a disbursement event, loans are given out and the participants are enrolled as members of the Akhuwat family to make them one of the torch bearers. |

This is a revival of the traditions of shura – mutual consent in Arabic, majlis – a Persian tradition of meetings, jirgah – a Pakhtun tribal tradition and panchayat – Punjabi rural tradition. These traditions were meetings and consultations for the solutions to day-to-day problems and resolution of conflicts.

Islam approves of this tradition in the best interest of mankind, as:

"And those who have responded to their lord and established prayer and whose affair is [determined by] consultation among themselves, and from what We have provided them, they spend". (Al-Quran: Surah; Ash-Shuraa (42:38) (Anon., n.d.)

Mutual consent has been mentioned alongside other religious obligations, which denotes its importance in the social life of mankind.

People who attend the ceremonies bear witness (shahadah), upholding the sanctity of a loan given as a benevolent act of divine favour.

Before giving the loan to the applicant, the loan managers speak to the gathering of borrowers as well as the guarantors, asking for a renewal of the pledge in the presence of Allah and within the vicinity of a holy place (sanctuary) to cultivate the spirit of Mawakhat and Ihsan. The loan then becomes a solemn pact of trust and solidarity between the borrower and donor (Akhuwat).

Akhuwat has the distinction of setting this tradition of loan disbursement inside sanctuaries. Furthermore, Akhuwat uses local mosque or church infrastructure as the centre for loan disbursement and community participation, which subsidises their operational and organisational costs as well as maintaining the mosque's status as a centre of good governance and good practice as per Islamic traditions. It ensures transparency and inspires people with accountability towards the Divine.

## 6 The ingenuity of a gift economy

From an integral 'South-Eastern' perspective, Akhuwat represents an ideal model of 'communitalism' (Chapter 1) as per Father Anselm Adodo's postulation of generating communal capitalism and as per Stephen Gudeman's byword, cited by Schieffer and Lessem (2014a).

> Stephen Gudeman, a graduate of both Cambridge University's School of Anthropology in the UK and also Harvard Business School in the US, is today a professor emeritus in the department of anthropology at the University of Minnesota.
>
> Per Gudeman, there is no one 'true' model of economy, but only multiple meaningful formulations within particular cultures, each with its own value domains, in which we need to reflectively immerse ourselves as researchers. Thereby, we uncover the origins of a particular community.
>
> As a representative of modern economic anthropology, a school of thought that uses anthropology to understand economy in human terms, he calls on us to understand 'local models'.

Though Akhuwat has exquisitely activated a whole community of donors, borrowers and volunteers by acting as an 'integrator' between those entities, the fact remains that Akhuwat depends on the generosity of Pakistan's civil society. For Akhuwat to solely depend on this 'gift economy' model, from a neoclassical economics perspective, is a casualty from the start, yet Akhuwat has survived for 17 years through benevolent sustenance. Amjad is encouraged by his faith in Pakistani society, people who are famous for generosity and charity-giving.

According to the Charities Aid Foundation (CAF) World Giving Index (Index, 2017), there has been a global decrease in giving since the last report. This follows a high point recorded by last year's Index, in particular for helping a stranger. The proportion of people across the world who reported donating money in 2016 – when the research for this year's report was conducted – is the lowest seen in three years.

Incidentally, a study by Pakistan Centre for Philanthropy (2017) confirms that philanthropy is universal in Pakistan, with nearly 98% of households reporting giving for various social causes in one form or the other, providing an opportunity for civil society organisations to tap into this practice of charitable giving and volunteering.

Whereas Akhuwat banks on charitable giving which is faith-based, i.e., zakat (obligatory) and sadaqah (voluntary) by people who have excess money to give, its reciprocal endowments engage people at the grassroots level to shoulder the burden of societal self-sufficiency.

Per Stephen Gudeman (2001), the word 'reciprocity' is used differently by economists and anthropologists. For economists, reciprocity refers to two-directional exchanges, monetised or not. Anthropologists use reciprocity for a more restricted set of practices – specifically, non-cash, non-market exchanges – and set it in opposition to commercial trade. Often anthropologists equate reciprocity with a gift on the argument that a gift obligates the recipient to offer a return, setting in motion a temporal, lasting cycle of obligations, which is reciprocity. But sometimes anthropologists avoid the term 'gift' because in market economy the gift has the connotation 'without obligation'. For economists, there are no free lunches; for anthropologists there are no free gifts.

*From Akhuwat's in-depth study and, now, Amjad's reassurances, also knowing my Pakistani culture, I can relate to this reciprocity which is rooted not only in religious commitment but also in cultural tradition. This tradition might become extinct owing to over-speculated scarcity infecting the world like a material plague. How is Akhuwat, then, preparing its future crop of benevolent donors and contributors in the coming generations?*

Karl Polanyi, a Hungarian American political economist (Polanyi, 1944), terms societies that practise reciprocity 'primitive'. For him, reciprocity in societies only exists where kinship is dominant. From his tripartite typology, redistribution comes second and is encountered in systems where political or religious institutions are dominant, such as 'ancient' societies.

*Looking at Pakistan's literacy rate, one can easily maintain that Pakistani society is primitive or ancient, as per any North-western definition. Furthermore, from a Western neoliberalist point of view, this might stand true, but the problem I find with these Western views is their total discard of an Eastern spiritual perspective which exists in this part of the world. For millions of Pakistani micro-entrepreneurs who are still grappling to find means to earn a living that can grant them three full meals, this model is no less than a divine intervention.*

This is when I, personally, find solace in Lessem and Schieffer's *Integral Economic* model, which brings culture and spirituality back into economic models (at the core) and works with any society's particular belief system. What is then needed is for Akhuwat to perpetuate its 'reciprocal' paradigm – explicitly defining it anthropologically, i.e., by its philosophy and principles as well as its redistribution model on an institutional and global level.

Incidentally, the process has begun, as Pakistan's government is now allocating funds for Akhuwat to disburse interest-free loans through their methodology to support micro-entrepreneurship and enterprise-building agendas.

*We believe this has helped our readers with the Mawakhat/solidarity redistribution model and its procedural process. As witnessed on many occasions and instances via my Akhuwat encounters, the entire process focuses on inculcating a spirit of 'sharing' and reciprocity – of Mawakhat – all the while embracing the local traditions and culture, i.e., Akhuwat staff documenting in the national language (Urdu) as well as communicating with their clients in their local languages. The 'divide' between the rich and poor remains.*

*For I wish to witness a day when the poor are not called 'poor' in my (Pakistani) society – a day when these 'unfortunate' ones realise the potential they hold within themselves to create their own fortunes (pool of abundance). Akhuwat has been steering them to that destination, but their lack of education and economic knowledge is hindering them from being the 'economic drivers' themselves instead of being subservient to the system.*

*Could there be one such day?*

## 7 Conclusion

Thus, we conclude this chapter with this intention: of seeing the effects of one such solidarity movement and reciprocity amongst these less privileged communities, of helping them be capable of developing their own original economic cultures without being steered by organisations or state machinery granting them 'micro-loans'.

Sahlins (2017), an American anthropologist best known for his ethnographic work in the Pacific and for his contributions to anthropological theory, calls this *Balanced Reciprocity: The Midpoint.* For him, 'balanced reciprocity' refers to direct exchange. For it is *less 'personal'* than generalised reciprocity, more *'economic'.*

Also, could this be possible through cultivating the intent of SOUL-idarity Hikma (wisdom) by realising the Transformational SOUL-idarity rhythm?

We aim to explore this further in our concluding chapter.

Now advancing towards our next chapter, we will briefly celebrate Akhuwat's many transformative acquisitions and achievements, thereafter narrating a few success stories of Akhuwat's clients and of the life-transforming effects resulting from the solidarity bond forged between Akhuwat's community of donors and borrowers.

Along these lines, it is our wish that the lending process chronicled above be perceived in this spirit, i.e., of redistributing abundance, as is (always) present within communities, spiralling through its four realms and the centre.

What keeps me fascinated with this model is the potential this reciprocity holds to generate indefinite barakah rounds, constantly churning in iterative circles. We only have to collectively SOUL-idify our inner Hikma and knowledge (Ilm) of the barakah silsilah (chain).

We will explore this further in our concluding chapter.

## Bibliography

Anon., 2017. *The State of Individual Philanthropy in Pakistan 2016.* Islamabad: Pakistan Centre for Philanthropy.

Anon., n.d. *Ash-Shuraa.* Available at: https://quran.com/42/36-39

Gudeman, S., 2001. *The Anthropology of Economy: Community, Market, and Culture*. Massachusetts: Blackwell Publishers Inc.
Index, C. W. G., 2017. *CAF World Giving Index 2017: A Global View of Giving Trends*. London: Charities Aid Foundation.
Polanyi, K., 1944. *The Great Transformation*. New York: Farrar & Rinehart.
Sahlins, M. D., 2017. *Stone Age Economics*. Abingdon: Routledge.
Schieffer, A., & Lessem, R., 2014a. Community Activation: Embeddedness. In: *Integral Development: Realising the Transformative Potential of Individuals, Organisations and Societies*. Abingdon: Routledge.
Schieffer, A., & Lessem, R., 2014b. *Integral Development*. Farnham: Gower Publishing Ltd.

# 8 The benevolence multiplier effect

## Akhuwat success stories

### 1 Preamble

Now, spiralling through Akhuwat's barakah (divine bounty) rounds and strengthening a bond of solidarity amongst the community of Akhwateers (Akhuwat's community of donors, borrowers and volunteers), we are edging towards the concluding part of our book. We believe it is time to draw on Akhuwat's real (tangible) success by providing some real-life stories of its successors as well as its multi-fold initiatives, all originating from a solidarity impulse – the core of our SOUL-idarity Hikma GENE. The next chapter, thereby draws on the Hikma noesis through our philosophical contemplation of this solidarity impulse, finally reaching its full effect.

Additionally, this chapter draws on the solidarity effect by narrating just a few success stories of many. Primarily, we start by presenting Akhuwat as a prime example of its own success by virtue of its philosophy now taking root in Pakistani society. What might seem like an abstract dream of idealism and passion is now an exceptional confederacy of Mawakhat between the two disparate classes of Pakistani society – those who give (Ansar) and those who take (Muhajiroun), only to progress and become Ansar themselves.

For Akhuwat, through its various initiatives, provides holistic and integrated solutions to the destitute, underprivileged segments of society in Pakistan by inculcating the spirit and philosophy of Mawakhat in the hearts and minds of millions of people locally and globally. It aspires to expand its outreach whereby it can provide financial, educational and health facilities to over 2.5 million families by the year 2020, through its own organisational initiatives and by promoting its replication model. It also intends to take its blueprint globally to alleviate the deprivation of impoverished communities in other regions, for example, the far-flung areas of Pakistan's North-western territory and Uganda.

As cited by Amjad in his Urdu book *Akhuwat ka Safar*, a question was asked during his visit to America in 2012:

'If people decide that they will spend their lives in accordance with the spirit of solidarity, is there anything that can stop them?'

Through the course of this book we have seen the widespread manifestation of the 'solidarity effect' and its spiralling circumvolution within Akhuwat's community – of creating more circles of reciprocity through the barakah rounds. On a wider/global scale, Amjad has prosperously reflected Mawakhat's philosophy of sharing with one's brothers, as was ordained by the Prophet of Islam, through Akhuwat's model sustaining itself for 17 years now. How this effect reflects on the global spectrum is what I aspire to witness. Through this book, could this paradigm shift perhaps be originated?

For I believe the world is still unwilling to face the reality of the current state of affairs, whereby we are obstinately fostering an economy that has lost its humaneness and human practicality. Could a model like Akhuwat's, then, have a global acceptance like other micro-lending models that are making business off someone's destitution?

We now relate Akhuwat's success story in Amjad's own words.

## 2 Akhuwat – a dream becoming reality

We start with Amjad's journey through America in 2012, narrating Akhuwat's story at a gathering at Maryland University, as cited by Amjad in his Urdu book *Akhuwat ka Safar* (Journey of Hope):

> 'We are all desirous of change', I said, beginning my talk. 'We wish to create such a world where there is no place for poverty, where the universal rules of justice and equality are honoured. There are many paths to this destination. *One of these is Qard-e-Hasan*, and the story of Akhuwat is affiliated with this vision of reviving this holistic tradition. Akhuwat has affirmed that solidarity is the name of a living, vibrant philosophy, that justice does not lie in the concentration of wealth, and neither is success based only on monetary acquisition. People do wish to help others and are sated with the zeal of volunteerism. The poor are reliable and giving out loans without interest is a potent possibility indeed. Further, the mosques or churches can be made the axis of social activities. All these things are worthy of importance in their own place, but the real achievement of Akhuwat is that it gave the poor the confidence that they are not alone. There are others shouldering their burdens and standing by them in their strife against poverty. For poverty is not just the name of deprivation of wealth; it is the name of being socially isolated. A man is poor when he has no well-wishers left. This world has become the centre of social and economic injustice – one person has 50 billion dollars, while another does not have even one. No decent society can even imagine such disparity. We do not believe in such a world where a child is unable to find his way to school, where his parents become desperate for medicine, where each door of justice becomes shut upon them, where people are deprived of even the glimmer of hope.
>
> The second reward of Akhuwat is that this institution has transformed beneficiaries into benefactors with a 100% rate of return on the loans, and in addition to that, donations also received from them. What's more, the

> Mawakhat philosophy is not borrowed from any Western capitalistic model. Rather, we have envisioned these dreams sitting in the shades of our own traditions, ultimately, finding guidance for our future generations by following in the footprints of our beloved Prophet Muhammad-e-Mustafa (peace be upon him).'

In Chapters 2 and 5 we researched Pakistan and Amjad's 4C (Call, Context, Co-creation and Contribution) phases of Akhuwat's integral development to fully CARE-ing for Pakistan and its communities and, ultimately, society. We demonstrated this through matching Akhuwat's four principles with integral CARE functions of Community activation, raising Awareness, Research-to-innovation and finally transforming Education.

We now aim to display the same CARE functions through Akhuwat's many initiatives to uphold their societal significance in a Pakistani context and to demonstrate their need as such and why Akhuwat had to engage itself in these. Notwithstanding the fact, the following examples focus more on Community activation, the initial tenet of the integral CARE model. How Akhuwat develops its other integral CARE functions remains to be seen.

## 3 Akhuwat initiatives – CARE sustenance 4 Pakistani society

Akhuwat, apart from granting loans, has an impressive portfolio of projects and initiatives for community welfare and societal betterment. For example, Akhuwat is the first organisation in Pakistan to focus on the plight of transgenders by starting an initiative for their wellbeing. The transgender community in Pakistan is a miserably neglected population. By employing them at Akhuwat's clothes bank, another of Akhuwat's 'circular economy' projects, recycling used clothing to be worn again, Akhuwat has set a new precedent of 'raising awareness' of this societal failing.

For us, this is the 'multiplier effect' of Ihsan/benevolence and Mawakhat/solidarity originating from Akhuwat's solidarity impulse as invariably explained by Amjad at many a gathering internationally and at local gatherings.

> The rapid growth that we have experienced in the past few years is not limited to granting Qard-e-Hasan (benevolent loan). There have been a few more initiatives. For example, Akhuwat Health Services is engaged in treating hundreds of patients completely free of cost, and a diabetes-specific hospital has been planned.
>
> The Akhuwat Clothes Bank was created to facilitate the transfer of household items such as clothes, shoes, and toys from the 'haves' to the 'have-nots'. We also felt that there was a crucial need to remove the stigma

attached to the transgenders or khwaja-siras. The Khwaja-sira Support Program was thus launched in partnership with Fountain House. Somewhere in the middle of this journey, it dawned upon us that the real solution to poverty alleviation is ensuring that each child is equipped with education.

Akhuwat Education Services (AES) was thus established. Students from underprivileged backgrounds were sent to the most prestigious medical and engineering universities of the country under Akhuwat's Educational Assistance Program.

The inception of Akhuwat Institute of Social Enterprise and Management resulted from the urgency to further develop students to become future leaders.

Akhuwat College and Akhuwat Faisalabad Institute of Research Science and Technology (FIRST) also began their operations in 2015. Both are residential facilities which have admitted the highest achievers from all provinces and corners of Pakistan through a merit-based admission structure, symbolising a 'Mini Pakistan'. Akhuwat FIRST is focused on research in biotechnology, recognising the capacity for excellence in this field.

A multidisciplinary university in Lahore and several Akhuwat colleges in various cities of Pakistan will be constructed in the near future.

Akhuwat book banks are being set up to facilitate the culture of reading and creation of knowledge. We have supplemented our efforts with a resolve to revitalise 150 non-functional government schools in the coming years. Our goal is to increase enrolment so that not even a single child is allowed to drown in the darkness of ignorance.

We hope that in this way we will be able to spread the message of hope, peace and brotherhood throughout and build a stronger Pakistan.

We now evaluate Akhuwat's many initiatives through an integral CARE process as proposed by Lessem and Schieffer.

## 4 The CARE-ing effect of Akhuwat's solidarity impulse

In Chapter 5, we elaborated on the integral CARE (Community activation, raising Awareness, Research-to-innovation and Embodied action) process, developed by Lessem & Schieffer (2013). As a prerequisite to my own PHD (Process for Holistic Development), and as per my own call-to-contribution (the 4C rhythm of Call, Context, Co-creation and Contribution), presenting Akhuwat and Amjad's collective call, I have sectioned Akhuwat's initiatives below as per the integral CARE process, classified according to their nature and effect on the societal level. Furthermore, this is to reinforce Akhuwat's certitude in institutionalising holistic integral development for their(Pakistani) community and, as borne of the solidarity impulse, other than a mere microfinance organisation as it is often contemplated. Notwithstanding the fact that Akhuwat, as an organisation, is still in need of embodying these four stages of integral development fully, this is my attempt to harness these functions in Akhuwat's prevalent practices.

Per Lessem & Schieffer:

> By engaging in the institutionalising CARE rhythm – in parallel to the 4C rhythm – of what we term a PHD, a particular PhD program becomes part of a Process for Holistic Development (PHD). The institutionalising, collective activities are geared to gradually building up communities and organisational structures that can sustain and further evolve the particular integral development impulse and give rise to new ones.
>
> Participants of such integral CARE process, thereby gradually 'stretch their personal development wings' into the larger organisational and societal arena, taking others with them on the journey, and ensuring that the personal development process can inform similar processes to follow. (Lessem & Schieffer, 2015)

This holds true for Akhuwat and its extensive sphere of societal development, which is institutionalising the CARE process through Pakistani society via their multiple initiatives ranging from raising awareness of societal issues, e.g., mistreatment of the transgender community, to innovating knowledge, e.g., Islamic Microfinance Network, an idea initiated by Amjad.

We now turn to Akhuwat's CARE-4-Society implementation process.

## 4.1 *Activating: community activation*

> The first component of the CARE process is *Community activation*. The guiding collective activity for activation is to *'form an inner circle and start building an outer community'*.
>
> At the heart of the activation of one's community is a *'healing component'* to restore the relational fabric within a particular person-and-community, required to release participatory potential.

### *4.1.1 Akhuwat Clothes Bank*

The Akhuwat Clothes Bank is an extension of Akhuwat Financial Services and benefits from the same model and philosophy which is applied in the financial services. The only difference is that the clothes are collected from well-to-do families, repaired, washed or dry-cleaned and then packed. The packed clothes are then given as a gift to the needy individual. Akhuwat aspires to collect and distribute on average over 15,000 pieces of clothing every month. This project primarily recruits transgender individuals, promoting dignified employment for this discriminated-against segment of society. Packed clothes are then distributed to the underprivileged communities with due honour and respect. Another important aspect of Akhuwat Clothes Bank is the engagement of transgenders in the processing of clothes collected from the donors. Clothes collected from the donors are sorted, repaired, stitched and packed by the transgenders employed at the organisation.

Through this circular model, not only do the clothes get upcycled and reused, but this initiative has helped transgenders to play a significant role in a prestigious organisation. Akhuwat does this by training transgenders (khawaja-sira) and then utilising their skills by employing them to be part of Akhuwat's innovative circular model of upcycling. In doing so, it has also restored the faith of this often ill-treated sector of society, providing them a platform to be functional citizens.

### *4.1.2 Akhuwat Volunteer Services*

The Akhuwat Volunteer Services Program promotes volunteerism amongst students and professionals. This program provides the volunteers with exposure in the areas of community service, disaster management, capacity building and event management. A network has been created whereby the volunteers can independently undertake projects across the country. In the future, individual chapters will be opened in different colleges and universities. The program will also expand internationally. It is envisioned that by the year 2020, Akhuwat will have more than 50,000 registered volunteers around the world.

Akhuwat has set a brilliant example of community activation by putting one of its distinctive core principles into practice: activating the spirit of volunteerism. This principle, conceptualised through the Islamic tradition of Ikhuwah and the local tradition of Bhai-chara (brotherhood), promotes a spirit of unity amongst the community. Akhuwat's young volunteers visit schools and localities providing their free support to those in need.

### *4.1.3 Akhuwat Food Bank*

The Akhuwat Food Bank aims to facilitate the transfer of meals from restaurants and catering services to needy families. The massive gap between the rich and poor in Pakistan is most evident in terms of food availability, as hungry street children continue to scavenge through garbage dumps, hoping to find a morsel of food to appease their empty stomachs. The Akhuwat Food Bank is an initiative targeted to bridge this rift. It aims to curtail the enormous wastage of food from marriage halls and food outlets by collecting excess edibles at the end of the day and distributing it amongst impoverished communities, prudently ensuring the sanctity of human dignity. A pilot project has been launched in Lahore, closely involving target communities. In future, lunch and breakfast will also be made available this way. Consequently, the provision of regular, nutritious, and plentiful meals to the needy will be guaranteed.

### *4.1.4 Akhuwat khwaja-sira (transgender) support and rehabilitation program*

The transgender (also referred as khwaja-sira) community is a group of people who receive the least amount of respect and rights in Pakistan. Due to the controversial nature and typical mindset of people, the subject of transgender rights in Pakistan is not even discussed in sophisticated circles. Most people do not even consider them as part of their community, and massive rejection is often faced by transgenders in almost all parts of Pakistan.

Akhuwat envisions a society where members of the transgender community are treated as equals without any discrimination. A way of implementing this is by building a support system. This is done by using funds that empower them socially, emotionally and economically. The program has several stages, starting with social engagement and provision of a small income supplement (Rs. 1,200/$10) to the most vulnerable. In its final form, we, alongside Fountain House, hope to be able to reintegrate the khwaja-sira (transgenders) to play a more active role in the community.

### *4.1.5 Akhuwat Health Services*

Akhuwat's benevolent loans are only one way to deal with poverty. Apart from loans, Akhuwat has started many initiatives, including Akhuwat Health Services. Quality treatment and medicines are provided free or at negligible cost through this service. The first clinic that was established through Akhuwat Health Services saved many lives. Akhuwat Health Services is a small clinic, but to date, thousands of patients with diabetes, blood pressure and hepatitis have been treated there. It is Akhuwat's resolve that this place turns into a large centre for the treatment and research of diabetes, where wounds are prevented from turning into a scourge, and where limbs are spared from being amputated. Through Akhuwat Health Services, Akhuwat Clinic has so far only been established in Lahore.

Akhuwat Health Services caters to the health needs of the poorest of the poor and Akhuwat's beneficiaries. It has developed a network of low-priced medical services by collaborating with different hospitals, clinics, diagnostic centres and pharmacies. Akhuwat has been able to develop its own clinic and diagnostic centres for the underprivileged society of Lahore and has also developed a partnership with Emergency Management Services (EMS) of LUMS, whereby it will catalyse this movement of low-cost provision of best health facilities to the deserving and needy. Akhuwat Health Services plans to replicate the EMS model in the other top universities of Pakistan. AHS has also initiated a tele-medical advice facility in the rural area and its outreach is gradually spreading across the province of Punjab. Health camps and health awareness programs are a regular feature of AHS across the country. It also plans to construct and establish a 300-bed diabetes-specialised hospital in Lahore.

#### *4.1.6 Punjab Welfare Trust for the disabled*

Punjab Welfare Trust helps four kinds of people: the blind, deaf and mute, mentally disabled and physically disabled. There is no other trust of this kind in Pakistan. To date, this trust has been of service to three million people. Many organisations working for special-needs people benefit from this trust, including LRBT, Amin Maktab, Rising Sun, Anjuman Bahali Maazooran, Fountain House, Rawalpindi Eye Donors Organisation (REDO), Aziz Jehan Trust, Roshni and Al Noor Trust. All these organisations have provided wonderful services for the disabled; with our support, the range of service has expanded.

The trust carries out work for the wellbeing of the disabled in collaboration with Akhuwat. As part of this initiative, interest-free loans are granted to three thousand people with special needs. The rate of return of these loans is also no less than 99%. Today, the trust is reliant on government resources. If these resources were to grow, so much more could be done for the betterment and rehabilitation of these people. The first test of a caring society is exactly this – how much does it love its members with special needs?

### *4.2 Raising awareness: building a catalytic innovation ecosystem*

Having activated the internal organisational and/or external societal community, the next step for Lessem and Schieffer would be to build a more wide-ranging, catalytical development ecosystem. The guiding collective activity for catalysation is to '*build up an interdependent innovation ecosystem to support your integral development with a view to alleviate imbalances*'.

#### *4.2.1 Islamic Microfinance Network (IMFN)*

Amjad's burning desire to establish a financial system that works in favour of the poor and needy gave birth to the idea of building an ecosystem (IMFN) where people could collectively explore other options. In his book *Akhuwat ka Safar*, he expresses his desire to provide the government with one such model:

> Why do we not open our minds to this lesson, especially when the Quran is found in a venerated niche of every house in our part of the world? There must surely be many among us who have read this verse of the Quran in which Allah has deemed the business of interest a declaration of war against Him and His Prophet Mohammed (peace be upon him). At every intersection of roads, however, large glittering boards boldly proclaim this war against the Lord. They reinforce their charm through newspapers and television. Why is this?
>
> People wonder how this banking system can be eradicated and replaced. Many tried to rework it in the name of Islamic banking, but here too, monopolist banks took the money from you, invested it where it pleased them, and handed

you a statement of the losses and profits. This money is lent to the government at 16% interest. Yet we remain smug that our rupee is secure from the Islamic point of view. Islam does not favourably view this kind of trade in which one has no idea whether the money is being spent, whether in legit or illegitimate business. If there is any vision of a bank in Islam, and if it can be established, then it is such an institution, which has a long list of enterprises, where capital can be invested. People make their own choices and invest themselves. The bank is there to look after their money like an employee and receives the salary for it. But no capitalist will want this to happen, and nor the government, because they are the winners in this prevailing situation. The money is another's, somebody else avails it, and the interest becomes the source of luxury for the bankers.

Our Lord has dictated only one path for the break of interest: Qard-e-Hasan. In this country (Pakistan) where *Akhuwat* stands as a glaring example, if the government asks how this system can be eradicated, one is surely surprised. This country, acquired in the name of Allah, endorses outlets to declare war on Allah. After all this, there lingers the expectation that there will be mercy upon us, no torment will befall us, and we will live our lives in peace.

Dr. Kamal Monnoo, an economic analyst from Pakistan, writes in his article for a Pakistani daily that the target market of the microfinance sector in Pakistan is estimated to be 25 to 30 million borrowers and the government has set the outreach goal posts to at least 15 million by 2020. Although the microfinance sector emerged in Pakistan with a delay of more than two decades (as compared to its other South Asian neighbours, Bangladesh and India), the sector today is growing tremendously – in fact outpacing the early entrants in South Asia. Notably, microfinance has failed to live up to its name, i.e., of helping the poor and in eradicating poverty. In Bangladesh, there is an active lobby which advocates that even the success story of Grameen Bank now stands exposed as an overblown claim. According to a 2007 study conducted by Q K Ahmad of Dhaka University, 1,189 out of 2,501 people surveyed could not pay back their micro-credit loans on time.

A study conducted by LSE economists cum anthropologists, Jason Hickel and David Roodman in their book *Due Diligence* claims that microfinance doesn't work. According to them 'The best estimate of the average impact of micro-credit on the poverty of clients is zero'. (Hickel, 2015)

Keeping this in mind, Akhuwat took the lead in setting up a platform to bring Pakistan's leading microfinance organisations to run a collective exploration into how Islamic microfinance – Shariah-compliant and interest-free – could help in tackling the poverty eradication challenge in Pakistan. In doing so, Amjad and Akhuwat have been playing a catalytic role in raising awareness of Islamic microfinance, a term used for Shariah-complaint methodology, as Amjad strongly believes and thus propagates a system which is close to people's beliefs and nature. Also, he strongly renounces the culture of making microfinance a business or making business from poor people's coercion.

Thereof originated the idea of IMFN – to bring forth Islamic microfinance and Shariah-compliant financial tools as a mechanism to eradicate poverty, Pakistan's biggest societal challenge after illiteracy. Therefore, IMFN serves as a platform for Islamic microfinance practitioners from Pakistan to jointly work towards benefiting the needy. IMFN is the hub of Islamic microfinance and works towards increasing both the demand and supply forces of the industry, creating awareness of the utility of the existing products, discussing the scope and potential of market growth, promoting innovation, increasing outreach and providing industry information. The Islamic Microfinance Network, IMFN, is dedicated to the development and promotion of the Islamic microfinance industry through innovation, Shariah-compliant product development, institutional capacity building, assistance in the development of donor linkages and up-scaling the Islamic microfinance institutions. The network serves as a platform for consultation and for the development of the most efficient, Shariah- compliant practices, with a special emphasis on social performance management. It also focuses on raising public and institutional awareness regarding Islamic financial systems.

### *4.2.2 Akhuwat replicators and partners*

Akhuwat supports all organisations engaging in the worthy endeavour of making Pakistan a poverty-free country. The organisation partners with others by developing a customised program for them, making all resources available for interested stakeholders in order to facilitate their transition or the first step into this field. This includes providing training to the affiliate staff in interest-free non-profit microfinance and lending their loan methodology literature to all those that require it to ensure the establishment and sustainability of all desiring ventures. Akhuwat's support for replicators is based out of their desire to expand the horizons and scope of pure interest-free microfinance throughout Pakistan and hopefully the world; thus without any interest in capitalising on market shares, they have invested their energy and resources into helping develop other organisations without detracting from their objective and actually significantly contributing to their ultimate vision of a poverty-free society.

A few examples of Akhuwat's model replication and partnerships with other organisations:

#### 4.2.2.1 KAWISH WELFARE TRUST

Kawish Welfare Trust is a social welfare organisation, started with the aim of providing free education and medical facilities for the poor and needy.

Their vision is to attain the above-mentioned objectives by providing primary and middle-level education, basic health facilities, interest-free loans facilities, skill development programs and disaster management. KWT are working to develop a literate, healthy and self-esteemed society ready to take on the challenges of life and support each other in the hour of need. The interest-free loans program at Kawish Welfare Trust is known as Al-Basit (one of Allah's 99 Divine names) Micro-Finance Project.

Through their micro-loans initiative, Kawish provides equipment to needy borrowers on interest-free plans – equipment that is able to generate more income for the household. The type of equipment given under the scheme to date has been cycles, motorcycles and sewing machines. After the successful implementation of the equipment-based micro-loans scheme, a livestock project has been started. Live Stock Project facilitates the poor villagers in the remote areas of Bahawalnagar as well as beneficiaries who are parents of poor students (studying in Kawish Schools), orphans, widows and old and poor deserving villagers.

The main purpose of this project is to improve the lives of those who are financially abused, abandoned and disregarded by society. A goat with offspring is given so that the beneficiary can fulfil one of the most basic amenities of life – milk for the members of the household, especially for children. He is obliged to return to KWT a goat after one year. These animals returned to KWT are then redistributed as part of a recycle process to broaden the micro-loans system tailored on the specifications suiting the local culture and trade.

#### 4.2.2.2 ISLAH TRUST

Islah Trust of Pakistan is established with the objective to reduce economic disparity and growing illiteracy in the society. Islah Trust of Pakistan has established Qard-e-Hasan (Infaq) disbursement mechanisms in poverty-hit areas of the country that are initially targeting areas in and around Rawalpindi and Islamabad. The target beneficiaries are poor, needy and marginalised segments of the society. Islah Trust successfully inaugurated its first branch in the Morgah area in December 2011 and subsequently opened four more branches in the Misrial, Shakriyal, Rawat and Barakuh areas.

Islah's Infaq Program envisions the economic and social wellbeing of the impoverished segment of the society. Islah works for poorest of the poor whose lives are beset with illiteracy, disease, and other adverse circumstances. With its interventions and community mobilisation, Islah strives to bring positive change to the lives of the poor masses. The hallmark of its strategy is the alleviation of poverty through its Qard-e-Hasan disbursement.

The philosophy behind its Infaq Program (interest-free loans) is to bring change to the society by improving the living standards of the poorest by providing them a platform to earn for themselves and their families with respect and dignity. It also aims to provide the country with future leaders who are inspired by Islamic teachings and are equipped through the access to every type of constructive knowledge of the faith and the world. The beneficiaries of the Infaq Program belong to the poor and needy segment of the society, and we as able citizens are the source to support them. The spirit behind this system of ibadah (rite) is to seek the countenance of Allah Most High and to bring economic equality to the society.

### *4.2.3 Akhuwat 'dreams'*

In 2008 the Akhuwat Dreams Project (previously 'Make a Dream' project) was initiated in order to cater to the 'dreams' of children suffering from life-threatening medical conditions. The majority of the children come from the most impoverished segments of society, with 'dreams' as simple as a bright toy car, a doll, or a trip to Wagha Border. Furthermore, the project operates through various hospitals (currently PIC and Mayo Hospital) that are also equipped with 'Akhuwat Dreams' playrooms. These playrooms offer bright, positive and playful environments for sick children, granting them attention that is otherwise lacking in drab and serious hospital environments. Scientific research has proven that such an environment that encourages play, attention, and granting of wishes to terminally ill children helps these stricken souls feel stronger, more energetic, and more capable in the fight against their illnesses. In addition to medical care, the experience of playing in Akhuwat Dreams playrooms and nurseries, as well as the fulfilling of wishes, aids in curbing the emotional and physical pain of being terminally ill.

With the activation of community and the subsequent catalytic build-up of a supportive innovation ecosystem, the foundation for a more thoroughgoing institutionalisation follows.

## ***4.3 Research-to-innovation: institutionalising integral development***

> The guiding collective activity for Research-to-innovation is to '*newly evolve – or link up with an existing – center/organisation to institutionalise, sustain and further leverage, research-and-innovation*'. Such an institutional process now builds on Co-creation, seeking to strengthen or establish a long-term structural foundation for integral development in one's society. The role of the CARE function 'Research-to-innovation' is to institutionalise ongoing scholarship, research and knowledge creation with a view to developing self and community, organisation and society.

One of Akhuwat's most emphatic success stories amongst many is the institutionalisation of its philosophy and methodology by the prime minister's office for their unemployment loan scheme. Through this partnership, Akhuwat have been able to disburse 5billion rupees to micro-entrepreneurs. For Amjad and his organisation, the adoption of Akhuwat's philosophy of not charging interest on loans, on an institutional level is a huge success. For now, the reciprocity of Akhuwat's barakah rounds is multiplying on a larger scale.

### *4.3.1 Prime minister's interest-free loan scheme*

The prime minister's interest-free loan is provided for expanding and establishing businesses, to poor people with a poverty score of up to 40 using the poverty score card (PSC). The poverty score card (PSC) identifies eligible households through the application of a proxy means test (PMT) that determines the welfare status of the household on a scale between 0 and 100. Small to medium-size loans are given to micro-entrepreneurs for businesses and setting small enterprise only. Loans are disbursed in places of worship including mosques and churches to ensure transparency and participation.

The same model is adopted by the governments of Gilgit Baltistan and KPK (Khyber-Pakhtunkhwa, formerly the North-West Frontier Province, or NWFP, along the border of Afghanistan). For Akhuwat to reach these areas is a phenomenal achievement, as there's always been an unstated conflict between the governments of Khyber-Pakhtunkhwa and Punjab, home to Akhuwat and its head office. Punjab, the largest province of Pakistan, has always been the blue-eyed child for rulers for the past seventy years. KPK has always been a severely neglected province.

By establishing an Akhuwat (brotherhood) link by helping the local enterprises and livelihood of people in that area, Akhuwat is not only helping with the development of KPK's poor people, but also acting as a bridge-builder for both the respective communities.

### *4.3.2 Knowledge creation through a sustainable ecosystem*

Akhuwat, in partnership with various organisations, periodically conducts conferences and consultations on matters related to promoting Islamic microfinance (Qard-e-Hasan). The objective of these discussions is to promote deliberation on the multi-fold relationship between poverty alleviation and Islamic microfinance. From the numerous events held to date, some hold considerable significance for Akhuwat. A conference titled 'Exploring New Horizons in Microfinance – Akhuwat' was held in 2011 to celebrate the journey of Akhuwat from its beginning to the disbursement of one billion rupees. Akhuwat and UCP (University College of Punjab) also organised a conference on 'Leveraging Qarz-e-Hasan to Alleviate Poverty' in November 2015, as part of the campaign to celebrate helping one million families to escape poverty and become self-sustaining entrepreneurs.

Additionally, in collaboration with Al Huda Center for Islamic Banking and Economics (CIBE), Akhuwat has organised five international conferences under the banner of Global Microfinance Islamic Forum to date. Seminars have been held in Pakistan, Dubai and, most recently, the 5th Global Islamic Microfinance Forum was organised in Kuala Lampur, Malaysia in November 2015 and was attended by numerous participants from 27 countries all over the world. The next global summit was conducted in November 2016 in Kenya. In this way, Akhuwat engages local and international practitioners of social entrepreneurship to ensure that its message of poverty alleviation and empowerment of the underprivileged communities is spread far and wide across the world. A series of workshops in partnerships with various universities such as Lahore University of Management Sciences, Institute of Business Administration, University of Central Punjab, University of Management and Technology as well as several Chambers of Commerce and Industry across Pakistan have also been executed.

### *4.3.3 Akhuwat-Ishtarak project*

Ishtarak, a business project initiated to develop and market research consultancy focused on the Middle East and African markets, collaborated with Akhuwat on the Akhuwat-Ishtarak Islamic Finance Project. Ishtarak provides funding to disburse and administer loans while Akhuwat provides operational support.

### *4.3.4 Musharaka project*

Musharaka is a branch of Islamic finance in which the capital is provided by two or more parties for project development. Akhuwat, in collaboration with Oxford University and Lahore University of Management Sciences (LUMS), is developing a tri-partite relationship to form the Musharaka Project.

*In addition to all the above, through my consultancy work Akhuwat's model of alternative finance has been presented to many organisations throughout the UK and South Africa. There seems to be a possible collaboration with my TRANS4M colleagues in Nigeria who initiated CISER (Centre for Integral Social & Economic Research). Team CISER have developed a model of integral banking (interest-free) and would like to replicate Akhuwat's model of interest-free loans as their microfinance arm for societal development and poverty alleviation in Nigeria.*

## ***4.4 Educational transformation and transformative education: integrally CARE-ing for the society***

The guiding collective activity for this final CARE function is to '*develop a transformative educational program delivered by the centre/organisation*'. Educational transformation and transformative education builds on Contribution, seeking to deepen and leverage, through fundamentally transformed education, the original development impulse. While this final educational stage is conventionally associated with learning establishments, formal or informal, school or university, and hence with 'individual education', in this case we see the new centre being a core 'delivery vehicle' of educational transformation and transformative education.

We now briefly explore the educational services Akhuwat is now offering by 'spreading its developmental wings', from providing loans to inculcating the spirit of solidarity as the final CARE function closes its transformational development round at *educational transformation*, which aids in transforming a community and/or society. With Pakistan's illiteracy rate at a dismal point, Akhuwat is playing a pivotal role by raising awareness and educating its wider community in its own localised way. Additionally, at the time of writing this book, Akhuwat is working towards building Pakistan's first *fee-free* university by applying the same formula of reciprocity and Mawakhat.

### *4.4.1 Akhuwat Institute of Social Enterprise & Management (AISEM)*

The Akhuwat Institute of Social Enterprise & Management (AISEM) is situated in the heart of Lahore. AISEM specialises in providing customised trainings which are based upon comprehensive training need analysis bridged with the needs and requirements of the concerned organisation. AISEM has a well-experienced and qualified training panel which includes experts in the areas of finance, audit, social development, leadership, communication, monitoring and evaluation, procurement, community development, volunteerism, social enterprise development, supply chain management, microfinance, community impact assessment etc. AISEM is also launching its annual training calendar for specialised modules focused on the social sector and is providing consultancy services to various social and public-sector organisations.

### *4.4.2 Akhuwat-Faisalabad Institute of Research Science and Technology (FIRST)*

This institute is the culmination of the education vision of Akhuwat. Their intention is to set up and develop a world-class university with the best facilities and the best faculty for the underprivileged sector of society. The university currently has one fully functional campus in Faisalabad. Most of the degrees and diplomas taught at the university are attuned and technically aligned with the latest global practices of pedagogy. It is the world's first free residential university with a world-class, practitioner-focused education for the talented needy students. Akhuwat FIRST is a state-of-the-art university complex with accommodation amenities for students. Akhuwat FIRST is completely dedicated to research and technology in Pakistan. It offers four-year undergraduate degrees in the sciences, with a special focus on biotechnology. This follows from the fact it is one of the most advanced and fastest-growing fields in the world today. To facilitate future scientists in their respective fields, Akhuwat FIRST wants to create a niche by being a top-notch research university in Pakistan. At present, 88 students are enrolled in the BSc. (Honours) Program. A custom-built 60,000-square-foot dormitory for 300 students is currently under development. Akhuwat FIRST aims to provide a holistic experience to its students. On the one hand, it aims to impart quality education of an international standard to the youth of Pakistan, and on the other hand, it hopes to inculcate in these students the values necessary to establish successful careers. The second, larger purpose-built campus, to be developed in Kasur, will encompass multidisciplinary faculties.

### *4.4.3 Akhuwat College*

Akhuwat has established a college in Lahore called Akhuwat College. It is a residential facility catering to students from all over Pakistan. Currently, 62 students from 40 districts of Pakistan, from Sindh, Punjab, Khyber Pakhtunkhwa, Balochistan, Gilgit Baltistan, Azad Jammu Kashmir, and FATA, are enrolled in the college. Moreover, it is a strictly secular institution – it does not discriminate on the basis of religion. Consequently, Hindu, Muslim, Sikh and Christian students all study together in perfect harmony, setting a marvelous example of religious tolerance for the rest of the nation to follow. Akhuwat College admits students from low-income backgrounds, paying special attention to the poorest of the poor (zakat deserving) and the marginalised strata of society. It grants admission to those who prove themselves to be deserving enough to study free of cost. Commitment to education is the key to progress; as a result, the process is highly competitive and only the crème-de-la-crème are accepted into the college.

Akhuwat College is a residential facility, the reason being that Akhuwat does not only want to educate its students in the fields of science and information technology; it also believes that it is the institution's responsibility to nurture the students' personalities and mould them into prolific human beings. Akhuwat aims to groom them to be able to secure admission in prestigious universities and, later on, use the same skills to succeed in life.

### *4.4.4 Akhuwat educational assistance program*

This program provides scholarships to the talented and needy students whereby they can study in the top medical, engineering and information and communication technology institutes around Pakistan. More than 605 students have benefited from this program, i.e., Akhuwat Leadership and Youth Fellowship Program. This unique program trains more than 300 interns and fellows per year through a rigorous practicum-focused four-week module, which familiarises the interns with multiple organisations in the development sector. In 2016, Akhuwat Leadership and Youth Fellowship Program trained over 315 interns in nine different cities of Pakistan. An expatriate-focused program has also been developed to instil compassion and empathy in global students. Links have been established with USM, UTM and UUM universities in Malaysia, with collaborations under consideration with other foreign universities. Customised Social Enterprise and Community Development (SECD) Programs have been developed and executed for IBA Karachi and Hasan Abdal Cadet College.

### *4.4.5 Kiran-Akhuwat School, Lyari, Karachi*

The Kiran-Akhuwat School was established in partnership with Kiran Foundation. Situated in the heart of Lyari, Karachi, the school provides a respite from the otherwise tense atmosphere of the locality. It serves as an educational platform for toddlers in Lyari, also ensuring simultaneously that their parents are equipped with the necessary knowledge to raise their voices when faced with challenges in life. Hence, it strives to provide a holistic training to the whole family to help them cope better with their surrounding circumstances and encourages toddlers to emerge as honest leaders of the future.

Pakistan has undergone a significant change in economic growth over the last few years. People living at subsistence level cannot afford the basic necessities of life. Considering such undesirable impacts of inflation, Akhuwat has embarked upon several projects to support the people of Pakistan. The need for household items such as clothes, shoes, toys etc. is being fulfilled by Akhuwat Clothes Bank along with the provision of books to the needy. To meet the public's need for books, Akhuwat is developing Akhuwat Book Bank and will establish outreach libraries for the underprivileged communities.

### *4.4.6 Akhuwat public school support program – Akhuwat mosque/church schools*

Akhuwat has adopted 100 non-functional government schools through a public-private partnership under the Public School Support Program. These schools are located in the Faisalabad and Jhang districts of Punjab and have been converted into properly functional educational institutions. School enrolment has increased where quality education is being provided through the implementation of modern pedagogical systems. Efficient frameworks have been set in place and defined processes have been outlined. These schools, which have unfortunately been neglected and suffer from improper utilisation of resources, will serve as a benchmark for other organisations that are capable of adopting and converting similar schools into fully functional educational institutions. With the support of civil society, 400–500 more schools will be transformed in the near future. Akhuwat has also undertaken the responsibility of educating street children that are commonly seen selling flowers or toys on busy urban roads. Instead of dedicated buildings, Akhuwat will utilise religious spaces in the form of mosques or churches to provide formal education to street children. In order to encourage attendance, a free morning meal will also be regularly provided. Through this endeavour, Akhuwat aims to not only provide education to children who are otherwise deprived of formal schooling, but also improve their health and well-being by serving a nutritious meal once a day.

### *4.4.7 Akhuwat University*

Pakistan has the highest rate of OSC (out-of-school children). Amjad and his board members believe that poverty or lack of resources should not be a deterrent to a child's basic human right to education. After providing loans for 17 years, Akhuwat has also undertaken the responsibility of providing free education to the deserving students who have no access to finance to continue their education.

There are a total of 163 universities in Pakistan providing their services in both the public and private sectors of education. Of these universities, 91 (56%) are working under the umbrella of public sector, whereas 72 (44%) are working under the supervision of the private sector. This menial number cannot cater to Pakistan's huge population of 200 million people, especially people with a limited access to resources. There is a dire need for more institutions to take a lead in educating youth from deprived areas, as they form the critical mass of Pakistan's population being denied their basic right to education, which is hindering their participation in making Pakistan economically stable and prosperous.

Through their university, Akhuwat aims to tackle this issue by making higher education accessible to those students who have been studying at Akhuwat College. Another overarching aim of this university is to inculcate the spirit of solidarity in students through the practical example of Mawakhat, i.e., extending support to the needy.

Importantly for Amjad, these students will then carry the Akhuwat philosophy forward by creating their own barakah rounds. According to Lessem and Schieffer, educational transformation and transformative education seek to deepen and leverage, through fundamentally transformed education, the original community development impulse.

Thus, as apparent from the above, Akhuwat has woven its extensive solidarity ecosystem through its Pakistani social fabric via its multi-faceted endeavours, from granting loans for poverty alleviation to educating the masses.

We now present some of Akhuwat's beneficiaries and their journey of Mawakhat/solidarity. These stories, in essence, aside from portraying a state of destitution and its dismal effects on Pakistani society, are shared to depict Akhuwat's patronage of local businesses and micro-enterprises.

This provides an overview of Akhuwat's communal CARE process through its many initiatives; we now share a few stories of success from Akhuwat's Qard-e-Hasan (interest-free loans) portfolio, its main feature of sustainable development amongst its community of borrowers. In doing so, our aim is to give our readers an insight into how these interest-free loans, regardless of their 'micro-ness' in financial terms, are contributing to Pakistan's economy by providing access to resources for its micro-entrepreneurs.

We now further demonstrate the manifestation of Akhuwat's solidarity effect through some success stories of its borrowers.

## 5 Akhuwat benevolent loan – success stories

The first ever story, and an extremely moving one, in Akhuwat's golden book of success is that of Hakim Bibi. Hakim Bibi, a 70-year-old, suffering from diabetes and high blood pressure, was forced to make ends meet with only the support of her husband's meagre pension of Rs. 600 ($6) a month.

Hakim Bibi and her husband are well into their seventies and eighties, hardly the age to live by the sweat of their brows. Her health did not allow exertion, but their expenses could barely be met. Both had reached the limit of endurance, but spreading their hands for alms was something they would never resort to. They bought baskets and jute (for charpoys) from the village so that they could sell them and keep a roof over their heads. Self-respect was hard to maintain, as that income hardly assured one meal a day. Just as they were on the verge of being crushed by abject destitution, somebody told Hakim Bibi about Akhuwat people reaching out to impoverished women with interest-free loans that were liable to be returned after a year. Hakim Bibi became part of a group of similarly hard-pressed women, called *Iqra*, and was given a loan of Rs. 10,000 ($100) the very next month. Along with the baskets, she was now able to have peppers brought from the village, and she ground and sold them. It turned out that there was sufficient demand for them in the neighbourhood. Neighbours and store vendors in the locality would come right to her doorstep to purchase the items. As these items began to sell, their situation started to improve. With this venture, not only were they able to repay their debts, but the income also contributing to the household expenses. Life is tough, especially at their age when just to seek two meals a day, Hakim Bibi and her husband had to work each day with their ailing conditions. Nonetheless, Hakim Bibi and her husband are grateful to the nobility of Akhuwat and its team for not only providing them with a loan, but also for extending their bond of solidarity to a destitute old couple.

The second story is that of Muhammad Saleem, as published in Akhuwat's monthly circular. Saleem is a resident of Basti Khokran in Bahawalnagar district. Saleem toils in scorching heat, the monsoon rains and chilly winter mornings to deliver milk to a number of households. 'Purchasing milk was something that was beyond my capacity; it was difficult to purchase in bulk quantities without any means of transport', Saleem says. He applied for a loan to purchase a bicycle. His application was accepted, and he was provided with a bicycle on interest-free monthly instalments. The bicycle helps Saleem to complete his job easily and quickly, and also enables him to reach more locations. After the addition of this asset in his business model, he easily purchases milk from one village and then re-distributes it conveniently in the village he targets. In fact, the loan brought more prosperity into his household. Due to the increase in monthly income, and eventual savings, Saleem has been able to open a milk and yogurt shop in the central marketplace of his village.

The third story that I would like to share is the one which was shared with me personally whilst I was doing a field round with Akhuwat's team to meet their borrowers in a residential colony in Lahore. A middle-aged lady named Sakeena Bibi told me that after her husband's death her son, who was 16 years old at that time, became the sole breadwinner for the family of five. The young boy used to toil day and night at a motorbike plant making plastic plugs for motorbikes. After learning about Akhuwat's interest-free loans, Sakeena suggested to her son that they should also take advantage of this opportunity. The first loan they took from

Akhuwat was 10,000 rupees ($90), and they bought a machine to make plastic plugs for motorbikes. After successfully repaying their first loan and seeing their business grow, Sakeena and her son went for a second loan of 20,000 ($180) to buy the second machine. They now own four machines and employ four women from their locality.

Such stories of hope and prosperity are aplenty in Akhuwat's portfolio, i.e., nearly 2.3 million families as of now.

Here I will narrate some more stories taken from Amjad's book *Akhuwat ka Safar* (Journey of Hope), as he cherishes all these stories which not only form a significant part of Akhuwat's bigger story but also occupy a large part of his own life story of being the catalyst to changing lives for many with his innovative model of alternative microfinance.

On a scorching afternoon last July in Lahore, near the canal, in the auditorium of a private educational institution, it was announced that the best entrepreneurs of Akhuwat were to be selected. A selection of those people who had started their businesses with Akhuwat's interest-free loans and had run them superbly were to be nominated for the award. This was a one-of-its-kind event. People came one after the other, shy, unpretentious, wearing scrubbed clothes. Even at first glance, one could tell that they were not used to an environment this 'formal'. Hesitatingly, they would start to speak, but as soon as their hard work and the ensuing success were mentioned, their tones assumed a special kind of pride. They would relate with dignity that they did not spread their hands before anybody and carved the path of their lives with their own toil. I was seated in the front row, awe-struck at them. Among them were women, the elderly, and disabled borrowers of Akhuwat's benevolent loan.

A motorcycle mechanic from Green Town came up. He told us that he had been working as a mechanic at Rs. 100 daily wage ($1) when somebody told him about Akhuwat. Taking a Qard-e-Hasan of Rs. 10,000 ($100), he got himself a shop, put in his hard work day and night, and managed to augment his income threefold.

An imam of a mosque in Dhoop Sarri, Sandah related that his only source of income had been the alms received during the Friday prayers. He was trying to make do with this, but with much hardship. At somebody's advice, he took a Qard-e-Hasan of Rs. 5,000 ($50) and began to sell shopping bags at Azam Cloth Market, in the centre of Lahore. In the beginning he would go on a bicycle, and then he bought a motorcycle on monthly payments. Each day, two to three hours spent there would earn him Rs. 150–200 ($2). Thus, life's hardships began to subside, and he even put his children in school.

Each story was more intense and astonishing than the one before. Women came up and related that, with a seemingly ordinary amount of money, they had started sewing and doing embroidery at home for income generation. One middle-aged woman set up a grocery store at her doorstep. With this income, not only was she able to get her children married, but also went on pilgrimage with her asthmatic husband.

There was one man, however, about 40–45 years old, whose story totally stunned us. He related, 'I was working at a private company and my children were studying at a middle-class private school. We were living respectably. One day, however, I got into an argument with the company manager. He complained to the owner, who, without considering my twelve years of service at his firm, fired me. This jolt proved so severe that my life changed completely. I am a college graduate but all efforts to get another job failed. Months passed by and all the savings were also spent. The neighbourhood storekeepers refused to give us groceries on credit. Friends and relatives got weary of lending to us and stopped taking our calls. My wife's few trinkets of jewellery were also sold, and one day we faced starvation.

'When my wife and children did not have food for the third time, I decided that death was better than this life of humiliation. I did not even have the money to buy poison. Suddenly, I remembered that we had once bought rat poison pills. I managed to find that packet of pills and made a powder out of it. I dissolved this powder into a *sherbet* and called my wife and children to me. My wife was surprised that we didn't have enough for *roti*, and I was serving this *sherbet*. I told my family to drink the concoction, and then wait for some great news. They were thrilled. I poured the *sherbet* into a glass and was about to give it to my elder daughter, when my four-year-old son leapt up and took the glass. His face gleamed with joy. He cried, "Father first I will drink, so that I can be the first to hear the good news".'

This man's speech reverberates to this day. I shudder to think that if that day, he had considered it beneath him to do menial work, his family's tragedy would have become another feature for newspapers and television channels. The real thing to do is turn such determined, courageous lives into beacons of the path.

More institutions like Akhuwat are needed, which provide interest-free loans. Despite 8–10 years of hard work, good name and credibility, Akhuwat has distributed Rs. 500–600 million rupees ($5–6 million). Its monthly disbursement is limited to a few million rupees. And then in our midst are people who lend on interest. This moneylending mafia hires thugs for recovery. In a city like Lahore, one can find blatant banners on streets where the 'good news' of pawning jewellery and assets for loans is proclaimed. It is surprising that there is no accountability for these extortionate moneylenders.

The question is, why, after all, does the government not make institutions that give out interest-free loans?

The government of Punjab can easily give institutions like Akhuwat one or two billion rupees. In the federal government, there was the Benazir Support Programme, for which 50 billion rupees (about 0.5 billion USD) were dedicated, an amount that will evaporate in a single year, having a negligible impact, if any. Is it not suitable that a part of this amount is donated to reliable charities and the rest spent on micro-credit, so that people are enabled to stand on their own feet? Similarly, from the National Treasury Fund, those people who are indebted to ruthless moneylenders must be freed. Remember that more than poverty, it is despondency that defeats a person. Giving people hope, giving them respite to breathe, is the work of the state. Charitable institutions that provide aid are doing their work, but transforming the system is the responsibility of the state'.

Aamir Khakwani, a journalist, wrote in 2010. Exactly a year later, in 2011, the government of Punjab decided to establish a Qard-e-Hasan fund with one billion rupees ($10 million) and handed over the responsibility and management to Akhuwat. This was a historic decision. It was announced at the shrine of Hazrat Data Gang Baksh, who is a source of grace to every person, ordinary or important. Perhaps this is a step towards interest-free banking.

This public-private partnership could be Akhuwat's biggest success, as this will pave the way to fully institutionalising a system of finance that is generated by revisiting Islamic history and the story of Mawakhat (solidarity) between those who 'have' and those who 'have-no-wealth'. As mentioned above in Amjad's statement, the government of Punjab finally realised that only by providing interest-free loans could they improve the economic situation of the very poor of the society.

This brings us to the close of this chapter, which expanded on Akhuwat's success stories, demonstrating their integral CARE (Community activation, raising Awareness, Research-to-innovation and Embodied action) impact as postulated by Lessem and Schieffer in their integral development theory. Our purpose in doing so is to, again, reinforce the belief that Akhuwat is doing more for the Pakistani community by not only providing interest-free loans to poor people, but also raising awareness of a) the issue of reliance on charity money and b) importance of supporting the local cottage industries and micro-entrepreneurs by giving them visibility in an almost feudalistic environment in which this section of the society has been considered as a serving class for the masters.

## 6 Conclusion

According to Amjad, over the years as our interaction with the community deepened, we realised that we were required to put in greater effort for a poverty-free society to be made a reality. Poverty is not only the absence of financial resources, but it encompasses all domains of life including health, education and social security. Hence, the reason Akhuwat initiated all the above projects to benefit society at large rather than just providing them with loans to earn a livelihood as many microfinance organisations are already doing in Pakistan and around the world.

According to a report generated by USAID-WHAM (Widening Harmonized Access to Microfinance) Project, in 2005 the number of active microfinance borrowers in Pakistan crossed the 600,000 threshold. This growth, from 60,000 in 1999, is the result of enormous investment on the part of international donors, the government of Pakistan, and motivated private organisations. Over this period, several providers experienced serious repayment problems. Akhuwat, on the other hand, claims a recovery rate of 99.9% and with no reliance on international donors. This proves two essential observations that Amjad came up with:

1) The poor are trustworthy (by providing them with interest-free loans).
2) The effect of solidarity is more solidarity; that is the multiplier effect of virtuous circles (barakah doing rounds).

Pakistan's microfinance industry faces some urgent choices. Under current conditions, microfinance could continue for a limited time but cannot grow much further nor sustain itself beyond the initial investment. Alternatively, Pakistan can consider the costs and benefits of raising interest rates, service charges or other fees necessary to become sustainable. Which poses the question of whether Akhuwat, as an alternative to microfinance, will be able to maintain its position in this field and, more importantly, does it present itself as a clear model for replication for other microfinance organisations around Pakistan to rid themselves of foreign aid reliance and instead adopt Akhuwat's model of reciprocal benevolence endowment and CARE model?

We believe, in light of all the exploration we have done throughout the course of previous chapters, we are now ready to explore Akhuwat's integral model of finance as per Lessem and Schieffer's model of integral economics, along with my other TRANS4M colleagues working collectively, yet in our own respective fields.

The next and concluding part of our book contemplates this through our SOUL-idarity Hikma postulation which came about after deeply observing the archetypal solidarity GENE rhythm of Pakistani and Islamic society, as also the inspiration came from the work of Islamic philosophers and thinkers like Muhammad Iqbal, who is also considered as the 'Thinker of Pakistan', and other Muslim philosophers and Sufi mystics who put a lot of emphasis on disciplining the nafs (false self), which is always demanding more and more. As per my research-to-innovation call, I suggest employing the inner (soul) wisdom/Hikma to create more SOUL-idarity and barakah (blessings) circles for societal wellbeing. For me, Akhuwat presents one such model, yet all too implicitly.

We now move on to our final round of the SOUL-idarity journey.

## Bibliography

Hickel, J., 2015. The Microfinance Delusion: Who Really Wins? *The Guardian*. Available at: https://www.theguardian.com/global-development-professionals-network/2015/jun/10/the-microfinance-delusion-who-really-wins

Lessem, R., & Schieffer, A., 2015. *Integral Renewal: A Relational and Renewal Perspective*. Abingdon: Routledge.

# Part IV

# The 4th P – The integral solidarity paradigm

## 1 Introduction: the final effect of solidarity circumvolution

As we have now reached the final part of our book, the task that remains is to have an overview of the soul of solidarity (Akhuwat) as per my postulation of the Hikma of SOUL-idarity.

For Amjad, unquestionably, it's love – of God and His holy Messenger (may peace be upon him) – that breeds solidarity amongst humankind. The following excerpt is from Amjad's Journey of Hope (*Akhuwat ka Safar*) as he travelled around the American continent in 2012, taking the message of brotherhood to many prestigious American institutions. The following narrates his Harvard experience/expressions:

> Institutions are shown through their students. Roman and David, both students at Harvard, were introduced to me through a friend, Imran Sarwar. They are both accomplished mountaineers. Roman is German while David is from Holland. I had been in touch with them many months before arriving. Together, they have established an institution called *No Mountain Too High* (NM2H). They have set their sights on scaling all the summits of Europe and America. When Imran told them about Akhuwat, their enthusiasm was such that they decided to spread the message of Akhuwat during their adventures. Thus, a spirit of cooperation was established between Akhuwat and NM2H.
>
> When I arrived at Harvard, Roman and David were immensely pleased. They introduced their girlfriends, Lorraine and Janet, an American and a Japanese. Germany, Holland, America and Japan – how people from unfamiliar cities and far-removed countries find each other. *Love works magic indeed.* Roman and David also hosted a dinner during which we spoke at length about mutual cooperation. At the end of the semester, they were heading to Alaska to climb a mountain of over 18,000 feet. They pledged to hoist two flags on the summit, one of NM2H and the other of Akhuwat. Not a single soul lives at this height in Alaska. Perhaps not even the enchantment of love exists there. Yet the flag of Akhuwat – solidarity of mankind – will be raised there.

> All journeys towards the heights begin with a single step. The step that was taken 17 years ago has accomplished great distances indeed.
>
> As the Quran affirms, 'And we made you custodians of the earth' And then, '*You are an ordinary, worthless, nameless creation; who gives you a revered status on earth? Who makes you a vicegerent of the Lord?*' It is nothing but His blessing.

*Incidentally, the journey started a year ago for me, when I summoned myself to narrate the Akhuwat phenomenon as an integral-spiritual mandate for the global community to acknowledge that this phenomenon exists in Pakistan. That the philosophy and its practices are existent in that part of the world was enough to excite me – for the love of my country. Pakistan, as previously mentioned, albeit ranking as an 'emerging economy' from the South-Asian region, still struggles with its global image perception. For me, the opportunity came as a duty to serve my country of birth in this capacity, as compared to the widespread recognition that the likes of Grameen as the microfinance pioneers entertain: that Akhuwat and Pakistan still lag behind on that scale.*

*My inspiration was threefold as I embarked on this journey*:

*Firstly, my fascination with the integral GENE model as proposed by Lessem and Schieffer, co-founders of TRANS4M, Centre for Integral Development, Geneva, in which Professor Ronnie Lessem, as my mentor and teacher, Trans4mation catalyst and supervisor, has played a huge role, not only by inspiring me endlessly, but also by guiding my way to a new dimension of 'integrality', which helped me unveil the implicit integrality in Akhuwat's case and how it is working to activate communities in Pakistan whilst innovatively institutionalising a model of communal self-sufficiency generating their own micro-solidarity economy.*

*Secondly, there was this dervish-like personality of Dr. Muhammad Amjad Saqib, founder and chairperson of Akhuwat – for every sitting with him opened up a new dimension in my heart and soul. The source of direct knowledge that I acquired form him – coming from a deeper, inner, divine source – has been the guiding light, connecting the integral-spiritual dots throughout my journey of the book. And to know one such integral-spiritual economic model exists affirms my belief that spirituality can be (practically) applied to financial models – the main premise of my research.*

*Thirdly, and building on the previous point, in the words of our beloved Bawa, Pir Zia* Inayat-Khan, *president of The Inayati International Sufi Order and grandson of Hazrat Inayat Khan, 'External divergences often conceal internal convergences. This is true of the revealed religions of the world. Exoteric distinctions tend to obscure the esoteric reality that the source and goal of all religions is the same'* (Inayat-Khan, 2017).

*In a secular, temporal world, where religious practices and rituals are considered essentially incommodious and primitive wherein the 'spirit' of religious ordination is defunct, those who hear the divine call become subservient to this 'calling' and take upon themselves this responsibility to serve a divine purpose. They become a vessel ready to receive the call and serve the call. From Amjad's words above, it becomes ever more evident, as he sees this as his duty and feels blessed to be able to deliver this divine purpose.*

*In a world of statistical complexity and tangible outcomes and analytical impact measurements, the call to serve somehow gets lost. The call of Mawakhat/ solidarity with the needy and destitute who are a statistical reality overshadowed by the vested interests of big organisations who identify them as 'customers'.*

In the words of my Canadian friend Mark Anielski, an economic strategist specialising in measuring the wellbeing and happiness of nations, communities and businesses, 'Models and words will always be inadequate. Love of God and neighbour seems so simple, yet we have created many human systems that reject these truths' (2007).

*Fewer, then, have the courage to embrace the truth fully and dare to define the truth in a practical way, as did Amjad and his colleagues. For such is the nature of truth.*

*In the case of Akhuwat, being such a beacon of hope for all those who needed a compassionate heart to share their pain and destitution, Amjad became one such source of hope and compassion. For time and again, all I hear him say is, distinct is the timbre of those tempered by love.*

*Though little did I know, this journey would reveal a process which could be perceived as a turn-key to a 'solidarity economic' model that could help communities to generate their own micro-economies rather than depending on grants from state institutions – something which comes as a hinderance, as practically experienced by my community organisation whilst working with migrant communities.*

*At the time of writing this book, and as part of my integral CARE (Community activation, raising Awareness, Research-to-innovation and Embodied action) journey of my PHD (Process of Holistic Development), I, along with my CIFE (Centre for Integral Finance and Economics) colleagues, are pursuing the option of applying Akhuwat's model of 'solidarity economy' to disadvantaged migrant communities within the UK so they can generate their own micro-economies, which can help them avoid financial-dependency entrapment.*

## *1.1 Section 1: the solidarity wisdom (Hikma)*

*In Chapter 1, we delved into the 'spirit' of communitas and what lurks in their midst. Through this journey of our book, we've made an in-depth exploration of the Akhuwat paradigm and the compelling outcomes, observed in previous chapters, of the spirit of Mawakhat, i.e., the activation of the barakah (abundance) present within communities to generate their own self-sufficiency pools of benevolent reciprocal endowment. Thus, in our concluding part, we will sum up the wisdom (Hikma) of solidarity – that which originates from the core of such Hikma.*

*Coming from an Eastern culture of 'sensing and feeling' (of soul and heart) rather than analysing (of mind), we believe that inner knowledge, which we term as Hikma, emanating in our inner recesses, comes from a deeper source, i.e., the soul; this is what guides us towards love, empathy and compassion for each other.*

*For we believe soul-wisdom can only be earned through the worldly experiences of the soul and not taught through applied knowledge. Writing this book, as per my calling, also came from that deeper source – to find a golden mean where the soul-wisdom could be applied to physical practices. I found that expression in Akhuwat's financial model – the only living example of such abridged wisdom.*

*My SOUL-idarity conclusion is a derivative of this soul-wisdom which can be applied to bridge the spirit and material divide. I believe that only by employing our soul-wisdom (Hikma) can we liberate ourselves from the shackles of populist theories and herd-like material existence, which is hindering societies from embracing the new-age transformation into a new era of peaceful co-existence.*

In the words of Pir Zia Inayat-Khan:

> Contrary to the assumptions of materialism, consciousness is not a latecomer to the universe. Revelation, tradition, and unveiling confirm: the cosmos was endowed with a soul and a mind before it obtained its corporeal form'. Dara Shikuh, the fifth Mughal Emperor and a Mystic, says, 'From love the Great Soul appeared, which is to say the jiv-atman, which is called the "Muhammadan Reality."' This alludes to the universal soul of the Chief of the Prophets, upon whom be peace and blessings
>
> (Inayat-Khan, 2017).

The first section of this part of the book thus establishes the link between this wisdom which comes directly from the soul, acting as the guiding light for SOUL-idarity – with Self and others (community). It is this wisdom which enables people, in the case presented here of Amjad and Akhuwat, to initiate or generate their own 'virtuous circles' and see (barakah) abundance all around.

We will hence proceed to our integral finance paradigm with this Hikma of virtuosity through our postulation of an awakened (soulful) integral SOUL-idarity noesis.

### *1.2 Section 2: SOUL-idarity with universality – an integral finance model*

Akhuwat and Amjad's vision, which is a reality now, has transformed many lives in the span of its 17 years of existence. Yet his dream of ridding Pakistan of poverty and social injustice has yet to materialise. Notwithstanding this fact, he's hopeful that the people (community of Akhuwateers) will carry this legacy forward. In his words:

'Averse to the rampant social injustice, and especially the inequitable distribution of wealth, we had longed for a change. Perhaps we assumed that change came from chanting slogans, or that revolution would rise over the horizon of student politics. Everybody's life changed since – but not that of Pakistan. Poverty, destitution, pain and sorrow; all remain the same. Individual change does not compensate for systemic change.

'We could not bring change, but the people whose lives improved as a result of their efforts and our undertaking will bring about change.'

Incidentally, Akhuwat's model of Mawakhat, Qard-e-Hasan (interest-free loans) and reciprocal endowment has now been adopted institutionally and replicated by many organisations in Pakistan. The question then arises of making this unique model universal and applicable to other communities. At a time when the world is going through an economic transitional phase of finding solutions in alternative models that can sustain our collective financial needs, could an Akhuwat-like model of reciprocity and solidarity provide an answer for the injustices committed against the less fortunate amongst us?

My primary quest remains to seek these answers, i.e., to apply this model to overcome the social and financial divide that exists between the UK's diaspora communities. But my reservations remain with people's acceptance of a model imbued with a spiritual philosophy as its guiding principle as per the general reticence that has engulfed people's faith in religions and spirituality. The Akhuwat model, however, though originating from a spiritual tradition in actuality, is not a religious organisation. What was observed in their case was a process of communal solidarity being generated as a result of their philosophical manipulation of a society's local culture and belief system.

Thus, my proposition of a 4P process which maps out a community's beliefs and culture – that which forms the moral core of their communal co-existence.

Therefore, the concluding part of our book aims to illustrate a universal effect of the soul of solidarity (SOUL-idarity) which I believe could be universally binding.

Additionally, we will postulate what could be a way for Akhuwat's solidarity paradigm to become a universal phenomenon. Regarding the integral 4C (Call, Context, Co-creation and Contribution) journey to CARE-4-Society model as developed by Schieffer & Lessem (2014), *how could one such model integrally care for a particular community or society?*

Thus, we invite our readers to embark on this journey of SOUL-idarity with us.

## References


Anielski, M., 2007. Building an Economy of Love Based on Genuine Wealth. *Celebrate*, 11, 11, pp. 6–7.

Inayat-Khan, P. Z., 2017. *Mingled Waters*. New Lebanon, NY: Suluk Press Omega Publications Inc.

Schieffer, A., & Lessem, R., 2014. CARE 4 Zimbabwe: Towards a Pundusto Centre for Integral Development. In: A. Schieffer, & R. Lessem eds. *Integral Development: Realising the Transformative Potential of Individuals, Organisations and Societies*. Gower Publishing Ltd.

# 9 The integral Hikma

## SOUL-idarity process

### 1 Preamble

> ***May this wayfarer's plea be heard.***
> In the beginning, a handful of people trusted this dream of Akhuwat (brotherhood).
>
> Perhaps there are always few in the beginning. Then followed a flood of supporters, the impact of this journey ingrained in their hearts. What we lost along the way we do not regret.
>
> In the accounting of passion and of *Ishq* (love), two and two do not equal four. The result is contingent only on intention. When the intention is noble, an extra zero can easily be added. Heaven knows when *Akhuwat's* next journey will take place, and whether or not we will be there for it.

*Thus, our journey of solidarity and brotherhood (Akhuwat), is edging towards its final part. Though the end is a beginning in itself, as expressed above in Amjad's sentiments, a new journey will begin in Akhuwat's association with a community of integral economists and finance innovators.*

*For we might not be here to witness the next (evolutionary) stage of this phenomenon, but the seeds have been sown by Amjad with the loving intention of seeing his country prosper. I have just returned from South Africa after attending an Integral Pan-African Roundtable. As a result of that and our CIFE (Centre for Integral Finance and Economics) conference outcome, Akhuwat – our solidarity paradigm – could be embarking on a global journey towards North-South. An integral SOUL-idarity economics research centre, to feed into other integral research centres, is already involved with knowledge creation for institutionalised research-to-innovation.*

*This includes our next book, which will serve as a bible of our Islamic to integral finance and economics postulation. As we believe, the world is now ready to embrace a model of finance, in principle and in practice, that proposes an integrated financial model which could aid in ridding the world of debt slavery and the Western 'mono-cultural' imperialistic model of materialism and wealth accumulation – an economy of SOUL-idarity and collabro-nomics.*

*Through our Mawakhat journey of this book, we have learnt that there could be a simple solution to our mostly over-speculated and complex financial problems that are challenging our very existence, socially, spiritually and ecologically.*

*The question remains: how willing are we to engage our heart and soul in making things better for ourselves and for our fellow humans?*

*For by consciously drawing on our innate wisdom of the soul (and heart), we are able to engage our communal 'solidarity impulse' and generate self-sufficiency and genuine wealth for communities that are often neglected by the state and big corporations, as presented in the case of Akhuwat's 'reciprocal endowment' model.*

*To be fully aware of this wealth and abundance (barakah), communities need to re-awaken their collective inner wisdom, as has been the case with Akhuwat, albeit implicatively.*

*In the opening chapter of our book, we introduced an integral Hikma (wisdom) process which came out of Akhuwat's 4I genealogy and practices.*

*Furthermore, as illustrated and presented through Akhuwat's solidarity GENE rhythm and 4I (Iman, Ikhlas, Ihsan and Ikhuwah) genealogy, the next phase of Akhuwat's innovative evolutionary stage, as indicated by Amjad in the note above, is to explicitly propagate the 4P (Philosophy, Principles, Practices and integral Paradigm) process that purposefully and soul-fully rekindles the soul of the 'solidarity spirit' amongst communities, thus universally radiating the effect of SOUL-idarity.*

*Thereby, we propose an integral SOUL-idarity rhythm which is borne out of this solidarity spirit within communities to then bring a transformative effect to societies trans-globally.*

## 2 Section 1: the Hikma of integral SOUL-idarity rhythm

> The way man harnessed the universe and disseminated the fruits of his toil, the Lord must surely be pleased. Thus, HIS abundance and blessings are scattered all around us, in the rising of the sun and in the chirping of the birds to herald a new morning. If the Lord has not despaired, then why are we hopeless about man's future?
>
> *Come, let's weave a dream* – for tomorrow. For what is life but weaving dreams and envisioning a better tomorrow for our fellow human beings?

For Amjad, to translate a dream into a living reality, hope and courage in one's divine abilities bring the desired results. Thus, he concludes his book *Akhuwat ka Safar* (Journey of Hope) with these words:

For him, man has achieved the apex of his self-actualisation by taming the seas and conquering the air – why then are we failing to justly distribute (and share) the God-given abundance on Earth amongst ourselves and especially to those who have been purposefully kept underprivileged due to an insatiable greed and lust for wealth?

In the words of Pir Zia Inayat-Khan, the contemporary mystic of our time, a Spiritual Guide and Founder of an inter-spiritual venture Seven Pillars House of Wisdom;

> The human soul comes to gather experiences on this earth and to leave a mark, which we often call – the legacy. we are constantly inscribing our signature on the tablet of nature. He directs our attention to contemplate; what is that signature that we will be leaving behind for our co-creative shared human-cause?
>
> (Inayat-Khan and Wisdom, 2014)

He then goes on by reminding us of the knowledge and wisdom humans have co-created:

> At special moments in human history people have come together to harvest the wisdom of the world. Examples of this enterprise include the *Library of Alexandria*, the *House of Wisdom of Baghdad (Bait-ul-Hikma)*, the interfaith *House of Worship of Fatehpur Sikri*, and the *Platonic Academy of Florence*.... In our time, the need for fresh vision is perhaps more urgent than ever before. The pace of history seems to be accelerating as the world is transforming on a dramatic scale. Our species has reached the height of its powers, but our might has out-paced our wisdom, and life on planet earth, the flower of four billion years of evolution, is withering before our eyes
>
> (Inayat-Khan and Wisdom, 2014).

Pir Zia Inayat-Khan emphasises that what is needed now is ‘a new house of wisdom, one for all of the great traditions of the world, as well as the burgeoning wisdom in science, in the arts, in all that comes from the heart of human experience’.

Meanwhile, around the world, it is reassuring to work with people who believe in this ‘togetherness’ as mentioned by Pir Zia and draw from their inner wisdom, spirituality and cultural traditions as they persistently work towards finding new solutions to the more deep-rooted problems of this world.

Amjad and Akhuwat found one solution for poverty eradication by generating a solidarity economy borne out of the Mawakhat philosophy. Dr. Emil Nothnagel, my TRANS4M colleague from South Africa, found his solution in Collabronomics – a green economy which offers communities more ways to stimulate business through finding alternative energy solutions. Daud Taranhike, another TRANS4M colleague from Zimbabwe, uses Nhaka-nomics to preserve his culture’s legacy and heritage. Furthermore, my Nigerian colleagues, Dr. Basheer Oshodi, Dr. Jubril Adeojo and Akeem Shina Oyewale are striving to set up an interest-free banking system based on Maqasid al Shariah to counter the overriding poverty challenge in Nigeria. Whereas my UK CIFE (Centre for Integral Finance and Economics) colleague, Robert Dellner, is proposing an I3 model of integral impact investment – from 'IRR to IIR' (Internal Rate of Return to Integral Impact Return).

The universe is virtuously conspiring to release humankind from the unbearable burdens of debt slavery and an overt culture of decadence and unappeasing greed and material fulfilment. This age is heralding an era of a trans-global solidarity bond of knowledge creation and SOUL-idarity amongst humankind.

We now turn to our 'integral bond of global solidarity', newly forming between a community of social, economics and finance innovators.

## *2.1 Solidarity bond – a case of integral finance and economics*

*After studying the Akhuwat model in depth whilst gathering the wisdom – from East, to West, to South (my recent trip to South Africa) – I am, evermore, attuned to this 'emerging' universal call to employ our collective wisdom to form a solidarity bond, working towards our common economic good.*

*As proposed by our TRANS4M colleagues and co-founders, Schieffer & Lessem (2010):*

> For micro-enterprise transformation is bound to be limited by the macroeconomic context to which organisations are required to adapt. This macroeconomic system is failing us to such a degree that we are collectively called upon to seek a more viable alternative. To those who claim that the existing system still works and may only have to be tweaked a bit here and there, we argue that it only works for an elite few, and that the time has come for us to develop an economic system that works for all of us and for the planet. We regard such a system as a crucial prerequisite for our collective survival.

*For economic systems to be integrally inclusive and be solution oriented rather than imposing debt slavery on to people, more so on the poor amongst us, the universal call is being heard, ever more audibly.*

As per Llewellyn Vaughan-Lee (2012), a Sufi mystic and lineage successor in the Naqshbandiyya-Mujaddidiyya Sufi Order, 'we are the only civilisation that has not had a relationship with the sacred within creation at its core,in the more simple and everyday activities; as a result the centre can't hold'.

*As we move away from the sacred core of our beings, the (man-made) systems that were created to serve us have now had us serving them, i.e., we are held captive by the systems – the economic system being the prime example. Incidentally, when these economic systems collapse, as per the recent 2009 crisis, even the experts of the field are incapacitated and fail to bring forth fundamentally new ways of thinking.*

*As part of my call to contribution, I am becoming ever more convinced that micro-enterprises, as presented in the case of Akhuwat's borrowers, might have little or no effect on the macro-economic system, albeit these micro-communities of micro-entrepreneurs have the capability of creating their own self-sufficient micro-economies which could eventually have an overall effect on a macro level.*

*Does this hold true for economically inactive migrant communities in the UK who are dependent on organisational grant money? Additionally, as seen in Akhuwat's case, there's an apparent strength in the values and beliefs that hold faith-based communities together, as observed in my experience of working with other faith communities in London.*

*Furthermore, by placing faith and/or cultural, traditional or moral values in the centre, or at the heart, of an economic wheel, it provides community members with a sense of communal purpose-ness and meaning.*

*Notwithstanding the fact, this very placement divides and segregates communities too, which often makes me wonder: could spirituality or the intersectionality of soul and solidarity, i.e., SOUL-idarity, be able to fill the segregational divide between spirituality/faith? Could this be our new-age economic renewal of oikos, the Greek word for economics? Wherein 'eco' is the whole ecology – a monetary eco-system that helps people 'manage' their household and, most importantly, work for all and not a select few.*

### *2.1.1 From econocracy to a SOUL-idarity monetary eco-system*

Per the economics student trio of the University of Manchester, "a century ago, the idea of 'the economy' didn't exist. Now economics is the supreme ideology of our time, with its own rules and language. The trouble is, most of us can't speak it". (Earle, Moran, & Ward-Perkins, 2017)

*The language is only understood by a 'select few' who can often tweak the language to their own benefits. Just as Muhammad Yunus, Bangladeshi micro-finance pioneer and founder of Grameen Bank, professed the case of poor people not being bank-worthy, I believe people are not even economics-worthy. Often, I've found this has been the case with the marginalised communities who have no or little knowledge of how 'eco-nomics' is impacting their survival.*

Whilst the whole government machinery rushed towards rescuing the big economies of the world after the 2008 economic crisis and, thereafter, more 'economic brains' gathered to predict the advent of any such future crisis, little, if any, attention has been paid to the fact that the danger still lurks by, with more serious challenges posed for any future economic overturn.

The people at the bottom of the 'pyramid' – the term often used for the less privileged – if not properly economics-educated, and by not playing their active role in economic upliftment, could in fact prove to be a big strain on future economies. A recent study (OECD, 2016) by the Organisation for Economic

Co-operation and Development shows that 69% of the population ranks below level 2 (with simple tasks like deleting an email considered 'level 1'). Complex skills are still hard to come by. 26% of people aren't able to use computers at all.

How do these groups of people, then, play an active role if economics remains a puzzling anomaly – not being mastered by the students who were expected to master it, as postulated by the student trio (Earle, Moran, & Ward-Perkins, 2017) who authored *The Econocracy: On the Perils of Leaving Economics to the Experts*.

As also maintained by Schieffer & Lessem (2010).

> Our painful observation was that after the demise of communism we were caught in one economic world – capitalism – and with it in one particular Western – or, better, Anglo-Saxon – frame of mind. Muhammad Yunus once commented that mainstream free market theory suffers from a conceptualisation failure, a failure to capture the essence of what it is to be human. And indeed, this was what some of Britain's leading economists – among them Geoffrey Hodgson, Paul Ormerod and Bridget Rosewell – admitted in an open letter to the Queen of England in August 2009, after the queen had publicly posed the question of why economists had not foreseen the financial and economic crisis the world was facing.
>
> The following excerpt from their letter is most illuminating. 'We believe that the narrow training of economists – which concentrates on mathematical techniques and the building of empirically uncontrolled formal models – has been a major reason for this failure in our profession.

Or in Mark Anielski'swords:

> 'Economics' comes from the Greek oikosnomia, or 'household stewardship.' In essence, true economics is the science of the well-being of the household. Aristotle distinguished oikonomia from chrematistics, refering to the art of getting rich or making money. Part of the problem is that our economic and business schools are graduating chrematists, not true economists.
>
> (Anielski, 2007)

*So what qualities are our economists lacking to create a monetary eco-system that works for all?*

### *2.1.2 Communal monetary ecosystems*

*Measuring with this yardstick, we ask the question: could communities, then, if made aware of the bigger plan (economy), which is out of their domain of comprehension, generate their own 'micro-SOUL-idarity' economies and become self-sufficient?*

Our collective call at this point in time thus becomes ever more 'present' and persistent. For according to the contemporary mystics and integral economists, an integrated model of finance and economics is the need of the hour – a system which is aligned with the sacred in nature (divine abundance) and within our innate nature and wisdom. A system borne out of 'Mawakhat' with our brothers and sisters. A sacred bond of solidarity and togetherness and not of charity towards the unfortunate ones, as is presently the case. A challenge Amjad and Akhuwat took upon themselves to prove, i.e., rather than being dependent on charitable offerings, given a chance, micro-entrepreneurs are capable of lifting themselves out of abject destitution and growing.

Given the above facts, this is the question posed by Pir Zia, Amjad and many of us: what is that signature that will leave a mark (legacy) behind? The question that arises for us is: how do we devise an economic system which is collectively sacred (spiritual) to all and, most importantly, people-worthy?

As per my own personal call-to-action or integral Research-to-innovation purpose, the question thus arises: could a model of economics be designed from the Hikma (wisdom) of SOUL-idarity which then generates 'the economics of happiness', thereafter building a 'genuine wealth' system for the wellbeing of communities, as per Mark Anielski? (2007)

Per Amjad, as his Mawakhat philosophy exemplifies, it is possible through creating 'virtuous circles' of Akhuwat and solidarity bond borne out of reciprocal endowment.

From an integral vantage point, according to Lessem and Schieffer's postulation of an integral economy: (Schieffer & Lessem, 2010)

> Implementing an integral economic laboratory as a local catalyst:
>
> This laboratory is at the centre of economic renewal. Its task is to contribute to an integral understanding of economics and to engage itself with the rich diversity of economic theory and practice from all over the world (using the integral economic map). It articulates the particular economic challenges of the specific society it is based in, and it needs to be interlinked with other similar laboratories from all over the world, to stimulate cross-fertilisation.

As per our collective call, now from Pakistan to Nigeria, the era of integral economics and finance is heralding and is here. For us, the time is now to have an integrated model of finance which is emerging from local laboratories (Akhuwat in Pakistan, Pax Herbals et al, in Nigeria) and integral research academies (CISER in Nigeria, CIFE in the UK and AFlead in South Africa) locally and globally.

This integral solidarity bond is created with a renewed transformative approach, as per Ronnie Lessem (2017), through recognising and releasing GENE-IUS (*local Grounding, local-global Emergence, newly global Navigation, and global-local Effect*), rooted in each one of our particular communities, organisations and societies.

As such it purposefully takes on the *rhythm* of the 'South', on to the 'East' and then the 'North' and 'West' in turn. In each case then, it is Grounded locally, most specifically now Emerging locally-globally, as well as Navigating newly globally and ultimately Effected globally-locally. It is such a rhythm, starting out structurally by actualising an innovative economic ecosystem.

How, then, is this solidarity transfigured into our SOUL-idarity Hikma? We are now ready to explore this further.

## 2.2 From solidarity bond to the wisdom of SOUL-idarity

In Chapter 1, we presented a new lexicon for the Hikma (soul-wisdom) of an Islamic archetypal community. As identified in Akhuwat's case, consequently emerging from their 4I genealogy of Iman (faith), Ihsan (excellence), Ikhlas (sincerity) and Ikhuwah (solidarity), setting in motion an integral Hikma noesis of; ishq, ilm, amal and akhuwah, the root words for Hikma in Arabic and Urdu.

In this section, we will further explore how, by applying the above Hikma, knowledge communities can develop their own self-sufficiency as indicated above. In my personal experience of working with deprived communities, the one thing these communities lack is access to finances or their lack of knowledge to generate such. On the contrary, one thing I noticed is that this spirit of solidarity – often circumstantial – binds them together. People in need and suffering, somehow, always stick together, as the pain of suffering or separation keeps people united in perseverance.

Could this appropriation be their guiding force to creating their own 'virtuous circles'?

### 2.2.1 The virtue of virtuous circles

Morality, goodness and virtue have always been of value to human societies. From religious scholars to philosophers to mystics and psychologists from the East and West – all have associated doing good deeds with morality and virtue.

Even though the virtuous merits differ from an Eastern philosophical perspective to the Western perspective, the end goal remains – spreading happiness for our common human good and welfare.

For example, per Iqbal, the Eastern mystic and philosopher:

> in order to have a moral point of view one has to rise above the level of conventional values, to a plane of existence which is not tinged with local hue derived from the ethos of a people. The moral law is, thus, essentially enacted by a man of vision. The moral legislator has to tear himself from the fetters of his culture and to seek contact with the roots of his own being. Iqbal describes such contact as 'travel into yourself'
>
> (Iqbal, 2000).

The vision of virtue that Aristotle provides in *The Nicomachean Ethics* is one in which virtue is the key to human happiness. 'Since happiness is a certain sort of activity of the soul in accord with complete virtue, we must examine virtue; for that will perhaps also be a way to study happiness better' (*Nicomachean Ethics*, 1102a).

Virtue, for Adam Smith, the Scottish economist, philosopher and author, is a matter of standards of conduct. Virtue, according to Aristotle, is a matter of the flowering of a certain possibility within human nature.

Whereas, virtue, for Iqbal:

> is a distinction between the efficient self and the appreciative self. The former is the practical self of daily life while the latter is one that we have in moments of deepest meditation – when the efficient self is held in abeyance. It is the inner centre of experience. We have freedom in the highest degree when we rise to the level of the appreciative self. Free choice is truly speaking choice exercised by the appreciative self. At this level the individual is in direct contact with the roots of his own being. His vision of life and values goes beyond the limitations of time and space.

*It is in this sphere of 'rootedness' in one's being that virtue flows naturally. It is in this state that a person thinks beyond one's personal gains, as is exemplified in the case of Akhuwat and Amjad, who have been perpetuating the 'virtues' of creating 'virtuous circles' – the spiralling effect of barakah that is continuously floating around us.*

*For communities to reach that level of rootedness in their own being, the wisdom that is needed comes by circumnavigating through an integral 'SOUL-idarity Hikma' GENE (Grounding, Emergence, Navigation and Effect) rhythm, as illustrated in Figure 9.1.*

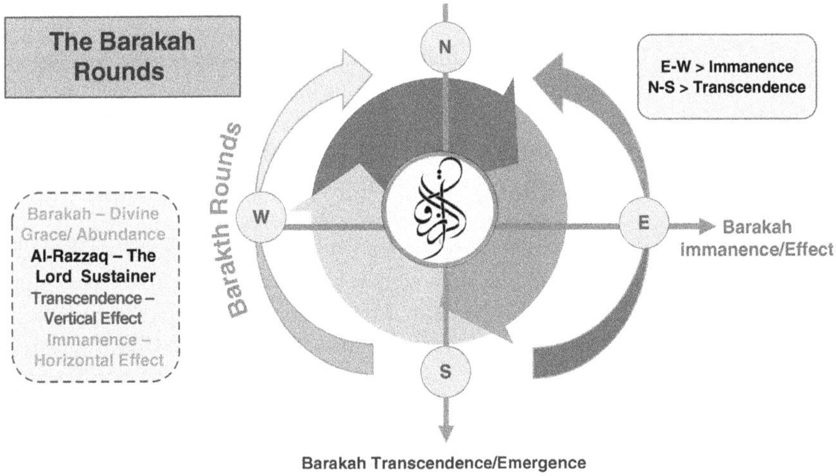


*Figure 9.1* The Barakah Rounds Circumnavigation

### *2.3 Circumnavigating through barakah/abundance*

Through examining Akhuwat's practical example of 'virtuous circles', which created a wealth of reciprocal endowment, we have seen the effects of a solidarity bond, generating abundance for a community of Akhuwateers. Figure 9.1, thus, depicts a lap around the circle of barakah – abundance which is ever-present around us.

In the case of Pakistan, being an Islamic society, this abundance comes directly from the inner source of Al-Razzaq – the Sustainer and Provider of all. In accordance with the cultural traditions of the region, Muslims, as well as Hindus and Sikhs, have always believed in this blessed abundance all around. In the indigenous culture of the region, particularly in Hinduism, *Maya* is an epithet for goddess, and the name of a manifestation of Lakshmi, the goddess of 'wealth, prosperity and love'. *Maya* is a spiritual concept connoting 'that which exists but is constantly changing and thus is spiritually unreal'. This abundance has always been revered in this region.

*But how does one become aware of this barakah that is around?*

From an Islamic metaphysical standpoint, creation is distinct from the Creator; in reality, the Creator is but creation is but the Creator. All are from one reality. Nay, it is but He who is the Only Reality, and it is He who manifests Himself in all these realities.

This concept is called *wahdat ul-wajud* (unity of being): the idea is that a knife and a sword, for example, are called by their respective names and are treated as distinct and separate items. But when their 'essence' moves *wara ul-wara* ('beyond the beyond', that is, beyond all forms and shapes), it is called steel. Similarly, God is considered as the Ultimate Reality, which is transcendent (beyond shape and form) but, in essence, immanent in creation.

*How does the human soul, then, acquire this knowledge?*

For Mulla Sadra (Kalin, 2010), an Iranian Islamic philosopher and theologian, the answer lies in his spiritual intellectualism, which is summed up in his oft-repeated idea that the soul is a physical entity in its origin and a spiritual and intellectual being in its subsistence. The more the soul knows, the more intense and simple it becomes in terms of ontological proximity to its divine source and nature.

The more it relies on the divine subsistence of its source, the more awakened it becomes to absorb the barakah (divine bounty) scattered around. Additionally, one becomes a vessel from which this barakah flows bountifully. Thus, the awakening of the soul to this divine bounty needs to be channeled through the Hikma noesis of SOUL-idarity, as per my postulation. An example of this abundance manifestation can be seen in Iqbal's insistence for a mu'min (believer) to eternalise a proprietorship of faqr (poverty) and spiritual neediness via qalandari/renunciation. A tradition of this type can be observed in Eastern mystics, e.g., Sufis in Islamic tradition, Yogis in Hinduism and Buddhist monks, etc.

### 2.3.1 From soul to SOUL-idarity

Per Dr. Omer Spahic (2017), associate professor at International Islamic University Malaysia, 'Islam with its unique Tawhidic (God's Oneness) worldview champions the fact that Muslims are brothers to each other and their similitude is like a wall whose bricks enforce and rely on each other'.

Indeed, it was due to all this that when Prophet Muhammad (peace be upon him) migrated from Mecca to Medina, aiming to create a dynamic prototype Islamic city and lay the foundation of the first example of sustainable Islamic architecture, sustainable Islamic urban development and, by extension, sustainable Islamic culture and civilisation, he focused first and foremost on human development. He taught that without adequate and holistic human development, no other development in the long and demanding community-building process will genuinely prove successful. He also taught that society is an organisation whose most basic and, at the same time, most significant substance is its people or individuals. For that reason, a relationship between society and its substance and basic units or blocks is a causal one – the latter, namely individuals as the basic social units, being the cause, and society, with its wide spectrum of tasks and aspirations, being the effect.

This means that the health or the development of a society depends mainly on the health and development of its substance and basic units or blocks, that is, its people, as human capital. An improvement in the minds and souls of individuals inevitably and proportionately leads to an improvement in society. Likewise, any degeneration in the minds and souls of individuals inescapably and proportionately leads to a degeneration of society. It stands to reason that the best method in diagnosing and remedying the ills of a society is by identifying the overall wellbeing and the contributions and roles of individuals as part of its focal interest, that is to say, the method that seeks out and deals with the root causes of a problem.

For the reason of creating and nurturing human capital in the nascent city-state of Medina, the Prophet (pbuh), upon arriving, disclosed to the assembled crowd some of the paths that invariably lead to Jannah (Paradise) in the hereafter, as well as to individual and collective felicity in this world. The paths are: 1) implementing and spreading peace and concord wherever possible and by whatever lawful means; 2) sharing and compassion; 3) maintaining good relations with relatives (as well as with others); and 4) praying at night when everybody else is asleep.

Thus, the soul of solidarity is, firstly, the awareness of one's reliance on divine sustenance (rizq), and secondly, as per the Sunnah/Tradition of the Prophet, communal sharing and compassion – Mawakhat, Akhuwat's philosophy of sharing for communal (ummah) wellbeing as found in Maqasid al Shariah.

We now expand on the integrality of our Hikma theory of the SOUL-idarity manifestation.

## 3 The Hikma (wisdom) of SOUL-idarity – integrality of solidarity

This brings us to our ontological postulation of solidarity – the wisdom (Hikma) in a soulful solidarity; the soul of our SOUL-idarity GENE (Grounding, Emergence, Navigation, Effect) rhythm as initiated in Chapter 1.

In this concluding part of our book, we set in motion our SOUL-idarity GENE as we assert a new economic discipline which is integral and spiritual in its nature and practice. A new paradigm of integral finance which has emerged from our Akhuwat exploration through our 4P model, the roadmap of which is fully illustrated in Figure 1.2 on page?

Philosophy, P1, is thoroughly represented in Chapters 1 and 3. Chapters 4 and 5 elucidate on Akhuwat's 4I (Iman, Ikhlas, Ihsan and Ikhuwah) genealogy and Principles (P2). Chapters 6 and 8 expand on the Practices (P3) – Akhuwat's Qard-e-Hasan (interest-free loans) and reciprocal endowment (borrowers becoming donors).

*What is thus mapped out in our 4P SOUL-idarity GENE (Grounding, Emergence, Navigation and Effect) Hikma fourfold is an emergent process, which revealed itself through my deep contemplation of Akhuwat's Philosophy (PI). Navigation then leads into its fourfold Principles (P2), immersed in Islamic philosophical and local traditions as per Akhuwat's Pakistani context – visibly translated into its fourfold Practices (P3).*

*What is left for us to further expound on is the solidarity rhythm of the integral paradigm (P4) – the wisdom of SOUL-idarity. We now turn to this.*

### *3.1 Solidarity or microfinance*

Akhuwat, as a distinctive model of Qard-e-Hasan (benevolent/interest-free loan), is, for us, a phenomenon – an alternative to microfinance. Yet throughout Pakistan, and often around the world, it is described as a microfinance organisation. In my view and that of my TRANS4M community, it surely is more than a mere microfinance organisation – a fact I have attempted to project in this book through a dynamic integral-spiritual lens. For had it been only a microfinance organisation, like many microfinance organisations within Pakistan or across the border, e.g., Grameen in Bangladesh, it would have made giving loans to poor people a business and not ventured into community activation and setting a precedent of reciprocal endowments, aka members donation program (MDP) or not ventured into free quality education services and free health care. Akhuwat University, as an institution for calculating the 'spirit of Mawakhat' would not have been borne out of its mandate of giving micro-loans to poor people. For in its stride, it has not only activated a huge community of borrowers, donors, volunteers and organisation replicators; it is playing a leading role on a national level in making solidarity (Mawakhat) and Qard-e-Hasan – an Islamic and Quranic ordinance – a concept in practice and not just a theory in Islamic textbooks.

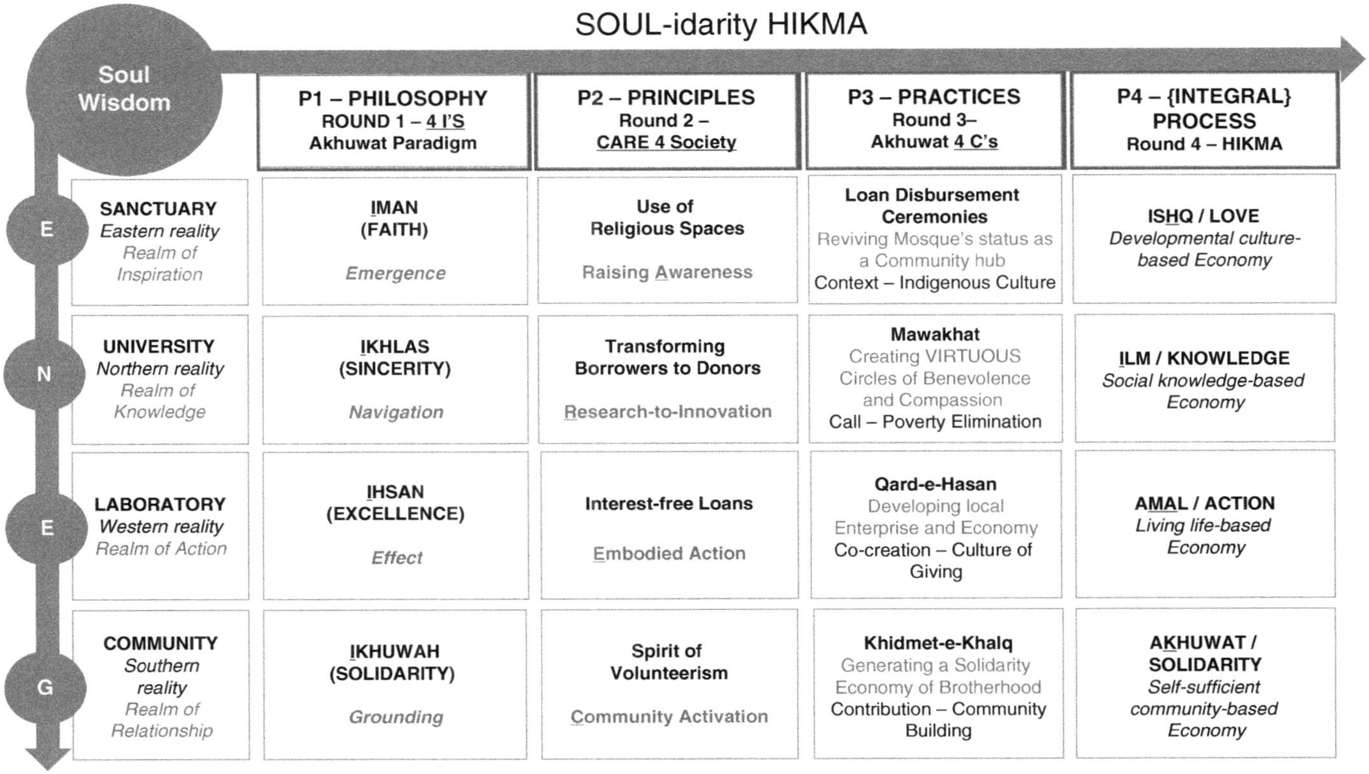


*Figure 9.2* 4 P's of SOUL-idarity Hikma

For Akhuwat to make solidarity possible, it held fast to its 4I (Iman, Ikhlas, Ihsan and Ikhuwah) philosophy. In Pakistan's local context, it remains a phenomenon of its own kind. From this end, whilst being fully immersed in its philosophy and fourfold principles, I have been pondering upon the Hikma – the wisdom of its solidarity paradigm which remains implicit, albeit fully patent to Amjad as the visionary and a social integrator, as per Ronnie Lessem (2016): *Such differentiation, and ultimately integration, that we are seeking arises out of both a personal individuation, that is, self-actualisation, and of societal acculturation, or organisational and cultural evolution.*

## 4 Section 2: the 4T SOUL-idarity GENE rhythm

For Amjad, Akhuwat is not only societal acculturation but self-actualisation too, as ever since his childhood, he grew up being enamoured by Sirat-un-Nabwi (life of Prophet Muhammad) and wished to exemplify it by practically emulating this way of life – the Sunnah of the Prophet – be it in however a small way, and carry the tradition in a practical way. History will now show a testimonial to his endeavour for exemplifying the Sunnah of the Prophet in the most practical way, something which islamic finance experts have merely theorised, to this day.

*The task that looms ahead of us in our collective call is to contemplate its philosophy further in a globally applicable way. My own call to contribution as part of my PHD is to adduce an integral-spiritual postulation of an integral finance model which subsequently closes the gap between spiritual and economic disciplines.*

*Incidentally, during my deeper immersion into the Mawakhat paradigm, I pondered more deeply on the alchemy of what propels this solidarity rhythm – the impulse of our SOUL-idartiy GENE circumvoluting through a 4T journey: of Transmutation, Transcendence, Trans-migration and finally Transformation, as sketched in Figure 9.3.*

### *4.1 Eastern orientation: transmutation of Ishq (love)*

**Holistic – Eastern – Sanctuary**

The belief is that the determining features in nature are wholes, that organisms progressively develop, are irreducible to the sums of their parts, but function in relationship to them.

Whereby, as per Schieffer & Lessem (2010), their 'Transformational GENE' (Grounding, Emergence, Navigation and Effect) rhythm activates 'inspiration' or the 'spirit'-level of a human system.

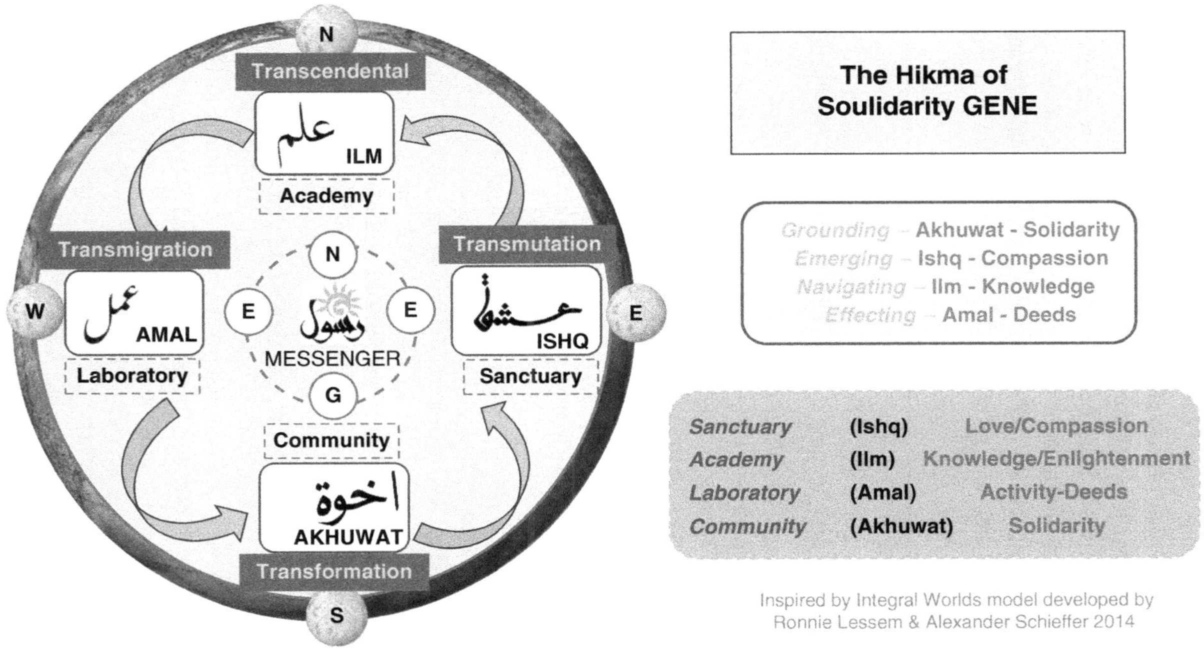


*Figure 9.3* The Alchemy of SOUL-idarity

Leadership is the name of faith. Some people say that it is an ideology, and others sincerity and sacrifice – a search for the truth, the elevation of character, stewardship, ardour and passion. In the words of Allama Iqbal, it is about 'the burning of fire-wood in your blood to ashes'. Pakistan may be a small country, but it is substantial in terms of its population, area and resources. It is currently beset by the most taxing years of its history, yet no leader has come forth: no Churchill, no de Gaulle, no Sir Syed, no Allama Iqbal, no Jinnah, no captain or visionary to lead this nation.

Sometimes, this itch and gnawing ache becomes intertwined with each step in my life journey.

We start with Amjad's words that echo his deep love and compassion for his country and his people, with a deep longing to find a cure for its many societal ailments:

*For the path of compassion which leads to soul transformation starts from the invocation of 'Ishq (divine love) impulse' – as repeatedly expressed by Amjad.*

*What, then, is this impulse of Ishq that drives Amjad, and many who volunteer with Akhuwat, or any such organisation that is working to make life better for the unfortunately neglected amongst us? And how does it drive us to solidarity with others?*

Ishq is an Arabic word – used in Arabic and Urdu, as well as many other languages – that means 'love'. The word is related to 'ashiqah, a vine. The common belief is that when love takes root in the heart of a lover, everything other than God is effaced.

Just as the word Allah has no plural, no opposite and no feminine, so the word Ishq has no opposite. Ishq is out of the boundaries of intellect just as Allah is out of the boundaries of intellect. Just as the Punjabi Sufi mystic, Sultan Bahu, wrote in Mohabbat-ul-Asrar (Revelation of Love), 'it should be clarified that the path of Ishq is not written in the books of laws of religion or community'. It is the supreme love that sets the seeker free of this world and its worldly demands.

And so we believe, in our esoteric traditions, those who are on this journey of love know that love is the one thing that every soul brings to Earth with it. As love is the source of creation (transcendence) and the real sustenance of all beings, so, if man knows how to give it – to the world around him as sympathy, as kindness, as service – he supplies to all, the food for which every soul hungers (Khan, 1914).

What we are suggesting here is, thus, Ishq/love is the driving force transmutating in the heart of a believer, igniting the flame of love which translates into a form of supreme knowledge (Ilm) which, coming from the land where Iqbal wrote in his poem, making a comparison between Ilm-o-Ishq (knowledge and love). For him, love is the essence of the creation of this universe, as he writes in his poetry book *Zarb-e-Kaleem*/The Rod of Moses-011:

*The universe is moved by the warmth of Love;*
*Knowledge deals with the Attributes, Love is a vision of the Essence.*

The attributes, as mentioned here by Iqbal, are the divine attributes which, of course, can be applied to physical things too. Per Iqbal, love/Ishq can serve as the vision which can 'sense' the essence – the essence of everything.

As observed in the case of Akhuwat and Amjad, his love/Ishq for Rasool (Prophet Muhammad) was the driving force for him to take the challenge of renewing the Prophet's legacy of Mawakhat in the community. Surely, love/Ishq as a vine takes root in the hearts of believers.

This phase also completes one's faith (Iman) – Akhuwat's first I of 4I (Iman, Ikhlas, Ihsan and Ikhuwah). The next stage that comes after Ishq is the transcendental and intuitive knowledge – Ilm.

### *4.2 Northern orientation: transcendence of Ilm (knowledge)*

As per Lessem and Schieffer (ibid): Northern 'navigation' is about activating the *mind*-level, the conceptualising prowess of the human system at hand.

The power to make logical inferences, whereby reason is a source of power independent of sense perceptions, is based on deduction through a priori concepts, rather than via empiricism.

The knowledge that has been acquired through the heart (Ishq/love), is now put into practice in this domain of Ilm (knowledge) – the source of which, notwithstanding, comes by engaging the mind/intellect faculty, but as postulated by Lessem and Schieffer above, it comes through priori concepts as expressed by Amjad whilst talking to a group during his Harvard Business School visit:

One gentleman asked whether Akhuwat's program was only for Muslims.

In reply, I asked, 'How could that be conceivable?'

The sentiment of solidarity is for all mankind. The state that was formed in Medina 1400 years ago was not a state only for Muslims. Followers of any religion were acknowledged citizens of that state.

In the modern world, two states were formed in the name of religion, Pakistan and Israel. In either of these states, is there freedom to differ in opinion regarding faith? The voice that praises another's God is brutally silenced.

Man always forgets the reality – that the eternal conquest is through the heart. There is no room for repression in faith (Iman); there is only humanitarianism. If we wish for peace in the world, we must honour each faith. The Prophet (pbuh) said on the occasion of his last sermon that his message was for all of mankind; Akhuwat's is the same.

For in Islam, Ilm is not confined to the acquisition of knowledge only, but it also embraces socio-political and moral aspects. Knowledge is not mere information; it requires the believers to act upon their beliefs and commit themselves to the goals which Islam aims to attain. The theory of knowledge from the Islamic perspective is not just a theory of epistemology. It combines knowledge, insight and social action as its ingredients.

This Ilm directly comes from a divine source, as the ploughing of the heart through Ishq transmutation as exemplified in Amjad's case – the revival of the prophetic tradition of Mawakhat and the Quranic ordinance of Qard-e-Hasan (benevolent loan).

The next stage after Ilm is amal – putting into action the knowledge acquired.

## *4.3 Western orientation: trans-migrational effect of amal (action/good deeds)*

From an integral perspective, as per Lessem and Schieffer (ibid), Western orientation is about pragmatically applying the new knowledge that has been developed, thereby actualising the innovation that it contains. The Western effect is, hence, about 'doing' and 'making it happen'.

**Pragmatic – Western – Laboratory**

The practical treatment of things, emphasising the application of ideas, whereby thought is a guide to action, and the truth is empirically tested by the practical consequences of belief.

The doctrine of *trans-migration* is usually held to imply the belief in the soul's rebirth. From our SOUL-idarity noesis, the solidarity-gene impulse originates at the Eastern-spiritual realm of Iman/Ishq, navigates through the Ilm/Intellect Northern realm and enters the Western realm of pragmatism – what we are calling the amal (action) realm. The trans-migration of the SOUL-idarity GENE at this stage is carrying with it the knowledge acquired in the previous realms, as it enters the realm of living-based economics, rebirthing a new paradigm.

In Amjad's case, his Ishq-e-Rasool (love for the Prophet) and reverence for the divine ordinances guided him to stand against riba (usury), which is considered haram (forbidden) in Islam. Thus, his passion for re-establishing the tradition of Qard-e-Hasan (a loan given to Allah).

He thus, writes:

Through Akhuwat, thousands of people have been granted loans and no interest is taken on these loans. This is a splendid beginning indeed towards interest-free banking.

There is just the difference of one letter, and an even smaller difference of one 'dot' (in the Urdu script), between Qard (loan) and Fard (obligation). To explain this point, we have come a long way. There are many destinies before the destination. Those who love their chosen paths and are empathetic towards their fellow travellers, they are not the ones who bring destinies to fruition; it is the destinies themselves that find the wayfarers. My companions are exactly these kinds of people.

In the sacrifice of life and wealth, the status of offering life is greater, but it is harder to part with wealth. Making this difficulty easier is the work of the compassionate. The compassionate seek the compassionate and they are able to find each other.

*For the whole philosophy of offering Qard-e-Hasan is concealed in the 'parting with wealth' test, as expounded by Amjad – time and again – as he considers this as the ill of the society. And this is what we term the realm of trans-migration, i.e., leaving behind or parting with material attachments with the Hikma (wisdom) of the soul.*

In the words of Iqbal, the mystical philosopher of the East (Bal-e-Jibril-156):
'Originality of thought and action creates miracles of life:
It turns pebbles into ruby stones.'

*For originality of thought with action (amal) can transform the destinies of nations, as per Amjad and Iqbal's philosophy. And this is the key to societal transformation, from self to organisation to community and society, translating as integral-spiritual development.*

*And thus, through our SOUL-idarity contemplation, we imply this trans-migration of the solidarity impulse which creates abundance (self-sufficiency), to then complete our SOUL-idarity-gene iteration by finally grounding itself in the community.*

### *4.4 Southern orientation: societal transformation through Akhuwat – solidarity*

From an integral perspective, as per Lessem and Schieffer (ibid), The secret of 'Southern' grounding is the issue at hand and the people involved are grounded in a particular nature and community, which need to be fully understood. For any living system, the Southern grounds represent its '*local identity*' and its connection to a common source of life.

**Humanistic: Southern: Community**
Asserts the dignity of (wo)man, promoting human and social welfare, incorporating the arts and humanities, fostering self-fulfilment in the context of collective and community relations.

Wherein, transformation, as a Sufistic principle, is the moment-by-moment alchemy of impulse. This may manifest itself as restraint in action and speech, as courtesy, self-discipline, generosity, subtlety or patience.

This is the fourth principle of *transpersonal integral development*, as per Lessem and Schieffer's Transformational GENE rhythm: 'All development levels – self, organization, society, and universe – need to be holistically and interactively included ('fully rounded')' (Schieffer & Lessem, 2014).

Finally, they argue (Schieffer & Lessem, 2014) that:

> the conventional discourse on development is primarily held at a generalised societal level, as well as, partly, on a community level. Usually not included are the transpersonal levels of individual development, at school and at university, and organisational, development, in-house and through external consultancy, alongside community and societal development, altogether in a particular context
>
> (Schieffer & Lessem, 2014).

*Thence, could this be possible through Akhuwat-like SOUL-idarity academies, to develop those skills of self-discipline, generosity, patience and compassion?*

At this point, at the final stage of our SOUL-idarity noesis, it arrives home by grounding itself in the community. In Akhuwat's case, this is its community of Akhuwateers who have been travelling the path of Mawakhat from Ishq to Ilm to performing amal and finally, grounding all the knowledge accumulated on the path to practise communal solidarity with a renewed Hikma of SOUL-idarity.

A living example of such is Amjad's own story in his own words, which expresses beautifully how the impulse of solidarity, once activated, keeps spiralling up and down dynamically – with a continual motion:

17 and 18 April 2004. These two days of my life were full of sorrow. On the evening of 17 April, death knocked upon the earthwork of my mother's life. She collapsed as she was standing in the kitchen having a glass of water and handed her life over to her Creator. This happened without warning, pain, or suffering. We rushed her to the hospital, but she had already passed on. At once, the gloom of departure overwhelmed me. It seemed as if I stood alone, helpless, as waves upon waves of sorrow struck me. My mother was a simple and compassionate lady who was deeply

attached to her faith. She was soft spoken, mild tempered, and full of sacrifice and altruism. It would be a great asset indeed if even a part of these traits were bequeathed to me.

On the 18th she was to be laid to rest. It was a strange coincidence that, on that very day, an *Akhuwat* event was to take place in the late afternoon. The 300 guests for this event, which took place at the Governor House, included the governor, the prime minister, and the corps commander. Also invited were scores of other guests including donors and a multitude of those brave families who had taken a loan from Akhuwat and forged their paths to prosperity. The president of Pakistan was the chief guest. Two trials faced me – participating in the final rites of my mother or fulfilling the responsibility that Akhuwat had placed on my shoulders. It was a painful dilemma indeed, choosing between a personal sorrow and a greater cause.

I decided to rise above the parapet of my personal pain. I committed my mother to the earth with my own hands, dusted off my clothes and arrived at the event. For two hours, I was sitting on the stage beside the president of Pakistan, being crushed under a mountain of sorrow. It seemed as if my mother was beside me and was happy that I had subdued my sorrow for her for the greater cause. Some people were surprised to see the dirt on my clothes, but nobody found out that I had arrived straight from the graveyard. The governor of Punjab and president of Pakistan appreciated the vision and service of Akhuwat and assured us of their co-operation. A lot of people pledged donations, including the president and his mother, who donated three hundred thousand rupees ($3000). As I thanked the guests my mother's cheerful and generous face was before me.

Those two hours taught me much – patience, composure and transcendence. It was that day that I found out how deep my love for Akhuwat really was, and that there is much fulfilment in transcending one's own sorrow. Some people were surprised at this decision of mine; others said it was exactly what I should have done. The event came to an end and I returned home to receive condolences. I felt heartened that Allah had saved the gift of compassion, which my mother had given, from being sacrificed to sorrow. It is none other than Allah who guides one to the right path, saves one from stumbling, and shows the way on dark nights.

From the above example, and as per our previous reflections on the *alchemy of communitas* – we believe the *solidarity impulse* – being the main driver for communities to generate their own self-sufficiency through reciprocity and divine bounty (barakah) – needs to be contemplated as such. The resultant multiplier effect, thereby, is a case of 'SOUL-idarity economy' – as presented throughout the course of this book in the case of Akhuwat's Mawakhat paradigm.

We now turn to further ascertain the *integrality of SOUL-idarity* from a finance and economics premise, contemplating the need for our prospective collective call to herald a new integral finance and economics paradigm.

## 5 From charity to solidarity (Mawakhat)

In Pakistan, philanthropy as ratio of GDP is one of the highest in the world. Social scientists claim that despite the inefficient state service delivery and complete lack of empathy on behalf of state and the pathetic state of governance, this virtuous and generous endeavour of citizens is what ensures a façade of stability and keeps the chaos at bay.

According to the findings of the study (2017), conducted by the Pakistan Centre for Philanthropy, the total estimated magnitude of household-level giving in Pakistan was Rs. 239.7 billion (2.7 billion $$) in the year 2014, which is more than three times larger than the estimate for 1998. The bulk of total giving comes from monetary donations, as zakat and non-zakat donations account for 13 and 32 percent, respectively, and the monetary valuation of time-volunteerism accounts for 21 percent of total giving. Plainly then, indigenous philanthropy in Pakistan is supported through local giving of time as well as money.

In many cases, the sporadic and disorganised nature of charity giving makes it difficult to reach the right kind of voluntary organisations who have the means and on-the-ground knowledge of how and where to utilise the grants for desirable communal and societal impact. The desired effects of philanthropy can only be achieved if the process is streamlined and a concerted effort is made at targeting specific social evils or economic ills of the society. The tragedy, sadly, in Pakistan is that most of the private charity ends up in minute distributions. And hence, any large-scale social or economic effect withers away.

*What could then be a consequential method of distribution to reap the benefits for the wider community in Pakistan?*

According to an article published in the March 2018 international edition of Accounting and Business magazine.

> It is widely acknowledged that small businesses can play a critical role in achieving sustainable growth in developing countries. This is especially true in Pakistan, where nearly 90% of companies are SMEs, most of them operating in the informal sector, according to SMEDA, the country's SME development authority
>
> (Klasra, 2018).

As Pakistan's government seeks to achieve its aim of becoming an upper-middle-income economy by 2025, helping these companies grow is a crucial effort to increase financial inclusion and reduce poverty. When the government launched

Vision 2025, it emphasised the importance of a development strategy for small business, highlighting in particular the need to improve access to finance and build financial literacy skills, and to simplify regulations to make it easier for people to set up and build a successful business. Reinforcing this, the State Bank of Pakistan sees microfinance as 'pivotal for inclusive and sustainable economic growth of the country, crucial to livelihood creation, and a key driver of grass-root-level development'.

*Is microfinance, then, an effectual solution for Pakistan's mammoth poverty predicament?*

Rudolf Steiner (1977), as mentioned in Chapter 5, in the early 20th century made the case for an autonomous, though interdependent, economic sector. Through the forces of economic life, people will develop the faculties which best serve the production and interchange of commodities. For Pakistan or any other country to believe that conventional microfinance, i.e., loading people with debt, can bring emancipation from poverty seems antithetical to say the least.

*Moreover, it is limiting to think that Pakistan can benefit from her home-grown solution – in the form of Akhuwat's Mawakhat and Qard-e-Hasan non-interest model – if you are thinking of such in microfinance terms. And this is what we have been indicating through the course of this book, for Pakistan and for Akhuwat to look beyond microfinance. Instead, by developing people's faculties of self-sufficiency, communities can be advanced to self-organise themselves – generating their own 'abundance' (barakah) funds and pools.*

*How can this be done?*

## 6 Conclusion

Finally, then, in the concluding part of our book, we are mindful that the way forward from here, for Amjad and Akhuwat and for myself, along with our community of integral researchers, into *integral finance* so to speak, is to migrate from an ill-conceived and miscalculated notion of microfinance. While intended to rid the world of the woes of poverty and adversity, it has instead imposed another societal entrapment onto an existent material captivity – the curse of debt slavery.

For Akhuwat to now postulate *Infaq* as their fifth principle and as their moral core defines them as an implementer of such an integrated model of finance which places 'giving and sharing' in the centre of their archetypal wealth-generation-plus-distribution design.

*Infaq* is an Arabic word mentioned in the Quran nearly 60 times. *Infaq* is one of the most important tools of income distribution. The Quran has placed special emphasis on the Muslim not only giving *Infaq* but giving as much as one can beyond the requirement.

In doing so, Akhuwat has taken one more step towards awakening the spirit of reciprocity and self-sufficiency – liberating the Pakistani society from micro-loans capitalisation.

What we then propose is to turn 'micro-loans' around and replace them with a contemporary form of communal solidarity/reciprocity – aiding communities to generate their own wealth of generosity/benevolence/Mawakhat through Infaq – fairly sharing abundance with those who are in need of it the most. This differs from the well-established decorum of 'a just and equitable wealth distribution' system as ordained by almost all the major spiritual and religious disciplines of the world who have ventured into the economic field. Yet from time immemorial, at least since the Palaeolithic stone-age times (Sahlins, 2017), there have hardly been any societies that modelled a pristine form of equitable 'wealth distribution' and 'balanced reciprocity'.

*What, then, has been illustrated through the course of this book and through our trans-disciplinary positioning of a transformational solidarity GENE rhythm, is the birthing of an integral paradigm of a SOUL-idarity economy which is dynamically barakah-oriented, that is to say, it is spiritual in its nature as per its philosophy (P1) and integral in effect as per its spiralling through its 4P (Philosophy, Principles, Practice, integral Paradigm) iteration.*

We strongly believe that for communities to be self-sustained and self-sufficient, this virtuous circle needs to be contemplated as such, from the donors to borrowers to employees and to volunteers, for that is our collective vocation – on Akhuwat's part and on our TRANS4M community's part. An integral finance and economics model which holds the potential to liberate us from the financial woes of the 21st century's augmented reality existence.

What would it mean for micro-communities to generate their own micro-economies by pooling their collective barakah (abundance)? For unless we feel this abundance and stop hoarding excess barakah for our individual habitude, nothing can ever be enough for us.

*How can this barakah of self-sufficiency be contemplated as such?*

We believe it is through Ishq (love for the Creator and creation) and Ilm (knowledge of the Self) and amal (putting the knowledge gained through this sublime love into action through good deeds) and eventually Akhuwat (communal solidarity), thus, closing our SOUL-idarity Hikma round.

For this is the transcendental *trans-formation* of the spirit of solidarity/Akhuwat through a contemporary discipline of integral-spiritual finance.

## Bibliography

Anielski, M., 2007. *The Economics of Happiness: Building Genuine Wealth*. Gabriola Island: New Society Publishers.

Anielski, M., 2012. Building an Economy of Love Based on Genuine Wealth. Celebrate! Winter 2012 edition.

Earle, J., Moran, C., & Ward-Perkins, Z., 2017. *The Econocracy: On the Perils of Leaving Economics to the Experts*. Manchester: Penguin.

Inayat-Khan, P. Z., & Wisdom, S. P., 2014. *The Seven Pillars: Journey Toward Wisdom*. New Lebanon: Seven Pillars House of Wisdom.

Iqbal, M., 2000. *Reconstruction of Religious*. Lahore: Sang-e-Meel Publications.
Kalin, I., 2010. *Knowledge in Later Islamic Philosophy: Mulla Sadra on Existence, Intellect, and Intuition*. USA: OUP.
Khan, H. I., 1914. Love, Human And Divine. In: H. I. Khan, ed. *Spiritual Liberty*. Delhi: Motilal Banarsidass Publishers Pvt. Ltd.
Klasra, K., 2018. *Microfinance is a Growing Business in Pakistan*. Available at: ACCA Global: http://www.accaglobal.com/in/en/member/member/accounting-business/2018/03/insights/microfinance-pakistan.html
Lessem, R., 2016. *The Integrators: The Next Evolution in Leadership, Knowledge and Value Creation*. Abingdon: Routledge.
Lessem, R., 2017. *Awakening Integral Consciousness: A Developmental Perspective*. Abingdon: Routledge.
Lessem, R., & Bradley, T., 2018. *Evolving Work*. Abingdon: Routledge.
Mance, E., 2011. *Solidarity Economy*. Available at: Solidarius: http://solidarius.com.br/mance/biblioteca/solidarity_economy.pdf
OECD., 2016. *Skills for a Digital World*. Mexico: OECD.
Omer, S., 2017. *The Qur'an, Sunnah and Architectural Creativity*. Available at: Medinanet.org: https://medinanet.org/
Sahlins, M. D., 2017. *Stone Age Economics*. Abingdon: Routledge.
Steiner, R., 1977. *Towards Social Renewal*. Edinburgh: Rudolf Steiner Press.
Schieffer, A., & Lessem, R., 2014. *Integral Development*. Farnham: Gower Publishing Ltd.
Schieffer, A., & Lessem, R., 2010. *Integral Economics: Releasing the Economic Genius of your Society*. Farnham: Gower Publishing Ltd.
Steiner, R., 2017. *The State of Individual Philanthropy in Pakistan 2016*. Islamabad: Pakistan Centre for Philanthropy.
Vaughan-Lee, L., 2012. *Prayer of the Heart in Christian & Sufi Mysticism*. California: Golden Sufi Centre.

# Epilogue

## 1 The age of integrality: SOUL-idarity in finance

*With this we reach the final destination of our SOUL-idarity round, for what started off as a quest for a financial model with a spirit and a culture of its own is now shaping up as a continuation of my call to undertake my role as an integral 'revivalist' between the physical (finance) and the spiritual as an extension to Amjad's work as being one such revivalist of the philosophy of Mawakhat and Infaq in an Islamic context.*

Per Abdolkarim Soroush (2000), an Iranian Islamic intellectual, Rumi scholar and former professor of philosophy at the University of Tehran, 'Revivalists are not lawgivers (shari 'an) but exegetes (sharihan).' According to him, 'that which remains constant is religion (din); that which undergoes change is religious knowledge and insight (ma'refat-e dini).'

We believe such knowledge (ma'refat) and insight arises from an integral awakening of higher consciousness – for only then can we act (amal) our role on this earth as per divine ordination. For Soroush, God manifests himself in each historical period according to the understanding of the people of the era.

*As this era calls for a financial (material) integration with the spiritual (sacred) to be inclusivist rather than exclusivist, i.e., serving a select few, we advocate a revival of the spirit (soul) of solidarity – that which I term an integral SOUL-idarity movement.*

*For me, finding such an integrable model, Akhuwat in Pakistan, was a source of jubilation to say the least, and then to consolidate with many a TRANS4M-ative kindred soul on our shared quest – wayfarers as I prefer to call them – has been an immense source of alleviation and indeed a true privilege. My quest to bridge the divide (and the reluctance in doing so) between the spiritual and the material took me to Pakistan, the country of my birth – towards an Eastern realm of spirituality and culture, as per the integral terminology. And then back to the Western realm of enterprise and economics.*

*This journey is now taking me to new frontiers of 'Self' and societal exploration, along with my fellow TRANS4Mers – the Southern realm of community. Together on a coinciding quest to transform and transpose new integral paradigms: our Northern realm of knowledge creation – for our world's ailing issues, from finance to social and cultural dis-integration. For what we are collectively seeking might sound like a fanciful approach to an altruistic idealisation, albeit the personal consolation, I gather, from this consequential synchroneity (solidarity) is the fact that we are forming a critical mass which heralds an age of integrality as postulated by Lessem and Schieffer, co-founders of TRANS4M, Centre for Integral Development, Hotonnes, France, with other existing and prospective integral research centres (CISER Centre for Integral Social and Economic Research from Nigeria; OFURE [Pax] Integral Research and Development Initiative from Nigeria; Pundutso Centre for Integral Development [includes: Kuona Centre for Integral Enterprise and the Mugove CIEA Centre for Integral Enterprise Agriculture]; AFlead Centre for African Local Economic Assisted Development from South Africa; TIA Transformation Institute of Africa from South Africa, CISER UK, CIFE (Centre for Integral Finance and Economics) Mark Anielski (Anielski Inc, Canada) and finally, Akhuwat Pakistan/UK, from around the four continents.*

## 2 The four journeys of an integral paradigm

To sum up our journey through the course of this book by employing the transformational **GENE** rhythm developed by Lessem and Schieffer (ibid), let us revisit our initiative call, i.e., **G**rounding myself in the Akhuwat paradigm to explore alternative models of spiritually based finance, on to the **E**mergence of a SOUL-idarity paradigm which assisted in our **N**avigation through the Hikma of my 4P postulation – Akhuwat's *Philosophy, Principles, Practices* and *-ntegral Paradigm* – to then quantify the **E**ffects of a *solidarity bond* formed through Akhuwat's dynamic *CARE* process of **C**ommunity activation through their various operations, e.g., volunteerism, therein raising **A**wareness around Islamic practices of Qard-e-Hasan, through institutionalising their innovative **R**esearch of providing loans for enterprise building and finally transforming and **E**mbodying action to educate the community by providing an alternative to microfinance for poverty alleviation.

Just as our dynamic yet compounded Akhuwat journey of a solidarity economy is interwoven, in a trans-disciplinary threefold conceptualisation, through integral-spiritual and our collective trans-personal journeys, this is to give an overview of our four journeys through an integral fourfold process.

We start by grounding our initiative call in Akhuwat's solidarity impulse.

### *2.1 Origination – grounding*

*As per my own inner calling and my Transformational GENE (Grounding, Emergence, Navigation and Effect) journey, I grounded my solidarity impulse into the soul of migration (hijrah) and what hinders the social integrational process of migrant communities, particularly the Pakistani diaspora as per my engagement with them, here in the UK.*

*Through my work in the social entrepreneurship sphere within the UK, I remained anxious to notice the state of deprivation and social isolation within the (Pakistani) diaspora community through not only the lack of resources but their lack of economical knowledge too, and the communal inertia around enterprise development in the real sense of the word, though there exist a few examples too, which are clearly not making a huge impact overall.*

*For clearly, the mainstream pool of (Western) knowledge and resources is not encouraging them to better their social visibility and upliftment. Hence, my guiding thought and question: how could these communities be mobilised to gain access to resources (and skillsets) which could come from their midst?*

*Indeed, the language, as observed, has been a great hinderance to adopting a new (Western) culture. And then, there is the hesitancy around religious beliefs too.*

*Incidentally, it dawned on me after my in-depth study of Akhuwat's model and my interaction with their community of Akhuwateers, what I am now beginning to realise could be lacking for diaspora communities in the UK. And most certainly through endless conversations with my TRANS4M-ational mentor Ronnie Lessem and research colleagues, which helped in awakening the realisation of the integral GENE (Grounding, Emergence, Navigation, Effect) process, that is strengthening my belief that a self-reliant Akhuwat-like model could be the way for micro-communities to generate their own micro-self-reliant solidarity (self-generated) economies. Whereby we refer to migrant communities as micro-communities here as per their nature of operating in clusters.*

*Thus, in my case study of the Akhuwat paradigm and by applying the integral lens, realities have started appearing as they are but have not been explicitly translated. Thereafter, the whole process unfolds a renewed perspective on Akhuwat as an integral paradigm of trans-local integrality which is dynamic in its nature of origination. Trans-local, as the philosophy of Mawakhat is borrowed from the prophetic tradition of solidarity, or sharing between brothers and sisters after his migration from Mecca to the city of Medina – the prototype Islamic community. This all equipped me with the tools required to unravel the Akhuwat paradigm through this perspective. The resultant unfolding through an extension of an existent soul awakening, owing to my allegiance on the path of Tassawuf (Sufism), now sets the impulse in systemic spiralling of a GENE-tic SOUL-idarity rhythm, that is, the soul iteration of the solidarity impulse.*

*As for the integral development process developed by Schieffer and Lessem* (2010) *through their 4R process, in the opening chapter I presented the 4P process leading to my SOUL-idarity GENE Hikma (wisdom) postulation, which has revealed itself whilst journeying through Akhuwat's fourfold Mawakhat paradigm in the course of this book.*

*For the sake of wrapping up our solidarity journey, the following is an applicative summation of our integral Hikma of SOUL-idarity economics, which is an ongoing journey, now translating into a bible on integral finance and economics and a potential centre for such global R&D endeavours.*

*Before I move on, let us first revisit the complementarity between the integral dynamics process developed by Lessem and Schieffer (ibid) and my rhythmic SOUL-idarity postulation, described as 'Unity-in-Variety' in their terms*:

Unity-in-Variety.

While the reality of 'communist' East and 'capitalist' West, if not also 'rich' North and 'poor' South, in political and ideological terms, have proved altogether divisive rather than mutually supportive, their symbolical importance in cultural and psychological terms is what is key to *Integral Dynamics*. Essentially, as we move from the politics of division to the psychology of integration, contradiction between opposing forces is replaced by complementarity between opposites, rivalry between factions is transformed into unity through variety, disintegration within and between worlds, and indeed growing inertia, is turned into duly integral dynamics.

How might this come about, internally and naturally, psychologically and culturally, as well as externally and politically, technologically and economically?

*Thus, the visible divide (and reluctance) between material (financial) and spiritual needs to complement rather than oppose each other's existence and usefulness, as suggested by Lessem and Schieffer as per their integrity of societal development. This complementarity could also support an integrative social cohesion for diaspora marginalised communities trans-local-globally.*

*Subsequently, and as per our initiative call, we start our grounding (**G**), i.e., in the micro-ness of microfinance and their emancipatory methodology as per Akhuwat's origination of Qard-e-Hasan (benevolent loans).*

### *2.1.1 From debt slavery to SOUL-idarity economics – the metempsychosis*

*Metempsychosis is a concept in Greek philosophy related to reincarnation and the trans-migration of the soul. It is a re-birthing of a new form.*

*In retrospection of our call, we intend to investigate: what does it mean to trans-migrate from our financial (greed-driven) soul to a soul-ful integrationof solidarity with SOUL-idarity? And how could that be applied to finance or economics?*

*For after residing in a debt-based society for some time now, and after intuitively studying and discovering Akhuwat's phenomenal Mawakhat/solidarity paradigm, I propose a universally transformed integral paradigm of trans-migration (moving away) from the misery of microfinance, that is, of 'granting' micro-loans to the poor and needy – to a self-generated autonomy of virtuosity.*

*How could this be generated?*

For Akhuwat to now place Infaq (spending in the way of Allah) as their fifth principle (5th I) and the core of their Mawakhat philosophy does not only propose to place a conceptualisation of Islamic values and faith back into the heart of communal living (Mashawrat), but also provides a mechanism for an equitable and fair system of wealth generation and distribution amongst various social classes, erasing the division that exists between them as a result. The relational epistemology of Akhuwat's 5 I's (Iman, Infaq, Ikhlas, Ihsan and Ikhuwah) as their foundational principles, in a Pakistani cultural and religious context, provides a practical framework for a full integral communal CARE (activation [*Ishq*], awareness [*Iman*], institutionalising research [*Ilm*] and embodied action [a*mal*]) paradigm, emancipating them from their dependency on microfinance.

As in the words of my TRANS4M colleagues and co-founders of CISER (Centre for Integral Social and Economic Research) from Nigeria, Basheer Oshodi and Jubril Adeojo:

> The primary purpose of Islam is the Maqasid al Shariah, which is founded on five elements. The human-self acts as the custodian of the remaining four rounds in a manner that allows the community to enrich prosperity by giving respect and love to others. Sanctuary transforms the enrichment of faith thereby believing in others to achieve communipreneurship. The university or research academy enriches the intellect by adding knowledge to the community. The laboratory transforms debt financial instruments to equity while expanding communal wealth through partnership ventures
>
> (Basheer Oshodi, 2018).

For Oshodi and Adeojo, communipreneurship is the new thinking of integral banking and finance, enabling environments to foster employment of self-and-community.

*Why are we suggesting such a model of integral finance, banking and economics?*

We have all witnessed the devastation debt servitude has brought upon our modern societies. When more than $100 billion in national debt was cancelled in the 2000s, many people thought the issue of debt was done and dusted. Instead, the debt payments of impoverished countries are increasing rapidly and are at the highest level for more than a decade. Closer to home, the number of households in persistent and dangerous debt continues to rise, and students leaving UK universities now face higher average debts than American students, with the average student graduating with more than £44,000 of debt.

These varying figures tell us that serious and systemic action is needed to make debt justice a reality, but lenders – the banks and richer governments – currently set the narrative on the issue, making it difficult for those suffering from unjust debts to be heard. All this while disadvantaged communities are suffering in silence with no one providing them with a solution to be self-sufficient through a balanced reciprocity as per Sahlins' (2017) postulation or by being self-enterprising as per Akhuwat's facilitation of Qard-e-Hasan (Benevolent Loans) as per Quranic ordinance and the Prophetic tradition of Mawakhat – sharing abundance (excess) with community (Ikhuwah).

Whereas the diseases of the soul, e.g., greed and wealth accumulation, can only be cured by disciplining the *Self*, organisations are rethinking the 'personal development' of their staff – little or no attention is paid on healing or liberating the '*Self*' *from the false self and its greed to accumulate and own more and more.*

Thus, it remains my call to integrate and heal the spirit of solidarity by (re)thinking it through the wisdom (Hikma) of the soul – *the SOUL of solidarity.*

Akhuwat's Mawakhat paradigm, coming from an Eastern philosophy, is a prime example of such a discipline based on its fourfold 4I (Iman, Ikhlas, Ihsan and Ikhuwah) genealogy, which has been generating a plausible financial upliftment for their micro-communities.

*How can this philosophy be integrated into an existent UK solidarity economy framework?*

We examine this in the next round of our integral SOUL-idarity GENE rhythm, which is the **E** of the integral **E**mergence.

## *2.2 Towards SOUL-idarity economics and finance emergence*

According to Euclides Andre Mance, a member of the Popular Solidarity Economy Network in Brazil, a philosopher and a popular educator since the 1990s, broadly defined, the term 'solidarity economy', names a grassroots form of cooperative economics that is working throughout the world to connect thousands of local alternatives to create large-scale, viable, and creative networks of resistance to the profit-over-all-else economy...

Per Mance, solidarity economy tries to avoid any kind of fundamentalism since it aims to promote a diversity of solidarity-based economic forms, taking into account diverse realities and cultures, with the purpose of promoting the 'well living' of all people and nations (Mance, 2011)

Veritably, there is a global revolution underway to collaborate and create networks to collectively rethink the human realities in economics. There are thousands of movements and millions of people who have begun weaving collaborative networks of economic solidarity, creating channels and connections with the potential to bring together and strengthen local and global struggles, whilst the UK solidarity economy movement is also gathering momentum by creating knowledge and empowering action to see a diverse UK economy that values the needs of all people and the planet above the creation of wealth for the few.

Furthermore, with a significant growth in Shariah-compliant Islamic finance products making their mark in the UK banking and finance sector, striving to cater to the UK's Muslim population of 2.5 million, there is a need for making the complex Islamic finance science more people-worthy, i.e., transcending the essence of Islamic finance philosophy. This is something Akhuwat has been practically doing through its self-sufficiently regenerative model of reciprocal endowment (Mawakhat) coming from its borrowers' pool of reciprocity.

*Which brings us to my contemplation of barakah rounds – emerging from Akhuwat's reciprocal endowment pool through Qard-e-Hasan (interest-free loans) and becoming self-sufficient, Akhuwat borrowers are now direct collaborators in generating barakah (abundance) for their less-privileged community members. This, by comparison, remains Akhuwat's unique contribution to wealth generation, serving the poverty-alleviation cause in Pakistani society.*

*Could this assist communities in emancipating themselves from the afflictions and 'micro-ness' of a microfinance loans-based model which has apparently not been too helpful in eradicating poverty on a macro level?*

## *2.3 Navigating through 4 P's of an integral SOUL-idarity paradigm*

Our integral compass at this point is pointing Northward, navigating (**N**) via a new praxis of universal Hikma (wisdom), which eventuates from our 4P mapping (*Philosophy, Principles, Practices* and [integral] *Paradigm*) of our **SOUL-idarity GENE** rhythm, spiralling in a recursive circumvolution.

Within Akhuwat's implicit inner wisdom of hybridity deeply embedded in its various initiatives is an interwoven process of its layered 4P orientation – uniquely drawing on

Akhuwat's philosophy and processes, thereby birthing binary affinity with the four rounds of integral dynamics conceived in Lessem and Schieffer's (ibid) integral GENE orientation. Thus, the 4P mapping in a GENE-alogical order is revealed as such:

- **The Philosophy (PI)** – Round I *(Self)*; the philosophy of Akhuwat/solidarity
- **The Principles (PII)** – Round II *(Organisational)*; Akhuwat's four principles
- **The Practices (PIII)** – Round III *(Community)*; Akhuwat's principles in practice
- **Integral (Hikma) Paradigm (PIV)** – Round IV *(Society)*; Akhuwat's integral SOUL-idarity paradigm

*How can the knowledge acquired through this 4P process be applied to a universal solidarity with integrality?*

### *2.3.1 The barakah rounds premise*

Through examining the 4P process in conjunction with Akhuwat's practical example of 'virtuous circles' – which has created a wealth of 'reciprocal endowment' – we quantified the effects of a solidarity bond generating abundance for a community of Akhuwateers for the past 17 years now.

This unique phenomenon, with all its hybridity implications on Pakistani society, reinforced our belief of the'presence and imminence' of abundance (barakah) and its regenerative nature as per the Quranic decree of Kun fa Yakun (Be and it is) and of the Iqbalian expression (Chapter 4) that the process of creation is still going on – that God substantiates the process of recurrent creation and an ever-expanding universe – by citing from the Quran: *'Every day is He (God Almighty) is engaged in some new work.'*

*Where is this knowledge and presence of abundance leading us to?*

## *2.4 The effectual integral SOUL-idarity*

*The barakah (abundance) realisation now takes us to the Western realm of* ***E*** *(Effect), as per our integral GENE dynamics* (Schieffer & Lessem, 2010).

Thus, we see the effects of Akhuwat's 4P process: Philosophy, Principles, Practices and (integral) Paradigm as narrated throughout the course of this book using the descriptive method of transcendental phenomenology. The transformational effects of their solidarity bond have emancipated 2.3 million Pakistani families from a life of destitution to self-sufficiency and God-reliance through institutionalising the Quranic ordinance of Qard-e-Hasan – transcending the essence of Islamic economics in effect – a task left undone by Islamic finance scholars and experts.

*How, then, is Akhuwat CARE-ing for the Pakistani society?*

## 3 The barakah (abundance) transcendence

From an Integral praxis, the iteration from the *Southern* realm of Community is towards the *Eastern* pilgrimage of revisiting *sanctuary* – the spirit and culture of a community.

*In the case presented here, I intuitively explored the barakah regeneration – Akhuwat's organisational and communal culture of reciprocity which overflows into their revolving fund-pool. For this, my intuitive knowledge guided me to navigate through the inner core of their economic model – the centre that 'holds' it, Infaq.*

*Through this, what emerged, for me, in the deeper ontological recesses of Akhuwat's philosophy was a Hikma (wisdom) of a solidarity paradigm, churning out new rounds of virtuosity of Islamic spiritual philosophy laced with the local wisdom traditions of the South Asian culture of giving, placing one's Iman (faith) in divine abundance and tawakul (God-reliance), and liberating people from the ills of debt, riba (usury) and needless wealth-accumulation in the form of zakat (obligatory contribution). From an Islamic perspective, charity is in the form of a sadaqah (voluntary act) without any obligation placed on the receiver, as a by-product of zakat. All for the benefit and wellbeing of the community. Akhuwat, then, meticulously funnels the voluntary streams running through Pakistani society, thereby generating self-sustained rounds of barakah pools. All this originates from a Pakistani genealogy of Akhuwat/Bhai-chara.*

### *3.1 The spiritual foundation of 4I genealogy*

All that emerged from there on pointed towards the Hikma (wisdom) of a 4I's (Iman, Ikhlas, Ihsan and Ikhuwah) GENE-a-logical rhythm, tracing its roots back to the Islamic philosophy of Shahadah – witnessing the God-reality in totality through Iman (faith) in divine supremacy (tawakul) to Ihsan (beauty) manifestation of divine imminence (barakah).

To find one such existent model with all its practical nobility reinforces the integral concept of 'Communitalism', as per Father Anselm's postulation (Lessem & Schieffer, 2012), prospering an integral community in the case of Anselm's 4 Paxes (Pax Spiritus, Pax Scientia, Pax Economia and Pax Communis).

Thereafter, a close investigation of Akhuwat's 4I epistemology unfolds a 4P paradigm of Hikma (is**h**q/love, **i**lm/knowledge, a**k**huwat/brotherhood and a**ma**l/action), of solidarity and divine barakah working through its four principles (engaging sanctuary, Qard-e-Hasan, reciprocal endowment and volunteerism) for communal prosperity.

This also supports our premise of faith-based societies thriving on their beliefs – binding them together in a 'solidarity bond', as was observed and presented in Akhuwat's case.

*Where is this leading us?*

### *3.2 Self-sufficiency through Hikma of a 4T SOUL-idarity noesis*

Now traversing through our 4P mapping, we reach our conclusive postulation of a SOUL-idarity which perpetuated the birth of a new integral paradigm of solidarity through a 4T process of: *Transmutation, Transcendence, Trans-migration* and eventually, *Transformation.*

What became apparent for us through Akhuwat's 4 I's (Iman, Ikhlas, Ihsan and Ikhuwah) in a genealogical order is an alchemy of ishq (supreme love), ilm (transcendental knowledge), amal (actioning by employing ilm) and akhuwat (communal solidarity), as per our Hikma (wisdom) of solidarity – a trans-disciplinary soul-full awakening of solidarity which I term SOUL-idarity.

*How can this process be relevant to an economy of solidarity then?*

*Referring back to my work with micro-communities – the small pockets of disadvantaged and under-represented migrant communities within UK, often dependent on the social services of the state – I suggest an Akhuwat-like SOUL-idarity mandate for these communities to become self-sufficient through a balanced and reciprocal endowment as demonstrated by Sahlins* (2017) *through his in-depth study of the 'Stone age Economics' model, or as observed in Akhuwat's model of reciprocal endowment – the two-way flow of reciprocity, i.e., borrowers contributing as donors after achieving a level of self-sustainability through Qard-e-Hasan.*

*Thereby, this 4T transposition develops the soul (self) faculties of CARE-ing (Community activation, Awakening consciousness, institutionalising innovative Research and Embodying transformative action) which, from a metaphysical transmutation, transpire from a soul Hikma (ishq, ilm, akhuwah and amal). The whole process can be applied to facilitate communities to generate their own self-sufficiency through a reciprocal culture of extending SOUL-idarity with each other.*

## 4 The end note – summation

To sum it up for the ease of our readers, I would like to reinforce in my end note the threefold conclusive narration of a self-generating model of abundance, Akhuwat (brotherhood), borne out of the Islamic and prophetic philosophy of Mawakhat (solidarity) and Infaq, Akhuwat's 5th principle, advocating a culture of giving and communal sharing in the way of Allah through emulating the Sunnah of Prophet Muhammad (may Allah's peace be upon him).

1) *Akhuwat's fourfold + one Islamic genealogy model of Iman, Infaq, Ikhlas, Ikhuwah and Ihsan, resulting in Akhuwat (solidarity).*
2) *Akhuwat's fourfold principles: Qard-e-Hasan, engagement of sanctuary, reciprocal endowment (Mawakhat) and volunteerism*
3) *Institutionalising Akhuwat's philosophy of self-sufficiency, resulting in a self-generative solidarity economy.*

*My journey through the book whilst mapping the phenomenal effect of this unique paradigm of solidarity emerging from Pakistan (East) has reinforced my belief in Akhuwat's philosophy of self-sufficiency through communal solidarity as often wilfully alluded to by Amjad:*

> As a philosophy, Akhuwat cannot fail; if the movement does not succeed, it will not be a failure of the principles and ideals that guide the organisation. Failure could only stem from the waning strength of men and the weakness of their resolve but never from the lack of strength in the idea of Akhuwat itself.

Per Ikujiro Nonaka (Nonaka & Takeuchi, 1995), the author of *Managing Flow* and a Japanese organisational theorist and professor emeritus at the Graduate School of International Corporate Strategy of Hitotsubashi University, best known for his study of knowledge management, speaking about practical wisdom (Hikma) and creating knowledge (Ilm), 'Without real exchange, you can't create knowledge. Knowledge creation is a human activity.'

*Whereas through human activity, organisations can create new knowledge and innovative ways of real exchange. For us, this knowledge is the basis of an organisational philosophy that can help start a social movement, as observed in Akhuwat's case through their bond of solidarity generated through communal reciprocity as a result of adhering to a faith-based philosophy of Mawakhat/reciprocity.*

*For once the solidarity impulse is honoured and decoded by divine intervention, it sets in motion a multiplier effect of barakah (abundance), self-generated by a community of people through SOUL-idarity.*

*In the end, I leave you with the impulse of a 'universal SOUL-idarity', a state wherein reciprocity radiates as an effect of a culture of benevolence of Mawakhat. An autonomous 'state of solidarity' and Bhai-chara (brotherhood/Akhuwat), wherein no one is called 'poor', thus, needy; instead everyone is a 'barakah (abundance) collaborator' extending this silsilah (chain) of SOUL-idarity Comm-Union.*

*And thus continues our collective SOUL-idarity journey.*

## References

Basheer Oshodi, J. A., 2018. Work Democracy: Integral Banking/Communipreneurship: CISER. In: R. Lessem, & T. Bradley, eds. *Evolving Work: Employing Self and Community (Transformation and Innovation)*. Abingdon: Routledge, Chapter 17.

Lessem, R., & Schieffer, A., 2012. *Integral Community: Political Economy to Social Commons (Transformation and Innovation)*. Abingdon: Routledge.

Mance, E., 2011. *Solidarity Economy.* Available at: http://solidarius.com.br/mance/biblioteca/solidarity_economy.pdf

Nonaka, I., & Takeuchi, H., 1995. *The Knowledge Creating Company : How Japanese Companies Create the Dynamics of Innovation*. Oxford: Oxford University Press.

Sahlins, M. D., 2017. *Stone Age Economics*. Abingdon: Routledge.

Schieffer, A., & Lessem, B., 2010. *Integral Economics: Releasing the Economic Genius of your Society.* Farnham: Gower Publishing Ltd.

Soroush, A., 2000. *Reason, Freedom and Democracy in Islam*. New York: Oxford University Press.

# Index

Page numbers in *italic* indicate figures.

Page numbers in **bold** indicate tables.